Developmentalist Cities?

Studies in Critical Social Sciences Book Series

Haymarket Books is proud to be working with Brill Academic Publishers (www.brill.nl) to republish the *Studies in Critical Social Sciences* book series in paperback editions. This peer-reviewed book series offers insights into our current reality by exploring the content and consequences of power relationships under capitalism, and by considering the spaces of opposition and resistance to these changes that have been defining our new age. Our full catalog of *SCSS* volumes can be viewed at https://www.haymarketbooks.org/series_collections/4-studies-in-critical-social-sciences.

DEVELOPMENTALIST CITIES?

Interrogating Urban Developmentalism in East Asia

EDITED BY

JAMIE DOUCETTE
BAE-GYOON PARK

Haymarket Books
Chicago, IL

First published in 2018 by Brill Academic Publishers, The Netherlands.
© 2018 Koninklijke Brill NV, Leiden, The Netherlands

Published in paperback in 2020 by
Haymarket Books
P.O. Box 180165
Chicago, IL 60618
773-583-7884
www.haymarketbooks.org

ISBN: 978-1-64259-072-2

Distributed to the trade in the US through Consortium Book Sales and
Distribution (www.cbsd.com) and internationally through Ingram Publisher
Services International (www.ingramcontent.com).

This book was published with the generous support of Lannan Foundation and
Wallace Action Fund.

Special discounts are available for bulk purchases by organizations and
institutions. Please call 773-583-7884 or email info@haymarketbooks.org for
more information.

Cover design by Jamie Kerry and Ragina Johnson.

Printed in United States.

10 9 8 7 6 5 4 3 2 1

Library of Congress Cataloging-in-Publication Data is available.

Contents

About *Developmentalist Cities?*

Ranging in topic from the "Gangnam-ization" of Korean urban space to the management of migrant populations in China, each essay in this collection is a fascinating and insightful case study in its own right. Taken as a whole, Developmentalist Cities? breaks important new ground by connecting the afterlives of Cold War developmentalism to new forms of neoliberal urbanism in East Asia. As these rich, interdisciplinary essays demonstrate, we cannot understand our urban present without understanding the histories, political economies and contested practices of developmentalist cities. This book is a timely and significant intervention into today's critical debates around urban growth and migration, gentrification and globalization, and the cities, zones and regions that mediate them.

> *Jini Kim Watson*
> New York University
> Author of *The New Asian City: Three Dimensional Fictions of Space and Urban Form*

While each chapter shows a distinctive urban process in the individual context of East Asian countries, this collection demonstrates the usefulness of *urban developmentalism* as a process that cannot be easily unpacked based on existing models of urbanization in Western countries. This book ultimately celebrates the vitality of scholarship that has called for methodological and conceptual innovation in order to understand East Asian cities as form, process, and imaginary.

> *Choi, Byung-Doo*
> University of Daegu
> Co-Founder of the East Asian Regional Conference on Alternative Geography

This original and provocative collection is the first critically to interrogate the nexus of urbanism and developmentalism in East Asia, mobilizing in the process the kaleidoscopic lens that is geopolitical economy. Highly recommended, the book inaugurates new ways of thinking about cities, urban theory, and (late) developmental states, both within the region and beyond.

Jamie Peck
Canada Research Chair in Urban & Regional Political Economy and Professor of Geography, University of British Columbia

Acknowledgements

This volume has emerged from a loose network of interdisciplinary scholars who have crossed paths on several occasions at academic events in East Asia and beyond. The East Asian Regional Conference on Alternative Geography (EARCAG) has been one of these key sites and has been bringing together progressive geographers and urban studies scholars in the region since 1999. More recently, the meetings of a spinoff group from EARCAG, the Geopolitical Economies of East Asia research network (known as EARCAG-GPE) has provided a further forum that has been integral to the development of the approach of many of the chapters in the current volume. In addition, the Center for Asian Cities (CAC) (previously known as the Social Science Korea (SSK) Project on East Asian Cities) at Seoul National University has also played an instrumental role in these activities by helping to host a bid for the Social Science Research Council (SSRC) InterAsian Connections V Seoul Workshop 2016 that the editors used to bring together most of the authors in this volume for the first time. The editors thus wish to thank both SSRC and the individual participants for helping to bring this volume to fruition.

The CAC has been generously funded by a National Research Foundation of Korean Grant funded by the Korean Government (NRF-2017S1A3A2066514) that the editors would like to acknowledge as a source of funding and support for the current volume. In addition, Jamie Doucette also thanks the Korea Foundation, in particular, which funded a Fellowship for Field Research (KF Ref.: 1022000–003867) during the winter and spring of 2016 that allowed him to spend a sabbatical semester at Seoul National University and to develop many of the ideas explored in the introduction to this volume and in his chapter with Seung-Ook Lee.

As mentioned above, the ideas and concepts explored in this volume have been developed through frequent meetings in the East Asian region, and especially the SSRC InterAsian Connections V event in Seoul. The interaction and discussions begun at this event have developed considerably over time, and were first explored in print through a special, double issue of *Critical Sociology* 44:3 [May] 2018. The chapters by Cartier, Choi and Glassman, Doucette and Park, Friedman, Gottfried, Hae, Hsu, Ip, Kim Chilcote, Kleibert, and Moon in particular are revised, extended and reworked versions of ideas that first appeared in that volume. The other contributions are by scholars who have also participated in the events described above but who were either not present at the SSRC InterAsian Connections workshop or did not participate in the special issue but pursued cognate ideas elsewhere. In particular, we thank Sage

Publications for permission to reprint sections of Hyun Bang Shin and Soo-Hyun Kim's article from Urban Studies. Finally, the editors would like to thank the artist Chang Chang Yoo for permission to use his painting (Earthquake), for the cover image of this volume. The editors also wish to thank the scss series editor, David Fasenfest, for all his help guiding the manuscript through the publication process.

Illustrations

Figures

Tables

Notes on Contributors

Carolyn Cartier

is Professor of Human Geography and China Studies at the University of Technology Sydney. She is chief investigator of the Australian Research Council Discovery Project, "Governing the City in China: The Territorial Imperative" (2017–2020). She has been a Fulbright Scholar in Hong Kong and a Research Fellow at the Centre for Interdisciplinary Research at the University of Southern California. She is the author of *Globalizing South China* (Blackwell, 2001, 2011) and co-editor with Alan A. Lew of *Seductions of Place: Geographical Perspectives on Globalization and Touristed Landscapes* (Routledge, 2005) and with Laurence J.C. Ma of *The Chinese Diaspora: Space, Place, Mobility and Identity* (Rowman & Littlefield, 2003).

Christina Kim Chilcote

holds a doctorate from the New School for Social Research in Anthropology. Her Ph.D. thesis is an ethnography of economic activities along the border of China and North Korea. Her recent work titled "Reworking the frame: analysis of current discourses on North Korea and a case study of North Korean labor in Dandong, China" is published in *Asia Pacific Viewpoint,* 56(3) (2015). She was a Jennings Randolph Peace Scholar at the United States Institute of Peace from 2015–2016. Her current work focuses on international security and defense regimes.

Young-Jin Choi

received her M.A. and Ph.D. in Geography Education at Seoul National University. Her dissertation *Geopolitical Economies and South Korea's Heavy industrialization in the late 1960s and early 1970s: case studies on "Hyundai Heavy Industries" and "Changwon machine-building industrial Complex"* examined the economic growth of South Korea in the 1970's from a geopolitical economy perspective as an alternative approach to the developmental state thesis. She coauthored the paper, "The *chaebol* and the US military–industrial complex: Cold War geopolitical economy and South Korean industrialization", *Environment and Planning A,* 46(5) (2014), with Jim Glassman, which won the Environmental and Planning A's 2014 Ashby Prize. Her current research interests combine the formation of industrial complexes and transnational business networks in East Asia during the Cold War period.

Jamie Doucette

is Senior Lecturer in Human Geography at the University of Manchester, where he coordinates the Cities, Politics, Economies Research Group and serves on the leadership team of the Manchester Urban Institute. His research interests include the study of East Asian developmentalism and democratization, labor geography, and the financial transformation of Korea's political economy since the late 1990s. His research has been published in journals such as *Transactions of the Institute of British Geographers, Political Geography, Geoforum, Capital and Class, Journal of Contemporary Asia, Journal of Asian Studies, Critical Sociology* and *Critical Asian Studies*, among others. He research on Korean politics was recently recognized with the *Journal of Contemporary Asia Prize* 2017 and a Leverhulme Trust Research Fellowship for 2018-2019.

Eli Friedman

is Associate Professor of International and Comparative Labor at Cornell University's School of Industrial and Labor Relations. He currently has two major research projects, the first of which looks at expansive worker unrest in China and state responses. The second project is a study of China's urbanization, with a particular focus on access to education for rural to urban migrants. He is the author of *Insurgency Trap: Labor Politics in Postsocialist China* (Cornell, 2014), as well as numerous articles on China's labor and development.

Jim Glassman

is Professor in the Department of Geography at University of British Columbia. His areas of research interest include the geopolitical economy of development, state theory, and military economies, with a particular focus on South Korea, Thailand, and the United States. He is the author of *Thailand at the Margins* (Oxford University Press, 2004), *Bounding the Mekong* (University of Hawaii Press, 2010), and *Drums of War, Drums of Development* (Brill, 2018).

Heidi Gottfried

is an Associate Professor of Sociology at Wayne State University. Her research focuses on gender, precarity and work. Publications include *The Reproductive Bargain: Deciphering the Enigma of Japanese Capitalism* (Brill, 2015); and *Gender, Work and Economy: Unpacking the Global Economy* (Wiley, 2013). She also has edited or co-edited several books: *Gendering the Knowledge Economy: Comparative Perspectives* (Palgrave Macmillan, 2007); *Equity in the Workplace: Gendering Workplace Policy Analysis* (Lexington Books, 2004); *Feminism and Social Change: Bridging Theory and Practice* (University of Illinois Press, 1996); *The SAGE Handbook of the Sociology of Work and Employment* (Sage, 2015);

and "Care Work in Transition: Transnational Circuits of Gender, Migration and Care" (with Jennifer Chun), forthcoming in *Critical Sociology*.

Laam Hae
is Associate Professor at York University. She studies and teaches on urban political economy and cultural politics, feminist urban theory and transformative urban activism. Hae has researched and written on popular struggles over gentrification, the post-industrialization of urban economies, the militarization of urban space, and the privatization of social reproduction, both in the U.S. and South Korean contexts. She is also an author of *The Gentrification of Nightlife and the Right to the City: Regulating Spaces of Social Dancing in New York* (Routledge, 2012).

Jinn-yuh Hsu
is a professor of Human Geography at the National Taiwan University. His research interests mainly include the inconstant geographies of capitalism in East Asian (post)developmental states, particularly the geopolitical economic impacts of state transformation. Currently, he is engaging in a book project to explore the historical transformation of special zones, including Export Processing Zones, Technology Parks and Free Economic Zones, and their geopolitical and geoeconomic implications for state transformation in Taiwan, in comparison with the case of South Korea.

Iam-chong Ip
is Assistant Professor of Cultural Studies at Lingnan University, where he teaches courses in Hong Kong society, cultural changes of Modern China, and social and cultural anthropology. His research interests include social activism, urban politics, independent media and modern Chinese intellectual formation. His publications have appeared in such journals as *Inter-Asia Cultural Studies*, *Critical Sociology*, *Cultural Dynamics* and *Asian Survey*.

Jin-bum Jang
is a Ph.D. Candidate in Sociology at Seoul National University. His research interests include citizenship, cities, poverty and labor. He is currently translating Herman R. van Gunsteren's *A Theory of Citizenship: Organizing Plurality in Contemporary Democracies* and Etienne Balibar's *Citizenship* into Korean (Greenbee Publishing Company, forthcoming).

Soo-Hyun Kim
is currently a Senior Secretary for social policy to President Moon Jae-in of the Republic of Korea, a position that involves managing social affairs that include

urban and housing issues. Before joining the government, he was a professor in the Graduate School of Public Policy at Sejong University in Seoul, Korea. He has studied squatters, poverty and housing issues, and published several papers and books, including *Over with the Real Property Society* (O-weol-eu-bom, 2011) and *Looking for an Ideal Housing Policy* (O-weol-eu-bom, 2017, co-author) among many others.

Jana M. Kleibert

is post-doctoral fellow at the Institute for Research on Society and Space (IRS) in Erkner and lecturer at the Humboldt University of Berlin. She is an economic geographer with research interests in globalization, global production networks, economic development and urban transformations in the global South. She holds a Ph.D. in Human Geography from the University of Amsterdam. Her research has been published in international peer-reviewed journals, including *Urban Geography, Environment and Planning A, Geoforum,* and *Regional Studies.*

Kah-Wee Lee

is Deputy Director of the Master of Urban Planning program at the National University of Singapore where he teaches history and theory of planning and qualitative methods. He works on the politics of urban development and planning practice in Singapore and other parts of Asia, as well as the spatial violence of colonial and nationalist projects. His current project examines the expansion of the casino industry in Asia through three cities - Singapore, Macau and Manila. Lee's research has been published in the *International Journal of Urban and Regional Research, Environment and Planning A* and *C, Geoforum,* and local professional journals. He is the author of *Las Vegas in Singapore: Violence, Progress and the Crisis of Nationalist Modernity* (The University of Chicago Press, 2018).

Seung-Ook Lee

is an assistant professor at the School of Humanities and Social Sciences of the Korea Advanced Institute of Science and Technology. His research focuses on the geopolitics and political economy of Northeast Asia, specifically China and the Korean peninsula. His works are published in journals such as *Critical Asian Studies, Environment and Planning A, Geopolitics,* and *Political Geography.*

Christina Moon

is an Assistant Professor in Fashion Studies in the School of Art and Design History, Parsons School of Design, The New School. Her research looks at the social ties and cultural encounters between design worlds and manufacturing landscapes across Asia and the Americas, exploring the memory, migration, and labor of cultural workers. She is a Social Science Research Council Transregional Research Junior Scholar Fellow, Graduate Institute of Design Ethnography and Social Theory fellow and member of the India China Institute The New School and Fashion Praxis working group at Parsons.

Bae-Gyoon Park

is a Professor of Geography in the College of Education at Seoul National University in Korea. His recent research focuses on geo-political economies of East Asian border regions and (post) developmental urbanism in East Asia. He is an editor of *Locating Neoliberalism in East Asia* (Blackwell, 2012) and several Korean-written books. He has also published papers in *International Journal of Urban and Regional Research, Critical Sociology, Political Geography, Economic Geography* and *Critical Asian Studies*.

Hyun Bang Shin

is Professor of Geography and Urban Studies at the London School of Economics and Political Science. His research focuses on the critical analysis of the political economic dynamics of speculative urbanization, the politics of displacement, gentrification, mega-events, and the right to the city, with particular attention to Asian cities. He is co-editor of *Global Gentrifications: Uneven Development and Displacement* (Policy Press, 2015), co-author of *Planetary Gentrification* (Polity Press, 2016), and editor of *Anti Gentrification: What is to be done?* (Dongnyok, 2017). He is currently writing a monograph *Making China Urban* (Routledge, forthcoming), and co-editing *Contesting Urban Space in East Asia* (Palgrave Macmillan, forthcoming) and *The Political Economy of Mega Projects in Asia: Globalization and Urban Transformation* (Routledge, forthcoming).

CHAPTER 1

Introduction: Interrogating Urban Developmentalism in East Asia

Jamie Doucette and Bae-Gyoon Park

1   Introduction

This book builds upon a broad, interdisciplinary effort that has sought to intervene in the study of the spatial forms, political economic processes, politics of representation, and planning policies that have animated East Asian urbanization.[1] This research – which includes contributions from geographers, anthropologists, sociologists, architects, cultural studies scholars and area specialists – has done so based on a shared feeling that urban studies would benefit from greater attention to the *geopolitical economic* context of East Asian developmentalism. For it is difficult to examine East Asian urbanization without taking the legacy of developmentalism into account, much less to study developmentalism without considering the role of the urban: as form, process and imaginary. And yet, to date, urban scholarship has neglected, or underappreciated, the spatial contours and processes behind what might be provisionally called *developmentalist cities*: urban spaces that have been inflected by a politics of developmentalism within Cold War and post-Cold War contexts. In contrast, the chapters in this volume all share an attention to the Cold War influence on urbanization in Asia, the ongoing transformation of its associated forms of development, and/or new forms developed in its aftermath. While many of these processes extend in geographical scope beyond the region *per se*, a critical focus upon them is particularly germane for understanding the historical roots of and contemporary challenges raised by urbanization in East Asia.

And yet, much of the classic literature on East Asian developmental states, for instance, has neglected the role of the urban in favor of national-level, state-centric examination of nodal planning ministries, strategic industrial policy, and state-business coalitions. The role played by urban space in materializing the planning ambitions of developmental state planners and their geopolitical

1   The authors benefitted from support from the National Research Foundation of Korea (NRF-2017S1A3A2066514) for the writing of this chapter.

partners, much less in providing a space of representation and contestation for various state building projects and patterns of capital accumulation has long been neglected in this literature (Hwang, 2016a; Hsu et al., 2018). However, East Asian states actively promoted the development of national urban networks to enhance the territorial integrity of the nation, and prioritized urban infrastructure to support mass production and economic growth, and to display political prowess. Under big push industrialization efforts across East Asia, urban processes took place very rapidly in strategically selected areas of political and economic importance. Iconic urban public spaces were built to accord praise on developmental politicians and various post-colonial nation-building projects. State-subsidized apartment and housing construction was used to create a new middle class and bolster the infrastructural capacities of select firms (Kwak 2015; Yang 2018). At the same time, social movements used urban space as a site of contestation against developmentalist regimes and urban inequalities (Mobrand 2016; Shin 2018). Urban protest has also shaped the design of public space as well as the form and patterning of residential and industrial growth in East Asian cities.

Likewise, many existing studies on East Asian cities have not been able to properly address the influences of national developmentalism, Cold War and post-Cold War geo-political economies on urbanization because they have often favored a localist approach that regards the city as a territorially contained and institutionally coherent object (Park, 2013). Their focus is too often concerned with describing cities in the abstract rather than on situating them in history, society and space. Alternately, while global and world cities scholars have paid attention to the globally networked character of East Asian cities, they too have neglected the dense entanglements of East Asian cities with national and regional dynamics of urbanization, especially the influence of Cold War developmentalism on the urban. There has been in many ways a missed encounter here between global cities research and East Asian regional context (see Hill and Kim 2000 and Sassen 2001 for notes on what 'could have been' an interesting debate); however, the recent advocacy of a geopolitical perspective on city regions might help further develop these topics in the future (Jonas and Moisio, 2016). This is a problem that also haunts the recent work on planetary urbanization in as much as its critics have noted a tendency to neglect forms of lived difference, including forms of urban difference that have been articulated within regional dynamics of urbanization (Buckley and Strauss, 2016). Meanwhile, postcolonial and ordinary cities literatures have recently called for greater attention to urban difference, but they too risk privileging a disjointed urban scale as their primary unit of analysis by downplaying important geopolitical economic forces and enduring national and regional contexts. The compressed temporality of urbanization (Kim, 2010; Wu, 2015) and intense cycles of creative destruction witnessed in many Asian locales; the spatial selectivity (Park et al., 2012) of Asian urbanism in the sense of the vast number of 'spaces of exception' such as enclaves, zones, and special regions that have shaped urban strategy (Ong, 2006; Bach, 2011; Neveling, 2015; Sidaway, 2007); and enrolment of migrants and Cold War expertise into patterns of urban development are just a few commonalities that might be considered germane for urban and regional research in East Asia.

In summary, there is a missing *urban* story to work on East Asian developmentalism as well as a missing *developmentalist* story in research on East Asian urbanization that this volume hopes to help rectify by laying the basis for further research. To do so, it promotes active research into the subject of *urban developmentalism*: a term that we find useful for highlighting the particular nature of the urban as a site of and for developmentalist intervention in various forms. We find this term useful for a variety of reasons. The term is useful in that it signifies that the urban process within the region does not easily fit into existing models of urban governance – such as the classic work on urban managerialism and urban entrepreneurialism – in as much as the inter-scalar and geopolitical dynamics of development and, by extension, the state-market nexus remain institutionally distinct in many East Asian contexts (cf. Lim 2016; Chattopadhyay 2017 for similar remarks in the context of South Asia). It is also a term that is able to capture East Asian urban development as not simply confined to the rapid physical development of urban infrastructures but also as a process that includes the production of space in multiple dimensions, including both physical spaces, but also space in the form of abstract imaginaries (in the sense of planning and ideology), everyday perceptions, and lived experience, as something imbued with memory and emotion (see Hwang, 2016b, Ji, 2016, Park and Jang, 2016, Watson, 2011 for a discussion).

Such an expansive understanding of space enables us to highlight the many actors involved in shaping urban developmentalism. For instance, the chapters in this volume foreground the roles played not only by the state and business in developing urban space but also by transnational networks of capital, migrants, and expertise. They focus on how interactions among these actors across scale, territory, networks and place have helped shape the form and content of East Asian cities as well as other scales of urban governance. In addition to cities per se, many of the chapters in this volume also pay careful attention to unique zoning policies such as special economic zones (SEZS) and other selective forms of urban districting that can be contrasted to traditional forms of urban governance in other parts of the world. One of this volume's signal contributions to the literature is to highlight the fact that in many cases of urban developmentalism the target of urban intervention is not the 'city', as conventionally understood, but other spatial units, such as special districts, export processing zones, science parks and Casino complexes. Provocatively speaking, *developmentalist cities* are not necessarily cities *per se*, in the sense of conventionally understood units of municipal or communal governance, but are often composed of spatial units existing above, below, alongside, and/ or within received units of urban governance. Finally, though much work is needed to flesh out the many varieties and articulations of urban developmentalism in East Asia, the term as it is used here is broad sense to describe forms of mass urbanization during the Cold War period as well as more neoliberal, speculative, and spatially-selective experiments with urban policy that have followed in its wake. The authors in this volume thus draw attention to enduring legacies of urban development under the Cold War and/or new institutions and networks that have transformed these in order to address new geopolitical and economic circumstances and to prefigure new imaginaries of the city and the urban in a post Cold War world.

While the inter-disciplinary research program that surrounds the idea of urban developmentalism is still being developed and, indeed, has much further room for expansion, this volume makes contributions to three key themes that we feel are essential to it and the more expansive approach to urban space advocated above: *geopolitical economies*, *spaces of exception* and *networks of expertise*. These are interconnected areas that, we feel, demonstrate some, but not all, of sorts of topics that should be included in its study. Furthermore, as the chapters come from an interdisciplinary group of scholars – most of whom were first brought together through the Social Science Research Council InterAsia Program's *InterAsian Connections V Conference* in Seoul, South Korea in April 2016 – they also suggest several potential methodologies for the study of urban developmentalism across disciplines. Each chapter below makes its own distinct contribution to the topic: some provide a critique of existing paradigms of East Asian urban research, while others focus on thickening existing approaches to urban development by putting urban theory into dialogue with the techniques of their respective disciplinary field. While the chapters are certainly worth reading in depth to identify the full range of their contributions to academic debate and connections to existing urban research, we offer a provisional introduction to their contributions here. To do so, in what follows we situate each in relation to the key themes identified above and discuss how they link up to one another across the various locales of their research and respective disciplines.

2   Geopolitical Economies

The predominant theme that runs through all of the chapters in this volume is the need to situate East Asian urban development within extended geopolitical and economic networks of capital, people, and expertise. There is a common view that the networks, territorial interactions, and inter-scalar relations that have shaped urbanization in East Asia have been profoundly influenced by Cold War and post-Cold War transformations that extend well beyond single cities and national territories. While the literature on geopolitical economy is still being developed, in our reading, the term is useful for three reasons: 1) it situates political economy as a geographic process; 2) it resists a clear separation between geopolitics (international relations) and (geo) economic forces (cf. Cowen and Smith 2009) and 3) it signifies that political economic processes are geographically expansive, that processes even at the urban scale are often shaped by relations that extend beyond it (Glassman 2018; Jessop and Sum 2018). The chapters in this volume develop upon this framework in a variety of ways. First, there is a clear strand of research that explicitly foregrounds the geo-political economic context of East Asian urban development. For example, Young-Jin Choi and Jim Glassman's chapter *Heavy Industries and Second Tier City Growth in South Korea: A Geopolitical Economic Analysis of the 'Four Core Plants Plan'* examines how second-tier city growth in Korea was driven by the enrollment of Korean firms such as Hyundai into transnational class alliances spurred by US military projects in Asia, rather than simply being a case of successfully planning by a national state. These findings, which build on recent work by Hsu et al. (2018) on industrial zones in Korea and Taiwan, directly contest the overemphasis by neo-Weberian scholars on the planning successes of the developmental state by highlighting the role of geopolitically embedded firms in realizing their own plans for sub-national urban growth. In a similar fashion, Heidi Gottfried's chapter *Eclipse of the Rising Sun? The Once and Future Tokyo* charts the rise of Tokyo as a global city under the influence of imperial decline and subsequent articulation of Japanese capitalist development within American geo-political networks. Gottfried identifies critical political conjunctures for class recomposition where new geometries of power emerged and where the balance of forces, and thus the form of urbanization, might have turned out otherwise. Looking at the contemporary, post Cold War context of China and Hong Kong, Iam-chong Ip's *The Fall of the Hong Kong Dream: New Paths of Urban Gentrification in Hong Kong* examines how Hong Kong's increasing politico-economic integration into China has produced a new form of state-led gentrification whereby the local city-state has used its new relations with the mainland to tap into global circuits of capital and develop the local property market. These chapters bring into focus the integral role of transnational class relations and their effects on urbanization. By extension, they also contribute to recent work in geography and urban studies (Walker, 2016; Schoenberger and Walker, 2016) that is critical of attempts to prioritize stylized forces of agglomeration (Storper and Scott, 2016) to the neglect of complex class processes and power relations.

But geopolitical economy is not confined simply to the study of formal class alliances in this volume. Three chapters in particular extend it down to the level of the built form as well as to the embodied level of family, memory, labor and emotion. Christina Kim Chilcote's *Waiting and Remembering: Economy of Anticipation and Materiality of Aspiration in Dandong, China* provides an ethnographic take on how urban development in Dandong has been fuelled by an 'economy of anticipation' that yearns for North Korea's eventual economic integration within the regional economy. To do so, older geopolitical memories of international solidarity and new special economic zones are materialized in the built form in order to reimagine North Korea as a capitalist frontier and help propel speculative investment. Jamie Doucette and Seung-Ook Lee's chapter *Volatile Territorialities: North Korea's Special Economic Zones and the Geopolitical Economy of Urban Developmentalism* complements Kim Chilcote's take on Dandong by noting how economic concerns and geopolitical imaginaries about the labor of North Korean workers in its special economic zones have helped configure them as *experimental* but *volatile* forms of territoriality of an uncertain duration. Likewise, Christina Moon's *Fashioning the City: Trans-Pacific and Inter-Asian Connections in the Global Garment Industry* also highlights the temporal aspects of SEZs and industrial districts by examining how migrants have negotiated a linked inter-Asian and trans-Pacific geography of family networks, production chains, and sites of labor and design. Similar to the chapters discussed above, Moon argues that the development of New York and Los Angeles as global fashion centers would not be possible without networks and skills first forged during the Cold War and transformed again in the years since. Furthermore, Kim Chilcolte, Moon, and Gottfried's chapters contribute to more than simply the study of geopolitical economic networks and their attendant yearnings and imaginaries. Their insights also extend down to the built form itself in their discussion of the role of spectacular architecture and infrastructure in materializing global city and modernist ambitions, and thus contribute to 'contemporary discussions on the role of iconic architecture within transnational class formation (Kaika, 2011; Sklair and Gherardi, 2012).

3   Spaces of Exception

The second theme to which the chapters in this volume make a significant contribution is the topic of spaces of exception, as mentioned above. This term include spaces such as special economic zones and other selective forms of urban development in East Asia. Over the last decade, there has been a growing literature (see, for instance, Arnold, 2012; Doucette and Lee, 2015; Easterling, 2014; Murray, 2017; Park, 2017; Ong, 2006) on East Asian states' efforts to develop zones (e.g. export processing zones, industrial complexes, apartment zones) through special and exceptional treatment and privileges, the spatial selectivity of which have often been politically justified by appealing to developmentalist rationality. Several chapters in this volume deepen and extend this literature. Doucette and Lee reveal how a 'topological' and geopolitical economic reading of such zones can reveal not only their deeply contextual configuration (which should not simply be reduced to neoliberal governmentality) and volatility (susceptibility to rapid change) in the context of the Korean peninsula. Carolyn Cartier's *From 'Special Zones' to Cities and City-regions in China* is perhaps the most ambitious of the chapters in really extending the debate on zones forward. Cartier critiques how the concept of zone has become code word for autonomous, neoliberal strategies in much of this literature, leading authors to decontextualize variegated forms of planning and governance. She argues that much of the literature on zones in China and Southeast Asia in particular assumes autonomy and ignores enduring structures of state authority and practices of territorial governance, for which the terminology of 'zones' is often used as an ill-suited analogy. In the process, Cartier revisits older debates in the philosophy of science and the production of geographic thought to question how the idea 'zone', like other geographic concepts before it, has been circulated and reproduced as an 'analog', an exemplar that has been detached from its pre-existing model or paradigm. Jana M. Kleibert's *New Spaces of Exception: Special Economic Zones and Luxury Condominiums in Metro Manila* complements Cartier's contribution by examining how Filipino elites have amalgamated residential and production zones to create 'exclusive developments'. Kleibert shows how rather than simply being examples of mobile neoliberal technology, such zones are conditioned by local class strategies in an elite-captured, 'anti-developmental' state that aims to create spaces of exclusion for luxury living. Jinn-yuh Hsu's *Zoning Urbanization: The Hsinchu Technopolis as an Enclave of Modernity in Taiwan* thickens the research on special economic zones even further in this volume. His chapter shows how zones themselves become objects of desire for the populations that are excluded from them. He does so by examining political contestation surrounding Taiwan's Hsinchu Science City, a project where local farmers-cum-landowners affected by previous zonal policies, rather than large domestic and transnational capitalists, have made demands for new zones from which they might benefit through retrofitting, real estate activities and/or speculative forms of urbanization (cf. Shin and Kim, 2016). Hsu's emphasis on the pressure for zoning from below provides a novel departure from top-down readings of zonal development.

Special economic zones are not the only spaces of exception dealt with in this volume. Eli Friedman's *The Biopolitics of Urbanization in China: Managing Migration and Access to Education* examines how the pursuit of rapid economic growth in China has created contradictory imperatives for Chinese cities to both draw in and expel workers by using a form of technocratic biopolitics that Friedman refers to as 'just-in-time urbanization'. Here it is the rural migrant worker laboring in the city that becomes a site of exception in as much as under this system, migrants can be granted access to urban citizenship and social reproduction if they fulfill a specific labor market need, or face exclusion and deepening educational inequality if they do not. Friedman's study resonates with Moon's chapter discussed above in as much as it foregrounds how migration has shaped rapid urbanization in East Asia. While Friedman reveals a process of pulling in and pushing out based on imperatives of capitalist accumulation, Moon, on the other hand, reveals how migrants' experience of working in enclave spaces, special economic zones, and industrial districts across cities has equipped some with the capability to shape capitalist globalization by negotiating diasporic networks and applying skills learned at various sites of the production and design chain in their favor. Finally, Park and Jang's chapter, *The Gangnam-ization of Korean Urban Ideology,* further complicates our understanding of spaces of exception by examining Gangnam's apartment complexes and the urban developments modeled after them. Park and Jang show how residents have themselves adopted forms of distinction and capital accumulation in these spaces that helped mold Gangnam as the primary ideological representation of the urban adopted by the Korean middle class. Gangnam is an exceptional space here in both the sense of how it has been targeted by the state to materialize developmentalist ambitions, but also in the manner in which middle classes have performed their own identity within the large and 'segmented' complexes (danji) of apartments that comprise it. In summary, the chapters in this volume provide both a new take on the literature of spaces of exception in Asia as well as suggest several novel entry-points into their further study.

4   Networks of Expertise

The third major theme of research into urban developmentalism that this volume contributes to involves the role of geographically extensive networks of knowledge and expertise forged during the Cold War in shaping urban developmentalism. As discussed above, Moon tackles this issue by looking at the embodied expertise of fashion workers who negotiate inter-Asian and trans-Pacific production chains and industrial districts, while other chapters explore the topic in a different register. For instance, Choi and Glassman look at how Hyundai's successful evolution into large, global firm was in large part due to its participation in US military offshore procurement, an experience that allowed it to accumulate both capital and expertise, as well as the ability to shape the pathway of urban growth in Ulsan, South Korea. Likewise, Gottfried discusses how US foreign policy networks and procurement policies shaped the institutional architecture and trajectory of Japan's developmental capitalism, giving prominence to Tokyo. In a different register, Hsu's chapter also describes how Taiwan's Hsinchu Science-based Industrial Park was designed to pull in highly-educated, returned migrants from US universities in order to build new industries and help transfer state-of-the-art technology from the US to Taiwan.

While this volume helps to document the role of geopolitical economic networks in shaping urban developmentalism during the Cold War, it also charts the influence of more recent flows of policy knowledge and expertise that have been transmitted across the Pacific. Kah-Wee Lee's chapter *Planning as Institutionalized Informality: State, Casino Capitalists and the Production of Space in Macau* charts how a network of planners, architects, and casino operators have created a planning regime that serves both China's geopolitical interests and the economic interests of competing fractions of local and international capitalists. This has been done through strategically ambivalent planning practices that embrace informality as a response to a political environment deemed unruly and through a particular politics of representation that depicts the past as chaotic in order to implement new planning regimes. In a complementary fashion, Hyun Bang Shin and Soo-Hyun Kim's *The Developmental State, Speculative Urbanization and the Politics of Displacement in Gentrifying Seoul* examines how various planning ordinances and redevelopment schemes have been assembled by property investors, state agencies, urban planners, and strategic business partners to displace poor urban residents and fuel property-led urban growth. In short, they provide a forensic exploration of the institutional expertise and planning practices that have allowed the urban ideologies explored by

Park and Jang to materialize, and that shape current geographies of gentrification and resistance in South Korea.

Laam Hae's *Translating a Fast Policy: Place Marketing and the Neoliberal Turn of Critical Urban Studies in South Korea* further enriches our understanding of the contested terrain of Korean urban development by taking up the interesting case of how progressive urban planners and urban studies researchers in Seoul, South Korea played a role in importing pro-gentrification policies from North America and Europe. Hae documents how critical urbanists saw reformist potential from place-marketing strategies that gave priority to local culture and identity. They argued that such policies could help address the problems of authoritarian urban developmentalism inherited from previous decades of urban growth. However, the culture-based strategies they promoted had the adverse effect of aiding real-estate speculation and undermining the welfare of local residents, spurring some urbanists to reject place-marking and search again for alternative policy circuits that might develop a more egalitarian approach to social justice in urban spaces (cf. Im and Križnik, 2017). Likewise, Ip's chapter on new urban developmentalism in Hong Kong examines how new financial networks between China and Hong Kong have influenced exclusive forms of state-led gentrification that undermine local residents' right to the city. Ip does an excellent job at foregrounding the use of quasi-state actors such as the Urban Renewal Authority in unsettling claims to property and installing new spatial forms in the landscape that pertain to 'better' the urban landscape but in fact act as vehicles for displacement and property speculation. The above chapters' analysis of the conjunction of the state, capital, and strategic private actors in a speculative process of gentrification and redevelopment here resonates with recent discussions about how to locate gentrification outside of the North Atlantic, especially in contexts where questions of land tenure are multi-layered, the urban commons complex, and where the state has played a strong role in marshaling resources for development and picking strategic partners (Shin and Lopez-Morales 2018; Ghertner 2015). Finally, what is also interesting about all of these chapters is that they reveal how expansive networks of knowledge and expertise, forged from geopolitical conflict and economic integration, continue to shape East Asian urban development after the Cold War, albeit in novel, often unpredictable, directions.

5   Conclusion

In summary, the chapters in this book draw our attention to the themes of geopolitical economies, spaces of exception, and networks of expertise in a variety of ways and disciplinary directions. The variegated forms of urbanization in the region, the geopolitical economic forces that have shaped them, and the transnational flows, aesthetics, and expertise from which they have been assembled are all foregrounded here. While there is much more work to be done in order to provide a fuller overview of urban developmentalism in East Asia, we hope that the efforts presented here stimulate further methodological and conceptual innovation and inter-disciplinary dialogue. For instance, the processes through which the urban strategies highlighted by each chapter have interacted with one another is a topic worthy of further attention, particularly in the current moment. It seems clear to us that in recent times trajectories of urban development have interacted, creating new networks, mutating urban forms, expanding the scale of city-building activities and creating new regional and transregional connections. Furthermore, the rise of neoliberal, market-friendly, and consumption-oriented processes of urban development has gradually become more influential than they were during periods of national developmentalism during the Cold War. How best to understand the contemporary moment? There is room for much further discussion on what the appropriate conceptual terminology to describe it might be. For instance, one might call the contemporary period in some East Asian contexts that of a new urban developmentalism, as Ip does for the context of Hong Kong, in as much as the process he describes details a rescaling of state-planning and a roll out of new capabilities in urban contexts. At the same time, the term post-developmental urbanism used by Gottfried to describe Tokyo's contemporary conundrums signifies a temporal shift away from industrialization, and perhaps a move towards de-industrialization: a tendency being witnessed in some of the other East Asian economies at the moment in formerly strategic sectors such as shipbuilding and automobiles (Hassink et al. 2017). We might also describe some urban processes in the region as post-developmental in another sense: that there are increased constraints on the capacity of both the local and national state to manage the urbanization process, whether it be through industrial policy and other policy measures (cf. Doucette 2016). Whichever term one prefers, it is clear that urbanization processes in the present are animated by the continued mutation of the institutional and material legacies of the Cold War period, but in a context where the regional, inter-Asian political economy is more integrated into the world market than in the past. Contemporary East Asia cities are spaces where global production networks and transnational flows of expertise, migrants and capital shape and pass through the urban in new ways, and where speculative development, urban displacement, divided cities, and struggles over public space are beginning to seem more intense.

It is our hope that further scholarship on this topic might aid in the development of a trans-Pacific and inter-Asian approach sensitive to how urban connections are being made and remade in the contemporary regional and global economy. This is a project that resonates both with Peck's (2017) recent call for a conjunctural approach to urbanism that is sensitive to the trans-Atlantic connections that shape urban austerity as well as recent discussions on using East Asian interconnections as a guiding research problematic (Chen, 2010; Paik, 2013). However, there is much more work to be done if this goal is to be realized. Beyond the complexities of the current moment, there is more that might still be extracted from historical and geographical inquiry into the role played by the city or the urban in wider scholarship on Cold War developmentalism and developmental states in general. As discussed above, the city is neglected in much of this literature, which is often more focused on national-level industrial planning and ideology. But as the chapters in this volume detail, developmentalism has also been an urban project. The urban is an important site in which developmentalist politics renders itself visible, in which the national state attempts to render populations legible and governable. The urban is a site where desires for development, modernity and urban living often become conflated and/or contested. It is a site where ruling powers try to legitimize their power but also accommodate some of the criticisms against it. As the urban story of developmentalism and the developmentalist story of urban development in East Asia have often been absent from both urban research and development studies, we hope that the present volume will help begin to address this lacuna alongside cognate attempts to better scrutinize the current moment.

Finally, while the chapters in this volume each explore urban developmentalism and point to areas for further engaging research, we might also further consider what some of the future methodological contributions to such a project might be. For instance, we feel that the ethnographic research on everyday practices of city making in chapters such as those by Moon, Hae and Kim complements the more institutional focus on urban development and/or archival research on Cold War planning networks by Choi and Glassman, Cartier, Gottfried, and others. Each method is used to explore geopolitical economies, spaces of exception and networks of expertise in unique ways. One open question, however, is how might these methods speak across their disciplinary boundaries in a more active fashion? What room is there for greater insights to be developed from an inter-disciplinary, mixed-method approach? While there are a range of insights in this volume that deepen the three main themes identified in this introductory chapter, we feel there is much more room for further development of the methodological aspects of this research. In particular, we are interested in exploring what insights might be gained through greater dialogue between the social sciences and the humanities in understanding the ways in which urban developmentalism takes place across institutions, networks, and scales but also through aesthetics, everyday practices, and the built form (for example, work by humanities scholars such as Watson, 2011, Lee, 2010 and by planning scholars such as Nam, 2011 provides an potential contact zone in these regards). It seems to us that the chapters in this volume open up several windows onto this topic and thus help set the basis for generating further critical discussion and urban research.

References

Arnold, D (2012) Spatial practices and border SEZs in Mekong Southeast Asia. *Geography Compass* 6(12): 740–751.

Bach, J (2011) Modernity and the urban imagination in economic zones. *Theory, Culture and Society* 28(5): 99–122.

Buckley, M and K Strauss (2016) With, against and beyond Lefebvre: Planetary urbanization and epistemic plurality. *Environment and Planning D: Society and Space* 34(4): 617–636.

Chattopadhyay, S (2017) Neoliberal Urban Transformations in Indian Cities: Paradoxes and Predicaments. *Progress in Development Studies* 17(4): 307–321.

Chen, KH (2010) *Asia as Method: Toward Deimperialization*. Durham, NC: Duke University Press.

Cowen, D and N Smith (2009) After geopolitics? From the geopolitical social to geoeconomics. *Antipode* 41(1): 22–48.

Doucette, J (2016) "The Postdevelopmental State: Economic and Social Change since 1997." In M. Seth (ed). *Routledge Handbook of Modern Korean History*. New York: Routledge, pp. 343–356.

Doucette, J and SO Lee (2015) Experimental territoriality: Assembling the Kaesong Industrial Complex in North Korea. *Political Geography* 47: 53–63.

Easterling, K (2014) *Extrastatecraft: The Power of Infrastructural Space*. London: Verso.

Ghertner, DA (2015) Why gentrification theory fails in 'much of the world'. *City* 19(4): 552–563.

Glassman, J (2018) Geopolitical economies of development and democratization in East Asia: Themes, concepts, and geographies *Environment and Planning A: Economy and Space* 50 (2): 407–415.

Hassink, R, X Hu, DH Shin, S Yamamura and H Gong (2017) The restructuring of old industrial areas in East Asia. *Area Development and Policy*, DOI: 10.1080/23792949.2017.1413405.

Hill, RC. and J.W Kim (2000). Global cities and developmental states: New York, Tokyo, and Seoul. *Urban Studies* 37(12): pp. 2167–2195.

Hsu, JY, DW Gimm and J Glassman (2018) A tale of two industrial zones: A geopolitical economy of differential development in Ulsan, South Korea, and Kaohsiung, Taiwan. *Environment and Planning A* 50(2): 457–473.

Hwang, JT (2016a) Escaping the territorially trapped East Asian developmental state thesis. *The Professional Geographer* 68(4): 554–560.

Hwang, JT (2016b) Building a developmental urban matrix: a Busan city case study. *Journal of the Korean Association of Regional Geographers* 22(2): 331–352. (In Korean)

Im, SC and B Križnik (2017) *Community-Based Urban Development: Evolving Urban Paradigms in Singapore and Seoul*. Singapore: Springer.

Jessop, B and NL Sum (2018) Geopolitics: Putting geopolitics in its place in cultural political economy. *Environment and Planning A: Economy and Space* 50 (2): 474–478.

Ji, JH (2016) The development of Gangnam and the formation of Gangnam-style urbanism: On the spatial selectivity of the anti-communist authoritarian developmental state. *Journal of the Korean Association of Regional Geographers* 22(2): 307–330. (In Korean).

Jonas, AE and S Moisio (2016) City regionalism as geopolitical processes A new framework for analysis. *Progress in Human Geography* DOI: 10.1177/0309132516679897.

Kaika, M (2011) Autistic architecture: the fall of the icon and the rise of the serial object of architecture. *Environment and Planning D: society and space* 29(6): 968–992.

Kim, IK (2010) Socioeconomic concentration in the Seoul metropolitan area and its implications in the urbanization process of Korea. *Korean Journal of Sociology* 44 (3): 111–128.

Kwak, N (2015) *A World of Homeowners: American Power and the Politics of Housing Aid*. Chicago: University of Chicago Press.

Lee, JK (2010) *Service Economies: Militarism, Sex Work, and Migrant Labor in South Korea*. Minneapolis, MN: University of Minnesota Press.

Lim, KF (2016) 'Emptying the cage, changing the birds': state rescaling, path-dependency and the politics of economic restructuring in post-crisis Guangdong, *New Political Economy* 21(4): 414–435.

Mobrand, E (2016) "Unlicensed Housing as Resistance to Elite Projects: Squatting in Seoul in the 1960s and 1970s." In F Anders and A Sedlmaier (eds) *Public Goods Versus Economic Interests: Global Perspectives on the History of Squatting*. Routledge, pp. 170–189.

Murray, MJ (2017) *The Urbanism of Exception*. Cambridge: Cambridge University Press.

Nam, S (2011) Phnom Penh: From the politics of ruin to the possibilities of return. *Traditional Dwellings and Settlements Review* 23(1): 55–68.

Neveling, P (2015) Export processing zones and global class formation. In J Carrier and D Kalb (eds) *Anthropologies of class - power, practice and inequality.* Cambridge: Cambridge University Press, pp. 164–182.

Ong, A (2006) *Neoliberalism as Exception.* Chapel Hill, NC: Duke University Press.

Paik, YS (2013) An interconnected East Asia and the Korean peninsula as a problematic. *Concepts and Context in East Asia* 2: 133–166.

Park, BG (2013) Looking for more space-sensitive Korean Studies. *Korean Social Sciences Review* 3(2): 157–193.

Park, BG (2017) State territoriality and spaces of exception in East Asia: Universalities and particularities of East Asian special zones. *Journal of the Korean Association of Regional Geographers* 23(2): 288–310. (In Korean).

Park, BG and JB Jang (2016) Gangnam-ization and Korean urban ideology. *Journal of the Korean Association of Regional Geographers* 22(2): 287–306. (In Korean).

Park, BG, RC Hill and A Saito (eds.) (2012) *Locating Neoliberalism in East Asia: Neoliberalizing Spaces in Developmental States.* Chichester: Wiley-Blackwell.

Peck, J (2017) Transatlantic city, part 1: Conjunctural urbanism. *Urban Studies* 54(1): 4–30.

Sassen, S (2001) Global cities and developmentalist states: how to derail what could be an interesting debate: a response to Hill and Kim. *Urban Studies* 38(13): 2537–2540.

Schoenberger, E and R Walker (2016) Beyond exchange and agglomeration: resource flows and city environments as wellsprings of urban growth. *Journal of Economic Geography* DOI:10.1093/jeg/lbw012.

Shin, HB (2018) Urban movements and the genealogy of urban rights discourses: the case of urban protesters against redevelopment and displacement in Seoul, South Korea. *Annals of the American Association of Geographers* 108(2): 356–369.

Shin, HB and SY Kim (2016) The developmental state, speculative urbanisation and the politics of displacement in gentrifying Seoul. *Urban Studies* 53 (3): 540–559.

Shin, HB and E Lopez-Morales (2018) Beyond Anglo-American Gentrification Theory. In L Lees and M Phillips (eds.) *The Handbook of Gentrification Studies.* Cheltenham UK: Edward Elgar.

Sidaway, JD (2007) Spaces of postdevelopment. *Progress in Human Geography* 31(3): 345–361.

Sklair, L and L Gherardi (2012) Iconic architecture as a hegemonic project of the transnational capitalist class. *City* 16(1–2): 57–73.

Storper, M and AJ Scott (2016) Current debates in urban theory: A critical assessment. *Urban Studies.* DOI: 0042098016634002.

Walker, RA (2016) Why cities? A response. *International Journal of Urban and Regional Research* 40(1): 164–180.

Watson, JK (2011) *The New Asian City: Three-Dimensional Fictions of Space and Urban Form.* Minneapolis, MN: University of Minnesota Press.

Wu, Fulong (2015) *Planning for Growth: Urban and Regional Planning in China.* New York: Routledge.

Yang, M (2018) The rise of 'Gangnam style': Manufacturing the urban middle class in Seoul, 1976–1996. *Urban Studies*, DOI: 0042098017748092.

Heavy Industries and Second Tier City Growth in South Korea: A Geopolitical Economic Analysis of the "Four Core Plants Plan"

Young-Jin Choi and Jim Glassman

1   Introduction

In 1973, the South Korean government announced the Heavy Chemical Industrialization Plan, which has since been regarded as the historical moment in which the *chaebol*-centered developmental path was firmly established. Neo-Weberian analyses of the South Korean developmental state attribute this developmental path primarily to choices by national state leaders (e.g., Amsden 1989; Evans 1995; Kim 1997). The resulting development of heavy and chemical industries not only transformed the Korean national economy, it was integral to the rapid growth of the southeast (*Yong-Nam*) region of the country, especially cities such as Ulsan (Jacobs 2011; Hsu et al. 2018), the growth of which has made South Korea a neo-Weberian model not only of rapid late industrialization led by a developmental state but of state planning for industrial dispersion and more regionally balanced growth (Markusen 1999: 74–79).

According to these kinds of statist theories of national and regional growth, (1) successful heavy industrialization in Korea was made possible by a strong and autonomous state that effectively disciplined and led the conglomerates, the *chaebols*, including by ordering firms to disperse activities to regions of the country outside of Seoul (Markusen 1999: 75–76); (2) some large capitalists positively responded to the state's projects because they believed that their cooperation with the state would provide them with an opportunity to expand their business into heavy industries by taking advantage of the government's preferential supports for state-targeted heavy and chemical industries, as well as the infrastructure being developed outside of Seoul for specialized industries (Markusen 1999: 76–8); and (3) the state's strong, disciplinary drive corresponded well with private sector actors' pursuit of their own interests—including their desire to locate plants in their home regions and areas remote from the border with North Korea (Markusen 1999: 79)—which was key to the success of heavy industrialization.

This line of reasoning, while having some merits, also has limitations. First, a strong bond between the state and Korean capitalists was not enough to generate heavy industry growth in dispersed locations; another condition was required. For their mutual agreement upon pursuing an export-oriented strategy to be effective, it was necessary that the state and capitalists should be able to tap transnational networks for sales opportunities, financing, and technology transfers; the conditions for growth of domestic capitalism cannot be confined to those that exist at the national-territorial scale. To the alliances between national actors (i.e., the state and domestic capitalists) we must add the alliances between these actors and transnational actors if we are to understand the success of heavy industrialization in Korea (see Woo 1991; Chibber 2003; Glassman 2018)—and all the more so if we want to understand the growth dynamics in second tier cities such as Ulsan.

Second, in our view, neo-Weberian approaches place too much emphasis on the planning *successes* of developmental states. Yet much that happens in the process of capitalist industrial and urban development happens because of numerous contingencies and social struggles that planning cannot control. These include the activities of capitalists who attempt to oppose or moderate the effects of state planning—a reality that has sometimes been undersold in analyses of the South Korean developmental state.

We take on these weaknesses of statist approaches through a case study of a core component of the heavy chemical industrialization process in the 1970s, the Four Core Plants Plan. Employing a geopolitical economic approach to national and regional growth, we show that the success of one of South Korea's premier *chaebol*, Hyundai, was an exception rather than a rule in that most firms did not prosper under developmental state planning. Moreover, the success that only Hyundai achieved, among the four companies selected for the Four Core Plants Plan, was not an outcome of the effectiveness of the state's developmental policy but, ironically, a result of the failure of the government's original plan. We show that the success of Hyundai and its growth into a powerful *chaebol* relied on its persistent efforts to substitute its own strategies for the state's plan, and on its enrollment into an expansive transnational alliance, based on its previous achievements in completing US military projects during the Vietnam War era (see Glassman and Choi 2014). In addition, we show that Hyundai's success was based in part on its specific opportunities in Ulsan, and therefore was not so much a model of national economic success as a model of transnationally mediated sub-national dynamism. We thus claim that what is considered Korea's success in heavy industrialization would not likely have occurred had it not been for both the US-led Cold War Alliance in East Asia and the localized urban connections of specific firms like Hyundai.

Our argument is structured as follows. In Section 2, we briefly outline the basic features of our geopolitical economic approach and note how we use it to address the growth of industry in second tier cities. In Section 3, we provide a brief outline of the Korean government's early policies promoting the machine industry, and we then examine the introduction, modification, and consequences of the Four Core Plants Plan, the first official blueprint for heavy industrialization. In Section 4, we compare the strategic responses and resulting historical paths of the four firms that were selected to pursue the Four Core Plants Plan. In Section 5, we highlight critical factors for the success of Hyundai Shipbuilding in Ulsan. In the conclusion, we briefly review our major arguments.

2   Rudiments of a Geopolitical Economy Approach

We call our analytical approach "geopolitical economy" (see Glassman 2018). A very brief word is in order, here, about how we use this term and what we mean by calling it an approach. At a very general level, "geo-political economy" calls attention to the dialectical interplay between geopolitical and political economic forces, with class relations being a constant mediator. In calling the attention we pay to this dialectic an approach we signal that we consider geopolitical economy to be as much an analytical perspective *on* geopolitics and political economy as a particular practice *of* geopolitics or political economy. Moreover, we think it is an analytical approach that has great historical scope and is useful for analyzing relationships between geopolitics and political economy in the pre-Cold War, Cold War, and post-Cold War eras. We also use the term "geo-political economy" as shorthand for "geographical political economy." In this we signal that, like other geographers, we regard the socio-spatial aspects of class and state relations as complex and frequently shifting, rather than as secure and antagonistic topologies of power. Thus, geopolitical economy as an approach requires attention to the interplay between geopolitics and political economy, as well as to the shifting socio-spatial terrain of this interplay over time and in different geographical contexts.

Our approach to geopolitical economy thus works from the contention that geopolitics, and state activities generally, condition economic development (and vice versa) across broad swaths of history; it also combines this contention with sensitivity to socio-spatial flexibility and the variety of scales at which political, geopolitical, and political economic processes develop. In our analysis of the Four Core Plants Plan and its consequences, we thus highlight both crucial geopolitical moments in the development of Korean heavy industry and the multiple scales at which this development occurs.

In both of these respects—emphasis on the dialectics of geopolitics and political economy, and on socio-spatial flexibility—the predominant neo-Weberian and institutionalist analyses of the Korean developmental state have been somewhat wanting (Glassman and Choi 2014). Focusing fairly narrowly on state policy-making within the nation-state container, and attuned especially to national indicators of economic growth, neo-Weberian scholarship has largely placed geopolitics in the deep background of the discussion (Woo 1991 being an exception), while also neglecting some of the crucial transnational class dimensions of development. These are weaknesses we believe a geopolitical economy approach can redress. We focus on how a complex of class and class-relevant socio-spatial processes in and around South Korea—running from transnational geopolitical and business networks, to national state policy-making, to local development alliances—shaped the distinctive outcomes associated today with Korea's developmental state and heavy industry complex.

In carrying out this analysis, we especially attempt to break away from the statist emphasis on national territorial framings of development. We do this by noting the importance of the *Yong-Nam* region—and Ulsan in particular—to Hyundai's growth and South Korea's heavy industry and petrochemical development.[1] This focus also places our analysis in conversation with recent debates between urban geographers such as Alan Scott, Michael Storper, Erica Schoenberger, and Richard Walker. Scott and Storper, for example, claim that forces of agglomeration play the major role in any processes of urban development (2014). In a critical geographical political economic rejoinder to this line of argument, Schoenberger and Walker argue that factors such as class processes and other power relations in which capitalists play central roles are also integral to urbanization (2016; Walker 2016). We are broadly in agreement with Schoenberger and Walker, and our analysis places significant emphasis on power relations, but we also bring a more overtly geopolitical perspective to bear in our analysis of capitalist elites like the owners and managers of Hyundai. Thus, like Ann Markusen, Yong-Sook Lee, Sam Ock-Park, and other scholars of Korean urbanization (Markusen et al. 1999), we highlight factors such as military considerations and funding in the siting of industrial projects in Korea. But in line with the points we make above, we also note the limited capacity of the Korean state to simply command Korean capital, whether in

---

1   See map of region at Wikipedia, "Gyeongsang Province," Available (consulted 26 January 2017) at: https://en.wikipedia.org/wiki/Gyeongsang_Province; and at the Perry Casteneda Map Library, "Korean Peninsula," Available (consulted 26 January 2017) at: http://www.lib .utexas.edu/maps/middle_east_and_asia/korea2001.jpg.

the fashion of a developmental state or in the fashion of a Cold War national security state. The story we tell, to which we now turn, is instead a story of transnational geopolitical economic networks, complex power relations, and numerous historical contingencies.

3   Early Attempts to Build a Machinery Industry: Plan A, The Dongyang Heavy Industry Plan

The South Korean government's first attempt to develop the machinery industry during the 1960s centered on construction of Dongyang Heavy Industries (Dongyang HI). The goal was to set up a new company that would take on subcontracted work from Japanese firms in the machinery industry. It was widely accepted that, unlike the steel industry, the development of the machinery industry required a well-structured production network. In this regard, Korean elites and businessmen agreed that entering Japanese-centered global production networks (GPNs) through subcontracting was a good starting point.[2] Japan was also thought to be the most feasible funding source. First, during the 1960s, Korean-Japanese assets in Japan were the most important for Korean business: prior to the Korea-Japan Normalization Treaty, the capital inflow of Korean-Japanese assets reached US$25.69 million, most of which was used for business creation (Nagano 2010, 54–6). Second, of the Japanese war reparations agreed upon as part of the normalization treaty, US$1.5 million were designated for developing small- and medium-sized firms in the machine industry (Kimiya 2008). Third, due to recent colonial history, Korean businessmen found the Japanese business environment familiar and easy to access. Fourth, for Japanese businessmen, Korea was a logical place—both economically and geographically—toward which to direct capital outflows: thus, 17.3 percent of total Japanese capital outflow to developing countries by 1970 was to South Korea (Woo 1991, 90).

After having gone through a series of changes in 1962, 1966, and 1967, and a further two revisions in 1968 (Choi 2015, 102–3), the final plan for Dongyang HI proposed that: (1) Shin Nippon Koki (SNK, owned by Son Dalwon, a Korean-Japanese businessman) and the Korean government (ROK) would jointly set up Dongyang HI with a 55:45 (SNK:ROK) ratio of ownership; (2) SNK, as the parent company, would subcontract to Dongyang HI in such a way that

---

2   Our use of the gendered term "businessmen," throughout, is intentional and accurately reflects both the complete dominance of men within the Korean business world of this era and the highly gendered character of the business culture.

70 percent of the product from Dongyang HI would be tagged as Shin Nippon Koki's product and exported through SNK's sales network; and (3) SNK would utilize the production networks that were already established in the Japanese machinery industry, so that Kobe Steel and Kawasaki HI would be responsible for supplying, respectively, the heavy machinery and industrial equipment for Dongyang HI (EPB 1968). By entering Japan-centered GPNs, Dongyang HI was expected to play a central role in attracting Korean-Japanese business participation in building the national economy, receiving the transfers of technology and management skills from Japanese firms, and forming a bridgehead for Korean firms to enter Japan-centered GPNs.

However, the Dongyang HI plan was not realized. Anti-Japan sentiment among Koreans made it difficult to obtain public support for economic cooperation with Japan. Additionally, SNK wanted to outsource only a part of their production process to Dongyang HI, so the transfer of technology and/or management skills was bound to be limited. Furthermore, it was alleged that the Korean government spent the war reparations received from Japan in setting up a secret fund (*Dong-A Daily Newspaper* 1964, April 2), and as a result, its promised share of 45 percent of the total investment never materialized. More importantly, Japanese businessmen and the Japanese government became pessimistic about the prospects of the plan. Japan's machinery firms preferred selling off aging capital goods (and upgrading) to having a Korean company within their subcontracting system (Choi 2011, 119–220). Moreover, Japanese capitalists thought that Korean machinery firms were not yet ready to fulfill the requirements of the hierarchical subcontracting system. The Japanese government also shared this opinion. According to the February 1969 inspectorate report on economic cooperation between Japan and Korea in the machinery industry, submitted to the South Korean government by the Economic Cooperation Bureau of the Japan Ministry of Foreign Affairs:

> There is a need for drastic investment in technology transfer. Facilities are falling too far behind and costs are poorly managed. They have inadequate foundry industrial facilities and immature fabrication technology of such a poor quality that they cannot meet the criteria for production in Japan. ... A more reasonable way of doing technology transfer would be through transferring capital goods from Japanese firms to Korean firms, rather than through direct investments from Japanese companies.
>
> cited in *Kyunghyang Daily Newspaper* 1969, February 27

The previous success of the hierarchical subcontracting system in light industry was not replicated in heavy industry. The Dongyang HI Plan had aimed to attract investment and technology transfers from large-scale Japanese firms by securing a channel of participation with Korean-Japanese businesses, such as SNK. However, Japanese businessmen saw the newly built company as a risky investment target because they did not consider the Korean machine industry ready to undertake work within their subcontracting system. It was also clear that the appeal to Korean-Japanese businessmen's patriotism was not effective in this case (*Donga Daily Newspaper* 1968, February 12). In sum, Japanese businesses thought investing in the subcontracting system was too risky and thus, in the end, the Japanese government did not approve this approach.

4   Early Attempts to Build a Machinery Industry: Plan B, The Free Export Zone as Heavy Industry Catalyst

After the failure of the Dongyang HI Plan, two opposing alternatives were suggested: (1) setting up a free export zone (FEZ) to attract Japanese foreign direct investment (FDI) in heavy industry, and (2) setting up the "Four Core Plants Plan", which involved large Korean capitalists as the main actors instead of Korean-Japanese businessmen. We will examine the Four Core Plants Plan in the next section; here we note why the FEZ approach failed.

By establishing a FEZ, the Korean government and domestic businessmen sought a way to attract FDI from Japan. The Federation of Korean Industries (FKI, a federation of major Korean firms) proposed creating an FEZ to attract FDI, using the Kaohsiung Export Processing Zone (KEPZ) in Taiwan as a model. Although the FDI policy seemed to be against large Korean capitalists' interests, such capitalists were enthusiastic about this policy because they believed FDI to be one way to induce technology transfer and capital inflow from Japan, thereby pushing them one step further into global markets (Choi 2008).

With the launch of the Masan Free Export Zone (MAFEZ), FDI grew from the equivalent of 5 percent of foreign borrowing in 1969 to 15 percent in 1970 (Woo 1991, 101). However, the FEZ/FDI Plan turned out to have two limitations: (1) FDI increased but fell short of the expected amount, and (2) the FEZ plan did not foster the growth of Korean domestic firms. Regarding the latter limitation, most Japanese companies operating in MAFEZ were labor-intensive, small- and medium-sized electronics companies. For example, Japan accounted for 91 percent of all FDI in South Korea by 1981, and 48.6 percent of this Japanese FDI was invested in the electrical and electronics sectors. Moreover, by this time (1980) 54 percent of the investments in MAFEZ were small-scale investments of less than US$1 million (MAFEZ 1997, 298, 302, 305). This Japanese approach of investing in simple processing and cheap labor performed well relative to its own goals, but had serious limitations for industrial upgrading (Lee 1974).

Realizing that it was impossible to follow the KEPZ model to develop a machinery industry within the Japanese subcontracting system, in which small- and medium-sized manufacturers produce items under OEM contracts (Choi 2015, 126), the Korean government went in the other direction and sought a substitute plan for MAFEZ. The new substitute strategy, called the Four Core Plants Plan, was aimed at the development of the machine industry based on large domestic firms.

This move, emerging only in the 1970s, shows that the strong bond between Park's administration and large domestic South Korean firms was not in any way natural or automatic. Rather, the government's favoritism toward large domestic firms emerged as a result of the government's strategic choices to counter the continuing failures of its previous plans. Seeing the failures of attempts to, first, insert South Korean firms into the Japanese machinery production subcontracting system through Korean-Japanese business networks and, second, to attract Japanese FDI in heavy industry through the FEZ, the Park administration called for large domestic firms to lead the charge of economic development.

5   The Emergence, Failure, and Afterlives of the Four Core Plants Plan

Following these failures, promoting the machinery industry increasingly became a state priority. Without a domestic base for machinery supplies, the growth of light industries in Korea was inevitably accompanied by an increase in capital goods imports from Japan. During the period of the second Five Year Economic Development Plan (1967–71), a three-fold increase of industry output raised the demand for machinery imports nearly five times (Korea Association of Machinery Industry 1980b, 18).

The share of Japanese machinery imports in total machinery imports rose from 52 percent in 1965 to 65 percent in 1968 (Park 2008, 101). As a result, the growth of light industries was dependent on Japanese capital goods, which increased the Korean trade deficit with Japan; and the import of general machinery from Japan was the main deficit-causing factor (The Korean Dredging Corporation 1973, August, 12). Eventually, the lack of a domestic machinery base became a bottleneck for further growth. Therefore, import substitution in the machinery industry became a pressing need for both accelerating growth and reducing the trade deficit (Lee 2009, 93).

The Four Core Plants Plan (1970–1), the next stage of the government's developmental strategy, was proposed as a solution for overcoming the bottleneck. It was the government's first official blueprint for Korean heavy industrialization (Woo 1991, 129). The Plan created a structure in which the heavy machinery complex was positioned at the center, and three other industries were related in terms of the input-output structure (see Figure 2.1). The Plan showed that the four core plants were to be built as industrial bases for digesting a large volume of steel that would eventually be produced by the Pohang Steel Corporation (POSCO)—under construction at the time. The Four Core Plants Plan, though modified several times and eventually cancelled, became a framework upon which Korean heavy industrialization was later based.

The main features of the Four Core Plants Plan can be summarized as follows: (1) the separation of conception and execution between the state and

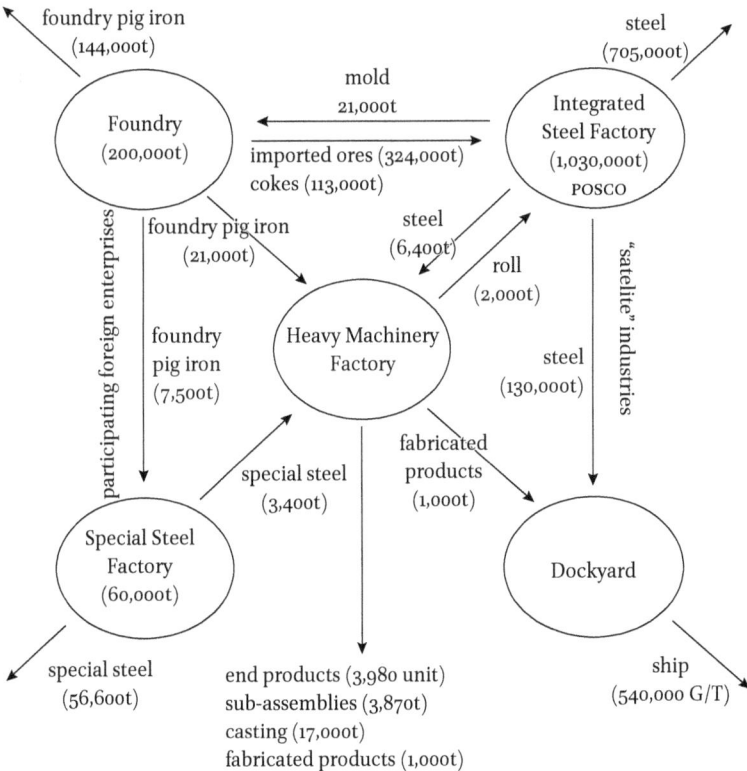

FIGURE 2.1   Four Core Plants Plan
SOURCE: KIST 1970, 126, FIGURE 3-1

private firms, (2) a Japanese-dependent financial structure (Kim 1999, 257), (3) a copied version of the Japanese heavy industrialization plan (Park 2008, 88–9), and (4) the respective assignment of four large domestic companies to the four selected industries.

The Korea Institute of Science and Technology (KIST) submitted a "Plan for development of Korean mechanical engineering industry" (1970) to the Economic Planning Board (EPB). According to the plan, which mainly suggested selection and concentration, nine industrial sectors were selected according to export and industrialization impact scores: ships, trucks, small work/passenger vehicles, machine tools, textile machinery, heavy electrical machinery, construction equipment, farm machinery, and automobiles. The government narrowed the nine candidates down to four core industries: foundry pig iron, heavy machinery, special steel, and shipbuilding. The government also selected four large domestic companies and assigned each one to one of the four core industries (see Table 2.1).

The Four Core Plants Plan was still critically dependent, both technologically and financially, on Japan's cooperation. It was a successor to the previous Dongyang HI Plan in the sense that it still basically pursued the strategy of inserting Korean machinery firms into the Japan-centered subcontracting network. To induce cooperation from Japanese capitalists and the Japanese government, the Korean government needed to show that the Plan was less risky than the previous Dongyang HI Plan and prove that the establishment of the subcontracting system would be mutually beneficial for both countries (Choi 2015, 120–3; Woo 1991, 129). Furthermore, the Plan needed to ensure that

TABLE 2.1   Target industries and firms in Four Core Plants Plan

Four Core Plants	Companies Selected	Company Subsidiary	Location
Foundry Pig Iron	Kangwon Coal Co.	Sampyo Heavy Industry Co.	Pohang
Special Steel	Daehan Heavy Machinery Industry Co., Ltd.	Daehan Heavy Machinery Industry Co., Ltd.	Changwon
Heavy Machinery	Shinjin Motors	Korea Machinery Co.	Changwon
Shipbuilding	Hyundai Construction Co.	Hyundai Heavy Industries	Ulsan

SOURCE: PARK 2008, 99.

the Korean government could push Korean domestic firms to upgrade their machinery tools and networks to the degree that they could fulfill the subcontract requirements.

The Park Chung-Hee administration put the Four Core Plants Plan on the official agenda at the 4th Korean-Japan Ministerial Meeting in 1970. In the meeting, Japan agreed to send an inspection committee to Korea to test the feasibility of the plan. However, Japan refused to discuss the possibility of aiding the Korean shipbuilding industry. Japan had promised to provide US$59 million in commercial loans for the construction of two of the proposed four plants (special steel and heavy machinery), but it then refused to include the promise in the official agreement. Later, Japan substituted US$80 million in export-import bank loans for the promised commercial loans but did not proceed with additional support. Eventually, Japan vetoed the Four Core Plants Plan over its support for the development of the special steel and machine-building industries (Woo 1991, 129).

The Four Core Plants Plan itself thus ended with no substantial achievements and was officially discarded. One of the main reasons for its demise was that the government failed to obtain cooperation from Japanese business sectors and the Japanese government for financing, technology transfers, and access to sales networks. The failure of the plan affected the future direction of heavy industrialization in Korea.

As the plan was scuttled, each of the core firm's responses and subsequent evolution differed, dependent upon the firm's position in global geopolitical economic networks. Ultimately, among the four large domestic firms that were selected under the Four Core Plants Plan, only Hyundai—at that time a large construction company—successfully metamorphosed into a *chaebol,* eventually gaining a dominant position in many sectors, such as shipbuilding, automobiles, and heavy industry. Looking at Hyundai's case and contrasting it with the other three cases, we will show that Hyundai's successful evolution into a *chaebol* was in large part due to its geopolitical economic positioning in the US Cold War alliance, based on its previous experience participating in US military offshore procurement (OSP), as well as its ability to cultivate growth in Ulsan.

During the old regime before the Four Core Plants Plan, the state acted as a planner responsible for the design and direction of economic growth (sometimes government intervention covered financing, human resources, management and sales), and private firms acted as the agents who passively executed the government's plans. After the failure of the Four Core Plants Plan, however, Hyundai developed an autonomous position from which it negotiated on an equal footing with the government concerning issues such as capital financing, joint ventures with foreign firms, capacity determination, and sales strategy, while pushing its own preferred strategies *through* government plans. In this regard, the Four Core Plants Plan serves as a window through which the change in power relations between the *chaebol* and the government can be observed. The *chaebol* grew to take the initiative in economic policies, and the government reset its role as an indirect supporter rather than a direct planner.

However, the transfer of initiative to the *chaebols* should not be understood as an example of the diminishing power of states but rather a result of a specific form of "strategic coupling" (Jessop 1990) between state actors and the *chaebol*, each pursuing their own accumulation strategies. The government still exercised life-or-death authority over the private sector by controlling distribution of the National Investment Fund and by selectively provisioning payment guarantees for foreign loans. Additionally, the growth of the *chaebol's* influence through heavy industrialization cannot be understood as the result of the economy becoming autonomous but rather was the result of political elites' choices for state projects, including the Four Core Plants Plan and the Economic Developmental Plan—which, coincidentally, were in line with the *chaebol's* interests in heavy industrialization. Once strategic coupling was established, it enhanced the mutual dependencies between the state and capital, which recursively reinforced the strategic coupling.

6   Historical Paths of Selected Companies

With the failures of previous plans as background, we now examine how the selected companies reacted to the government's Four Core Plants Plan, and then evolved after the plan was cancelled. The histories of these firms show how their businesses and geopolitical economic networks affected their strategies and actions.

7   Kangwon Coal and Foundry Pig Iron

Kangwon Coal, which was selected by the government to undertake the foundry pig iron plant, was the largest coal mining company in the 1960s, but it had no experience in working with raw pig iron. Despite the company's lack of experience, the government expected the company's large cash holdings to be effectively invested in the plant when combined with government financing. To satisfy the requirements of the Plan, Kangwon Coal founded Sampyo Heavy Industry in Pohang in 1970. However, no further progress was made because the government failed to gain an agreement from Japan to fund the plan and failed to provide its own funds. Seeking another funding source was difficult for Kangwon Coal, which had been operating on a purely domestic production basis. After the Four Core Plants Plan was cancelled, the foundry pig iron project was partially undertaken by POSCO in 1973.

8   Daehan Heavy Machinery Industry and Special Steel

Kansai Machine Works, which used to be a Japanese firm during the colonial period, was sold to Kim Yeon Kyu after liberation and was renamed Daehan Heavy Machinery Industry (Daehan HMI). Being the only machine-tool production company in Korea, Daehan HMI was constantly supported by the government through USAID loans in 1957, the Promotion of Daehan HMI in 1965, and other state mechanisms (EPB 1965). Owing to the government's favor, Daehan HMI grew to be the 4th largest company in Korea during the 1950–1960s (Kim 1997, 125, Table 4.1).

Kim, one of the leaders of the Korean machinery industry in the 1960s and 1970s, was a key player in the Korean Association of Machinery Industry, which represented the interests of private firms in the machinery industry. Using his strong ties to Japanese businessmen, he also played a role in inserting Korean machinery firms into Japan-centered GPNs (Korea Association of Machinery Industry 1980, 53).

Unfortunately for Kim, Daehan HMI went through phases of stunted development similar to those of Kangwon Coal. No significant steps were taken under the Four Core Plants Plan because the promised government funding never materialized. When the investment fund was financed at a low interest rate under the heavy industrialization plan in 1975, Daehan HMI moved to the Changwon complex and took its first step in constructing a special steel plant. However, Daehan HMI suffered from financial difficulties and was finally acquired by Kia Special Steels in 1986 (Korea Development Institute 2011, 135).

9   Korea Machinery Industries and Heavy Machinery

Chosun Machine Works, which was a Japanese company during the colonial period, was confiscated by the Korean government and then operated as a state-run enterprise under the name Korea Machinery Industries (KMI). It was the largest machinery factory in Korea in the 1960s and a special law (No. 1227) was enacted in 1963 to officially support it. The company produced goods such as diesel engines, lift cars, and trains. It was one of the two largest state-run heavy industry companies (the other being the Korea Shipbuilding and Engineering Corporation).

KMI was privatized and sold to Shinjin Motors in 1968 at far below market value, under Park's directives (Parliamentary Inspection Report 1968; see Choi 2015, 111–5). However, after acquiring KMI, the Shinjin group had a conflict with the state over whether automobiles or heavy machinery would become their core project for funding (Park 2015, 632). When the government found in 1975 that Shinjin was not carrying through on its promise to expand the plant's capacity—an expansion meant to serve as the basis for its running KMI—it placed the company under legal management by the Korea Development Bank. "Giving" a formerly state-owned company to a *chaebol* as a favor, without any concerns over efficiency, has been one of the typical routes to *chaebol* growth under state favoritism. This presents a vivid example of the corrupt alliance that strategically coupled state elites and "political" capitalists.

10   Hyundai Construction and the Shipbuilding Industry

Hyundai Construction was selected to lead the shipbuilding industry under the Four Core Plants Plan, instead of state-owned Korea Shipbuilding and Engineering (KSEC), which, at the time, was Korea's largest shipbuilding firm and had been showing good performance and steady growth. The reason Hyundai was selected instead of KSEC was unclear, although KSEC did have disadvantages, such as a strong union, a weak governance structure, a lack of management ability, and a reluctance to pursue an export-oriented strategy (Nam 2013). Although Hyundai had no prior experience in the shipbuilding business, its achievements in many construction projects abroad were likely taken into account. Unlike the other three firms examined here, Hyundai sought a breakthrough abroad instead of relying on the government's support when faced with financing problems, and in doing so it successfully established itself in the shipbuilding industry.

Each of the four firms differed in its strategy for overcoming financial problems, and the different strategies were conditioned by the scope and geographic scale of their business networks. Hyundai, unlike the other firms, was able to maximize the potential gain from its transnational business networks because it was neither confined within national economic space nor dependent on Japan-centered GPNs. Instead, Hyundai's networks were globally formed, integrated into the geographically expansive US military-industrial complex (MIC) that emerged through Cold War alliances. We will now examine the stimulus provided by Hyundai's participation in this alliance.

11   Hyundai's Success and Cold War Alliance

We outline several factors that affected Hyundai Heavy Industries' (HHI) evolution into one of the world's largest shipbuilding companies. First, we will show that HHI's success in the shipbuilding industry lay in its successful mobilization of foreign capital. Second, we will show how HHI developed its own growth strategy and emerged as an autonomous player in spite of state planning setbacks. Third, we will show that the technology, knowledge, and business networks that Hyundai Construction accumulated from its participation in OSP for the US MIC became a base for Hyundai's expansion into the global market. Finally, we will show that all of the above factors were closely related to Hyundai's geopolitical economic position in the globally formed US Cold War Alliance, which also facilitated its ability to grow in Ulsan, for historically specific reasons.

12   Successful Mobilization of Capital

Unlike the other three firms, Hyundai managed to access substantial financial resources for pursuing its task under the Four Core Plants Plan. Table 2.2 shows the financing sources for HHI's investment in building shipyards. HHI obtained 84 percent of its total capital financing through its own financing routes, while only 16 percent of its total financing came from direct government support. The returns for Hyundai Construction's participation in the Vietnam War project, along with total foreign loans, accounted for 23 percent and 61 percent, respectively.

Hyundai Construction received a total of US$178 million from Vietnam War contracts, a portion of which was used as seed money for building the shipyards (Amsden 1989, 266; Glassman and Choi 2014). Although the government failed to obtain loans from Japan, HHI successfully contracted for a

TABLE 2.2   Capital financing for building shipyard in 1970–73

Source	Amount (1,000 US$)	Ratio (%)
Hyundai	30,480	23
Korean Government	21,020	16
Foreign Loan	79,770	61
Total	131,280	100

SOURCE: HHI 1992, 262, 272

US$51 million loan from Barclays Bank, which provided additional funding for building shipyards (Amsden 1989, 309; Kim 1999, 102). Eighty million US dollars, the total amount of Hyundai's foreign loans, amounted to one-sixth of Korea's total foreign exchange reserves in 1971.

Hyundai thus showed more capacity for finding its own sources of financing than the other companies involved in the Four Core Plants Plan. Hyundai Construction had accumulated considerable engineering experience and had built strong geopolitical economic networks through US military OSP during the Vietnam War, which became the major basis for HHI's success in mobilizing foreign loans.

Figure 2.2 shows the personal connections of Hyundai CEO Chung Ju Yung in the Cold War alliance that Hyundai utilized for obtaining foreign loans. HHI was a newly born company; therefore, proving its competence and ability to successfully fulfill contracts was necessary for its investment projects to be approved by foreign lenders. Charles Brooke Longbottom, CEO of the English consulting firm A&P Appledore International, Ltd., was a key actor for launching Hyundai's project. Based on the observation of Hyundai Construction's previous achievements with US OSP projects both in Korea and Vietnam, Longbottom was convinced that Hyundai met US military engineering standards. Being an influential expert in the shipbuilding industry, he wrote a recommendation letter to Barclays Bank for Chung, attesting to Hyundai's capacity as a shipbuilder (Kirk 1994, 97). Longbottom also introduced Chung to George Stravros Livanos, a Greek shipping magnate, and influenced Livanos' decision to place an order with Chung for two 260,000 ton ships, even before the shipyard was built, a time when placing an order and making an advance payment was highly risky (Shim 2010, 39). When he placed the order, Livanos made an advance payment of 140 million KRW. This advance payment was used as the proof of the actual order that was required for Hyundai's foreign loan application to Barclays Bank to be approved by the Export Credit Guarantee Department in the UK (Hyundai 1997, 516).

A US loan broker named Davis, who was a key actor for USAID in Korea in the 1950s and 1960s, introduced Chung to Longbottom (Hyundai 1997, 514–516). In addition, James Van Fleet, a former US military commander in the Korean and Greek Wars, became another key economic bridge between the United States and Korea during the 1960s and 1970s (Braim 2001, 327, 347). He founded the American-Korean Foundation in 1953 and The Korea Society in 1957. Van Fleet attempted to help the Park regime consolidate its legitimacy with the Kennedy administration, and he acted as a bridge between Park and US and Korean capitalists when they began undertaking a number of industrial projects in the 1960s, including the Ulsan industrial complex, the first and the largest complex

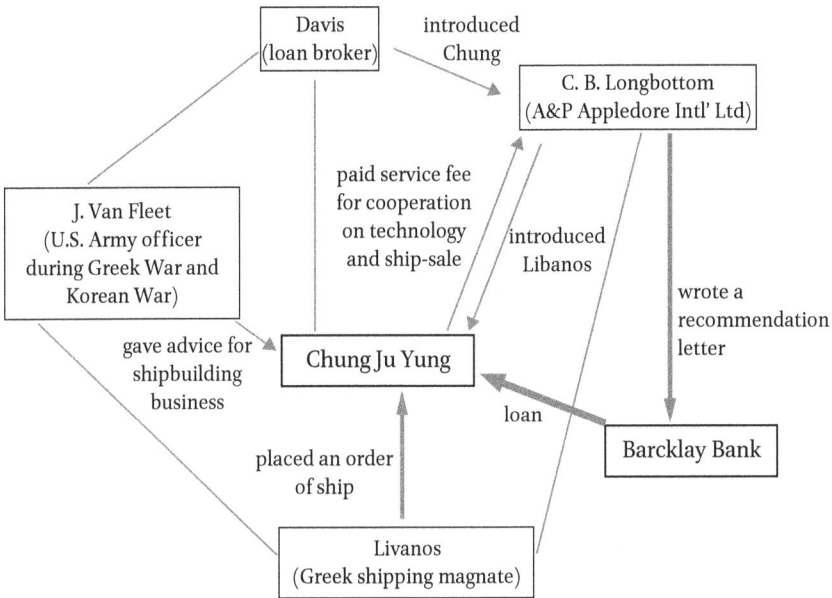

FIGURE 2.2   HHI's successful startup and Cold War class alliance
SOURCE: CHOI AND GLASSMAN 2018, 413

of its kind (Hsu et al. 2018; Glassman 2018). Van Fleet personally introduced Chung to some US shipping businessmen at the Keiser Shipyards when Chung was looking for business ventures other than construction, which made Chung think that the Keiser path—starting from the construction business and moving to shipbuilding and automobiles—was a model that Hyundai could follow (Hyundai 1997, 508).

The story of how Hyundai—with neither previous experience in shipbuilding nor evidence to prove their ability to undertake the orders and repay foreign debt—could successfully obtain foreign loans from Barclays Bank and receive actual orders, shows that these feats would have been impossible without Hyundai's involvement in the US Cold War alliance. Hyundai's crucial networks, as it moved into shipbuilding, were based both directly and indirectly on participation in US military OSP in Korea and Vietnam.

13   Substitution and Modification of the Government's Plan

Although Hyundai undertook the project outlined for it in the Four Core Plants Plan, it also gained the ability to shape the government's original plans according to its own interests. First, HHI pushed forward an export-oriented strategy instead of the government's original import-substitution strategy. Second, instead of following the state-led growth path, HHI sought to become both financially and technically less dependent on Japan-centered GPNs and found substitute technological and financial sources among European shipbuilding companies.

After the Four Core Plants Plan was officially cancelled, alternative measures for fostering the shipbuilding industry were discussed. Following successive modifications, Hyundai submitted the final version of its plan for shipyards in 1973. Table 2.3 shows the differences between the government's plan, as reflected in the Four Core Plants Plan, and HHI's proposal in 1973.

When the Korean government created the Four Core Plants Plan, the Korean government set a goal of constructing a shipyard with 200,000 DWT for import substitution of ships (KIST 1970, 148). Hyundai initially proposed a shipyard with 500,000 DWT, followed one year later by a 1 million DWT capacity proposal, which was five times larger than the government' original plan and would allow the building of vessels larger than or equal to very large crude oil carriers. Although the Korean government announced that its plan was export-oriented, the shipyard's capacity was in fact planned to be just enough to meet growing domestic demand (see KIST 1970, 148, Figure 4-6; Korea Development Institute 2002, 94, Table 12). Yet Hyundai had global ambitions and independently pursued an export-oriented strategy by constructing the shipyard with a 1 million DWT capacity.

In its original plan, the government proposed a joint venture between Hyundai and Mitsubishi Heavy Industries that would allow for technology transfer. However, the Korean government failed to induce agreement from

TABLE 2.3   Government's original plan and Hyundai's modification

	Government's Original Plan (1970)	Hyundai's modification (1973)
Shipyard's capacity	DWT 200,000 Import substitution	DWT 1,000,000
Main purpose	Domestic-oriented	Export-oriented
Capital financing for the plant construction	Joint venture with foreign firms	Foreign loan (to secure control of the company)
Technology transfer partner	Japanese shipbuilders	European shipbuilders

SOURCE: HHI 1992, 254, 320; CHOI 2015, 145–146

Japan. When the government's attempts to build a shipyard with Japan's cooperation reached an impasse, Hyundai, realizing Japan's reluctance to cooperate lest technology transfer boomerang against it (Woo 1991, 129), instead sought European technology transfer partners. European shipbuilding companies intended to gain profits from technology transfer rather than from increasing sales volume because their market share had shrunk against Japan's in the world market. Hyundai, as a newcomer in the shipbuilding business, urgently needed a chance to learn any available technology through European partners (Hyundai 1997, 379–380). Hyundai pushed through a deal with A&P Appledore and Scott Lithgow in the UK for technology transfer and the use of their sales networks (Korea Development Institute 2002, 100). Based on this contract, Longbottom wrote the recommendation letter to prove Hyundai's competence in pursuing shipbuilding business, which allowed Hyundai to receive a foreign loan from Barclays Bank.

14   Hyundai Construction as a Prerequisite for HHI's Growth, and Vice Versa

The birth and growth of HHI cannot be considered without taking into account its relationship with Hyundai Construction. As mentioned earlier, the government's plan to set up HHI to undertake the shipbuilding project could not be justified without its belief that Hyundai's achievements in many construction projects, both domestically and abroad, could be repeated in the shipbuilding industry. Chung Ju Yung also thought that the knowledge and skills accumulated from Hyundai's construction business could be easily applied to the new business because the "shipbuilding business can be regarded as an extension of construction business as shipbuilding process is indeed similar to the one in construction industry" (Chung 1992, 114–116). Therefore, HHI's plan of aiming at the global market can be understood by taking into account Hyundai Construction's ongoing and future projects in the global market. In this regard, the achievement of Hyundai Construction was a prerequisite for the success of HHI, and Hyundai Construction could take advantage of running HHI.

There were a number of dimensions of this process. First, as noted above, the earnings from Hyundai Construction's Vietnam War OSP were crucial to the startup funding for HHI, as were the loans obtained from European banks, which valued Hyundai Construction's previous achievements in Vietnam. Second, Chung was correct that equipment, basic technological skills and management abilities obtained from previous experience in the construction business could be utilized for the shipbuilding business, in part because Hyundai

Construction, with its main production plants already located in and around Ulsan, was an assured source of demand for HHI. Hyundai Construction, while running construction projects in the Middle East in 1970s, placed orders for equipment, such as steel structures and cranes, with HHI, instead of placing orders with nearby producers. Through these internal transactions, Hyundai Construction bought equipment at cheaper prices, and HHI could maintain a volume of orders necessary for a smoothly running business, which is unusual for a new company (Eum[3] 2009, 128–129; Kim 1999, 167; HHI 1992, 163–165). HHI and Hyundai Construction were stable buyers and sellers for each other and mutually gained benefits through technology transfer, exchange of human resources, and the sharing of business networks (HHI 1992, 161–165; Kim 1999, 167).

Third, Hyundai Construction came to the aid of HHI when it was in trouble due to a series of cancellations of ongoing orders. When Livanos, Japan Line, and CY Tung cancelled their orders while the ships were being built, HHI was on the verge of bankruptcy (Eum 2009, 78). To save HHI, Hyundai set up a shipping company, Hyundai Merchant Marine Company, and took over the ships that the above three shipping companies did not take (Bruno and Tenold 2011, 212). Hyundai Merchant Marine Company began to use the ships to carry cargo, including construction tools and other equipment, to Hyundai Construction's construction sites in the Middle East. This relocation strategy was possible because Hyundai Construction was operating major construction projects in the Middle East, projects in which it became involved through the US MIC (Hyundai 1997, 585–586; Glassman 2018).

15   Hyundai Construction and Cold War Alliance

HHI's growth depended on Hyundai Construction's business in the Middle East, which, in turn, depended on Hyundai's geopolitical economic position in the Cold War alliance, which it gained through the many US military projects it had been involved in throughout the Vietnam War and post-Vietnam War periods (Glassman and Choi 2014).

Table 2.4 lists the main projects that Hyundai Construction undertook during the early stage of its growth in the Middle East. Whereas Hyundai Construction's previous experience in building the Ulsan shipyard in Korea and in military construction for Vietnam might have been regarded as proof of

---

3   Author interviews with Yong-Ky Eum, former CEO of Hyundai Mipo Dockyard (1988-9), and
      former Vice President of HHI (1983-8), January 2013.

TABLE 2.4   Projects that Hyundai Construction undertook during the early stage of the
Middle East project

Projects	Location	Ordering Organization	Construction period	Contract value (million, US$)
Arab Shipbuilding & Repair Yard	Bahrain	OAPEC	1975–77	144
Saudi Naval Expansion Program, Offshore Facilities	Saudi Arabia	Saudi Arabia Minister of DefenseUS Corps of Engineers	1975–78	220
Bandar Abbas Mobilization and Training Shipyard	Iran	Persian Gulf Shipbuilding Corporation	1975–76	10
Jubail Industrial Harbor	Saudi Arabia	Saudi Ports Authority	1976–79	940

SOURCE: HYUNDAI 1982, 2102–93

Hyundai's technological capacity to handle the construction projects in the Middle East, its technological and engineering skills could not at this point provide a complete answer as to how Hyundai could win out in severe competition among other international construction companies with more experience in such projects.

The first construction project that Hyundai undertook in the Middle East was the construction of the Arab Shipbuilding & Repair Yard in Bahrain. Hyundai joined the project as a subcontractor for the consortium of the English firm Sir Alexander Gibb & Partner, which was responsible for dockyard design, and Lisnave Shipyard, which was in charge of construction supervision and management. Sir Alexander Gibb & Partner gave Hyundai the opportunity to bid on the project, even though the deadline for the prequalification had passed (Eum 2009, 102–110; Hyundai 1982, 2102–2103). The completion of the subcontracted work was the stepping-stone toward other construction projects in the Middle East, such as the turnkey-based contract for Bandar Abbas Mobilization and Training Shipyard in Iran and other construction projects in Bahrain (Hyundai 1982, 2118).

By virtue of its performance in the Vietnam War and Bahrain projects, Hyundai was also invited to join the Saudi Naval Expansion Program Offshore Facilities in Jubail, Saudi Arabia, by the US Corps of Engineers (Eum 2009,

111–117) and the Jubail Industrial harbor construction project, which brought huge profits to the firm.

The opportunity to enter the bidding process for the Jubail Industrial harbor construction project was only given to companies that could prove their financial integrity by paying a deposit, which amounted to 2 percent of the estimated total cost and was equivalent to US$20 million, an amount larger than the foreign reserves of South Korea at that time. Half of the required deposit was paid, upon Hyundai's request, by Bahrain National Bank, without any collateral security for the loan, and the other half was paid, upon Bahrain National Bank's request and the Saudi Arabian government's approval, by Saudi National Commercial Bank (Hyundai 1997, 2175).

This story thus shows that it was Hyundai's enrollment in the US MIC-based geopolitical economic network, not Hyundai Construction's productivity nor its technological capacity, that enabled it to gain orders for the projects operating in the Middle East.

16   Ulsan: Hyundai's Company Town

Hyundai's dynamism was not exclusively a story of either national or transnational growth. To a great extent it was, instead, a transnationally enabled and nationally mediated process of trans-local growth, with Ulsan—the site of Hyundai's shipyards and automobile production—being the key locale for this growth. We cannot do justice here to the entire story of Hyundai's development in Ulsan, but we highlight a few major features of this development that are brought out by a geopolitical economic approach.

Hyundai was not originally based in Ulsan, Chung Ju Yung having been born in the north of Korea and having based his original business ventures in Seoul (Kirk 1994). Ulsan had long been part of a series of southeastern ports, based primarily around Pusan, that had grown through trade with Japan, but as of the early 1960s it was still comparatively small and limited in industrial development, even compared to Pusan. Ulsan came onto the map of the Korean developmental state's industrial planning at that time, as part of the more general efforts of the Park Chung Hee regime to disperse crucial industrial activities—including military production—as far from the border with North Korea as possible (Sonn 2007; Jacobs 2011). In this context, the *Young-Nam* region, including cities in a belt along the coast from Pohang and Ulsan through Pusan to Masan and Changwon, became some of the most rapidly growing industrial cities in the country, with Ulsan leading the pack and experiencing a stunning 334 percent increase in population between 1970 and 1990 (Markusen 1999, 77).

Ulsan was targeted as a growth pole by the Park regime through activities such as those of the 1962 Van Fleet Industrial mission, which led to the establishment of the Ulsan petrochemical complex (Glassman 2018). Moreover, as with other sites in the *South-east area*, Ulsan became a growth pole and a site of industrial promotion because of Park's personal military and intelligence connections—Korean Central Intelligence Agency director, Hu-Rak Lee, being from Ulsan (Shin 1994, 120). Thus, the foundations for Hyundai's growth in Ulsan had a doubly geopolitical character: on the one hand, the growth of the firm's assets and capabilities owed much to its participation in the US war effort in Vietnam, and, on the other hand, the growth of Ulsan as crucial base for its industrial operations was spurred by geopolitical considerations such as distance from North Korea and cronyism among military and intelligence leaders.

Once Hyundai established its heavy industry operations in the Ulsan industrial district—particularly its automotive and shipbuilding plants—it quickly became the dominant economic actor and employer in the city, Ulsan becoming virtually a Hyundai company town. Class dimensions of this process, and especially Hyundai's despotic labor practices in the 1970s and 1980s—deeply enabled by the Cold War context—were crucial. As one Korean politician noted of Ulsan in the early 1990s, "This is the Kingdom of Hyundai, and Chung Ju Yung is King" (cited in Kirk 1994, 230). The Hyundai "monarchy" effectively extracted enormous surplus from discontent Korean workers, keeping laborers and the city under control with state-backed, Cold War-style surveillance and repression (Ogle 1990, 117–125). In this sense, the Cold War geopolitics we have noted as crucial to Hyundai's growth—and thus to South Korea's industrial growth and dispersion—is deeply intertwined with the class processes and power relations that Schoenberger and Walker rightly highlight as a foundation of urban development.

17   Conclusion

Our case study of South Korea's heavy industry growth in the wake of the Four Core Plants Plan shows that the development of crucial lines such as shipbuilding was neither the result of a developmental state disciplining capital nor the result of the simple expansion of the global market. Rather, as a geopolitical economic approach emphasizes, geopolitics played a crucial role in spurring a socio-spatially complex political economic development process, one in which class and class-relevant forces operating transnationally, nationally, and locally intertwined to generate unanticipated and highly idiosyncratic results.

Hyundai Construction, based on the technology and business networks built through its participation in US OSP projects in Korea and Vietnam, expanded its businesses geographically from Korea to Southeast Asia and to the Middle East, and industrially from the construction field to heavy industries, including shipbuilding and automobiles, all the while growing especially dynamically in its adopted home base of Ulsan. Of course, Hyundai is only one firm—but it is not just one among others; rather, it is one of a small number of giant *chaebol* whose growth has been central to Korea's development of a highly unique "construction state," one of the few cases of "late" industrialization featuring world-beating heavy industry growth centered in the dynamism of the construction sector. And as our discussion of Ulsan also makes clear, it is uniquely important to South Korea's process of industrial dispersion and second tier city growth. This makes the Hyundai case particularly important— and it is a case where it is clear that the firm's economic achievements were made possible by its enrollment in the transnational class alliance organized by US leaders during the Cold War. In other words, Cold War geopolitics was deeply embedded in the Korean developmental process.

References

Amsden, A (1989) Asia's Next Giant: South Korea and Late Industrialization, New York and Oxford: Oxford University Press.

Braim, P (2001) *The Will to Win: biography of General James Van Fleet.* Daehun: Republic of Korea Army Training & Doctrine Command

Bruno, L and S Tenold (2011) The Basis for South Korea's Ascent in the Shipbuilding Industry, 1970–1990, *The Mariner's Mirror* 97(3): 201–217.

Chibber, B (2003) *Locked in Place: State-building and Late Industrialization in India,* Princeton: Princeton University Press.

Choi, WY (2011) "Korea-Japan Normalization and private commercial loan", in Reillumination of Korea-Japan relation in Park Jung Hee Era, Eds, Seoul: Sunin, Institution of Japanese Studies.

Choi, Y-J (2008) "Capital-State Relations and the Spatial strategies of Developmental State: A strategic-relational view on the development of MAFEZ in the 1960s and 1970s", MA thesis, Seoul National University.

Choi, Y-J (2015) Geopolitical Economies and South Korea's Heavy Industrialization in the late 1960s and early 1970s: Case studies on Hyundai Heavy Industries and Changwon Machine-building Industrial Complex", PhD thesis. Seoul National University.

Choi, Y-J and J. Glassman (2018) A geopolitical economy of heavy industrialization and second tier city growth in South Korea: Evidence from the 'Four Core Plants Plan'. *Critical Sociology*, 44(3): 405–420.

Chung, JY (1992) *There may be distressing events but no such thing as failure*, Seoul: Hyundai Culture Press.

Dong-A Daily Newspaper (1964) "The Republican Party receives 20 million USD for the election from Japan," April 2.

Dong-A Daily Newspaper (1968) "Editorial column: questions to the Heavy Machinery plan," February 12.

Economic Planning Board (EPB) (1965) "Promotion plan for Daehan Heavy Machinery Industries", National Archives of Korea, file name: floatation of foreign loan (Daehan HMI), No.BA0139444.

Economic Planning Board (EPB) (1968) "Feasibility test of the promotion plan for Machinery Industry: A.T. Kearney's report to Economic Planning Board", *National Archives of Korea,* file name: Loan for Dongyang Heavy Industries, No. Gongcha 321–3256.

Eum, Yong-ky (2009) *Fly over the sea without lighthouse*, Seoul: Yiyagikkoch.

Evans, P (1995) *Embedded Autonomy: State and Industrial Transformation*, Princeton: Princeton University Press.

Glassman, J (2018) Drums of War, Drums of Development: The Formation of a Pacific Ruling Class and Industrial Transformation in East and Southeast Asia, 1945–1980. Leiden and Chicago: Brill and Haymarket Press.

Glassman, J and Choi, Y-J (2014) "The chaebol and the US military-industrial complex: Cold War geopolitical economy and South Korean industrialization," *Environment and Planning A* 46(5): 1160–1180.

Hsu, J, Gimm, DW and Glassman, J (2018) A tale of two industrial zones: A geopolitical economy of differential development in Ulsan, South Korea, and Kaohsiung, Taiwan, *Environment and Planning A* 50(2): 457–473.

Hyundai (1982) *35th Anniversary History of Hyundai Construction*, Seoul: Hyundai Construction Company.

Hyundai (1997) *50th Anniversary History of Hyundai Construction*, Seoul: Hyundai Construction Company.

Hyundai Heavy Industries (HHI) (1992) History of Hyundai Heavy Industries Seoul: Hyundai Heavy Industries Company.

Jacobs, A (2011) Ulsan, South Korea: A Global and 'Nested' Great Industrial City, *The Open Urban Studies Journal* 4: 8–20.

Kim, EM (1997) Big Business, Strong State: Collusion and Conflict in South Korean Development, 1960–1990, Albany: State University of New York Press.

Kim, JH (1999) State-business relations in developmental state: a critical study of
industrialization in the Korean ship-building industry and the thesis of support-
discipline, PhD thesis, Seoul National University.

Kimiya, D (2008) *The Park Government's Choice*, Seoul: Humanitas.

Kirk, D (1994) *Korean Dynasty: Hyundai and Chung Ju Yung*, New York: M.E. Sharpe.

Korea Association of Machinery Industry (1980) Visit to Daehan HMI's Changwon
plant, *Machinery Industry* 46(0): 53–55.

Korea Development Institute (2002) Construction of the Shipbuilding Industry: A
Model for Korean Industrialization, *Reference paper: knowledge partnership project*.

Korea Development Institute (2011) 2010 Modularization of Korea's Development Experience: private Sector Development, *Knowledge Sharing program*, Ministry of
Strategy and Finance.

Korea Institute of Science and Technology (KIST) (1970) *Plan for Development of Korean Mechanical Engineering Industry Volume I.*

Korean Dredging Corporation (1973) *Examination Report Developmental plan for Heavy
and Chemical Industry Complex*, August.

Kyunghyang Daily Newspaper (1969) "Inspectorate's report for economic cooperation
between Japan and Korea in machinery industry and our future," February 27.

Lee, CB (1974) "Special report: real condition of MAFEZ", *Quarterly Changbi* 9(4):
1191–1259.

Lee, DJ (2009) The economic policies in the era of Park Chung-Hee government: political economy of a double-edged sword, *Yoksa Wa Hyonsil: Quarterly Review of Korean
History* 74: 79–112.

MAFEZ (1997) 25th Anniversary History of Masan Export Zone, Administration Agency of Masan Free Trade Zone.

Markusen, A (1999) National Contexts and the Emergence of Second Tier Cities, in
Markusen et al. (eds) *Second Tier Cities: Rapid Growth Beyond the Metropolis*, Minneapolis: University of Minnesota Press: 65–94.

Markusen, A, YS Lee, and S DiGiovanna (ed.) (1999) *Second Tier Cities: Rapid Growth
Beyond the Metropolis*, Minneapolis: University of Minnesota Press.

Nagano, S (2010) *Korea's Economic development and Korean-Japanese Enterprenuers*,
Seoul: Malgulbichnaem.

Nam, H (2013) *Building ships, building a nation: Korea's democratic unionism under Park
Chung Hee*, Seoul: Humanitas.

Ogle, G (1990) South Korea: Dissent within the Economic Miracle, London and New
Jersey: Zed.

Park, YG (2008) Process and Character of 4 Core Plants Plan, *Korean Economic History
Society*, 44(1): 81–107.

Park, YG (2015) *Machinery Industry Research Report in Korea's Heavy and Chemical Industrialization*, Seoul: Haenam.

Parliamentary Inspection Report (1968) National Assembly Minutes, 7th (1967.07.01–1971.06.30), Kukjungkamsa, 1968, Korea Machinery Co. (1968. Oct. 08).

Schoenberger, E and R Walker (2016) Beyond exchange and agglomeration: resource flows and city environments as wellsprings of urban growth, *Journal of Economic Geography*, advance publication DOI:10.1093/jeg/lbw012.

Scott, A and M Storper (2014) The nature of cities: the scope and limits of urban theory, *International Journal of Urban and Regional Research* 39(1): 1–15.

Shim, TY (2010) Korean Inc.: Building PreEntrepreneurship in Korea, in T Y Shim(eds) *Korean Entrepreneurship: The Foundation of the Korean Economy*, NY Palgrave: Macmillan.

Shin, DH (1994) The Impact of Industrialization on the Quality of Life in Korea: Case Studies of Ulsan and Kyungju, PhD thesis, University of British Columbia.

Sonn, JW (2007) Insulation with Solidarity as a Political Condition for an Implementation of Polarised Development Strategy: The South Korean Experience and its Theoretical Implications, *International Planning Studies* 12(3): 221–240.

Walker, R (2016) Why Cities: A Response, International Journal of Urban and Regional Research, advance publication DOI:10.1111/1468-2427.12335: 164–180.

Woo, JE (1991) *Race to the Swift: State and Finance in Korean Industrialization*, New York: Columbia University Press.

CHAPTER 3

Eclipse of the Rising Sun? The Once and Future Tokyo

Heidi Gottfried

1 Introduction

Tokyo's once gleaming office towers announced its ascendance as a global city, rising like a phoenix out of postwar ruins.[1] The ascendance of Tokyo was neither obvious nor assured. Tokyo seemed to be an unlikely contender for the status of a global city in the aftermath of carpet-bombing of whole swaths of the city and the decimation of productive capacities. By sifting through the rubble, this chapter lays the groundwork for understanding the rise and subsequent decline of Tokyo in the world economy.

A closer examination of Sassen's (2001) classic conception of generic global cities, in the first section, will reveal that Tokyo is a global city both similar to and different than global cities in the West and emergent global cities in East Asia. By definition and function, Tokyo fits the statistical portrait of what makes a global city. Tokyo, like New York City and London, operates as a nodal command position in the circuits of capital in the world economy. Yet Tokyo's origins as a global city remain obscure – born fully formed, as if by Immaculate Conception. A more dynamic picture can crystalize by specifying the connected histories and geographies of Tokyo and cities in the region (Saito, 2003; Saito and Thornley, 2003; Hill and Kim, 2000; Wang, 2003; Hill et al., 2011; Fujita, 2003; Park et al., 2011). Using inter-Asian and trans-Pacific lenses, also deployed by other contributors in this edited volume, highlight the logics of urban developmentalism shaping distinctive political-economies that condition urban forms among these 'Tiger' economies.

Tokyo's dizzyingly disarrayed built environment, however, almost defies rendering an interpretation of the representational space of the city. To do so, in the next section, the chapter puts forth a geography of power approach that imposes order on the urban grid for analyzing Tokyo, both as a symbolic

---

1 The reference recalls the mass mobilization in celebration of May Day 1946 described by an Asahi reporter: 'a powerful step toward reconstruction of a democratic Japan, rising like a phoenix out of the devastation of war' (cited in Dower, 1999: 262).

space and as a terrain of struggle. Introducing a geography of power perspective excavates local geographies and buried histories informing urbanism as inter-scalar processes "from intra-urban neighborhoods to global city systems" (R. Walker, 2016: 174). The next section establishes the historical setting, suggesting that residues of empire shaped the geo-political economy and infrastructural connections in the region.

The global ascendance of Tokyo was made possible by the state's developmental economic projects materialized in massive infrastructure and architecture built during two critical historical conjunctures. The first period brackets the end of the Second World War to the beginning of the 1960s that put Japan on its economic path. In the early post-war period, contentious labor and geo-politics influenced the compressed pace of urbanization. In the second period between the 1970s and 1980s, the state purposely intervened in a political-bureaucratic project positioning Tokyo at the strategic center of its capitalist growth regime. Against this backdrop, radical politics disrupted the veneer of consensus. Distinct urban forms defined each era: modernization of the Imperial railway system and an extensive subway network, symbolized by the Shinkansen bullet train, anticipated the 1964 Olympics that thrust Tokyo back on the world stage; and public works patronage, high rise development, and an international airport at Narita elevated commercial sites in and around Tokyo. At these critical conjunctures, the fate of the city could have turned out differently. A postscript looks forward to the 2020 Olympics for a comparison to the national(ist) project aimed at regaining Tokyo's global stature, after being battered and buffeted, this time as a result of enduring economic crisis. In summary, the production of urban form associated with Tokyo as a global city – its airport, its public spaces, the type of export-oriented financial activities that go on there, and the domestic bubble – need to be situated within the geo-politics of the era and the social struggles that animated it. Rather than positing one generic global city, the narrative of Tokyo's origin story in this chapter pays greater attention to the trans-Pacific and East Asian regional political economy that was being constructed at the time, as well as domestic struggles over urban space. A geo-political economy analysis of Tokyo's origins as a global city can offer insights into the dynamics of East Asian capitalism and its urban landscapes.

2   The Origins and Characteristics of Global Cities

With the shift to 'postindustrial' production, a select number of city centers in New York, London and Tokyo were positioned as administrative hubs of regional and the global economy. The attempt to define shared characteristics of global cities, however, has masked the historical origins and regional distinctive political-economic governance that differentiate Tokyo, and other East Asian cities from the Anglo-American prototypes. The concept of urban developmentalism unpacks the politics of economic planning that repurposes the built environment for capital accumulation in East Asian cities (see Doucette and Park in this volume). Juxtaposing Tokyo and New York can distinguish the specificities of comparative cases, and thereby rethink the relationship between the logic of capital in general and the logics of 'the concrete situation' (G. Walker, 2016: 70).

3   What Makes a Global City?

Global cities concentrate finance and producer services and multinational corporate headquarters. An economy-wide diagnostic uncovers the heavy presence of manufacturing employment and R&D functions servicing large manufacturing companies in Tokyo in contrast to NYC (Fujita, 2003: 258). In this sense, Tokyo is not fully post-industrial, but rather reflects 'neo-industrial' urban development (Fujita, 2003: 258). Whereas industrial production has almost disappeared in NYC, plummeting to only 6 percent of employment in 2000, manufacturing remains a core economic activity in Tokyo, making up 15.2 percent of employment (Fujita, 2003: 257). Statistically, Tokyo's service employment jumped from 17.9 percent in 1970 to 31.9 percent by 2000, while functionally finance and service industries are subordinated to manufacturing technology innovation. Japanese companies locate their R&D and development of alternative product lines in Tokyo, and increasingly outsourcing material production to lower-wage sites in neighboring countries (Fujita, 2003: 254–5), initially in Malaysia, Thailand and Vietnam, then relocating the lion's share in China (Harvey, 2005: 139). Districts around Tokyo retain a significant concentration of manufacturing produced by a large number of medium and small-sized firms (Fujita, 2003: 270).

The financial industry is embedded in distinct symbolic economies. NYC's Wall Street and London's eponymous 'City of London' are synonymous with global finance. Japan's main financial institutions (the Stock Exchange, the Bank of Japan, headquarters of major banks, such as the Bank of Tokyo-Mitsubishi and Nomura Securities) reside tucked away in the less conspicuous southeastern part of Tokyo near the main Tokyo Station, whereas foreign banks rent office space in high rises clustered around the regional Asakasa Station. This geographic dispersion of 'domestic' and 'foreign' financial institutions in

Tokyo spatially mirrors the specific relationship between Japanese capital and the developmental state.

The representational space of the city stakes out its global status and stature concretized in the built environment, following the dictum, as succinctly stated, "the city is never a mute artifact of economic activity" (R. Walker, 2016: 173). Both out of necessity and by design, the national government and Tokyo Metropolitan Government (TMG) promoted large-scale infrastructure projects and curated globalized districts differentiating each to attract tourists and businesses. From below, labor and students asserted alternative visions by erecting their own 'temporary' monuments (tent village) in the parks.

Capital and labor flows also distinguish Tokyo from NYC. Japan imposed high tariffs until the 1980s, limiting foreign direct investment (FDI) in the country. As a result, Japanese-owned and operated firms make up the majority of the world's largest firms based in Tokyo (Saito and Thornley, 2003: 668). This national character of and the intimate liaison between finance and industrial capital, undergirded by the economic policy architecture linking business and bureaucratic elites in the Ministries of Finance and Economy, Trade and Industry – a holdover from the early post-war restructuring of inter-corporate networks – sets Tokyo apart from NYC. In Tokyo, Japanese firms serviced by Japanese banks form a felicitous relationship that generated astonishing export-led expansion throughout the postwar period until the late 1980s, and then fell victim to its own success when financialization became the engine of growth of the world economy in the 1990s (Harvey, 2005: 89–90). A combination of the transnationalization of Japanese corporations, spiking land prices and the booming stock market, boosting the accumulation of capital, catapulted Tokyo into a financial center for international capital transactions (Machimura, 1998: 186). Trade protectionism in turn was the unwitting handmaiden of immigration controls, staunching the flow of migrants whose cheap reproductive labor provide local amenities to elites in other global cities. The low-levels of inward flows of both capital and labor led some to characterize Tokyo as an 'immature ... world city' (Kamo, 1992: 10, cited in Saito and Thornley, 2003). State bureaucrats and technocratic policy in tightly coupled economic governance – an institutionalized public/private partnership, defined developmental urbanism.

4   A Global City with a Difference: Tokyo, the West and the Rest Debate

Definitions of what makes a global city, as Saito suggests, "run into problems when it moves beyond describing the characteristics of global cities and tries to explain the processes and governance that created and sustained them" (2003: 285). East Asian scholars correctly, and unavoidably, bring the state back into the analysis of developmental capitalism in this region (Wang, 2003: 311–12; Saito, 2003; Park et al., 2011; Fujita, 2003). Wang's (2003: 311–12) assessment re-balances the perspective when he notes that global cities are always already embedded in national contexts, which have consequences for the specific fea-tures of each global city. Even in market-centered cities, despite more porous borders due to less regulation over capital flows and more labor mobility, the state, both local and national, conditions the structures and processes of ac-cumulation. Further, the developmental state and global cities constantly in-teract with each other rather than being in opposition to each other (Wang, 2003: 311–12).

At the same time, a hierarchy places Tokyo in a command and control posi-tion relative to other cities in the region, and relative to New York and London at a global scale. The brief for an East Asian perspective on urban develop-mentalism informs the materialization of global processes in the production of urban forms. Differences between Tokyo and New York and London are con-sequential in determining trajectories of change and points of friction. It is important to ground analysis of the politics of scale and the repurposing of space in the histories of specific cases and the particular colonial and post-colonial histories in East Asia. The literature on global cities is insufficiently inter-scalar, largely ignoring contentious politics, underestimating the role of geopolitics, and underexploring the logic of specific places. Adopting a geog-raphy of power perspective, the next section seeks to make visible these inter-scalar interactions.

5   Geographies of Power: An Inter-Scalar Approach

A geographies of power perspective entails inter-scalar processes that are in-terdependent, linked, contradictory, complex, multifaceted, and uneven in effects across time and space (Gottfried, 2014). It considers how, and through what political practices, actors and institutions produce scale (Herod and Wright, 2002: 11) and define space. This geographies of power perspective high-lights the political and ideological borderlines racializing national groupings and calls attention to the shifting hegemonies that shape urban space. For in-stance, to analyze Tokyo, area specialists have brought a regional sensitivity to understanding what makes East Asian global cities distinctive. Too often, how-ever, their construct of region is taken-for-granted. Contiguous nations bound together in Asia share more than a common physical geography; they occupy different positions of power relative to each other and against other world regions. In the early modern period, Asia signified the naming practice given to racially differentiate the East from the West. Prior relations between cities in East Asia arose separately from encounters with Europeans (R. Walker, 2016: 175). Regionalism accompanies globalization, notably evinced in the emergence of trading blocs (ASEAN), but also in the circulatory forces and networks facilitating the exchange of goods, ideas and people (Duara, 2015: 16). Japan's hegemony over neighboring countries through occupation and military force also instantiated geographies of power at a regional scale. The region is a "critical transmission scale that has mediated and facilitated circulations beween the world and the nation or locality" (Duara 2015: 240).

Geopolitics aligns a cartographical practice and discourse about inter-scalar relationships concerned with power struggles among states and empires, involving "borders, lines, distinctions beween cores and peripheries; in short, (re)territorialization" (Steinmetz, 2012: 13). The postwar period saw a different regional mapping of East Asia carved out of the new geo-political world order; in particular, the US security apparatus policed borders and boundaries of East Asia (see Choi and Glassman in this volume). Its Janus-face of isolationism and internationalism, directed inward and outward, defined Japan's singularity.

An analysis of geographies of power renders more visible the historical construction of this imaginary East Asia. To use the term 'imaginary' does not mean that Asia did not or does not exist. Rather, it destabilizes the taken-for-granted geographies of economies by unpacking power relations between 'colonized' and 'colonizers'. Colonial residues and historical memories inform fraught political relationships within the region, echoed in the race among cities to gain a dominant place as the next global technology powerhouse.

Furthermore, a geography of power perspective is well suited to help us understand why inter-Asia and globally, the 'center of gravity' pivots from a single polar axis in Tokyo to multiple axes in Hong Kong, Singapore, Seoul and Beijing. It shows us how the politics of producing scale-restricting capital and labor mobility was inherently fragile, pushing both Japanese and global capital to move to other globalized outposts in the region, while limiting in-migration and restricting pathways to citizenship within a Japan deprived of a pool of low wage labor that could be exploited. Tokyo as a global city has suffered from a familialistic reproductive bargain that stifled the development of an infrastructure in support of social reproduction and the restriction on migrant care workers who cater to amenities expected and enjoyed by the global elite in other global cities (Gottfried, 2012).

Finally, historicizing the origin of Tokyo requires a longer view than the aftermath of the Second World War. The idea of critical turning points is compatible with comparative historical approaches to "conjunctural contingent causality," as an historical dialectic in which "underlying powers, tendencies, and structures.... combine in contingent ways with one another and with additional causal mechanisms ....in producing empirical events" (Steinmetz, 2014: 217). The historical antecedents show how Tokyo already achieved its stature with the establishment of empire. The role of empire is more than historical background for contextualizing colonialism and post-colonialism. Empire was the means by which the Japanese state created an infrastructure for economic and military expansion. Residues of empire can be detected in the current constellation of forces in the region.

6   Historical Setting: From Empire to Developmental Capitalism

6.1   *In the Shadows of Empire*

The railroad and the airport are symbolic and functional hubs emblematic of Japan's modernity; both represent sites of private and state interventions projecting empire, building the modern nation-state, and sites of post-war contentious politics over the economic fate of the nation. At the turn of the 20th century, Japan built an extensive railway system throughout the colonies, consolidating the physical empire and supporting the circulation and transmission of art, material culture, and cross-border exchanges in spaces around Tokyo already prefigured in 'the floating world' (Kleeman, 2014: 7, 18). Railroads are legacies of the prewar military complex and the dismantling of the post-war military machine: the infrastructure for industrial modernization, thrusting empire into their territories and epitomizing the iconic Japanese corporate networks (*keiretsu*) that own rail-lines to combine transportation with urban commerce in department stores at the terminus (Gottfried, 2015).

Japan's postwar model crystallizes in the twin development of rail and air transport. To ensure reliable transportation in their effort to rebuild capitalist productive capacity in 1949, the US General Headquarters (GHQ) issued a directive to reorganize much of the rail system by forming the Japanese National Railways (JNR), a state-owned public corporation. The Liberal Democratic Party realized its postwar economic agenda, introducing and expanding high-speed rail including the line from Tokyo's main stations to Narita Airport, with little input from unions and despite strikes and protests throughout the 1960s. The airport, upon closer inspection, reveals a turbulent history of the post-war settlement in the shadows of its imperial entanglements. Pitched battles pitted farmers and student allies against the police force for control over land use. In the expanse between the airport and Tokyo lies a forgotten history, also a part of the revved up engine that propelled Japan's muscular economy to its global zenith. Using the powers of eminent domain, the state expropriated farmers' land in the mid-1960s, and then privatized the airport authority in the early years of the new millennium. Following a neoliberal playbook, JNR was dismantled and privatized in 1987.

Current literature on imperial formations has tracked the genealogies of empire, both its historical antecedents and its contemporary 'imperial formations' (Stoler, 2013: 3; Steinmetz, 2013; Hardt and Negri, 2000). Empire marks both the symbolic and material role of Japan's military and economic domination in the region. What's left behind has escaped notice in much of the analysis of Japan's present crisis and the sliding fortunes of Tokyo. Stoler reminds us that imperial power resides in often overlooked and seemingly imperceptible residues. Japan's vestiges of colonialism cast a long shadow on the scarred lives and landscapes within and across countries in East Asia. Through the lens of imperial formations, it becomes possible to see how the Japanese state established its economic hegemony and then lost its way in the twilight of the 20th century.

Japan's imperial project both emulated and rejected Western models of empire. On the one hand, Japan's political elite commandeered the idea of gunboat diplomacy from the West (Chae, 2013: 402) in order to accomplish the annexation of colonies in Asia at the turn of the 20th century (Kleeman, 2014: 1–2). On the other hand, the state articulated both an ethno-historical discourse that emphasized a common Asiatic cultural and racial identity and a colonial narrative in which Japan claimed control over ancient Korea to justify its colonial rule (Chae, 2013: 404–5). Though Japan's territorial expansion was more limited in scale and in scope than either the British or French empires, the close geographic proximity fostered more frequent flows and exchanges of people, ideas, and material culture within what became defined as the East Asian region (Kleeman, 2014: 2). More specifically, these dual aspects of Japanese expansion entailed what Kleeman (2014: 4) calls 'colonial disregard', to describe 'the process of erasure' whereby the Meiji administrative powers concealed internal colonization of peoples from Hokkaido to Okinawa; and 'colonial regard', to describe the 'mimicry of Western superpowers'. The legacy of imperialism resonates in contemporary nation-building.

Empire is inscribed in the rise and decline of Tokyo from its heights as a global capital. Japan's conquest seeded the geopolitical and infrastructural connections that aided and abetted economic (under)development in the region. Tokyo was the symbolic center of and the transportation nexus for the far-flung empire. The fight over land use also expressed local concerns about the direction of development. Regional dynamics further cannot be understood without reference to the postwar settlement forged during the Cold War. From Tokyo the US Occupation forces stabilized the Japanese political-bureaucratic apparatus and quelled political dissent.

7   Contentious Politics: The Making of Developmental Capitalism in
      Post-War Japan

At the end of the Second World War, America played a pivotal role in the establishment of the Japanese employment and political systems and in laying the
groundwork for Japan's accelerated economic growth. Tokyo assumed the role
of administrative and political capital of the globalizing capitalist network. In
this view, Japan's economic miracle was neither an inevitable outcome of a
collectivist ethos derived from Confucianism nor of hierarchical relations inherited from feudalism (West, 2003: 3). Instead, geo-politics paved the way for
Japan's spectacular postwar economic ascent.

Internationally, the Cold War climate fostered US foreign policy goals vis-à-
vis Japan: the US saw Japan as a strategic partner in Asia, as a key geo-political
location for stationing American troops, and as an ideological bulwark against
communism looming in China and the Soviet Union. The outbreak of war in
Korea helped to jumpstart Japan's flailing manufacturing sector,[2] propping up
industries from textiles, vehicles, raw materials, and primary metal products to
medicines: special procurements injected an estimated $2.3 billion into Japan
and the influx of military personnel and their families stimulated further construction and services, especially in Tokyo (Dower, 1999: 541–2; see also Choi
and Glassman in this volume). Many Japanese companies invested their windfall profits by upgrading equipment and "acquir[ing] of rights to American
commercial licenses and patents ... that the US government strongly supported as crucial for the economic well-being of its still-fragile cold War associate"
(Dower, 1999: 543). After the war ended, "the US allowed Japan to participate
in ... the US-directed reconstruction of South Korea" (1999: 542). Around the
same time, a treaty signed in 1951 gave the US the right to establish military
bases in Japan and to call on Japan for aid in case war broke out in the region
(Global Nonviolent Action Database) – the renewal of this treaty has sparked
mass demonstrations provoking episodic waves of protest in front of the Diet.

America's role also shaped the institutional architecture and trajectory
of Japan's developmental capitalism, giving prominence to Tokyo. In "the
fortress-like Dai-ichi Insurance building" (LSA, 2013: 55), a setting resonant of
muscular military strength, the Supreme Commander for the Allied Powers
(SCAP), General Douglas MacArthur, oversaw the writing of a new constitution
and labor laws, modeled on the US National Labor Relations Act. Militant class
conflict might have changed the course of history if the Occupation forces had
not prohibited a general strike in Tokyo, canceled by the organizers on the eve

---

2   TMG recognizes the role of geopolitics in its official account of Tokyo's history.

of the mass mobilization in February 1947, and if the US military presence had not posed as a potent deterrent. SCAP's takeover of the imposing white colonnade facade in sight of the Imperial Palace staked a symbolic position in Chiyoda at the heart of the new and the old seats of governmental power in Tokyo.

In the wake of the Second World War Japan teetered on the brink. Tokyo resembled a war zone. Housing shortages, food scarcity, and rampant exploitation catalyzed radical grassroots movements among students, workers, and housewives (Dower, 1999). Socialist and communist parties channelled discontent into dramatic symbolic actions, most prominently in and around Tokyo. In 1946, workers seized control over the means of production in coal mines, newspaper offices, electric railways, and machine shops concentrated in Tokyo. While protests roiled satellite cities, Tokyo was a privileged site for enacting protests because of its public spaces accommodating large crowds, because of easy access as a transportation hub connecting participants from outlying areas, and because of the symbolic importance of the city's political landmarks. For example, a labor-farm alliance, along with cultural groups, mobilized 70,000 to attend a 'people's assembly' in Hibiya Park in central Tokyo, and May Day rallies in Tokyo marshalled half a million people waving red flags and carrying banners with slogans calling for 'equal wages for men and women in equal work' (Dower, 1999: 262). This revolutionary fervor inspired several million workers who pledged to honor the call for a general strike in the early months of the following year. MacArthur could not abide a general strike. A work stoppage of this magnitude could have brought down the fragile government. Acting to preserve the status quo and to keep a lid on worker's mobilization, General MacArthur banned the strike. Radical labor groups upped the ante in the months that followed. In the midst of the Cold War and in response to the communist/socialist inspired movements, the Occupation forces reversed course, rescinding public employees' right to strike (Dower, 1999: 271–2). Suppression and repression of domestic communist parties, left-leaning unionists and students was a part of the domestic 'security' alliance.

The Cold War exerted a lasting influence over the state bureaucratic apparatus, The Supreme Commander for the Allied Powers promoted administrative 'rationalization' that concentrated and strengthened an already centralized national state (Dower, 1999: 27). The Japanese bureaucracy came in handy as a means of implementing General MacArthur's mandates. One of the major governmental reorganizations gave birth to the powerful Ministry of International Trade and Industry (MITI, later METI) in 1949. Already by 1927, the Ministry of Finance effectively 'controlled' the financial system (Murphy, 2009), and Japanese authorities maintained monetary independence even during the Occupation (Metzler, 2013: 72). As a consequence, "six such major concentrations of economic power had emerged, all centering on city banks ... and all but one represented reclusterings or reconfigurations of the old zaibatsu" (business conglomerate) by the early 1950s (Dower, 1999: 546). MITI, along with the Ministry of Finance, rendered technical decisions cast in the national interest, but in fact served the dominant alliance between the state and business interests. Unions exerted little leverage at the national level, weakened by the red purges.

Political alliances brought together conservative politicians and business interests expressed in the newly-founded Liberal Democratic Party (LDP) formed by the merger of two competing conservative parties in 1955 (Tsukamoto, 2012: 401). The LDP secured more than 60 percent of the seats in the 1958 election of the Lower House, and dominated electoral politics for the next 50 years (Samuels, 1981). However, Horiuchi (2013) expresses skepticism that the LDP's victory alone was the decisive factor explaining double-digit growth on the eve of the next decade. In this account Horiuchi persuasively argues that the new security relationship forged with the US fundamentally altered Japan's economic prospects. An adjunct to the security alliance was an economic pact in which the US absorbed a large share of Japan's exports, facilitated bank loans, and provided subsidies, relieving the Japanese state of considerable outlays for defense spending. The ruling LDP then directed 'savings' toward domestic economic purposes to shore up political patronage, solidifying their hold on government power. Overall, the economic miracle was rooted in 'good' institutions and favorable policies, but also enjoyed exceptional international circumstances providing the conditions for sustained growth (Horiuchi, 2013).

By the end of the decade a massive protest against the security treaty threatened the fragile alliance between Japan and the US (Horiuchi, 2013). Prime Minister Nobusuke Kishi, one of the architects of the LDP's conservative industrial and foreign policy (Samuels, 1981), had made strengthening and ratifying the security treaty with the US foremost amongst his top priorities. Despite mass mobilizations, the Diet passed the treaty in short order after Kishi authorized the police to extricate Socialist Party MPs from the parliament on 19 May 1960. Protests continued and intensified, sparking strikes and culminating in a rally of more than 120,000 people. Organizers chose the National Diet Building to stage the largest rallies. Smaller skirmishes did occur elsewhere but did not have the dramatic impact of the gathering amassed around the Diet. In the face of mounting pressure Kishi resigned, defusing this politically volatile situation. By 1960 the LDP was ensconced in office, propped up by US economic aid.

To effectively subdue the remnants of social movements, the state had to secure consent for its ruling authority. Once the LDP had solidified power, the state dictated rapid modernization aimed at building physical infrastructure for the reconstruction of the economy. A national(ist) narrative filtered modern subjects through the binary of Japanese/non-Japanese based on the exclusion of (colonial) 'Others'. To sustain this juxtaposition, the modern state reinvented a tradition of an authentic monolithic culture. In particular, the construction of Japaneseness erased the recognition of other subject positions and fostered a kind of historical amnesia for forgetting Japan's colonial past. Through the Immigration and Control Law and strict enforcement the state created a border regime, regulating the mode of entry, the movement of bodies within and across nations, and restricting the terms and conditions of living and working in Japan, that undergirded this inward turn. Institutionally embedded in the enterprise, unions stood to benefit short-term from submerging their class solidarity and merging their interests with the firm's. Consensus bargaining provided male union members with real economic gains, but only as long as the company prospered from the arrangement. Going forward, neutered unions narrowed their claims on realizing company citizenship rights, effectively surrendering their claims on rights to the city. A quelled radical opposition left the developmental coalition to rebuild Tokyo.

This brief political history has highlighted the inter-scalar politics that put Japan on its economic path. The US Occupation forces along with US economic aid and special military procurements fueled the expansion of manufacturing and buttressed the establishment of the LDP's stronghold on the levers of national government. Furthermore, the relation between Japan and the US has continued to influence Japanese urban development long after the Cold War in the form of providing export markets for goods but also swelling currency reserves. Bubblenomics, a term coined by R Taggart Murphy (2009, 2014), historicizes how the felicitous networked relationship between banks, the state bureaucracy and the export industry that fueled the economic miracle's virtuous cycle later fed the vicious downward spiral, due to the sclerotic institutions staying the course despite growing signs of weakness. A policy based on combining systemic suppression of domestic demand with the deliberate channeling of financing into internationally competitive export industries ran up trade surpluses and accumulated US dollars. When US currency reserves reached the point where they began to have serious effects on Japan's ability to conduct monetary policy, the authorities deliberately cultivated asset bubbles in an attempt to counteract the dollar build-up. Japan's political economy, closely aligning and entwining the state with financial and industrial capital, provided the institutional backing for the developmental coalition and the unique type of financial arrangements that are reflected in the kind of services located in Tokyo.

8   Tokyo: Turning East and West

Tokyo experienced major growth spurts later than the more mature economies of New York and London. In the aftermath of the war, the state's infrastructure projects absorbed surplus capital and labor (Harvey, 2011: 202). Tokyo's sprawling and dense built environment grew up and out in bits and pieces, fits and starts, from the ashes of war destruction. Allied bombing had eviscerated whole neighborhoods, wiping out nearly 65 percent of all buildings in an uneven grid across the city.[3] Pockmarked land lay waste where poor residences, small machine shops and factories once stood, while the wealthier quarter survived 'largely undamaged' and was replaced downward by "'little America', the home to MacArthur's General Headquarters" (Dower, 1999: 47). Rebuilding Tokyo accelerated when political actors cleared the path, readying urban space for its developmental agenda.[4]

Construction for the Olympics jumpstarted urban renewal on the eve of the 1960s, and enhanced the image of Tokyo and the nation to the world (Martin, 2013). Before leaving office, Prime Minister Kishi spearheaded the winning bid for the 1964 Olympics and funneled substantial funds to pay for massive infrastructure and 'public works' projects. In the lead-up to the opening ceremonies, the state modernized the imperial railway network and subway system, and fashioned bold venues for the sporting competition. The location of the Olympic Village has a military provenance, occupying a former Japanese military field that the US government converted into American military family housing, in an area called Washington Heights (Tomizawa 2015).[5] The award brought prestige to Japan, as the first Asian nation to host the Olympics, and showcased Tokyo's modernity and technological progress, most notably symbolized by Japanese-designed architecture (e.g. Kenzo Tange's elegant Yoyogi National Gymnasium) and by high-speed Shinkansen. The bullet train hurtling across the island nation became an emblem of national pride, and did the work of shedding vestiges of Japan's aggressive war image. At the time Tokyo's destiny as a global city was not assured. However, its stature as the symbolic center and as the rail hub made it the likely candidate.

---

3   *Year Zero*, Ian Buruma's (2016) history of 1945, depicts the harrowing image of life among Tokyo's ruins in the one-year span after the armistice.
4   The new housing authority, the Japan Housing Corporation, set up in 1955, erected public-subsidized apartment complexes (*danchi*). Its utilitarian architecture rerouted social interactions on the streets into the anonymity of isolated apartments for the growing middle classes living in nuclear families.
5   The US government returned the land to Japan in exchange for a commitment by the Japanese government to pay for the housing in other US military bases (Tomizawa 2015).

During the 1970s, the state shaped the urban landscape to withstand the economic tsunami rippling globally. Japanese capitalism, based on manufacturing, would remain the focal point of the growth regime. Finance capital continued to support export-led production. Intensified global competition pushed the state toward a technology-centered approach to urban development, a process discussed in more detail by Fujita (2003) and Saito (2003). Their otherwise excellent analysis of urban planning politics does not fully explain the historical and geo-political factors that both propelled and later stalled the economic miracle, that is, the inherent tensions to developmental capitalism.

The second turning point occurred in the midst of contentious politics at the end of the 1960s and 1970s, student protests, including struggles against the expropriation of land to locate Narita Airport, and public sector strikes. Suppression and the enduring class compromise weakened these movements. Photos of the 1960s era capture the roiling struggles between helmeted police and protesters alike. Early years of the 1970s saw an uptick of strikes, involving public sector unions, and hotbeds of former student radicals – echoes of the late 1940s. Unlike the previous period of contentious politics redolent of revolution from below, most unions remained in the embrace of consensus bargaining. Consensus bargaining enabled exported-oriented firms to manufacture consent among its core workforce, which contributed to a relatively quiescent working class. Throughout the 1970s and 1980s, when oil shocks reverberated in this oil-dependent nation, there was a relative decline of manufacturing, while financial capital consolidated its base in Tokyo. Employment mushroomed an astonishing 28 percent in finance, insurance and real estate; whereas employment in manufacturing declined 15 percent even though a small percentage of new manufacturing jobs became available in other parts of Japan. Nonetheless, Japanese banks financed export-oriented production by Japanese companies.

Although less dramatic than the 1964 Olympics, the 1980s' commission of a new landmark city government building coincided with the state's promotion of Tokyo's global ambition. From the choice of Japanese architect, the location in the vibrant shopping area anchored at Shinjuku Station, to the structure's Lego-like exterior, the 48-storey building sought to present Tokyo as a world-class city. Tokyo Metropolitan Government again turned to renowned Japanese architect Kenzo Tange, whose aesthetic referenced 'tradition' and 'modernity', East and West, and integrated digital imagery mimicking the computer chip. The visual elements fittingly concretized technological prowess epitomizing modern Japan. Not coincidentally, the choice of a Japanese architect also signaled Japanese know-how. Finished in 1990, this pre-bubble building, the tallest in Tokyo until 2006, rendered the cityscape in the veneer of an 'invented' Japanese tradition and a Japanese casting of modernity.

Attesting to the construction industry's importance as a political boondoggle, the ruling party of the Liberal Democrats subsidized the building explosion even after the country's economy took a tailspin during the Lost Decade of the 1990s. A construction boom in Tokyo created jobs for working-class men, whose employment rose by 23 percent from 1985 to 1997. Industrial areas were replaced by postmodern office buildings, housing for high-income residents and complexes eliding commercial shopping malls with cultural institutions such as museums and concert halls (Machimura, 1998: 186). Land speculation and the subsequent plunge in land prices was the model's undoing. As reported in *The New York Times*, beneath the surface of civil engineering projects is political pork spending that fueled economic growth in the postwar period, sustaining the Liberal Democratic Party in power for most of the past half century (Tabuchi, 2009: 4).

Economic malaise lingered into the 21st century. Urban developmentalism in Japan changed from the public works orientation to increasing neoliberal influence over urbanization processes. Private enterprises, in partnership with local authorities, sought to restructure space surrounding the Tokyo Station in the central business district of Marunouchi. This locale accommodated 230,000 workers toiling away in high-rise office buildings mostly owned by Mitsubishi, one of the biggest corporate conglomerates currently controlling nearly 40 percent of the land (Languillon-Aussel, 2014). After the asset price bubble collapsed, private developers actively looked to redefine public spaces (Languillon-Aussel, 2014). New sub-centers and industrial clusters brand districts around the city. During the past two decades, Japanese capitalism has morphed into a neoliberal dreamscape for private interests.

The Tokyo Municipal Government wielded 'global city' as a sign in policy discourses, harkening to its Japanese uniqueness while projecting an international (Western) future(ist) vision of Tokyo. It's origin myth twines a history of heroic reconstruction efforts in the face of devastating disasters and infrastructural projects boosting Tokyo's rise as a global city (TMG, 2017a). Their zealous pursuit of changing the built environment was motivated by an ideological and political commitment to the growth machine and the structural necessity for expanded capital accumulation (Machimura, 1998: 188). The very obsession with local uniqueness to attract global investment centered on cooling the overheated economy, but it could not reverse the downturn.

Developmental urbanization could not rescue the economic freefall. In a last-ditch effort to jumpstart economic growth and to shore up Tokyo's attractiveness as a place for business, the Diet promulgated the National Strategic Special Zones Act (NSSZA) of 2013/14. This initiative created subnational spaces of exception by reconfiguring the boundaries of the Tokyo zone from Tokyo metropolis, Kanagawa prefecture, Chiba to Narita city. Designating an enclave gave the Tokyo Metropolitan Government and Abe's coalition the rhetorical shield to 'realize its Tokyo Global Financial Center vision' by drawing together the clusters of financial entities and institutions along the bounded corridor and to provide incentives for business investment by deregulation and by easing entry of skilled 'guest workers' and expats applying for temporary residence. TMG endorsed the special zones to "create a more comfortable environment for foreign businesses and their employees," lauding their achievement of "now dominat[ing] the No. 1 spot in the global city rankings as a livable city overall for foreign nationals" (TMG, 2017a: 42). Tokyo zone exemplified the neoliberal shift redefining geographies of power, that is, how international business functions in the newly formed urban configurations. Rather than a move toward autonomy, the zone signified the state's prioritizing spaces "free" from the enforcement of regulations (see Cartier in this volume).

Like its predecessor in 1964, the successful bid for the 2020 Olympics is a platform for government shaping of Tokyo's representational spaces. *New Tokyo. New Tomorrow, the Action Plan for 2020*, lays out a vision of Tokyo's future. The action plan reveals an obsession with rankings among global cities. Toward the end of the promotional document, "Tokyo in the World" presents its relative position on a number of metrics. In bold print, the overall ranking shows Tokyo elevated to 3rd place from 4th place a year earlier in 2015 (TMG, 2017b). TMG seeks "to restore Tokyo to its position as Asia's No. 1 financial city... [by declaring that] we will promote bold measures to revitalize the financial industry" (ibid) –hinting at competition with other cities in the region. The 'Tokyo brand' mixes cutting-edge "fintech," digital media, and fashion with traditional crafts and agricultural produce 'harvested' in Tokyo. In the run up to the Olympics, the attempt to transform the city has precipitated another building boom resulting in gentrification and unsold inventory. In Tokyo's Kachidoki area proximate to planned Olympic venues, prices for apartments had surged 25 percent, yet a large inventory of property remained on the market (Chu, 2017), in part due to the Chinese government making it harder for citizens to move money offshore and the yen's volatility (Chu, 2017).

The built urban environment is not merely a façade behind which the real economy must be analyzed. Global urban spaces concretize capital accumulation in both form and function. The Japanese state cannot build itself out of the crisis, and the increasing sourcing of production outside of the country and in the Tokyo zone are the latest spatial fixes attempting to maintain capital accumulation, which undermines the consensus bargain that had anchored the material conditions of the model.

9   Changing Geographies of Power: Tokyo and its Discontents

9.1   *Emergent Global Cities in East Asia*
Seemingly distant work conditions and processes ripple from one location
to another as a result of increasing global and regional interconnections. Financialization of assets, heretofore in place by the 1970s, generated a crisis of
capital accumulation on a global scale. From the 1980s onward, the surplus
absorption problem fueled speculation and boosted property prices, inflat-
ing an already overextended housing bubble (Harvey, 2008). Meanwhile, the
financial elite parked capital in construction sites of earlier global cities, or
erected crystalline cityscapes in emergent regional global cities in India and
China. The process of financialization bids up real estate properties, making
it expensive to conduct business in New York, London and Tokyo, which in
turn undermines the appeal of these leading global cities. As a consequence,
certain global functions are transferred from distinctive financial districts in
city centers to nearby cities or off-shored to countries with cheaper rents and
lower wages. And changes in the labor process enabled by computer technologies extend the global reach of finance and banking. For example, call centers
relocate work to lower wage areas and enclaves in globalizing cities and to
English-speaking countries in the Caribbean, and to India and the Philippines
(see Jana M. Kleibert in this volume). Transnational corporations faced with
high costs of doing business move operations to cities in the cheaper Global
South.

Rival cities in the region now compete for prominence in the global economy, threatening Tokyo's position in the hierarchy of global cities. Tokyo's vul-
nerability is rooted in the connected histories of the region. The operation and
orientation of finance capital in Tokyo is more closely bound to the nation and
to the region than the finance industry in NYC and London. Recently, Shanghai,
Beijing, Singapore, Hong Kong, and Seoul have emerged as regional global cities, or as 'second tier' mega-cities (Gugler, 2004: 3). These cities are considered
global to the extent that finance and other business services operate on a dena-
tionalized but primarily regional scale. However, they are considered second-
tier based on the relative density of transnational headquarters, at levels
higher than most cities but still lower than in older global cities. The location
of these cities in poorer nations, without the social and physical infrastructures
to support the large number of people arriving in search of jobs, differentiates
these second-tier global cities from the first-tier. Such rapid in-migration produces mega-cities with enormous populations, drawing mostly on migrants
from their own domestic hinterlands.

Older global cities repurpose the built environment to accommodate shifting economic functions; up-and-coming global cities in East Asia rely on state-directed development efforts to transform the built environment – quick spatial fixes offer instantaneous cosmopolitanism by hiring 'starchitects' whose brand names and styles convey global prestige value and aspirational status in the symbolic economy. Tokyo's bid in the architectural sweepstakes worked in a more confined footprint for repackaging luxury goods inside of the upscale district of Shibuya: Herzog and de Meuron's bubble-wrapped Prada building in 2003; Toyo Ito and Associates' branching clad exterior for Tods in 2004; and Creative Designers International's expressionist Audi Forum in 2006. These buildings are modest in comparison to the monumental scale and proportion of properties, epitomized by Zaha Hadid's undulating Dongdaeman Design Plaza in Seoul at the bulldozed site, forcing the relocation of 900 merchants (Meyer, 2014).[6] Such accelerated economic modernization projects in these second-tier global cities appear as if watching the cityscape emerge through time-lapse photography. Urban developmentalism in these East Asian globalized cities derives its velocity and its form from being embedded in a different constellation of geo-politics – one in which Japan's hegemony is waning in a reformed geography of power.

The trans-border system of cities and regions occasion the rise of struggles over and in urban spaces. Tokyo, like Seoul, London, and New York, has witnessed the flare-up of contentious politics among dispossessed workers and the unemployed in public spaces, such as encampments in parks. In Tokyo's Hibiya Park, 500 temp workers erected a tent village to protest their precarious existence made worse after the collapse of Lehman Brothers in 2008. Organizers drew on local idioms of day laborer's makeshift domiciles glimpsed in city parks for their symbolic protest. What makes the event spectacular is the relative invisibility of the homeless whose blue tarp tents are tethered between trees hidden away in forested areas of city parks. Though only a temporary installation, the tent village occupied a representational space for gaining recognition in the city. Recurring large-scale anti-nuke protests recall mass mobilizations at the heart of Tokyo's government district (Andrews, 2016).

Finance capital still concentrates global command in the triumvirate global cities, while increasingly extending these functions across a wider

---

6 Landing like a spaceship, Zaha Hadid's winning design for the 2020 Olympic stadium drew instant criticism from Japanese architects who dubbed the building as a monstrosity and as "a turtle waiting for Japan to sink..." while other critics reproved the project as depriving Tokyoites of an expansive green space (McCurry 2015).

range of urban places. In Tokyo finance capital is nation-bound, connected to manufacturing through intra-corporate networks. Through technocratic guidance state industrial and monetary policy elites fostered an export-oriented growth model protecting Japanese firms from direct foreign competition and reinforcing the felicitous relationship between Japanese banks and manufacturing. Urban developmentalism gave national capital a boost, but in doing so created the conditions for its undoing. Both the (trans)national and regional contexts shaped the rise and the decline of Tokyo as a global city.

10   The Rise and Decline of Tokyo: Urban (Post)Developmentalism?

To understand what makes a global city requires an account that goes beyond enumerating and quantifying the number of transnational corporate headquarters and banks clustered in an urban center. A global city is not analogous to a recipe – add ingredients, mix and stir. Rather, theories of global and globalizing cities must excavate shifting spatial logics of capitalism by considering the specific histories and geographies producing urban forms. Origin stories unfold narratives of events, actors, institutions, and places.

Tokyo can be read as a palimpsest. Stripping away layers of its own origin story reveals a Janus-like city: double-faced, both inward-oriented and extended outward. Tokyo's story is best discerned from an inter-scalar geography of power perspective, focusing on the national(ist) in relationship to the region. An archaeology of Japanese empire uncovered colonial residues beneath the surface of the Japanese economic narrative, and archived the historical infrastructure, most emblematically represented by railroads and airports, undergirding Tokyo's ascendance to global city status. The echoes of empire reverberated in Japan's prewar colonialism and vis-à-vis its postwar 'security' relationship to the US.

Though Japan's imperial ambitions were extinguished in the ashes of defeat, the Japanese state embarked on an ambitious modernization project in an effort to rebuild the war-torn nation and to ensure an adequate supply of 'native-born' labor channeled into burgeoning industrial sectors. The state's investment in economic infrastructure and productive capacity, decimated during the Second World War, occurred in the context of that country's imperial entanglements and complex histories bound to the region and to the United States' Cold War security apparatus. Japan's institutional architecture and infrastructural networks, prefigured in the war machine, were molded by the US Occupation forces that buttressed the Japanese bureaucracy and the establishment of the Liberal Democratic Party's (LDP) stronghold over the levers of government.

Against that backdrop the phoenix rose in a moment of disruption that might have changed urban policy and the broader political economy. Contentious politics and the settlement between labor, capital and the state made a difference in the way that Tokyo achieved global city status. At the time, protests and strikes seemed on the verge of radically challenging capitalism. The suppression of radical movements and the unions' retreat into company bargaining institutions left a political vacuum in which the developmental coalition could operate. Company unionism submerged workers' interests with that of the enterprise, narrowly negotiating the realization of company citizenship rights rather than rights to the city.

During the 1970s Narita Airport became the next battleground where the state and opposing forces clashed over the direction of urbanization. This transportation hub secured Tokyo's position as a global city in the circuits of capital. It also symbolized the developmental state's use of public works projects for partisan gain. Likewise, to explain Tokyo's decline, it is necessary to interpret spatial logics at multiple scales. The Japanese state's inward-focused but export-oriented growth model sheltering Japanese capital, and a relatively egalitarian bargain between labor and capital, became the source of its own undoing. Massive construction and public works' projects, that had kept afloat jobs and wages, fueled an asset bubble undermining the terms of the consensus bargain. Bubblenomics, though not inevitable, has its origins in the closely intertwined relationship between financial institutions, state bureaucracy, and industrial development.

Neoliberal planning policies and national enabling legislation sought to revive Tokyo's fortunes but faced a new competitive regional milieu. What makes global cities' local spaces attractive has the contradictory effect of heating up housing prices, and ever more construction in the competition to win investments from the same transnational firms. In East Asia, municipal and national economic projects vie for dominance in designing and assembling technology of the future. Tokyo remains a global city despite seeing its fortunes decline, but the political bureaucratic project has little room to maneuver and an infrastructural fix no longer has a palliative effect for fueling economic growth after cooling off asset bubbles. Neoliberal policies inspire new spaces of exception where capital can operate according to off-shore principles onshore. New strategic zones encompassing Tokyo and its surrounding areas are yet another quixotic quest by the local and national state to build itself out of the straightjacket of its own making. Similarly, zombie cities sprouting up in China raise questions about that country's construction boom. At the same time ascendant cities in the region offer capital new geographically proximate locations for investment. The future of Tokyo as a global city is not assured.

Is Tokyo's position eclipsed by the city's loss of centrality due to changes in the global economy? In part, the answer lies in understanding the role of regionalism bred and reconfigured by geographies of power. The region is a 'transmission scale,' mediating flows between the local, the national and the global (Duara, 2015). From this perspective, regional geopolitics shaped Tokyo's past and will influence its future. Japan's winning bid for the 1964 Olympics occurred at an early turning point for the city and for the nation. Tokyo was the first Asian city to host the games, a badge of honor promoted by the national and metropolitan governments. The 2020 Olympics can be seen as a nationalist effort to reassert Tokyo to its position as the primary global city in the region, aspiring to being '#1 in Asia.' This aspirational goal recognizes the trans-border shift to a multi-polar system of global cities in the region. An analysis of regionalism points to the tensions inherent to inter-scalar dynamics, raising the question: Why does Tokyo's slide seem so much more precipitous than the other nodal cities of NYC and London. London's current precarious position also stems from regional tensions, but of a different kind. For London, challenges have a political as well as an economic origin brought about by the self-immolation of Brexit. The global status of London is undermined by the tug-of-war between 'national(ist)' interests and the competing logic of regional governance by the European Union. In Europe, Frankfurt and Paris stand in the wings. By contrast, NYC faces no similar regional contenders, either from the likes of Los Angeles in the US or Sao Paolo in the hemisphere. This examination of Tokyo's past and what the future holds provides us with a greater understanding of how global cities are dependent both on policies and practices locally initiated, and on the shifting terrains of rising regional challenges.

Future research must delineate inter-scalar linkages and resulting contradictions and tensions. What spaces of struggle will result from the trans-border shifting system of global cities? Can Seoul, Shanghai, or Hong Kong escape the fate of Tokyo? Has urban developmentalism reached its nadir? Or, are we headed into another phase of post-developmental urbanism? This edited volume addresses many of these themes through detailed case studies in the region.

Acknowledgements

Thanks to Jamie Doucette, Bae-Gyoon Park, and other participants' lively discussions during the SSRC InterAsia Connections workshop, at the Seoul National University, 26–30 April 2016. Their comments on previous drafts crystalized a number of themes running throughout the chapter.

References

Andrews, W (2016) *Dissenting Japan: A History of Japanese Radicalism and Counterculture from 1945 to Fukushima*. Oxford: Oxford University Press.

Buruma, I (2016) *Year Zero: A History of 1945*. New York, NY: Random House.

Chae, O (2013) Japanese colonial structure in Korea in comparative perspective. In: G Steinmetz (ed.) *Sociology and Empire: The Imperial Entanglements of a Discipline*. Durham, NC: Duke University Press.

Chu, K (2017) Realtors say Tokyo's Housing Boom Fading as Sales to Chinese Slow. Bloomberg (consulted 10 Septmber 2017) at: https://www.japantimes.co.jp/news/2017/02/24/business/economy-business/realtors-say-tokyos-housing-boom-fading-sales-chinese-slow/#.WfSPpjBrxEY

Dower, J (1999) *Embracing Defeat: Japan in the Wake of World War II*. New York, NY: Norton.

Duara, P (2015) *The Crisis of Global Modernity: Asian Traditions and A Sustainable Future*. Cambridge, UK: Cambridge University Press.

Fujita, K (2003) Neo-industrial Tokyo: Urban development and globalisation in Japan's state-centred developmental capitalism. *Urban Studies* 40(2): 249–281.

Gottfried, H (2012) *Gender, Work and Economy: Unpacking the Global Economy*. Cambridge: Polity Press.

Gottfried, H (2014) Rescaling labor and gender politics: New geographies of power and resistance. In: *Geschlecht und Transnationale Raeume: Feministische Perspecktiven auf neue Ein- und Ausschlusse*, J Gruhlich and B Riegraf (eds.). Muenster: Verlag Westfaelisches Dampfboot, 119–135.

Gottfried, H (2015) *The Reproductive Bargain: Deciphering the Enigma of Japanese Capitalism*. Leiden: Brill.

Gugler, J (ed.) (2004) *World Cities beyond the West: Globalization, Development and Inequality*. Cambridge: Cambridge University Press.

Hardt, M and A Negri (2000) *Empire*. Boston, MA: Harvard University Press.

Harvey, D (2005) *A Brief History of Neo-Liberalism*. Oxford: Oxford University Press.

Harvey, D (2008) Is this really the end of neo-liberalism? Counterpunch, 7 April. Available (consulted 11 November 2010) at: http://www.counterpunch.org/harvey03132009.html

Harvey, D (2011) *The Enigma of Capital and the Crisis of Capitalism, 2nd Edition*. Oxford: Oxford University Press.

Herod, A and M Wright (eds.) (2002) *Geographies of Power: Placing Scale*. Malden, MA: Blackwell.

Hill, RC and JW Kim (2000) Global cities and developmental states: New York, Tokyo and Seoul. *Urban Studies* 37(12): 2167–2195.

Hill, RC, B Park and A Saito (2011) Introduction: Locating neoliberalism in East Asia. In: B Park, RC Hill and A Saito (eds.) *Locating Neoliberalism in East Asia: Neoliberalizing Spaces in Developmental States*. Malden, MA: Wiley-Blackwell.

Horiuchi, Y (2013) *America's role in making Japan's economic miracle: New evidence for a landmark case*. Paper presented at the Center for Japanese Studies Noon Lecture, 21 November, University of Michigan.

Kleeman, FY (2014) In Transit: *The Formation of the Colonial East Asian Cultural Sphere*. Honolulu, HI: University of Hawaii Press.

Languillon-Aussel, R (2014) The burst bubble and the privatization of planning in Tokyo. *Metropolitiques*. Available (consulted 8 June 2014) at: http://www.metropolitiques.eu/The-burst-bubble-and-the.html

LSA (Literature, Science and the Arts) (2013) Far flung fieldwork. Alumni Magazine (College of Literature, Science, and the Arts, University of Michigan), Fall: 54–56.

Machimura, T (1998) Symbolic use of globalization in urban politics in Tokyo. *International Journal of Urban and Regional Research* 22(2): 183–194.

Martin, A (2013) The 1964 Tokyo Olympics: A turning point for Japan. The Wall Street Journal, 5 September. Available (consulted 1 October 2016) at: http://blogs.wsj.com/japanrealtime/2013/09/05/the-1964-tokyo-olympics-a-turning-point-for-japan/

McCurry, J (2015) Tokyo Split over Zaha Hadid's gigantic white elephant Olympic Stadium. The Guardian (consulted 15 September 2017) at: https://theguardian.com/world/2015/jan/17/tokyodenounce-zaha-hadid-olympic-stadium.html

Metzler, M (2013) *Capital as Will and Imagination: Schumpeter's Guide to the Postwar Japanese Miracle*. Ithaca, NY: Cornell University Press.

Meyer, U (2014) Dongdeamun Design Plaza. Arcspace, 23 April. Available (consulted 3 October) at: http://www.arcspace.com/features/zaha-hadid-architects/dongdaemun-design-plaza/

Murphy, TR (2009) Bubblenomics. New Left Review 57 (May/June). Available (consulted 15 June 2016) at: https://newleftreview.org/II/57/r-taggart-murphy-bubblenomics

Murphy, TR (2014) *Japan and the Shackles of the Past*. Oxford: Oxford University Press.

Park, B, R Hill and A Saito (eds.) (2011) *Locating Neoliberalism in East Asia: Neoliberalizing Spaces in Developmental States*. Malden, MA: Wiley-Blackwell.

Saito, A (2003) Global city formation in a capitalist development state: Tokyo and the Waterfront Sub-Centre Project. *Urban Studies* 40(2): 283–308.

Saito, A and A Thornley (2003) Shifts in Tokyo's World City status and the urban planning responses. *Urban Studies* 40(4): 665–685.

Samuels, R (1981) Kishi and corruption: An anatomy of the 1955 system. Working Paper No. 83, Japan Policy Research Institute. Available (consulted 29 May 2014) at: http://www.jpri.org/publications/workingpapers/wp83.html

Sassen, S (2001) *The Global City: New York, London, Tokyo*. Princeton, NJ: Princeton University Press.

Steinmetz, G (2014) "On the articulation of Marxist and non-Marxist theory in Colonial Historiography. Vivek Chibber's Postcolonial Theory and the Spectre of Capital." *Journal of World Systems* 20(2): 282–288.

Steinmetz, G (ed.) (2013) *Sociology and Empire: The Imperial Entanglements of a Discipline.* Durham, NC: Duke University Press.

Steinmetz, G (2012) Geopolitics. In *Encyclopedia of Globalization*, George Ritzer (ed.). Routledge.

Stoler, A (2013) *Imperial Debris: On Ruins and Ruination.* Durham, NC: Duke University Press.

Tabuchi, H (2009) Rising debt a threat to Japanese economy. *The New York Times.* Available (consulted 15 June 2016) at: http://www.nytimes.com/2009/10/21/business/global/21yen.html

Tomizawa, R (2015) The Olympic Village in Washington Heights: Athletes Get a Taste of Americana in Tokyo. The Olympians from 1964 to 2020. (consulted 1 October 2017) at: https://theolympians.co/2015/09/03/the-olympic-village-in-washington-heights.html

Tokyo Metropolitan Government (2017a) About Our City. Tokyo's History, Geography, and Population (consulted 3 October 2017) at: http://www.metro.tolyo.jp/ENGLISH/ABOUT/HISTORY/history02.html

Tokyo Metropolitan Government (2017b) New Tokyo, New tomorrow. The Action Plan for 2020. (consulted 29 September 2017) at: http://www.seisakukikaku.metro.tokyo.jp/actionplan_for_2020/english/index.html

Tsukamoto, T (2012) Why is Japan neo-liberalizing? Rescaling of the Japanese developmental state and ideology of state-capital fixing. *Journal of Urban Affairs* 34(4): 395–418.

Walker, G (2016) *The Sublime Perversion of Capital.* Durham, NC: Duke University Press.

Walker, R (2016) Why Cities? A Response. *International Journal of Urban and Regional Research* 40(1): 164–180.

Wang, C (2003) Taipei as a global city: A theoretical and empirical examination. *Urban Studies* 40(2): 309–334.

West, M (2003) Employment market institutions and Japanese working hours. University of Michigan Law School, Paper #03-016. Available (consulted 1 November 2013) at: http://law.bepress.com/umichlwps/olin/art22/

The Biopolitics of Urbanization in China: Managing Migration and Access to Education

Eli Friedman

1 Introduction

In 2014, some of China's megacities initiated a wide-ranging effort to expel rural migrants.[1] Shanghai's Minhang and Pudong districts incorporated population reduction quotas as a key metric for appraising the work of street-level cadres, while Baoshan district demanded that officials reduce population within their jurisdiction by 5 to 10 percent.[2] In Beijing, Mayor Wang Anshun commented, 'Beijing is not at present a livable city. But there is still a mad scramble of people to come here, so controlling the population is the single biggest problem for the government'.[3] In order to support urban districts with this task, the municipal government promised more than one billion Yuan (≈US$160m) to promote industrial restructuring and population control, and nearly 10.4 billion Yuan (≈US$1.7b) for 'slum redevelopment'.[4]

Cities adopted various strategies to reduce their migrant populations, including adjustments to housing policies and forcing labor-intensive industries to relocate. But perhaps most troubling was a strategy pursued with great zeal in the capital: 'using education to control the population'. Children of rural-to-urban migrants in Beijing had never enjoyed the right to public

1   This research was supported by Cornell University's Institute for the Social Sciences. This chapter has benefitted from feedback from many colleagues, including Jia-Ching Chen, Diana Fu, Greg Distelhorst, Jamie Doucette, Peter Evans, Christina Kim, Zach Levenson, Mike Levien, Thonghong Lin, Jonas Nahm, Marcel Paret, Bae-Gyoon Park, and Ed Steinfeld. I also received very useful comments during presentations at InterAsian Connections V (held at Seoul National University, South Korea), as well as National Tsing Hua University in Taiwan. I would like to thank Ling Tao, Hao Zhang, Magic Peng, Christine Wen, and Andi Kao for invaluable research assistance.
2   20 November 2014. Renkou tiaokong zhengce chujian chengxiao, lai hu renyuan zengsu mingxian xiajiang. Laodong Bao.
3   24 January 2015. Beijing shizhang Wang Anshun: yiju zhi du shi women de mubiao. *Zhongguo Qingnian Bao*.
4   Ibid.

education, and tens of thousands had long been relegated to a wildly inferior system of private education. But migrant parents whose children had been lucky enough to get into public schools suddenly found that the bar for entry had been raised. The result was that thousands of parents had the impossible decision of whether to send their children back to the village alone, or accompany them and forsake their jobs in the city.

This effort to remove migrants from the city would seem to be at odds with recent central government policy. Indeed, the government has for several years been talking about shifting from a model of growth dependent on low-cost exports and debt-financed investment to one based on increased urbanization, which is seen as likely to catalyze domestic consumption and growth in the service sector. But on closer inspection it is apparent that the state is developing a highly variegated system whereby certain kind of people are encouraged to move to certain kinds of cities. State policy in recent years has been oriented towards institutionalizing a socio-spatial citizenship regime in which large wealthy cities can selectively pull in specific kinds of labor power from smaller cities and the countryside to respond to labor market demands, while relegating less desirable people to less desirable places. The 2014 population control campaigns in Beijing and Shanghai were aimed at removing this latter population.

All processes of capitalist urbanization involve a dilemma: on the one hand, cities need to pull in labor power in order to fuel their factories and construction sites, to take care of children and the elderly, to prepare and serve meals – in short to *work*. But on the other hand, urban elites fear overcrowding, social chaos, and the costs associated with reproducing the workforce. In other words, the pursuit of rapid economic growth almost always implies growth of population, but there are contradictory imperatives to both draw in and expel workers. Although this urban growth dilemma is a general tendency under capitalist urbanization, the specific politics are of course shaped by a huge array of historically, culturally, and spatially specific conditions.

In this chapter I argue that the Chinese state is responding to the tensions generated by the urban growth dilemma by attempting to develop a form of technocratic biopolitics I refer to as 'just-in-time (JIT) urbanization'. As with the Toyota Production System (TPS), of which JIT is a constituent element, large Chinese cities have sought to avoid the costs associated with the production, warehousing, and social reproduction of workers. Under this system, migrants can be granted access to urban citizenship if they fulfill a specific, state-determined, need in the labor market, thereby giving them access to subsidized reproduction (e.g. public education, social insurance). The hope is to be able to precisely deploy specific kinds of labor power as needed, at as low a cost as possible, while avoiding waste, overpopulation, and (presumed) attendant political chaos.

But this attempt to prevent over-accumulation of people in the spaces of rapid capital accumulation encounters limits. While the Chinese state exercises impressive capacity and a willingness to use highly coercive means to achieve its ends, human movement inevitably exceeds the logic of technocratic biopolitics embodied in JIT urbanization: peasants from impoverished areas need jobs, and capital in the cities needs cheap labor. And while the right to state-subsidized reproduction remains tied to specific places, migrants are free to sell their labor anywhere in the country. The question then becomes: in what specific way is inclusion in the city socially segmented? I have found that urban governments have developed relatively predictable sorting mechanisms, characterized by a positive association between migrants' levels of economic, social, and cultural capital and their access to public goods. In focusing on primary education, I find that the consequence of this politics of urbanization is deepening educational inequality and reconstitution of an increasingly rigid class structure.

2   The Specificity of Chinese Urbanization

For the purposes of this research, scholarship on the process of urbanization can be broadly categorized into two currents: that which sees a tendency towards progressive inclusion of rural migrants into the economic, political, and social life of cities, and that which sees on-going forms of exclusion. The former we can call, somewhat imprecisely, a 'modernization' perspective, which emerged in the 19th century and was dominant until the mid-late 20th century. 'Southern urbanism', on the other hand, grew out of late 20th century studies of the former colonies in Africa, Asia, and Latin America, which emphasized the distinct historical trajectories of the South. As descriptive approaches, at least, each of these perspectives captures some of the dynamics of contemporary China.

Cold War-era scholars in the Durkheimian tradition theorized a basically universal tendency for progressive inclusion of the working class into the market, which they saw as causally linked to emergent citizenship rights. T.H. Marshall famously delineated a teleology of rights, in which all citizens were gradually granted civil, political, and then, in the 20th century, social rights (Marshall 1950). Parsons (1964: 353–6) saw democracy and civil society organizations as playing a key role in politically integrating the working class, while Lipset (1959) was confident that increased economic growth would result in a full extension of democratic rights. In each of these cases, the economic process of the universalization of wage labor was directly linked to the extension of citizenship rights. While this literature is not concerned with the urban per se, it is assumed that modernity and urbanization are parallel processes.

Since at least the 1970s, scholars have worked to identify the distinctive features and dynamics of Southern urbanization and proletarianization. Early work on Africa and Latin America identified informality as a distinctive feature of the economy (Hart 1973), a phenomenon that defied expectations about a progressive absorption into wage labor (Bradshaw 1987). It is now beyond doubt that the former colonies have experienced a radical disjuncture between the production of proletarians, i.e. those dispossessed of non-market forms of reproduction (Denning 2010), and capital's demand for labor power. This shift in the socio-economic dynamic of capitalist development has resulted in growth of urban population without a concomitant growth in formal labor market opportunities in the city. Durable informality – be it in the labor market, housing, or social services – suggests *exclusion* as a fundamental political dynamic of the Southern city.

In recent years, scholars have turned to a synthesis of Foucault and Marx in thinking about the politics of inclusion and exclusion. In his lectures at the Collège de France, Foucault defined biopower as 'the power to "make" live and "let" die' (Foucault 2003). In his formulation, 'race' is the axis of differentiation by which certain social groups are 'made' to live, while others are 'allowed' to die. In synthesizing Marx and Foucault, scholars such as Michael McIntyre and Heidi Nast (2011) have elucidated the racialized delineation of population and surplus population – the former becoming the object of an affirmative biopower while the latter is condemned to what Achille Mbembe has called the 'necropolitical' (2003). Tania Li provides an explanation for why this racialized differentiation is a feature of Southern urbanization: contemporary dynamics of capital accumulation favor (largely rural) dispossession over (largely urban) exploitation (Li 2010). The result has been the production of a population that is simply superfluous to the needs of capital, either as workers or consumers. The vision we are left with is of a mass of humanity accumulating in the cities that are treated as 'waste' (Bauman 2004), and subject to myriad forms of state-sponsored violence and expulsion (Sassen 2014).

But when we turn to China, some very different dynamics are at play. To begin with, the politics of racialization are not quite what this literature might lead us to expect.[5] In China, the biopolitical distinction between population and surplus population is interpreted primarily through the lens of space,

---

5   In my view, Foucault's conception of race is so capacious as to be vacuous. By including both colonialists and socialists as 'racist' (the latter because of their advocating violence against

not race (Wang 2005; Zhang 2001). From the perspective of the urban state, it is the rural migrant worker who is seen as expendable and is excluded from life-affirming biopower. The overwhelming majority of such workers are Han, as are urban elites. Certainly racism plays a fundamental role in the Chinese state's efforts to control and urbanize peripheral regions such as Tibet and Xinjiang (Fisher 2008; Joniak-Lüthi 2013). But in the eastern megacities it is place of origin and access to property – not race – that divide population from surplus population.[6]

When we look at economic processes, each body of thought has something to contribute to accounting for China's experience. Modernization theory has been rightly maligned for decades, and there is no need to rehash why an evolutionary approach cannot explain the politics of contemporary capitalist development. But we should not overlook the fact that among countries in the South, China's developmental experience comes the closest to repeating the historical trajectory of the North. Indeed, hundreds of millions of people have left agriculture and have been absorbed by industries such as manufacturing and construction. The Chinese state has enacted a raft of labor legislation to regulate and formalize employment relations and extend social insurance coverage. Chinese cities have relatively few slums (Wallace 2014). Scholars and government officials may grossly underestimate the scope of the informal economy (Huang 2009), but it certainly pales in comparison to other large Southern countries. While there are some very important ways in which China differs significantly from the North, most importantly with regards to the delinking of the market and liberal democracy, the 'Southern urbanism' vision doesn't quite comport with China's reality.

But when we leave the sphere of production and move to an analysis of social reproduction and politics, we do see ongoing forms of exclusion. And while it is true that vast swathes of the population continue to be treated as potentially, or imminently, surplus, excluded from the full benefits of urban citizenship, we also see that dynamic capitalist growth has required huge volumes of labor power. Thus, a rigid inclusion/exclusion binary cannot account for the experience of migrant workers in China. Building on the work of Mezzadra and Neilson (2013), I am interested in the particular way in which migrants' insertion into urban space is segmented. While modernization presumes

---

the bourgeoisie), he robs the term of any analytical specificity. His conception of racism, then, is really no different from what would typically be thought of as a generic othering.

6   It is true that othering of migrant workers can take on racialized undertones, as they can be described as dirty, of 'low quality', or backward. While recognizing the porousness of all racial categories, 'migrant' is a relatively escapable form of social designation, and therefore should not be considered a race.

progressive inclusion and literature on Southern urbanism and surplus population focuses on on-going exclusion, the perspective of segmented inclusion
highlights the peculiar ways in which Chinese migrants are tethered to the city
as labor power and expelled as social beings. From this perspective, then, we
must ask how and why the urban state attempts to enforce a particular segmentation of inclusion of various social groups.

3   The Urban Growth Dilemma

In his classic formulation, Harvey Molotch argued that cities are, 'for those
who count, a growth machine' (1976: 310). For Molotch, 'growth' is a category
that encompasses both economic expansion and population increase, and
these two goals constitute the decisive orientation of urban elites. But when
we look at China's cities – and, I suspect, many other cities – it is not apparent
that these two types of growth can be neatly categorized together. If we are
to assume that the capitalist urban state is oriented towards the inter-related
goals of accumulation and domination, then it follows from this that the state
faces some tension in managing economic and population growth.

Clearly, cities must admit populations if they are to grow economically –
and just admitting wealthy or highly educated people is insufficient. Labor-
intensive manufacturing is still the most reliable route to development, even
in the 21st century. In order to attract such industry, urban governments must
be able to pull in large volumes of cheap and docile labor. As was shown to be
the case over the past 35 years, this capacity has proven decisive in allowing
China to industrialize and post historically unprecedented rates of growth year
after year (Chan 2009). Even without large-scale manufacturing, many service
industries (e.g. food and beverage/hospitality, health care, child/elder care,
sanitation, sex work) will demand low cost labor.

But admission of newcomers is not without its drawbacks from the perspective of the state. Given that the wage rarely constitutes the full cost of labor
power, the state is almost always on the hook for some of the costs of social
reproduction of the workforce. City governments may be reluctant to provide
major new fiscal outlays for public housing, health, and education for recent
arrivals. Politically, urban elites may fear that new arrivals will undermine
the social fabric of the community, bringing with them crime, drugs, and dis-
ease. The possibility for social dissolution or political chaos looms large in the
consciousness of the urban state – particularly so in China where concerns
about the 'carrying capacity' (*chengzaili*) of cities are a key feature of state
discourse. The state's *perception* of economic and political pressures owing

to overpopulation constitutes what I refer to as the 'Malthusian crisis'.[7] It is precisely this sense of crisis that has led cities like Beijing to employ various methods to eject migrants.

Expulsion of populations, while perhaps effectively responding to nativist sentiment, engenders other problems for capital and the state. Aside from the obvious point that this process itself can trigger social unrest, an effective reduction in population poses risks to profitability. With a tighter labor market, capital may face rising wages and more assertive workers. While these dynamics are certainly sectorally uneven, inability to pin down sufficient labor could lead capital to flee to areas in which labor is more abundant. This in turn would lead to falling tax revenue for the state. This 'profitability crisis' may then push the state back in the direction of admitting populations.

The urban growth dilemma refers to the competing imperatives faced by the state in managing high-speed economic growth and urbanization (see Figure 4.1). Over-accumulation of people in the cities raises the specter of a fiscal crunch and social chaos. But every attempt to address the Malthusian crisis simultaneously hastens a profitability crisis by depriving capital of its lifeblood – labor. These are crisis *tendencies* and are not necessarily discrete and diachronic events. But urban governments must constantly negotiate this uncertain terrain, pulled in one direction by fear of chaos and nativist sentiment, and pulled in the other by capital's demands for an abundant and pliable workforce. While cities face widely heterogeneous local political arrangements, as well as a differential capacity to respond, this tension is a central motor force of the politics of urbanization.

The question then becomes, how specifically have Chinese cities responded to this dilemma? What sorts of strategies have they developed in an attempt to reduce human waste and overcome spatio-temporal disjunctures in the distribution of capital and labor? And what are the social consequences of these practices?

4   Just-in-Time Urbanization?

My central claim is that Chinese megacities are pursuing a JIT approach to urbanization in an attempt to overcome the political and economic problems posed by the urban growth dilemma. In what ways does this constitute a JIT approach? Taiichi Ohno, the person most responsible for the development of

---

7   It is important to emphasize that this is a *perception* on the part of the state. I am not making any claim about the actual carrying capacity of the city.

TPS,[8] provides the following definition: 'Just-in-time means that, in a flow process, the right parts needed in assembly reach the line at the time they are needed and only in the amount needed' (Ohno 1988: 4). When considering urbanization, of course, the parts in question are not material objects, but labor power. This raises a particular concern, as labor power is inalienable from the worker. So rather than thinking about how companies organize the production and movement of commodities through the supply chain, here we are concerned with how cities (and especially China's wealthy megacities) regulate the movement of workers into urban space. While the analogy with auto production is imperfect in a number of respects, the basic impulse remains the same: megacities are attempting to develop a technocratic apparatus capable of regulating the flow of workers in accordance with demands of the market, such that specific types of labor power can be delivered in the right quantity at the right time to capital.

Aside from these general similarities, there are some more specific parallels between JIT production and JIT urbanization. To begin with, there is a similar focus on a reduction of warehousing. JIT production sees warehousing of parts as wasteful and costly, as it requires additional expenditures on space as well as labor to maintain the stores. 'Warehousing' of people is also costly and includes housing as well as other costs associated with social reproduction. But JIT urbanization aims not just for economic efficiency, but also to

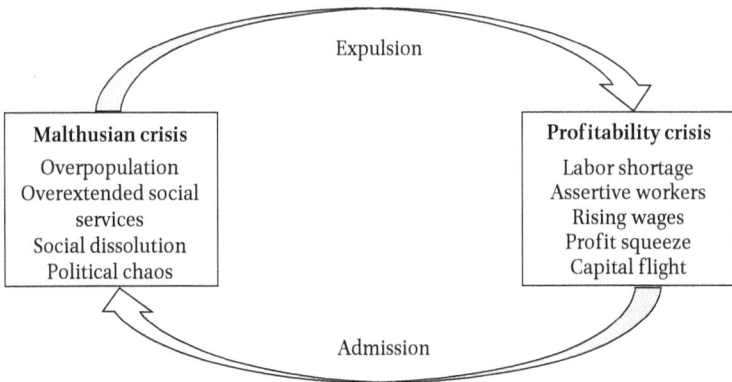

FIGURE 4.1   The urban growth dilemma
            SOURCE: BY THE AUTHOR.

---

8   The relationship between JIT, TPS, and lean production is complicated. Lean and TPS are broadly similar, though the former is concerned with all sorts of production, not just autos. JIT refers more precisely to coordinating the quantity and movement of products in space and time, i.e. managing *flow*, and is a component feature of lean and TPS.

address the potential political problems associated with warehousing people. As is well-established in the literature, Chinese urban elites have long subscribed to a neo-Malthusian worldview which associates overpopulation with political chaos (Anagnost 1997; Wallace 2014). By keeping surplus population at bay in the countryside or smaller towns, megacities intend to draw in workers on a strictly as-needed basis, thereby serving both economic and political ends.

A second parallel is a concern with the reduction of waste (Womack and Jones 2010). For TPS, Ohno holds that, '"waste" refers to all elements of production that only increase cost without adding value – for example excess people, inventory, and equipment' (Ohno 1988: 54). Both JIT production and urbanization are oriented towards reducing costs and improving productivity 'through the elimination of various wastes such as excessive inventory and excessive workforce' (Monden 2011: 4). Michelle Yates postulates the emergence of the 'human-as-waste' under late capitalism, suggesting that huge swathes of the population are 'structurally and biologically redundant to global accumulation and the corporate matrix' (Yates 2011: 1679). But again, China is somewhat different from much of the South in that capital actually has employed hundreds of millions of people. So in this case, a human that was 'waste' yesterday may be the bearer of a viable labor power today. The point, from the perspective of JIT urbanization, is to eliminate any responsibility on the part of capital or the urban state to underwrite social reproduction for that person during a 'waste moment'. When workers are deemed superfluous – a fundamentally political rather than economic designation – the state reserves the right to expunge them.

A final related similarity is the tendency towards maintaining flexibility through dualization. While more associated with TPS and Japanese employment relations in general rather than JIT in particular, workforce flexibility is central to achieving JIT production (Monden 2011: 311). Toyota and other Japanese firms were at the forefront in dividing the industrial workforce into a stable, unionized core, which enjoyed strong job security and generous benefits, and a contingent, temporary workforce that could be utilized and discarded with minimal friction. JIT urbanization envisions a core group of citizens who enjoy a variety of rights (most notably for this study, the right to public education), surrounded by a contingent workforce that may be included in certain spheres of social and political life and not others. This latter group experiences access to social services as a revocable privilege rather than a right. This rupture in the citizen-worker nexus (Barchiesi 2011: 62) gives cities greater flexibility in deploying the right kinds of labor power at the right time, without having to bear the costs associated with maintenance and regeneration of workers. Furthermore, as denizens, these expendable workers have no right to political representation or participation in the city.

But there are some important differences between JIT production and JIT urbanization, a brief discussion of which will be useful in highlighting the specificity of the latter. The fundamental difference owes to the different character of the commodities in question. According to Yasuhiro Monden, author of the definitive work on TPS, 'it is the principle aim of the Toyota Production System to control overproduction – to ensure that all processes make products according to the sales velocity of the market' (Monden 2011: 6). But cities' biopolitical capacity, i.e. the ability to regulate the production, maintenance, and circulation of people, is inevitably much more constrained than would be the case in material production. The Chinese state has developed highly competent biopolitical machinery, the chief example of which is the notorious birth control policies (Greenhalgh and Winckler 2005). But despite megacities' position at the apex of the Chinese political economy, they do not have the capacity to actively control the production of labor power, to say nothing of determining the appropriate quantities, qualities, and circulation thereof. Cities are dependent on the hinterlands to produce workers for them, and unlike the lead firm in JIT production, they exercise little control over their suppliers. So while cities will still try to regulate the flow of people according to demand in the local market, they cannot directly control production.

The second related difference is that the object of JIT urbanization is people rather than things. Workers' place-specific sociality and frequent demands for respect and autonomy pose a whole host of problems that are irrelevant for JIT production. Since there will always be a coordination problem between the production of proletarians and capital's need to employ human labor, inevitably some labor powers will be underutilized – and given nearly universal market-dependence, this can create social friction. In short, when we consider urbanization as the process of condensation of human settlement under conditions of capitalist transformation of both city and countryside, *politics* matter in a way that is simply not the case for JIT production. Workers are not merely objects, and their subjectivity and need for community and survival pose a challenge to JIT principles.

It is precisely for this reason that JIT urbanization refers to a utopian vision rather than an empirical reality. And yet, even if this vision can never be fully realized in practice, the state's pursuit of JIT urbanization has major social consequences. I will now turn to a discussion of the tools the state has at its disposal, as well as the social consequences.

5   From Rigid Exclusion to Segmented Inclusion

Following the 1949 revolution, Chinese cities experienced a major population influx from the countryside. Although the peasantry had been the social foundation of the revolution, the Communist Party quickly moved to a Soviet-inspired model of development predicated on extraction of surplus from the countryside and investment in heavy industry in the cities (Hung 2015: 43, 50). But in 1958, on the eve of the Great Leap Forward, the government established the *hukou* system. Although household registrations had historical precedent under the imperial system, the modern incarnation was much more specifically focused on a particular end: controlling the mobility of the population (Dutton 1988) and keeping peasants out of the cities.

Taking its cues from the Soviet internal passport *propiska* system (Chan 2009: 199), *hukou* status is passed from parents to children and can only be changed with official approval. *Hukou* controls movement by tying the provision of a variety of goods to a specific place. During the period of the command economy, this included nearly everything someone would need to survive: not only health care and education, but also housing and even food. Leaving one's place of registration without official approval would imply forsaking access to state-provided goods. A rural resident that wandered into the city could face police harassment, detention, and even deportation back to the countryside. From its inception in 1958 until the initiation of market reforms, the consequence of the *hukou* was a radical demobilization of labor.

But with the introduction of foreign capital and private enterprise beginning in 1978, the government initiated a gradual process of relaxing controls on internal movement. The export-oriented firms popping up in special economic zones such as Shenzhen needed workers, and the low cost of labor had been a primary point of attraction. Surplus workers from the countryside were able to secure temporary permits to live and work outside their area of *hukou* registration, provided that the firm was willing to provide proof of employment. As during the Mao era, those who wandered away from their workplace without their papers were frequently subject to police harassment, and even deportation. Such a system has been compared to the apartheid 'pass laws' in South Africa (Alexander and Chan 2004), and as in South Africa it was crucial in the production of a low wage, pliable workforce (Wolpe 1972).

Throughout the 1990s and 2000s, however, this system came to be increasingly relaxed. Whereas in the 1960s it would have been very difficult to survive without state approval, by the turn of the millennium, market exchange and dependence were nearly universal. This meant that people could now survive outside of their area of *hukou* registration, as they were less dependent on state-provisioned goods. However, leaving one's area of registration also implied forsaking any rights to said goods, including education, subsidized housing, health care, and pensions. Given the highly uneven economic geography of contemporary Chinese capitalism, most ruralites had to go to the cities to find work. The consequence of these various developments was, in effect, a passive privatization of social reproduction for 270 million migrants. While there is no longer the rigid exclusion that characterized the era of the command economy, rural residents face the choice of subpar public services and poverty in the countryside, or marginally better economic opportunities without guaranteed access to public services in the cities.

It is important to remember that *hukou* affects not only poor migrants but elites as well. Most of the time this will not pose a problem for someone with the resources to purchase high-quality education, housing, and insurance on the market. But there are certain decisive moments, notably the university entrance exam, which have been subject to rigid status-based closure by those with full urban citizenship. Thus, the state has been moving to refine the citizenship regime, not necessarily to make it more inclusive, but to incorporate market-based metrics in distributing nominally public goods. The consequence is that processes of sorting the population are increasingly predicated on the basis of class rather than status.

6   The New Urbanization Plan and Point-Based Citizenship

2014 was an eventful year in the development of migration policy in China. The National New Urbanization Plan (2014–2020), intended as a blueprint for China's shift to urbanization-driven development, was unveiled in March. The plan aimed to move 100 million people to cities by 2020, under the belief that this would reduce inequality, increase domestic consumption, and promote higher-value-added production and ecologically sustainable development. In addition to encouraging people to move to cities, with the stated goal of a national urbanization rate of 60 per cent by 2020, the new plan aimed to reduce the percentage of people living in cities without local *hukou*.[9] The plan was also quite forthcoming in acknowledging inequalities that had emerged over the previous decades:

> Disparities in access to public services between local and migrant populations have produced ever more apparent contradictions in cities' dual

---

9 "Guojia xinxing chengzhenhua guihua (2014–2020)," gov.cn, last modified 16th March 2014, http://www.gov.cn/zhengce/2014-03/16/content_2640075.htm.

structure. The model of primarily relying on unequal public services to minimize expenses and promote rapid urbanization is not sustainable.[10]

Then in July, the State Council released the 'Opinion on Promoting Reform of the Residency System', a document intended to complement the move to urban-led development. The key feature of the Opinion was a call to 'unify the rural and urban *hukou* registration system' and 'comprehensively implement a residential permit system'.[11] The former was hailed as an indication of the end of the apartheid-like features of the system that made transferring from rural to urban *hukou* (*nongzhuanfei*) particularly difficult. The residential permit was intended to replace the 'temporary resident permit', a designation that allowed migrants to stay and work in the city while denying them access to social services. The residential permit, on the other hand, was supposed to allow for migrants to enjoy similar (though not necessarily identical) rights to those of people with local *hukou*.

Yet, a closer analysis of these and related policies points to an important nuance: the government was encouraging certain kinds of people to move to certain kinds of cities. Item Six of the urbanization plan is titled, 'promoting the transfer of rural to urban hukou for *those who meet certain conditions* [emphasis added]'.[12] As had been the case previously, the central government did not dictate to the municipalities any specifics as to the conditions for accessing local *hukou*. But the types of conditions that were generally applicable included 'number of years of employment, number of years of residence, and number of years of participation in urban social insurance', adding that both employment and residence should be 'stable and legal'. Crucially, the central government did not promise any fiscal restructuring to accommodate these new arrivals. Given that municipalities would largely be on the hook for increased outlays in social services, there was reason to doubt their willingness to embrace full integration of new migrants.

Although the center did not directly dictate conditions for admission to various kinds of cities, the urbanization plan gave some indications about how cities of different sizes should proceed. Specifically:

---

10   Ibid.
11   "Guowuyuan guanyu jin yi bu tuijin huji zhidu gaige de yijian," gov.cn, last modified 30th July 2014, http://www.gov.cn/zhengce/content/2014-07/30/content_8944.htm.
12   "Guojia xinxing chengzhenhua guihua (2014–2020)," gov.cn, last modified 16th March 2014, http://www.gov.cn/zhengce/2014-03/16/content_2640075.htm.

... townships and small cities should comprehensively relax restrictions for attaining local *hukou*; cities with a population of 500,000–1 million residents should relax restrictions in an orderly manner; large cities with a population of 1–3 million should reasonably relax restrictions; large cities with a population of 3–5 million should reasonably establish conditions for attaining local *hukou*; extra-large cities with a population of more than 5 million should strictly control the scope of their population.[13]

Definitions of 'reasonable' and 'orderly' were not provided, and establishing the specific conditions for accessing local *hukou* was explicitly left up to the municipalities. What is clear is that the center did not envision significant *hukou* liberalization in large cities – precisely the places with the most dynamic economies (see Figure 4.2) and most generous social welfare provision (see Figure 4.3).

Of greatest relevance for our understanding of JIT urbanization has been the center's promotion of point-based *hukou* schemes (*jifen ruhu*). These schemes have been implemented in the extra-large cities that are the focus of our investigation. Cities in Guangdong province were early adopters of the point-based *hukou* application system, but other municipalities have recently been devising their own schemes. While there is significant variation between various cities' approaches, the basics are the same. Any citizen is eligible for consideration – there are no place-based exclusions. Applicants accrue points based on various characteristics, and after meeting some point threshold they are then allowed to apply for local *hukou*. This gives cities a concrete administrative system for including certain kinds of migrants and excluding others.

As of the end of 2015, point-based *hukou* schemes existed in only a limited number of cities. Programs had been unveiled in the Guangdong cities of Guangzhou, Shenzhen, Dongguan, Zhuhai, and Zhongshan. Elsewhere, Tianjian and Shanghai had plans in place, while Beijing was in the process of drafting up guidelines. The State Council's Opinion had said that cities with a population over 5 million should establish point-based schemes. On the other hand, the Opinion says that cities with a population of 3–5 million 'can' establish point-based systems. Both Zhuhai and Zhongshan have fewer than 3 million people, but given their location in the Pearl River Delta they have a relatively high proportion of migrants. Clearly there is no prohibition on smaller cities developing such schemes, even if they are not required to do so.

In general, the intent of the programs is captured by the first article of Guangzhou's 'Measure on Point-Based *Hukou* Management', which states

---

13   Ibid.

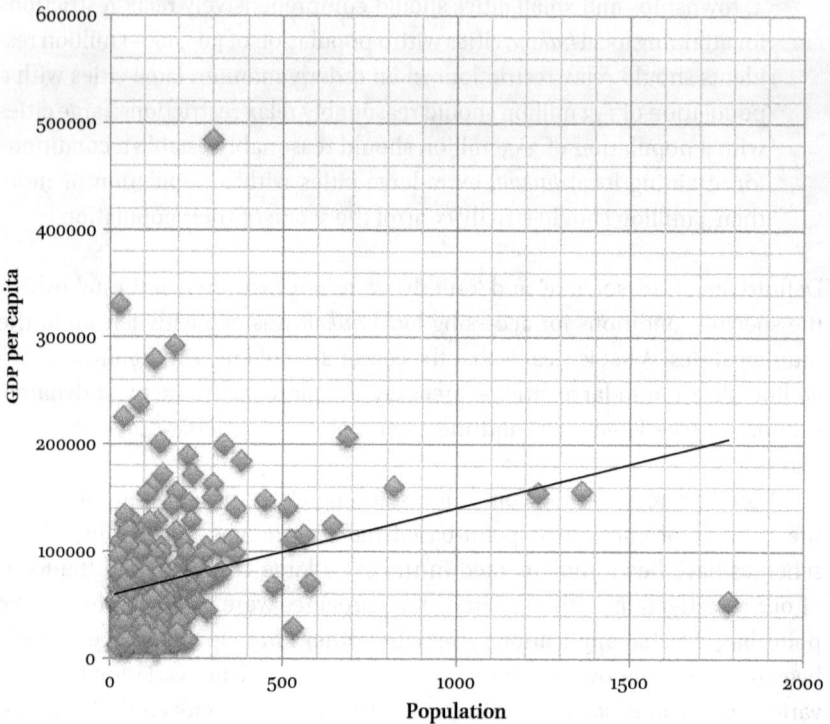

FIGURE 4.2 Gross Domestic Product (GDP) per capita and city size, 2013
SOURCE: 2014 ZHONGGUO CHENGSHI TONGJI NIANJIAN.

that the Measure has been established to 'reasonably control the scope of the population, improve the population structure, improve the quality (*suzhi*) of the population, and coordinate development between the population and the economy, society, resources, and the environment'.[14] The single most important criterion for accruing points is level of education. Although each city assigns different numbers of points for different types of degrees, in general the higher the academic accomplishment the more points an applicant can accrue. Guangzhou assigns points for technical degrees, while Shanghai's system favors those with PhDs as well as graduates of the prestigious '211' universities.[15] In general, cities assign points for various kinds of skills that are in demand in the local labor market.

14   "Guangzhou shi jifen ruhu guanli banfa," gz.gov.cn, last modified 26th October 2016, http://www.gz.gov.cn/gzgov/s2811/201610/540802a006b34b8280f02d4af8b48a7f.shtml.

15   This refers to a group of over one hundred elite universities in China that receive additional government support.

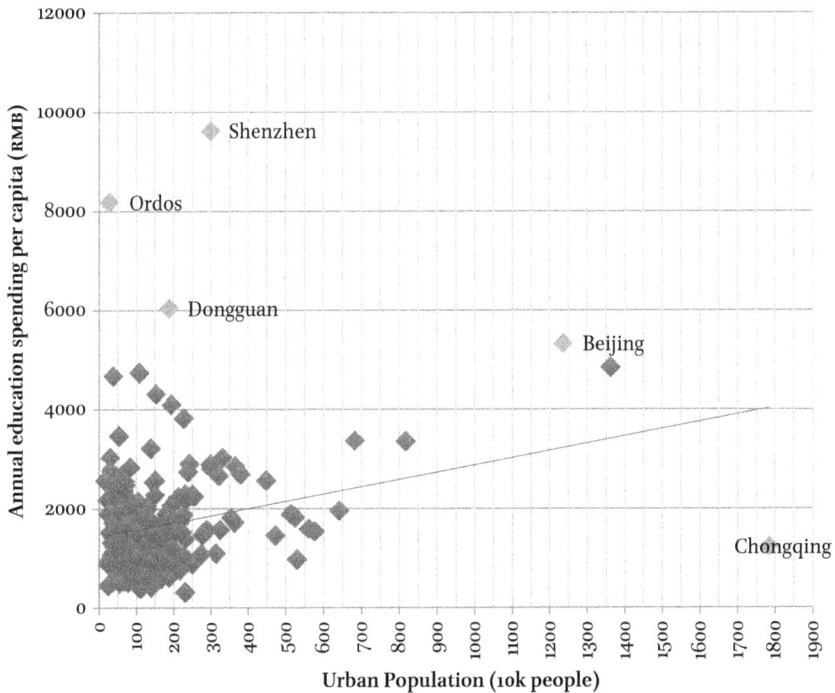

FIGURE 4.3 Education spending in urban China, 2013
SOURCE: 2014 ZHONGGUO CHENGSHI TONGJI NIANJIAN.

The point-based systems contain a variety of other provisions that are oriented towards including specific kinds of people. As is recommended in the central government's Opinion, applying for local *hukou* will almost always require that migrants can produce labor contracts and leases – thereby excluding anyone working in the informal sector or living in informal housing (Huang 2009).[16] Most cities assign points based on the amount of income tax applicants have paid within the municipality. For instance, Guangzhou and Tianjin both assign points for applicants who have paid at least 100,000 Yuan in income taxes over the previous three years, whereas Shenzhen has an elaborate system that awards progressively more points for more income tax paid. Most cities assign points for the number of years that applicants have paid into the local pension fund. As an increasing number of labor conflicts in recent years have demonstrated, migrant workers rarely receive (legally mandated) pension contributions from their employers. Guangzhou, Shenzhen, and Tianjin bar applicants who have any criminal record or who have violated the birth control policies.

---

16   Huang has estimated that there are 168 million informal workers in China's cities.

And people over 45 are either barred completely from applying or receive point demerits for each year over age 45. Cities are clearly only interested in extending social welfare privileges to young, educated, and relatively wealthy people who will presumably contribute to the economy for many years.

The point-based schemes are an attempt to formalize and make transparent the highly unequal methods large cities have used for distributing rights to local services for many years. And there is no doubt that these plans are emerging as key administrative tools in cities' efforts to get the right kind of labor power delivered, in the right quantity, and at the right time.[17] In conjunction with the more coercive measures to expel undesirable migrants, this suggests an urbanization strategy imbued with the logic of JIT. The problem, however, is that such a technocratic vision of perfect control over human movement can never be realized in practice, particularly in a country which already has a national labor market. By attending to one side of the urban growth dilemma, i.e. avoiding overpopulation, the state would simultaneously deprive capital of a cheap workforce. Furthermore, rural residents are no longer categorically bound to the countryside. But while a national labor market has been institutionalized, citizenship is still constituted at the local level. To put it another way, China has realized freedom of movement for labor power but not people. The consequence is there are more than 270 million migrants that are moving 'out of plan'. How then are these people included and excluded in urban social space? More specifically, for those who are living in the city but have no chance of securing local *hukou*, how do they go about getting access to education for their children?

7   Inverted Means Testing

Shifting our focus from the labor market to the sphere of reproduction, we see massive spatial inequality in social spending. Again, in general, the larger the city, the more generous the social service provision (Chan 2009: 214). As can be seen clearly in Figure 4.3, there is a clear positive correlation between the size of the city and education spending per capita. High land values in larger cities cannot account for this inequality, as schools occupy public land. Cities are simply spending much more on better teacher salaries, physical plant, educational technology, and recreation facilities.

Gaining local *hukou* guarantees access to local public education; but many – most, perhaps – migrants in the megacities must earn the *privilege* to send

---

17   The definition of what counts as the right qualities and quantities of labor is flexible, and cities can continually adjust in response to labor market or political demands.

their children to public schools. Since 2001, central government policy has been captured by the slogan 'the two primaries', meaning that receiving areas are primarily responsible for paying for migrant children's education, and that these children should primarily be placed in public schools. The 2006 revision of the Compulsory Education Law reaffirmed that receiving areas should 'provide conditions for equal education' for migrant children (Ge 2009: 1). The government claims that 70 per cent of migrant children nationwide are in fact enrolled in public schools. While this number is suspect for a variety of reasons, it is certainly true that many migrants do end up in public schools. The question then becomes, what is the sorting mechanism whereby some people can access public education while others are relegated to the free market?

In general, the greater a family's access to cultural, economic, and social capital, the better the chance that they will be able to obtain the public good of primary or middle school education. It is important to remember that the population of non-*hukou* holding residents in the megacities is highly heterogeneous in terms of class composition. Although there are different procedures in various cities, there are some common requirements used to exclude working-class migrants. The first requirement is that parents produce a *hukou* for their children from their home region. This seems like a simple enough request as all Chinese citizens are supposed to have *hukou*. However, this requirement ends up excluding 'surplus children' (*chaoshengzi*), which refers to those born in violation of the birth control policies. These children are denied *hukou* unless their parents pay a fine, the amount of which is determined (seemingly arbitrarily) by local birth control officials. Although surplus children are a relatively small portion of the population, they are severely overrepresented in migrant schools.

The second item public schools will typically demand of applicants with non-local *hukou* is a legal employment contract from the parents. Some cities demand multiple years of contracts within the city. Once again, this excludes the poorest migrants, namely those employed in the informal sector. Since the implementation of the Labour Contract Law in 2008, an increasing share of workers has received employment contracts. However, huge swathes of the lower end of the labor market remain fully unregulated. As just a few examples, construction workers, domestic workers, sex workers, street hawkers, drivers, and own-account workers would be very unlikely to be able to produce any kind of labor contract.

The final item that is formally required in most places is a lease or deed to an apartment within the city. China certainly does not have slums on the scale of many countries elsewhere in the global South, and city governments have not shied away from mass evictions and demolitions (Zhang 2005). Nonetheless, informal housing has persisted in many peri-urban spaces. And it is precisely those migrants with the fewest social or economic resources who are most likely to end up in such informal housing (Logan et al. 2009). Securing a legal lease is thus not a straightforward proposition.

More recently, a number of cities have been experimenting with point-based systems for public school admissions. This approach is not yet widespread, but they are in broad terms similar to the point-based *hukou* schemes. As with the *hukou* schemes, applicants accrue points based on their years of legal residence, property ownership, payments to local insurance system, and receiving official state awards (e.g. being a 'model worker'). Such plans have emerged in Pearl River Delta cities such as Guangzhou, Shenzhen, and Dongguan, but also in Yangzi River Delta cities including Suzhou and Kunshan. Such systems allow public schools to attach numerical scores to each student, thereby giving them a quantitative basis for ranking and admitting students based on the number of openings.

Aside from these formal procedures, there are a number of informal factors that impact migrant children's ability to get into public schools. The first is the practical necessity to bribe school administrators. Since 2010, public schools have been banned from charging educational fees (*jiedufei*) to non-locals. But this formally discriminatory practice has by all accounts persisted in less overt manners. Parents I interviewed in Beijing reported having to pay at least 20,000 Yuan (≈US$3000) to get into public schools. This is a sum equivalent to one year's salary for many migrants.[18] And 20,000 is merely entry-level: the better the school, the higher the cost, with some schools running as high as 60–100,000 Yuan for entrance. In many cases personal connections with education department officials or school administrators prove decisive in securing admission. Given that working-class migrants do not travel in the same circles as school administrators, few have the social capital necessary to gain an audience.

In sum, we have two distinct moments in the process of sorting migrants. First, there is the question of whether migrants will be integrated as full citizens (or 'core' members, in the language of JIT). Those places with the most generous social services are also the places that have the highest bar of entry. The second moment consists of contingent admission of those migrating out of plan (or the 'flexible' members), where certain children can gain access to public schools while others are relegated to the market. These administrative processes can be considered an inverted means test in that accessing publicly provided goods is facilitated by an accumulation, rather than a deficit, of means. This is one of the key measures urban governments have to incorporate

---

18   Minimum wage in Beijing for 2016 is 1720 yuan/month, which equals 20,640 per year.

some migrants in the sphere of social reproduction while excluding others. Whether those excluded will return to the countryside is another matter – they are not categorically *compelled* to leave. But the state has developed a set of market-based metrics to ensure that life in the city will be incredibly difficult for those included only as labor power.

8   Conclusion

This chapter has been centrally concerned with assessing the state's attempts to manage the flow of people in the process of large-scale urbanization. Chinese cities have required huge volumes of labor power and hundreds of millions of people have been incorporated in the labor market. The urban growth dilemma refers to competing imperatives to pull people in as labor power but expel them as social beings. The urban state has responded to these contradictory impulses by employing JIT principles in managing the flow of people, with the intention of reducing economic costs and political risks associated with warehousing human waste. But the technocratic aspirations of such an approach can never be realized: while JIT is oriented to a temporality in which the commodity labor power is to be delivered according to fluctuations in the market, human sociality unfolds in a radically different spatio-temporal nexus. The social and political friction resulting from this disjuncture has resulted in cities taking ad hoc approaches to managing surplus population, and extending the public good of education on a contingent basis. Inverted means testing for inclusion in the sphere of social reproduction enhances educational and other forms of inequality, and will almost certainly lead to a rigidification of the class structure.

The question remains as to why Chinese cities are pursuing JIT urbanization. I do not claim that there has been a conscious attempt on the part of state actors to emulate TPS. There are similar pressures coming to bear on the managers of capitalist firms and capitalist cities to reduce costs and foreclose political contestation, and it is possible to imagine that broadly similar techniques would be applicable in both settings. But if these pressures are more or less general in nature, the capacity to manage the flow of people is remarkably uneven in different national settings. Certain historical anomalies have endowed Chinese urban managers with much greater capacity to regulate human movement than is the case in other countries. Most importantly, the state-socialist *hukou* combined with a highly rationalized bureaucracy oriented primarily, if not exclusively, towards economic growth are highly effective tools in pursing JIT urbanization. But these tools are constantly being refined: the state has also increasingly moved towards regulating inclusion in urban space on the basis of class rather than status.

This dystopian vision of social organization is hardly frictionless, and indeed there have been signs of growing resistance. Social exclusion in the places where migrants can find work has resulted in a crisis of reproduction and dissolution of the family. Nearly 40% of rural children do not live with their parents,[19] and are raised either by grandparents or warehoused in state-run boarding schools. Lack of access to adequate health care is resulting in widening health inequalities, and millions of migrants are nearing retirement age with no pension or savings. Suffering by no means translates mechanically into resistance. And yet, recent sporadic protests in Beijing, Shenzhen, and elsewhere by parents excluded from public education suggest a willingness to act in demanding equality in the sphere of reproduction. Every attempt by migrants to establish durable community and to ensure social reproduction throws sand into the gears of JIT urbanization. Try as it might to enforce a smooth and efficient biopolitics, the state can never fully vanquish social resistance.

Is JIT urbanization in China indicative of a broader historical trend in managing the movement of labor? While these comments must remain speculative, there is growing evidence that JIT-like strategies are emerging in other post-Fordist cities. With the massive expansion of guest worker programs globally (Surak 2013), it is clear that political, social, and even civil rights have been peeled away from the right to work in a variety of national settings. Led by rapidly growing cities in the South (particularly city-states such as Singapore and Hong Kong along with the Gulf states), these workers now constitute absolute majorities of the workforce in certain sectors. Other places in Asia such as South Korea, Taiwan, and Japan have implemented sizable guest worker or 'training' programs, although these account for a smaller relative share of the workforce. But in all cases, inclusion in production is paired with on-going exclusion in the spheres of politics and reproduction. As in China, the state reserves the right to expel such workers should they be deemed extraneous. China is somewhat unusual in that the expendable portion of the workforce is recruited domestically and is generally part of the dominant race. But in all cases the common and decisive element is that cities have enhanced their technocratic capacity to reduce waste by admitting and expelling workers in response to labor market dynamics. In contrast to the 20th century Fordist city, a growing share of the workforce now has no value as either consumer or citizen.

19   "Woguo nongcun liushou ertong, chengxiang liudong ertong zhuangkuang yanjiu baogao," people.com.cn, last modified 10th May 2013, http://acwf.people.com.cn/n/2013/0510/ c99013-21437965.html.

References

Alexander, P and A Chan (2004) "Does China Have an Apartheid Pass System?". *Journal of ethnic and migration studies* 30(4): 609–629.

Anagnost, A (1997) *National Past-Times: Narrative, Representation, and Power in Modern China*. Durham, NC: Duke University Press.

Barchiesi, F (2011) *Precarious Liberation: Workers, the State, and Contested Social Citizenship in Postapartheid South Africa*. Albany, NY: Suny Press.

Bauman, Z (2004) *Wasted Lives: Modernity and Its Outcasts*. Cambridge, UK: Polity.

Bradshaw, YW (1987) "Urbanization and Underdevelopment: A Global Study of Modernization, Urban Bias, and Economic Dependency." *American Sociological Review* 52(2): 224–239.

Chan, KW (2009) "The Chinese Hukou System at 50." *Eurasian Geography and Economics* 50(2): 197–221.

Denning, M (2010) "Wageless Life." *New left review* 66: 79–97.

Dutton, M (1988) "Policing the Chinese Household: A Comparison of Modern and Ancient Forms." *Economy and Society* 17(2): 195–224.

Fischer, AM (2008) "'Population Invasion" Versus Urban Exclusion in the Tibetan Areas of Western China.' *Population and Development Review* 34(4): 631–662.

Foucault, M (2003) "'Society Must Be Defended": Lectures at the Collège De France, 1975–76'. edited by Mauro Bertani, Alessandro Fontana and David Macey. New York, NY: Picador.

Ge, X (2009) "'Liang Wei Zhu" Zhengce Zhong De Zhengfu Touru Zeren Tanxi.' *Research in Educational Development* 2: 1–7.

Greenhalgh, S and EA Winckler (2005) *Governing China's Population: From Leninist to Neoliberal Biopolitics*. Stanford, CA: Stanford University Press.

Hart, K (1973) "Informal Income Opportunities and Urban Employment in Ghana." *The journal of modern African studies* 11(1): 61–89.

Huang, PCC (2009) "China's Neglected Informal Economy: Reality and Theory." *Modern China* 35(4): 405–438.

Hung, HF (2015) *The China Boom: Why China Will Not Rule the World*. New York, NY: Columbia University Press.

Joniak-Lüthi, A (2013) "Han Migration to Xinjiang Uyghur Autonomous Region: Between State Schemes and Migrants' Strategies." *Zeitschrift für Ethnologie* 138(2): 155–174.

Li, TM. (2010) "To Make Live or Let Die? Rural Dispossession and the Protection of Surplus Populations." *Antipode* 41(s1) 66–93.

Lipset, SM. (1959) "Some Social Requisites of Democracy: Economic Development and Political Legitimacy." *American political science review* 53(1) 69–105.

Logan, JR, Y Fang and Z Zhang (2009). "Access to Housing in Urban China." *International Journal of Urban and Regional Research* 33(4): 914–935.

Marshall, TH (1950) *Citizenship and Social Class: And Other Essays*. Cambridge, UK: Cambridge University Press.

Mbembe, A (2003) "Necropolitics." *Public Culture* 15(1): 11–40.

McIntyre, M and HJ Nast (2011) 'Bio (Necro) Polis: Marx, Surplus Populations, and the Spatial Dialectics of Reproduction and "Race"'. *Antipode* 43(5): 1465–1488.

Mezzadra, S and B Neilson (2013) *Border as Method, or, the Multiplication of Labor*. Durham, NC: Duke University Press.

Molotch, H (1976) "The City as a Growth Machine: Toward a Political Economy of Place." *American journal of sociology* 82(2): 309–332.

Monden, Y (2011) *Toyota Production System: An Integrated Approach to Just-in Time*. New York, NY: CRC Press.

Ohno, T (1988) *Toyota Production System: Beyond Large-Scale Production*. Portland, OR: Productivity Press.

Parsons, T (1964) "Evolutionary Universals in Society." *American Sociological Review* 29 (3): 339–357.

Sassen, S (2014) *Expulsions: Brutality and Complexity in the Global Economy*. Cambridge, MA: Harvard University Press.

Surak, K (2013) "Guestworker Regimes: A Taxonomy." *The New Left Review* 84: 84–102.

Wallace, J (2014) *Cities and Stability: Urbanization, Redistribution, and Regime Survival in China*. New York, NY: Oxford University Press.

Wang, FL (2005) *Organizing through Division and Exclusion: China's Hukou System*. Stanford, CA: Stanford University Press.

Wolpe, H (1972) "Capitalism and Cheap Labour-Power in South Africa: From Segregation to Apartheid 1." *Economy and society* 1(4): 425–456.

Womack, JP and DT Jones (2010) *Lean Thinking: Banish Waste and Create Wealth in Your Corporation*. New York, NY: Simon and Schuster.

Yates, M (2011) "The Human-as-Waste, the Labor Theory of Value and Disposability in Contemporary Capitalism." *Antipode* 43, no. 5 (2011): 1679–1695.

Zhang, L (2005) "Migrant Enclaves and Impacts of Redevelopment Policy in Chinese Cities". In *Restructuring the Chinese City: Changing Society, Economy and Space*, edited by Laurence JC Ma and Wu Fulong, 218–233. London: Routledge.

Zhang, L (2001) *Strangers in the City: Reconfigurations of Space, Power, and Social Networks within China's Floating Population*. Stanford, CA: Stanford University Press.

CHAPTER 5

Zoning Urbanization: The Hsinchu Technopolis as an Enclave of Modernity in Taiwan

Jinn-yuh Hsu

1   Introduction

The Hsinchu Region, the Hsinchu Science-based Industrial Park (HSIP) and its neighboring highway extending all the way to Taipei, is often praised as one of the most successful technopoles in the world. Also referred to as "a Silicon Valley of the East" (Hall & Castells, 1994; Mathews, 1997), the HSIP can be conceived of as a paradigmatic example of how a late developer has met the global industrialization trend (Hsu, 1997). Currently, the area is home to Taiwan's most rapidly growing microelectronics industries, such as those of Integrated Circuits (IC) and Personal Computers (PC). Before the establishment of the HSIP, however, Hsinchu County contained only a rudimentary amount of industry, one based largely around lighting manufacture and natural gas. In the sixteen years between 1964 and 1980 the amount of light bulb factories in Hsinchu grew from only 3 to over 500. In 1980, the Hsinchu area manufactured over 80% of total light bulb exports from Taiwan, making Taiwan the number one light bulb exporting country in the world. Seeking to promote Hsinchu's industrialization further, the Taiwanese government established the HSIP on the edge of Hsinchu City, starting a brand-new chapter in local industrial history. The resulting economic success of the project led to social and economic disparity between the HSIP and its neighboring areas. In order to address this contradiction, local governments subsequently created two new technopolis projects in sequence. Accordingly, the special economic zones such as the HSIP turned from an industrial enclave to an urban megaproject, or zone-city.

Such an urbanization process has become phenomenal in East Asia, where states have used zoning technology to maintain exportist regimes of accumulation (Jessop and Sum 2006). The Tsukuba Science City in Japan and Taedok science Town in Korea, in addition to the HSIP, are well-noted early examples (Castells and Hall 1994), and New Songdo City in Korea and Taoyuan Aerotropolis Project in Taiwan are recent ones. These technopoles have not only been designed for the growth of high-technology industries, they have also become one of the key types of new urban spaces for attracting and shaping the fantasies of and aspirations for modernity in new urbanities (Bach 2011). Modernity is projected into these spaces through fantasies of technological superiority and social ordering that have been mobilized by urban designers. Such social-technical imaginaries or dreamscapes of modernity (Jasanoff 2015) have been supported not only by the advancement of technology, but more than often are also inspired by the will to improvement by the local people and governments in the zone-city areas.

But, the imaginaries of zone-cities are not without their contradictions. A number of cases have showed that speculative forms of urbanization have shaped technopolis-based megaprojects into elaborate real estate hoaxes; the development of zone-cities thus faces the suspicion of land grabbing despite its apparent guise of high modernity. Worst of all, financial liberalization, the backbone of speculative urbanization for East Asian urban redevelopment, has aggravated the issue of land redistribution, arousing social struggles that haunt the development of the zone-cities and their modernist planning and lifestyle (Easterling 2014, Shin and Kim 2015). It seems that the politics of space production in the zone-city revolves around the dialectics of the desire for regional improvement and the greed of land speculation; their symbiosis of and confrontation against each other poses an ethical and practical challenge to critical approaches in urban studies.

Concerned by the politics of space in the zone-city, this chapter will focus on answering the following three questions. First, given the social context of late industrialization, to what extent can the HSIP materialize the imagination of a Silicon Valley in Taiwan? Second, what is the impact of the HSIP's success on the neighboring areas in different stages? Finally, how do local governments and people respond to the impact of the HSIP? While answering these questions, it is important to realize that the search for modernity and the will to improve almost always constitute a desire for development for "underdeveloped" people. The pursuit of this desire often brings forth divergent trajectories of economic and spatial development that are often contradictory, evoke differing imaginations of modernity, and are thus important to attend to.

The rest of the chapter is organized as follows. The next, second, section examines the key concepts and the theoretical framework. The third section offers an empirical investigation of the imagination of Silicon Valley in Hsinchu. Section four will then explore the contradictions caused by the development of the HSIP and the consequent projects proposed to ameliorate them. Finally, the fifth section summarizes the findings, offers concluding remarks on the politics of imagination surrounding the HSIP, and wraps up the chapter.

2   Modernity, Development and the Desiring Subject

For a considerable period of time, dominant geopolitical thought has perceived development as constituting a unilinear sequence of societal change, from the traditional to the modern and from the barbarian to the civilized. More importantly, it has converted time into space. In terms of ideas, it provided a natural link between the European past and the global present outside of the modern world. Moreover, this link was defined in terms of what the latter lacks and the former has to offer to make up for this deficiency (Agnew, 1998; Escobar, 1995; Ferguson, 2006). As such, in the mainstream geopolitical worldview, the world is binary divided into the "West" and the "Rest". All the rest can or should do is follow in the past footsteps of the West. Hence, the Western past is the Rest's present and mainstream thought tends to totalize the comparison between the two parts. By doing so, the development of different people in different localities is not judged by their own condition, but instead categorized along the stages of the Western developmental trajectory. As such, since human rationality is associated with the modern, or modernity, the Western context has become the universal history for the people in the Rest to pursue or imitate (Amsden, 2001; Mitchell, 2000).

But, as Harvey (1996) and Mitchell (2000) pointed out, modernity, or modern civilization, was not a product of the West, but a result of its interaction with the non-West (the Rest) during western colonization. After the colonial encounter, modernity was created and internalized in Western societies, and then imposed upon the Rest as Western technological, ideational, and civilizational superiority. In a sense, the de-colonization of later times became tantamount to the acquisition of modernity, or Western civilization (Kothari, 2005; Wagner, 2012). Consequently, particularly after the colonization era, aspirations of modernity became to constitute one of the key drivers of societal change within the countries of the Rest, explaining the emergence of the postcolonial national will to catch up. The rise of the "Rest", as Amsden (2001) calls it, became one of the phenomenal changes in the last half of the twentieth century. It was so special because it was the first time in history in which so-called "backward" countries industrialized without proprietary innovations. To establish its modern industries, the "rest" was initially totally dependent on the commercialized activities of the West, making it a process of "pure learning". Hence, the desire for development in the latecomers (the "Rest") was shaped through imitating or learning from advanced Western countries' technology, knowledge, values and institutions.

Consequently, in many ways latecomer countries engaged in policies and institutional transfers to "modernize" and comply with "international" standards

(Peck & Theodore, 2015). Few of the imported policies and technologies could be implemented turnkey, though. Instead, they often had to be adjusted to fit local contexts. At best, they were hybridized while, on the one hand, highlighting the superiority of the "original" devices and ideas, and, on the other, demonstrating that they possessed flexible enough capabilities to solve local issues. Sometimes, though, transferred/imported things became white elephants and led to waste and even disaster for the localities.

One of the most dazzling things imitated from the West is the so-called special zone, which refers to a space of experimentation within the Rest (Easterling, 2014; Neveling, 2015). The zone could either constitute a cultural quarter, a new town with a distinct social life, a new business district, or even an urban megaproject. Usually, government agencies or public-private partnerships (i.e. land developers and architects) initiated the zones and in the design of the so-called "West in the Rest" (Mitchell 2000) directly copied the geographical configurations of modernity from the West. But, more intriguingly, while special zones presumed to exhibit the world as it was in advanced countries, they often represented an imagined social and urban "modern" order that did not necessarily reflect Western reality. As such, the special zones created a sort of dream utopia of a rationally ordered society where nature and society were assumed to fit into precise, manageable categories that could be productively manipulated to enhance the civilization level (Bach, 2011; Easterling, 2014).

Nevertheless, despite their deficiencies, the imported devices –machinery, lifestyle, or even space– were usually regarded as delivering upon the promise of modernity and the utopian imagination in the lands of the Rest. In fact, they created their own effects on reality. On the one hand, the representation of modernity became a precious commodity that distinguished itself from those traditional ones. On the other, they created new desires to follow for people discontent with the poor quality of local infrastructure and technology. As argued by Mitchell (2000, p. 18), though, a representation can never become an original because by nature it always makes a double claim: first, it denies its own essence and defines itself by what it is not. In other words, its lacking and immateriality separate it from the real thing. Second, in asserting its own lack, a representation claims that the world it replicates, enacts, or endows with meaning and structure must be, by contrast, original or real. In effect, the zone-city becomes a tidy heterotopia, an actually existing utopia or an alternative "other space" clearly separated from neighboring chaotic cities. Murray (2017) underscores this by arguing that spatial segregation and social exclusion usually characterize zone-cities located next to ordinary cities in the Global South.

3   The HSIP: The Hybridization of Nationalism and Transnationalism

One of the key motivational factors behind the development of high-technology industries and the HSIP was the search for modernization and the will to catch up to the West. The techno-bureaucrats only managed to succeed with the political support of the new leader, Chiang Ching-Kuo, which gave the development of high-technology, as well as the HSIP, a political flavor. It was not just an economic affair, though. For Chiang, the construction of the semiconductor industry, as well as other key component industries such as the petrochemical and the steel industries, was part of a "nation-building" project critical to the survival of the economic system and the revival of the nation to combat the People's Republic of China (PRC) (Xu 1995). The idea was that the modernist values represented by the establishment of the high-tech industries, which were assumed to be only embraced by the advanced industrial countries at that time, could validate the superiority of the KMT regime over the Chinese Communist Party (CCP), which had just led mainland China through the destructive Cultural Revolution. Thus, as Yang and Chen (1996) demonstrate, the HSIP represented the search for technological leadership in a crisis time for "Free China". In this sense, the emphasis on a modernist and progressive image as distinguished from the "backward" and "traditional" became the dominant design and planning principle of the HSIP.

The idea of the HSIP appeared after the visit by key bureaucrats such as Minister Li Kuo-ting and Mr. Xu Xian-xiu, the Director of the national Science Council in the mid-1970s, to the US. During their visit they identified the Stanford Science Park in North California as the model Taiwan should follow. Minister Li even translated a special issue of Fortune Magazine (1974) about the development of Santa Clara Valley (later Silicon Valley) in order to induce popular acceptance of a special zone of science-based industries. Doubtlessly, the establishment of the HSIP aimed to imitate the development of the Silicon Valley (SV). However, it was clear from the start that Taiwan was an industrial latecomer, making it difficult to develop into the same kind of innovative powerhouse as SV. Therefore, the original plan mixed the successful experiences of the Kaohsiung Export Processing Zone and the industrial cluster in SV (Li 1986).

In its early stage before the 1990s, the HSIP mainly hosted national firms that had spun off from the public lab. However, as demonstrated by Saxenian and Hsu (2001), growing numbers of US-educated Taiwanese engineers returned to Taiwan in the 1990s. They were lured primarily by the promise of economic opportunities as well as the desire to return to families and contribute to their home country. The numbers only kept rising. Whereas in the early

1980s approximately 200 engineers and scientists returned to Taiwan annually, a decade later, that number had risen to 1,000. According to the National Youth Commission, by 1998 more than 30% of the engineers who had studied in the US returned to Taiwan, compared with only 10% in the 1970s. The flow of graduates back to Taiwan in the 1970s and 1980s went hand in hand with an aggressive transferring policy of state-of-the-art technology from the US to Taiwan by government agencies. As such, the development of the HSIP created a venture capital industry in Taiwan long before it became fashionable elsewhere in the world, causing the HSIP to host many startups by returnees.

Consequently, in 1997 almost half of the companies in the Science Park (97 companies) were started by US-educated engineers, many of whom had considerable managerial or entrepreneurial experience in Silicon Valley (HSIP, 1998). Taiwan's global links with the Californian technology hub unfolded mainly in three ways: 1) Taiwanese companies recruited overseas engineers; 2) they set up listening posts in Silicon Valley to tap into the brain power there, or 3) successful overseas engineers returned to Taiwan to start up their own businesses (Hsu & Saxenian, 2000).

The Hsinchu region case thus demonstrates the interplay between the top-down developmental state and the bottom-up technical community in the governing of global production networks. It also incarnated the hybridization of the nationalist will with transnationalist technology. The HSIP was directly supervised by the central government, was located in an enclosed area with gated control, and special regulations were put in place for environmental protection, site planning and labor affairs. The government purposely separated the HSIP from the neighboring communities, and produced an enclave to attract capital, people, and firms to the high technology industry. The HSIP became an icon for the "Free China" that was closely related to Western values and the Silicon Valley lifestyle. All this clearly distinguished it from communist China with its perceived "political cruelty" and "economic backwardness" (HSIP 1998). In other words, the establishment of the HSIP was simultaneously supported *by* and mobilizing *of* a national identity (cf. Crane, 1994).

4   The Geographical Configuration of Hsinchu's Silicon Valley

The modernist image created by the designers of the HSIP was not only meant to differ the Republic of China (ROC) from its political rival Communist China, but also aimed to represent a divergent and better environment compared to the neighboring communities, which were traditional Hakka villages. As a special zone, the HSIP was an isolated area with gated control. A special permit was required for visitors to enter. Moreover, the HSIP was run by a special administrative bureau that took care of the change of land use and environmental regulations. This led to a situation in which the HSIP with its neat and tidy land layout represented the modern, and the neighboring towns with their chaotic and crowded streetscapes the traditional. The modernity of the HSIP was also represented by the architectural forms of the buildings of its high-technology firms, which were usually shelled with glass curtain walls. It might therefore not come as a surprise that Mr. Tsai Jen-Chien, the former Major of the Hsinchu City, complained that "the inside of the HSIP was like the USA, and the outside world like the Philippines." (Lin, 2001) As a space for modernist fantasies in the developing world, the HSIP came to represent the West within the Rest (Easterling, 2014).

Despite being acclaimed as a "Silicon Valley of the East", the physical characteristics of the HSIP stood in stark contrast with its counterpart in the Bay Area. Whereas SV had emerged spontaneously through a bottom-up social network, the HSIP was the result of top-down state dictate. The state developed the master plan, allocated the land, and reviewed all the firms by administrative procedure. As a result, the location of firms was very concentrated in the HSIP, while those in SV were relatively dispersed.

Moreover, while SV firms focused on design innovation, the heavyweights of HSIP specialized in manufacturing. The largest high-technology firm in the HSIP is the foundry provider Taiwan Semiconductor Manufacturing Corporation (TSMC), which was founded as an Electronics Research & Service Organization (ERSO) spinoff in 1986. TSMC was set up to concentrate on manufacturing for other companies, not compete with them in the chips market. Currently, TSMC has become the most successful semiconductor company in Taiwan, and the top leader in the foundry business in the world.

In fact, for TSMC the exclusive focus on manufacturing is its innovative business model. According to TSMCs 2014 yearly report, 17,124 out of 43,591, or 40% of its employees are shop-floor operators. At the same time, 18,552 engineers, or 42.5%, are hired for wafer fabrication jobs. In this sense, jobs within TSMC are polarized, and almost equally distributed on the top and bottom tiers respectively. Indeed, these numbers reflect actual job distribution within the HSIP as a whole. Rather than the powerhouse of innovation with knowledge and design intensive activities that SV is, the HSIP employs thousands of low-skilled workers whose wages are just slightly higher than those of their counterparts in the traditional sectors. Even so, to lower costs some electronics firms in the HSIP would like to hire guest workers from Southeast Asia. This is an indication that the contrasts between rich and poor are sharp in the HSIP. While the high-ranking engineers and managers drive posh cars to the office, the low-skilled workers ride on motorcycles or commuting buses to their plants. Therefore, whereas one typically associates a job in the HSIP with an engineer wearing cleanroom overalls in a state-of-are lab, the inconvenient truth is that much of the work within HSIP is done by groups of low-skilled, mainly female workers.

Among the high-ranking engineers and managers, some of them, particularly returnees from the US, live with their families in the residential area of the HSIP, which is known as 'Bamboo Village' and includes 645 households housing 960 individuals. As Chang (2003) observes, HSIP's Bamboo Village is a more self-sustaining community than most typical American suburbs. Surrounding the village are a small supermarket, a post office, a bank, a petrol station, a clinic, a garage, a bilingual school, parks and open spaces, as well as a recreational area with a swimming pool and tennis courts. Interestingly, a lake with a Chinese bridge and garden design, called the Lake of the Peaceful Heart (*jing-xin-hu*), is located in the center of the residential area. Low-density housing is spread around the lake to accommodate the returnees and their families. Similar to everyday life in Taiwan, but unlike suburban life in SV, HSIP residents can reach all their conveniences within a comfortable walking distance. Moreover, a bilingual high school is established to deliver quality education to the children of homecoming scholars and foreign employees. Such an international school is critical for attracting returnees, as children's education is one of their key concerns when debating to move back or not.

In fact, the HSIP administrative bureau has consciously created the American lifestyle and landscape as one of its marketing strategies. In the introductory remark of the HSIP, the chief of the HSIP administration writes, "[d]orms adorned with lush greenery as in the American suburbs provide a cozy haven for tenant employees to call home" (HSIP 1988:2). The Silicon Valley – Hsinchu connection is constructed through a dense social network and cultural (image) reproduction with technology flow. Consequently, Hsinchu's Silicon Valley becomes more of a hybrid, or in-between, space, as imagined SV space comes to life in the real place Hsinchu. Indeed, new constructions in the Hsinchu technopolis usually claim themselves to be "red-brick and white-wall California style" in order to attract engineers, as shown in Figure 5.1. Thus, the HSIP represents Silicon Valley by design, making its constructed modernity a transnational one.

But, as Mitchell (2000: xiv) argues, "no representation can ever match its original, especially when the original exists only as something promised by a multiplicity of other imitations and repetitions". The modernity presented by the perceived technological superiority and landscape rationality of Silicon Valley is used to highlight the contrast with the "tradition" and "backwardness"

FIGURE 5.1   The red-brick and white-wall California style construction in Hsinchu technopolis
SOURCE: CREATED BY AUTHOR

of the Hsinchu area before its transformation into a modern science park. SV as such becomes a model of "what the modern should be" for the Hsinchu technopolis. Consequently, in terms of outside appearances, the neat and tidy streetscape, the glass-curtain-walled buildings, the neighboring universities and research institute, and even the California-style housing in the limited special zone are copied directly from SV. In terms of culture, the transnational bottom-up networks between the SV and Hsinchu are mobilized to bring forth the SV lifestyle. SV itself, however, has never had such a clear-cut landscape and homogeneous social composition (Saxenian and Hsu 2001). This makes the HSIP not just a recreation of the Bay Area only, but also an interaction between a Taiwanese projection of what should constitute SV style modernity and SV in Taiwan.

5   Contradictions and Harmonization Projects: The HSC project of the 1990s and the UJP project of the 2000s

The implementation of Taiwan's SV project has not been without contradictions. The first and foremost tension appeared in the interaction with the neighboring Hakka communities, for example the *Chin-Shan-Mien* Village, as shown in Figure 5.2. The village is over a hundred years old and is connected through strong social and ethnic networks, established long before the arrival of the HSIP. Since it is located close to the HSIP area, a special zone with its

FIGURE 5.2   The neighboring Hakka communities of the Hsinchu Science-based Industrial
Park
SOURCE: PHOTO BY AUTHOR

own system of rules, to the village the HSIP soon turned into a monster affecting the daily life of the mostly peasant residents.

In addition to the rural-urban contradiction, the village faces a housing
shortage and traffic congestions appeared in the village because of the HSIP.
A more controversial issue arose due to the planned expansion of the HSIP, a
plan that would expropriate part of the village's land and result in serious water and environmental impacts. As a consequence, even without an officially
declared drought and water shortage, paddy farms growing rice might face insufficient water resources as a result of the water supply being prioritized for
the HSIP. Therefore, peasants, local historians, and Hakka groups organized
a number of protests against the unfair expropriation of the water resources
(Tsai 2015).

One of the key appeals of the groups is to preserve the integrity of the village's traditional culture and history. Mr. Wu, one of the local community
leaders, complains that "[t]he HSIP has forced some people to move out and
demolished some old houses. Moreover, some of the HSIP workers moved into
the village. The problem is that they have nothing to do with the local people

and culture besides the fact that they accommodate here. This will hurt the traditions of local culture" (Wu 2007:1). Wu's complaint reflects tensions between the local community and the HSIP outsiders that are ongoing and have yet to be resolved.

But, as more and more HSIP workers, not only from other counties in Taiwan but also those from overseas, move into the region and become the dominant group there, it becomes a thorny issue to tell apart the local from the transnational, the inside from the outside, and the modern from the traditional. While the HSIP tries hard to paint itself as a product of modernity, it also takes the local villages as representing "contra-modernity" or the "traditional". Such a categorization has led to a series of protests from the local villagers, and has produced a movement to protect "local tradition". Therefore, the hybridization of the local and transnational in the HSIP is still a work in progress.

To "harmonize" the tensions between the HSIP and its neighboring villages, the central government proposed the "Hsinchu Science City" (HSC) plan in 1993 to "integrate the success of the HSIP and the development of its neighboring counties". The plan was expected to enhance the spread effect of the HSIP by benefiting both the local urban and rural economies. The plan anticipated the HSIP to propel the entire Hsinchu region forward, not just in terms of economic gains, but also in terms of cultural transformation by bringing forth more "high-quality" talent with cultural capital. In addition, the HSC plan targeted the development of producer service sectors, such as financial, accounting and law services. Amongst others it proposed to expand the residential area to house more immigrating engineers. Consequently, land speculation in the Hsinchu region boomed, causing real estate prices in the neighboring counties, especially Chubei (North Hsinchu) and Chudong (East Hsinchu), to go through the roof.

The intention of the plan was to incorporate the neighboring areas into the special zone and to solve the problem of land shortage caused by the booming industries. Despite naming it "science city", the urban life in the proposed plan has little, if anything, to do with the use of digital technology to improve the quality of life, but instead "modernized" through the introduction of department stores, shopping malls, luxurious residential buildings and the revitalization of the river waterfront (Huang 2013). The HSC plan, together with the expansion of the HSIP, would further spur the immigration of high-skilled laborers and engineers to the neighboring areas. For example, Chubei grew from a town with a population of 90,000 in 1994 to a city of 160,000 in 2013. Hence, the HSIP and its neighboring counties became the model for other local governments in Taiwan, as similar plans might increase the land prices and employment opportunities. The proposal of the HSC plan to reinforce the expansion of the HSIP to other areas was soon suspended, however, when the late 1980s witnessed the processes of democratization and liberalization in Taiwan.

In fact, the HSC project was a planning blueprint without any legal implementation plan that would have involved various levels of government and the HSIP Administrative Bureau. The implementation of the project would have needed the strong political will of the central government to coordinate the different governing bodies involved in the industrial and residential development. Without the strong support of the central government, the HSC plan was nothing but a blueprint of a daydream (Chen 2000). Still, although the central government was no longer keen to consolidate the development of the HSIP and neighboring Hsinchu City, it would engage in the dispersion of the success of high-technology development into other regions in Taiwan in the 1990s. Although at the time the government used the rhetoric of regional equalization resulting from pressure due to democratization, more important was that the dispersion was used to compensate for the losses incurred by not allowing capital investments in, at the time, cheap land in China. This also spurred the government to eagerly offer land subsidies and fiscal benefits to keep businesses in Taiwan[1]. Consequently, a new science park in Southern Taiwan, the Tainan Park, was planned and launched in 1995 (Hsu, 2011). The dispersion of the science park to the south of Taiwan reduced the imminence of finding a solution for the problems between the HSIP and its neighboring areas.

But, the spreading effects of the thriving HSIP still aroused concerns from the local governments and communities. On the one hand, the industries and the employees they attracted were hungry for land expansion of the HSIP to improve the crowdedness of firm agglomeration and housing quality within the HSIP area. On the other hand, the discrepancy between the developed industrial areas and the undeveloped rural ones within the Hsinchu region became an issue of social and spatial justice for the local residents. To respond to this situation, the Hsinchu County Government, after persuasion from National Chiaotung University (NCTU), initiated the Taiwan Knowledge-based Flagship Project or Unpolished Jade Project (UJP) in 1999 under the KMT regime. Its goal was to combine the expansion of industrial locations, high-quality

---

1 From the late 1990s on, Taiwanese investments in China have shifted from labor-intensive and small-scale to technology-intensive and large-scale after China's entry in the World Trade Organization (WTO). This raised concerns about the possibility of the hollowing out of Taiwan's high value-adding activities. It led the government to legally prohibit high-tech firms to invest in China, punishing, even jailing, those who broke the law (Hsu, 2005).

residential buildings and high-end university and industrial laboratories together under the slogan of "knowledge-based industries". The project would
have expropriated more than 446 hectares of farmland for commercial, industrial and residential uses.

In the beginning, the UJP was supported by the Democratic Progressive
Party (DPP), which had come to power after the Presidential election in 2000,
much to everyone's surprise. Newly inaugurated president Chen Shui-bian
even proclaimed the UJP as the flagship of "National Development and the
Knowledge-based Economy Plan", which would be fully supported financially
and administratively by the central government. However, as the DPP president decided to implement the "Silicon Island" Plan to establish a third science park in central Taiwan for electoral reasons (Hsu, 2011; D.Y.-R. Yang, Hsu,
& Ching, 2009) Huang 2013), the UJP gradually lost its attractiveness for the
new political regime. As a result, the UJP project was suspended indefinitely.

But, the suspension of the UJP caused fierce protests from the nearby residents, mainly small farmers who had been living in the villages for generations.
In order to voice their support for the UJP, they organized a pro-UJP group,
the Self-help Group for the UJP. In a recent public hearing, the leader of the
pro-UJP group claimed that "we are divided by the highway; on one side is the
booming HSIP with its modern buildings, while the other side, the side we live
on, is a place lacking proper infrastructure and full of old and broken houses.
We are simply treated as second-rate citizens!" Moreover, he complained that,
"the promises made in the past of infrastructure improvement and employment increase were broken. Each time the government raised our hopes, and
each time they let us down again. We only wanted the development of our
community!" (Luo 2015).

In fact, a series of plans for local development were proposed by governments at various levels. In addition to the two grand projects above, other
small ones were raised by the government to target the spillover effect of the
HSIP. One of the more attractive ones from a local perspective was the "Plan to
Expand the HSIP", which was proposed soon after the success of the HSIP. The
plan promised to appropriate funds to the development of the neighboring
lands and create high- quality residential life for the local people. Although
infrastructure in the shape of new roads, water systems and retrofitted houses
belonged to the basic elements of the plan, none of which were realized due
to insufficiency of the fund (Luo 2015). Thus, repeatedly dreams of prosperity
by the locals were created and then broken by the public agencies. Under-
standably, after recurring disappointments during the past two decades, some
of the local people gave up their dreams and adopted a lukewarm attitude

towards new projects. Still, others continued fighting for their interests, although they often merely achieved small improvements for the local areas. Their appeals though, clearly demonstrated a desire for development and modernity.

In contrast to groups supporting the UJP, a rival group was organized to protest against it. Rather than describing the current situation as "backward", this group argued that the preservation of local farmland and culture was valuable, and that the expropriation of land by the UJP would destroy local culture. To enhance their legitimacy against the supporting group, which encompassed the majority of the residents, the anti-UJP group tried to portray the pro-UJP group as a group of people manipulated by land developers outside of the Hsinchu region. Interestingly, to fight against the argument of collaboration with outside developers, the SGUJP in its place accused the anti-group of mainly mobilizing those social movement groups, such as the Front of Farmland Protection and Anti-expropriation Group, that came from outside of the region and enjoyed the preservation of farmland for these urban groups' recreation (Luo 2015). These kind of mutual accusations occurred repeatedly in social media, public hearings and official meetings at various governmental levels. The core issue always revolved around development: whose development and what kind of development?

It might have been true that some of the farmlands were already sold to land developers who were just waiting for permission to grab the windfall from land speculation (Tsai 2015). However, it was also true that the gaps, in terms of income, social status, infrastructure and landscape, between the people in the HSIP area and those in the farmlands the UJP was focused on were so obvious that the development of the living circumstances for those who felt deprived of opportunities in the early round should not be compromised upon (De Vries, 2007). At the same time, some of the anti-UJP groups, particularly environmental ones, propagated resistance against modernity. In their view, agrarian life was a possible alternative to the modern economic order, and in particular the developmental mentality revolving around the HSIP. The confrontation was thus divided along two conflicting views and dominated by binary oppositions: traditional/modern; backward/advanced; sustainable/unsustainable, etc. As a result, the debate is still unconcluded, although almost 17 years have passed since the UJP proposal in the early 2000s. It seems that the UJP rests a similar fate as the early HSC: indefinite suspension as no consensus is visible in the near future. But, the issue is that it is somehow considered fair to fail the desire for development repeatedly without providing any alternatives. Moreover, the anti-groups always accused the pro-groups of being driven or deceived, or victimized, by land speculation, but never took the emotions of this group serious. Similarly, the pro-groups conceived of the anti-groups as farmland conservationist without facing the infrastructure shortage and low-income problems. This lack of concern for each other's worries inhibited constructive dialogues and led to the stalling of the UJP plan. However, the possibility of the development of the neighboring areas of HSIP in fact did exist, only an alternative had to be found that could satisfy or transform people's desires for development, which are not necessarily about land speculation. The existence of the desire for development itself is politically and ethically legitimate and must therefore be taken serious. As such, more geographical and social imaginations for the development seem urgent for the development of the UJP in the near future.[2]

Indeed, in the past decades, urban and regional planners in East Asian contexts have often used the construction of zone-city or new-build gentrification to fulfill the demands of local populations, as shown both in the UJP case as well as in for example the redevelopment of Seoul in Korea (Shin and Kim 2015). These cases differ significantly from the New Town planning of the 1960s in Western Europe or North America, where the idea of urban planning was conducted for social reform (cf. Hall and Castells 1994). Taking the Western standard as the norm, critical scholars and social movements usually contest speculative coalitions to be the key drivers behind the urbanization processes in East Asian cities. However, treating the desire for improvement of the local farmer-cum-landowner as the same as the greed of non-local landed-business-groups does not necessarily reflect the principles of social and spatial justice. In light of the UJP case, a more challenging issue for critical scholars in East Asian cities would be to conduct a more nuanced and subtle social analysis of the differentiated processes of speculative urbanization. Perhaps through such a method an interstice between differing motivations for development could be discovered and a distinction made between the desire for improvement and the greed of speculation. Such knowledge might finally provide the fertile ground upon which to construct a truly united front of social and spatial reform for the new towns.

---

2 For example, it is possible to encourage the conversion of local farms into organic farms that provide their goods directly to the people living within the HSIP for a prime price. This way modern organic farmers can continue living in a traditional way while engaging in their farm work, and the HSIP engineers can enjoy healthy food. It ultimately hinges on the dialogue and negotiation between the local groups to find out the way to turn the will to improve into practice.

6   Concluding Remarks

The HSIP was established under the KMT government as a way to catch up to advanced countries through technology-led industries. In other words, it constituted a pursuit of modernity. Rather than dedicating resources to developing domestic technological capabilities, the developmental state relied on technology transfers from overseas Chinese technical communities to Taiwan to foster local spinoffs and exploit the latecomer advantage in the global market. Against the claim that techno-globalism would contradict with the development of techno-nationalism (see Ostry & Nelson, 1995 for details), the HSIP case demonstrates that transnational socio-technical networks can constitute an in-between space of technology transfers and as such are able to produce a synergy in the global-local interplay. It also supports the argument, in line with Ernest Gellner's account of nationalism remaining an international phenomenon (Gellner, 1983), that modern nationalism was vital to modernity, not as a way of escaping from a globalized cosmopolitan modern world, but as a means of participating in it, and indeed creating one's capacity to participate (Edgerton, 2007).

The HSIP as a project of modernity is not only represented in its technological excellence, but also in the gated community of the industrial park. To attract overseas experienced engineers and entrepreneurs back to Taiwan, the HSIP imitated Silicon Valley's production facilities and residential amenities, in a sense portraying western modernity as Europe had once portrayed the non-western "world-as-exhibition" (cf. Mitchell, 2000). By doing so, the HSIP became a social-technical imaginary that was supported by the development of advanced technology. As such, it constituted a publicly performed ideal vision of the future of employment and lifestyle, or a dreamscape of modernity (Jasanoff, 2015).

In fact, the Hsinchu technopolis exemplifies a zone-city in the Global South that functions as a heterotopia –i.e. an alternative "other space" that seeks to compensate for outside untidy realities and "urban problems", such as the lack of urban amenities, traffic congestion and secured communities, caused by the existing planning system, which could not meet the abrupt rise of the zone-city. Instead of engaging in the management of the old city center and its issues, the HSIP zone-city provides a fast solution to its problems by constituting a publicly performed ideal vision of the future of employment and lifestyle. In other words, starting from a blank plate the HSIP constructed a dreamscape of modernity in which new communities could form. By doing so, it mobilized an imaginary that inspired the local people to desire improvement in the shape of modernization. This earned the government political legitimacy to plan and realize the heterotopia project of modernity without having to deal with existing urban problems. Accordingly, waves of regional harmonization projects demonstrated that the format of zoning urbanization is becoming the *modus operandi* of building new cities and a way to deal with the imagination of disconnection with local problems of urbanization such as broken facilities and environmental chaos. As such, the development of Hsinchu technopolis has led to the formation of an enclave of modernity spatially separated and socially excluded from the ordinary city.

References

Agnew, J (1998) *Geopolitics: Re-visioning World Politics*. London and New York, NY: Routledge.

Amsden, AH (2001) *The Rise of "the Rest": Challenges to the West from Late-industrializing Economies*. Oxford: Oxford University Press.

Bach, J (2011) Modernity and the urban imagination in economic zones. *Theory, Culture & Society* 28(5): 98–122.

Castells, M and Hall, P (1994) *Technopoles of the World: The Making of the Twenty-first Century Industrial Complexes*. London: Routledge.

Chang, S (2003) Transcultural home identity across the Pacific: A case study of high-tech Taiwanese transnational communities in Hsinchu, Taiwan, and silicon Valley, USA", In: A Erdentug and F Colombijn (eds) *Urban Ethnic Encounters: The Spatial Consequences*. London and New York, NY: Routledge.

Chen, LJ (2000) [The myths of Hinchu Science city]. *NTNU Journal of Geography* 32: 125–145. (in Chinese).

Crane, GT (1994) 'Special things in special ways': National economic identity and China's special economic zones. *The Australian Journal of Chinese Affairs* 32: 71–92.

De Vries, P (2007) Don't compromise your desire for development! A Lacanian/Deleuzian rethinking of the anti-politics machine. *Third World Quarterly* 28(1): 25–43.

Easterling, K (2014) *Extrastatecraft: The Power of Infrastructure Space*. Brooklyn, NY: Verso Books.

Edgerton, DEH (2007) The contradictions of techno-nationalism and techno-globalism: A historical perspective. *New Global Studies* 1(1): Art. 1.

Escobar, A (1995) *Encountering Development: The Making and Unmaking of the Third World*. Princeton, NJ: Princeton University Press.

Ferguson, J (2006) *Global Shadows: Africa in the Neoliberal World Order*. Durham, NC: Duke University Press.

Fortune, Magazine (1974) "California's Great Breeding Ground for Industry", June 1974.

Gellner, E (1983) *Nations and Nationalism: New Perspectives on the Past.* Ithaca, NY: Cornell University Press.

Hall, P, M Castells (1994) *Technopoles of the World: The Making of 21th Century Industrial Complexes.* London and New York, NY: Routledge.

Harvey, P (1996) *Hybrids of modernity: Anthropology, the Nation State and the Universal Exhibition.* Hove: Psychology Press.

HSIP (1998) [*Year Report of Hsinchu Science-based Industrial Park*]. Hsinchu: HSIP. (In Chinese).

Hsu, JY (1997) A late-industrial district? Learning network in the Hsinchu science-based Industrial Park, Taiwan. Unpublished doctoral thesis, University of California, Berkeley.

Hsu, JY (2005) A site of transnationalism in the "Ungrounded Empire": Taipei as an interface city in the cross-border business networks. *Geoforum* 36(5): 654–666.

Hsu, JY (2011) State tansformation and regional development in Taiwan: From developmentalist strategy to populist subsidy. *International Journal of Urban and Regional Research* 35(3): 600–619.

Hsu, JY, A Saxenian (2000) The limits of guanxi capitalism: transnational collaboration between Taiwan and the USA. *Environment and Planning A* 32(11): 1991–2005.

Huang, WJ (2013) Spatial Planning and High-tech Development: A comparative study of Eindhoven city-region, the Netherlands and Hsinchu City-region, Taiwan. Unpublished doctoral thesis, Delft University of Technology.

Jasanoff, S (2015) Future Imperfect: Science, Technology, and the Imaginations of Modernity. In: S Jasanoff and SH Kim (eds.) *Dreamscapes of Modernity: Sociotechnical Imaginaries and the Fabrication of Power.* Chicago, IL: University of Chicago Press. 1–33.

Jessop, B. and N-L. Sum (2006) Beyond the regulation approach: putting capitalist economies in their place. Cheltenham: Edward Elgar.

Kothari, U (2005) *A Radical History of Development Studies: Individuals, Institutions and Ideologies.* London: Zed Books.

Li, GD (1986) [The establishment and Practice of the EPZs in Taiwan]. *Newsletter of EPZ* 21(12): 136–142. (In Chinese).

Lin, MY (2001) The connection between technology and humanality: Who changes the face of Hsinchu City? *Cheers* 9(1): 3–6.

Luo, XL (2015) [The Pu-Yu Project will make a big change in Hsinchu area], *United News*, May 24, 1015. (In Chinese).

Mathews, JA (1997) A Silicon Valley of the East: creating Taiwan's semiconductor industry. *California Management Review* 39(4): 26–54.

Mitchell, T (2000) The stage of modernity. In: T Mitchell (ed.) *Question of Modernity.* Minneapolis, MN: University of Minnesota Press 1–34.

Murray, M (2017) *The Urbanism of Exception: The Dynamics of Global City Building in Twenty-First Century.* New York: Cambridge University Press.

Neveling, J (2015) Free trade zones, export processing zones, special economic zones and global imperial formations 200 BCE to 2015 CE. In: I Ness and Z Cope (eds.) *The Palgrave Encyclopedia of Imperialism and Anti-Imperialism*. New York, NY: Palgrave Macmillan, 1007–1016.

Ostry, S and RR Nelson (1995) *Techno-Nationalism and Techno-Globalism: Conflict and Cooperation*. Washington, DC: Brookings Institution Press.

Park, SO and A Markusen (1995) Generalizing new industrial districts: A theoretical agenda and an application from a non-Western economy. *Environment and Planning A* 27(1): 81–104.

Peck, J and N Theodore (2015) *Fast Policy*. Minneapolis, MN: University of Minnesota Press.

Saxenian, A and JY Hsu (2001) The Silicon Valley–Hsinchu connection: Technical communities and industrial upgrading. *Industrial and Corporate Change* 10(4): 893–920.

Shin, HB and SH Kim (2015) The developmental state, speculative urbanisation and the politics of displacement in gentrifying Seoul. *Urban Studies* 53(3): 540–559.

Tsai, YL (2015) Behind the economic success of Taiwan's Hsinchu Science Industrial Park: Zoning technologies under neo-liberal governmentality, ongoing primitive accumulation, and locals' resistance. *Journal of Contemporary Asian Development* 14(1): 41–75.

Wagner, P (2012) Modernity. In: *Wiley Online Library*. Available at: http://dx.doi.org/10.1002/9780470670590.wbeog400.

Wu, QJ (2007) [Not for economy, but for culture]. *Holka Special Report*: 1–2. (In Chinese).

Xu, XX (1995) [Remembering the ins and outs of the establishment of the Hsinchu Science-based Industrial Park—This paper would like to commemorate Ching-kuo Chiang]. Regal Tao (notes), *Biographical Literature* 66(6): 23–28. (In Chinese).

Yang, DY, JY Hsu and CH Ching (2009) Revisiting the Silicon Island? The geographically varied 'strategic coupling' in the development of high-technology parks in Taiwan. *Regional Studies* 43(3): 369–384.

Yang, DY and HL Chen (1996) [*Companies Compete, the Fittest Survives*]. Taipei: China Times. (In Chinese).

CHAPTER 6

New Spaces of Exception: Special Economic Zones and Luxury Condominiums in Metro Manila

Jana M. Kleibert

1 Introduction

Many cities in the twenty-first century are best understood as assemblages of 'spaces of exception', discontinuous patchworks of island-like enclosures that form interlocking urban archipelagos (Murray, 2017). Taking an aerial view of the Philippines, we can see a natural archipelago comprised of several thousand islands. From this vantage point, a second archipelago structure, a manmade one, becomes visible that shows unevenly distributed islands of elite spaces that peak into the sky in the form of central business districts with skyscraper office towers and gated communities with high-rise luxury condominiums. The current real estate boom gripping the Philippines manifests itself through the relentless rise of new office towers, special economic zones and information technology parks, large-scale residential condominiums and townships, colossal malls, luxury hotels, and casinos, adjacent to tourist resorts and golf courses.

Considerable urban transformations, in particular in and around Metro Manila, the Philippines' capital region, are visible. Several integrated megaprojects are under construction, such as a new central business district, Bonifacio Global City, and a casino-tourism resort on reclaimed land, Entertainment City. This chapter engages with the question of how to explain the fragmented landscape that characterizes the Philippines economic development in general, and Metro Manila's neoliberal urbanization trajectory in particular.

Despite constituting a seemingly diverse set of spaces, the above-mentioned production, entertainment and residential spaces share some important commonalities. All of them can be conceptualized as 'islands', which are spatially distinct globally connected spaces for elites, which aim at distancing themselves or 'escaping' from the immediate national or urban surroundings through referencing globality, modernity, and exclusivity. While they perform different functions as economic enclave spaces for production (in the case of special economic zones), or consumption and leisure (in the case of residential enclaves and/or malls), they all act as key nodes for articulating the Philippines into transnational flows of capital. Finally, they all constitute 'spaces of exception', which function according to special rules and laws and have the power to exclude and/or regulate the entry of different population groups.

As globalized production and consumption enclaves are empirically converging and overlapping, it is useful to bring together two sets of literatures that have so far remained largely disconnected, namely the literature on special economic zones (SEZs) on the one hand, and that of gated communities on the other hand. SEZs have been used by many governments as a strategy to attract foreign direct investment and industrialize by creating favorable conditions for investments to articulate local economies into global production networks, often becoming sites of labor exploitation. Scholars have analyzed the rise of these production sites as neoliberal 'zones of exception' and 'graduated sovereignty' (Ong, 2006). Over time, SEZs have changed their form and function considerably, transforming from export-processing zones to knowledge and information technology parks, to adapt to the new demands of the post-industrial economy (Bach, 2011; Easterling, 2014; Neveling, 2015).

Concurrently, but in a largely disconnected debate, urban scholars have discussed the secession of primarily urban elites into gated communities, more recently developing the concept of 'enclave urbanism' (Douglass et al., 2012; Wissink et al., 2012). Providing a case-study of exclusive developments in the Philippines' mega-urban region of Metro Manila, this chapter engages both approaches to generate a meaningful understanding of the rise of different types of integrated mixed-use enclaves that combine an export-oriented strategy of enclave development with upper-class spaces of living, consumption and entertainment. The creation of new enclave spaces needs to be better theorized, and requires, above all, a closer engagement with historical and contemporary political, economic and social contexts, as well as key actors operating at multiple scales.

Enclave spaces are crucial sites of capital accumulation, based on the attraction and capture of transnational capital flows both for production and consumption purposes. Spatially uneven development on a macro-level can be explained through global, and potentially even planetary, processes that accompany the extensification and intensification of global capitalism, such as neoliberal urbanization and gentrification (see e.g. Lees et al., 2016). To these structural perspectives, this chapter adds a grounded perspective of a situated analysis of "actually existing spaces of neoliberalism" (Brenner and Theodore, 2002), based on the case of a post-colonial state in Southeast Asia.

The Philippines, dubbed an 'anti-development state' (Bello, 2009), constitutes a contrasting case to the developmental states in East Asia, which have been discussed as exemplary SEZ policy users. SEZs are often portrayed as a mobile technology that spreads around the world (Ong, 2006; Easterling, 2014), which this case aims to amend with a more contextualized analysis. I argue that the rise of enclave spaces in the Philippines is best understood as a historically rooted process of fragmented development, which has recently intensified into exclusive 'spaces of exception 2.0'. The argument advanced in the following is that contemporary enclave spaces in Metro Manila epitomize an urban and national development model of 'exclusive development', based on post-industrial capital accumulation in enclosed spaces organized by an elite-captured state.

The findings presented stem from data collected during several months of fieldwork between June 2011 and May 2013, with additional data collection in November 2016. I conducted interviews and a focus group discussion with policy makers, real estate advisors, consultancies and brokers, real estate developers and their marketing divisions, to understand the ongoing urban and economic changes in Metro Manila. Moreover, I attended presentations and high-level events on foreign investment policy and on urban planning in Metro Manila. In this chapter, I draw on information from ten qualitative interviews, one focus group discussion, and observations during extended stays in three different areas of Metro Manila (the central business district of Makati, Eastwood City, and Bonifacio Global City). Secondary data was compiled from government and corporate bodies and from the annual reports of real estate developers.

The structure of the chapter is as follows. The next section connects different bodies of literature that are relevant for an analysis of Philippines' enclave development trajectory. Following the genealogy of the Philippines' socio-spatially exclusive development trajectory empirical illustrations of Metro Manila's 'spaces of exception 2.0' are presented. The penultimate section discusses the critical and expanding role of (urban) real estate, before the final section concludes by demonstrating the usefulness of the notion of 'exclusive development' for further research.

2   Revisiting Spaces of Exception: SEZs and Enclave Urbanism

Special economic zones are "spatial capital accumulation machines" (Bach, 2011), created by states to attract foreign investments. They provide an attractive regulatory environment and select infrastructure adapted to the needs of foreign investors. The first export processing zone (EPZ) was opened in 1959 in Shannon, Ireland, but since then the policy-tool of geographically demarcated tax incentives and special legislation to facilitate production for world markets has spread around the globe and has, in particular, been used by developing countries as a way to attract foreign investments (for a genealogy of SEZs, see e.g. Bach, 2011; Easterling, 2014; Neveling, 2015). Following a global reorientation from more inward-looking development policies towards export-oriented development advocated by key international institutions, free trade zones, EPZs and SEZs were promoted as the preferred policy option for developing countries to become articulated in global supply chains of labor-intensive sectors, such as textiles and electronics (see e.g. UNIDO, 1971).

Above all, SEZs have become associated with China's ascendance as a world leader of production through the experimental, gradual and selective opening of its economy. SEZs were initially conceptualized as *temporal* and *spatial* exceptions, intended as a temporary instrument to kick-start economic development. They were envisioned to be capable to spread gains to the entire national territory and would, after a few years, dissolve into the national state. Primarily developmental states, eager to fast-track national economic development based on exports, introduced SEZs. Drawing on examples of SEZ creation by developmental (or strong) states, Ong (2006) uses the concept of 'spaces of exception' to explain the state's sovereign creation of positive exceptions for privileged groups in society, thereby leading to a flexibility of state practices. Ong's use of the term is quite different from the original notion of 'exception' based on Schmitt's (1985) assertion that "sovereign is he who can make an exception"[1]. The question arises, however, to what extent it makes sense, in the case of a weak state like the Philippines, to understand the creation of enclave spaces as a sovereign Schmittian 'exception' or whether the zones should rather be interpreted as a reflection of a weak state's inability to act independent of elite interests.

Originally a temporal concept, Agamben (1998: 169) argued that the exception is used to divide between included citizens and excluded outsiders and added a spatial component through the example of the concentration camp, which arose out of state of exceptions, became normalized and "given a permanent spatial arrangement". Diverting from Agamben's focus on the camp as a space of 'bare life' and the suspension of all rules, this chapter sees exceptions not as lawless and devoid of rules but rather as the sites of alternative rules and regulations, arranged in spatially fragmented forms that constitute the contemporary spatialities of the urban. It is precisely an 'urbanism of exception' expressed in "multilayered cities consisting of multiple intersecting, overlapping, and interlocking 'spaces of exception' ...not as isolated territories

---

1   Schmitt referred to Hitler's suspension of existing legal order in the Weimar Republic by declaring an *Ausnahmezustand* (state of emergency).

but as integral features of contemporary urbanism itself" (Murray, 2017: 310), which include economic zones, gated communities, and integrated enclave forms, that this chapter seeks to interrogate.

SEZs have proliferated across the globe. In 2006, an estimated 3500 SEZs were in operation in 135 countries (Farole and Akinci, 2011); more recent figures estimate a total of 4500 SEZs globally (The Economist, 2015). The seemingly universal uptake of SEZs as a global strategy obscures the substantial variations in geographical spread, size, and type of zones. China is responsible for the predominant share of SEZ employment, accounting for approximately 40 million workers out of a total of 66 million (data for 2006, in Neveling, 2015). SEZs range in size from entire cities, such as the Chinese mega-city of Shenzhen in the Pearl River Delta, to large-scale industrial parks, to individual factories and buildings. Moreover, they cater to different industries, fulfill variegated purposes, and take on various shapes, from sweatshops to high-tech research and development facilities. Bach (2011) argues that SEZs can be read along a continuum from low-wage export-processing 'modular zones' to high-end 'Ex-Cities', such as Shenzhen, Dubai or New Songdo City (see also Easterling, 2014). Most analysis has focused on the former zones for manufacturing production to the neglect of urban SEZs, despite zones increasingly occurring in and even constituting the urban through "'nested exceptionalisms' - [the] interplay of exception and rule that creates intersections for networks, markets and political rule [...] these intersections turn the Zone into a form of new urban imagination" (Bach, 2011: 100). As SEZs become more urban, they increasingly coincide, or start to overlap, with other types of urban enclave spaces, suggesting a fruitful avenue to discuss them in relation to the literature on enclave urbanism.

Gated communities constitute visibly secured 'exceptions' to the general public urban environment. Inside, privatized services and security are offered to affluent residents, while entry for non-residents is restricted. Urban enclaves, however, are not limited to segregated residential spaces. Caldeira (1996: 308), for example, defines enclaves as "privatized, enclosed and monitored spaces for residence, consumption, leisure and work, which tend to be socially homogeneous environments, that serve primarily the rich, middle and upper classes." The concept of "enclave urbanism" is similarly broad, including work, leisure, shopping and housing as constitutive elements of enclaves (Wissink et al., 2012: 161).

Despite the capacious definition, empirical investigations of enclave urbanism have almost exclusively focused on residential enclaves. Gated communities in the global South are often aggressively marketed as 'exclusive developments', offering a superior standard of living for a select few amidst a sea of poverty and informality. Explanations for the rise of gated communities have primarily been sought at the urban scale (e.g. as a response of urban middle and upper classes to fears of crime and the desire for security, status, privacy, and the reliance of private rather than public service delivery), with little attention to the (national) state's role in remaking cities as a strategy to attract global flows. Malls and entertainment hubs clearly draw on global flows, but increasingly even gated communities become dependent on transnational flows of people and capital (Ortega, 2016; Pow, 2011).

Enclave urbanism and SEZ development, previously largely understood as two disparate processes, occur simultaneously in mixed-use urban enclaves and are indeed related phenomena. Zoomers (2010) has argued that SEZs, tourism enclaves and foreign capital flows into residential gated communities, among others, are elements of the 'foreignization of land'. This is a very fruitful starting point to conceptualize both production zones (such as foreign-leased agricultural zones for food and biofuels, industrial and service-based SEZs) and consumption zones (tourism resorts, overseas retirement homes, and housing financed by remittance flows) as imbricated processes.

Given a transition to services-based economies, SEZs and enclave urbanism have increasingly converged in the creation of urban mixed-use enclaves, which combine 'live, work, play' functions (Kleibert and Kippers, 2016, Hsu, 2018). These integrated developments constitute 'spaces of exception 2.0', which are not fundamentally new, but signal an intensification of a development trajectory based on socio-spatial exclusions and exceptions and are qualitatively different from earlier mono-functional enclave spaces. Following this brief discussion of the genealogy of an enclave-strategy to development globally, we now turn to how this policy has been used and adapted in the Philippines.

3   The Anti-Developmental State

The Philippine state differs significantly from its East Asian 'developmental state' neighbors, which managed to engineer socio-economic transformations through state-led policies (e.g. Amsden, 1989; Wade, 1990; Woo-Cumings, 1999). Combining infant-industry protectionist policies with strategic integration into the global economy Japan, South Korea, and Taiwan managed to develop competitive export-oriented economies. The core of these countries' developmentalist strategies was a strong bureaucratic state led by a technocratic elite, which intervened in the economy to support and, at the same time, discipline domestic industrialists.

The absence of a strong state in the Philippines coupled with powerful elites has limited opportunities for economic development. The Philippines has for long time been recognized as an outlier in the region with respect to its economic development outcomes, which "have been disappointing by any yardstick" (Balisacan and Hill, 2003: 4). When compared to its neighboring countries and, in particular, the East Asian developmental states, the failure of the Philippines to industrialize and achieve economic growth is striking (King, 2007; Medalla et al., 1995). Real per-capita GDP in 2000 in the Philippines was on the same level as in 1980, and has, since the 1950s, been overtaken by Korea, Taiwan, Thailand, Indonesia and China (Balisacan and Hill, 2003). Several explanations have been advanced to explain the developmental failure of the Philippines, which can broadly be distinguished as exogenous and endogenous factors. Whereas scholars differ in the weight they attribute to external geopolitical and internal political factors, most agree that colonialism, debt repayment, and cronyism *in combination* have prevented the Philippines from achieving economic development.

The Philippines was a Spanish colony (1565–1898) and was subsequently ruled by the United States until 1946 (with increasing autonomy from 1935 onwards). Following the stated aim of colonial 'exceptionalism' and 'benevolent assimilation', the US created political institutions and an education system modeled on its own (Diokno, 2011; Hedman and Sidel, 2000). Bello (2009: 4) argues that installing a US model of government has precluded the formation of an East Asian-type 'developmental state', and instead brought about an 'anti-development state': "The American pattern of a weak central authority coexisting with a powerful upper-class social organization [...] was reproduced in the Philippines, creating a weak state that was constantly captured by upper-class interests and preventing the emergence of the activist 'developmental' state that disciplined the private sector in other societies in postwar Asia". Debt repayment is seen as the most critical factor preventing Philippine economic take-off by Bello, and Abinales and Amoroso (2005: 16) similarly argue that today's economic development policies are seriously impeded by a lack of state resources due to foreign debt accumulated during the Marcos era and "the state's inability to collect taxes from well-connected corporations and wealthy families".

Elite families have played a crucial role in controlling economic and political power in the Philippines and undermined efforts at economic development to protect personal gains (McCoy, 1994; Krinks, 2002). The political clout of powerful land-owning elites has effectively blocked much-needed agrarian land reform, leading commentators to argue that, "the Philippines is probably the most extreme example of land policy dysfunction in Southeast Asia"

(Studwell, 2014: 39). Political scientists have grappled with the role of elites and oligarchs in the Philippines and developed a multitude of concepts describing their strong influence over the political economy of the Philippines such as 'crony capitalism', 'cacique democracy', 'booty capitalism', or 'bossism' (Anderson, 1988; McCoy, 1994; Hutchcroft, 1998; Sidel, 1999).

Corruption and crony capitalism, however, are not unique to the Philippines, and were also prevalent in 'Tiger' economies like South Korea (Kang, 2002). Development outcomes, therefore, do not depend on the individual ambitions of elites but on the institutional settings in which they are embedded. The existence of extractive institutions instead of inclusive institutions in the Philippines is essentially what Acemoğlu and Robinson (2012) identify as the cause of 'why nations fail'. In the Philippines, elite interests have persistently been able to dominate the Philippine political economy (Raquiza, 2011; Van Helvoirt, 2009). Domestic entrepreneurs have concentrated their efforts on obtaining protection and subsidies from the state through rent seeking, rather than competing based on production capabilities and technological innovation.

Given a lack of employment opportunities within the country, the political economy of the Philippines has come to largely depend on a system of state-brokered labor migration that deploys millions of Overseas Filipino Workers (OFWs) in low-paying labor-intensive service jobs abroad, whose remittances are the single most important contributor of foreign-exchange (Rodriguez, 2010).

4   SEZ Policy: From Manufacturing to Services

Land-owning elites have been able to substantially evade land redistribution by converting their land into SEZs (Bello, 2009; Kelly, 1998; Ortega, 2016). SEZ creation in the Philippines thus, is intimately related to political power structures and has always also been a vehicle to prevent land reform and secure the power-position of elites, in addition to its function as a tool for attracting foreign direct investments and spurring industrialization. Other, non-economic and geopolitical rationales also play a role in the creation of SEZs in Asia, as for example in the border zones of North and South Korea and in the Mekong Region (Arnold, 2012; Doucette and Lee, 2015). The geopolitical situation of the Philippines paved the way for the development of SEZs on former US military bases. Subic Naval Bay was the first converted base, in 1991, to be transformed by the Subic Bay Metropolitan Authority into a hub for Korean investments and the Hanjin Heavy Industries Shipyard (Casanova, 2011). Since 1995 neoliberal policies in the Philippines have shifted SEZ development from the public to the private sector. With this step, the number of sezs increased drastically, leading to an "intensification of the 'enclave economy' approach" (McKay, 2006: 60).

sez development in the Philippines has thrived tremendously over the past decade, despite questions about the relevance of sezs as an economic tool and reports of illegal activities facilitated through their existence, e.g. smuggling in free ports and money laundering in casinos (Manasan, 2013). In total, 348 sezs (including 234 information technology parks and centers, 19 tourism economic zones, and 2 medical tourism parks) operated in the Philippines in July 2016, with an additional 148 under development (PEZA, 2016). Whereas manufacturing sezs were largely concentrated in the suburban provinces surrounding Metro Manila, the new generation of sez-spaces is predominantly found in the central business districts of Metro Manila, where they often occupy several floors in the most expensive high-rise buildings. The spectacular rise of service-based sezs is related to a structural economic transformation into an urban service-based economy. Three newly promoted service sectors, dependent upon global capital flows and incentivized through sez policy, are information technology and business process outsourcing (IT-BPO), health and retirement tourism, and casino complexes.

5   IT and Business Process Outsourcing

Since the turn of the millennium, the Philippines has managed to attract investors in the IT-BPO sector exporting services to the United States and several other countries. This relatively new sector is primarily driven by lower-cost English language skills and 'cultural affinity', resulting from the period of US colonization and its enduring legacy. In a little over a decade, the sector has risen to employ one million workers (in 2014), the majority of whom are middle-class urban graduates. IT-BPO zones are heavily concentrated in Metro Manila and other urban agglomerations. To allow for the creation of smaller-scale sezs within the existing urban high-rise office buildings (instead of Greenfield investments into large-scale industrial parks) a reduction of the minimum size requirement for sezs and a creative re-interpretation of space from horizontal to vertical space was introduced (Kleibert, 2015). The recent real estate boom is heavily dependent on the IT-BPO sector, which is estimated to account for 95 per cent of total new office demand between 2005 and 2012 (Interview with country head, real estate consultancy firm, March 2013).

6 Health and Retirement Tourism

In addition to incentivizing tourism enclaves and beach resorts through the creation of tourism-SEZs, the Philippine Board of Investment has identified overseas health and retirement tourism as a valuable strategy for economic development and as an opportunity to generate employment for the large number of unemployed Filipino nurses and caretakers (Padojinog and Rodolfo, 2004). The Philippine Retirement Authority (PRA), a dedicated government body operating under the Department of Tourism, was founded with the mission "to attract foreign nationals and former Filipino citizens to invest, reside and retire in the Philippines [...] providing them the best quality of life in the most attractive package" (PRA, n.d.). Japanese, Chinese, Korean and English-language forms are available online for potential retirees (of a minimum age of 35 years). 'World class' hospitals complying international standards (such as St. Luke's in Bonifacio Global City, a classified SEZ) have opened to cater to the global market. Real estate firms have started to construct 'retirement villages', which take the shape of enclaves, mimicking the style of the retiree's home country. Megaworld's Mactan Boulevard development in Cebu is one example catering to Japanese seniors which features, in addition to a medical facilities, a bonsai garden, a koi pond, a Japanese-style tea room, and origami and ikebana rooms (Kacho, 2013). So far, however, the strategy of attracting health and retirement tourists has not proven very successful and the sector remains small.

7 Casinos

Casino development has recently become a strategy to attract foreign money and tourists, especially tapping into the market of Chinese gamblers who escape increasing restrictions in Macao (Dela Peña, 2015). A boom of integrated casino developments has engulfed Metro Manila (e.g. Entertainment City, Resorts World in Newport City). Despite the social costs of the casino industry (Hannigan, 2007; Wu and Chen, 2015), the development of these enclave spaces is incentivized by the Philippine Economic Zone Authority (PEZA). The integrated resort spaces have some resemblance with the themed urban landscapes of Las Vegas and Dubai, where privatized urban planning and a heavy investment in the tourism and real estate sectors have led to a proliferation of privately owned casino-cum-hotel landscapes. The casino complexes form artificial "stimulus-intensive surrogate worlds" (Schmid, 2006: 347) that cater primarily to foreign tourists and consumers. Large-scale real estate construction

in hotel and resorts is required to create the infrastructure to support the Philippine's bet to become the fourth largest casino destination globally by 2018
(Philippine Daily Inquirer, 2016).

8   Urban Enclaves: From Gated Communities to Luxury Condominiums

Metro Manila's history of enclave development dates back to colonial times,
when the Spanish ruled the city from the walled city of *Intramuros* ('within the
walls'), excluding native Filipinos and other Asians, who were bound to live in
segmented spaces of the Extramuros. The first 'modern' gated communities
were developed after the Second World War, most famously Forbes Park, the
elite enclave inhabited by upper class Filipinos, American military and expatri-
ate diplomats (see Hogan et al., 2012). The restrictions have thus always been
based on both class and race. More exclusive gated 'villages' or 'subdivisions'
followed suit in the 1960s, such as Dasmariñas and Bel-Air in Makati. Private
urban development has traditionally been very strong and the entire neighborhood of Makati was privately developed by Ayala Land Incorporated, a Filipino
conglomerate. Murphy and Hogan argue that the legacy neo-patrimonial
power has played a crucial role in transforming Metro Manila into "the world's
most fragmented, privatized and un-public of cities" (2012: 28). Metro Manila's
profound transformation under neoliberal urbanization has been well documented by urban scholars (Choi, 2016; Michel, 2010; Shatkin, 2008, 2011; Van
den Muizenberg and Van Naerssen, 2005). Since the 1990s, countless gated
communities have arisen in Metro Manila's peri-urban fringe, marketed as
exclusive, secured and privatized Western-themed suburban dreamscapes
(Connell, 1999). Ortega (2016) argues that neoliberal suburbanization critically
depends on transnational real estate investments by overseas Filipino workers
and on accumulation by dispossession (Ortega, 2016). The struggle for urban
space, similarly to developments in Jakarta, can also be understood as 'contested accumulations through displacement' (Leitner and Sheppard, 2018).

In addition to suburban, gated communities of low-rise housing, luxurious
and highly securitized housing proliferates in the form of skyscraper luxury
condominiums in inner-city areas. Condominium development in the Philippines forms part of a larger trend of 'condo-ism' that redirects growth to the
urban core and favors densification in post-Fordist cities (Rosen and Walks,
2015). The transition towards urban living of elites not only reflects a de-
mographic life-style choice of consumers, but has been driven by increased
revenue opportunities for land owners and a re-orientation from farmland

to urban land as a source of profit in the 21st century. Condominiums have been constructed at fast speed and are often composed of very small units, an apparent mismatch given the average family size in the Philippines. As in Jakarta, a 'perfect storm' of traveling neoliberal urban policy models, emerging middle-class aspirations, national real-estate developers and global finance emerged that transforms urban lands for condominium development (Leitner and Sheppard, 2017, 14).

The Philippine boom has also been enabled by the Condominium Act of 1996, which enables foreign ownership of units within apartment-complexes in the previously fully protected domestic housing sector. Developers have focused on constructing upper-class condominiums, leading to an undersupply of social housing units in Metro Manila (Cardenas, 2011). Despite legislation that stipulates augmented requirements for social housing development, between January and May 2016 an overwhelming 37,631 licenses to sell were issued by the Housing and Land Use Regulatory Board in the mid- to high-end condominium segment, in contrast to only 1,365 low-cost condominiums (Colliers International, 2016).

The condominium boom can be understood as part of the aspirational and symbolic remaking of cities and it is primarily transnational labor migrants who are buying and investing into these properties at home. Overseas Filipino Workers (OFWs) are specifically targeted by real-estate marketing of condominiums and segmented into different economic categories based on the countries they work in. The highest-end developments targeting OFWs based in North America and Europe, the medium-and mixed developments for those in Singapore and Hong Kong, and low-end, or 'affordable housing', reserved for those based in the Middle East. The hierarchy of geographies of work destinations is thus pro-actively translated into a spatial stratification within urban condominium projects, even by the same developer (Focus group discussion, November 2016).

9 Spaces of Exception 2.0 in Metro Manila

'Spaces of exceptions' in various shapes have existed for a long time in the Philippines, and new ones often overlap with or supersede earlier spaces of exceptions, such as former military zones. Private sector interests have historically been able to realize their own interests in Metro Manila, given weak (metropolitan) state authorities unable to steer and control the urban development process. But what is new in the 21st century enclave urbanism in the Philippines? The argument advanced here is that we currently witness an intensification and amplification of the enclave strategy to economic development, which is more urban-focused, more pervasive and all-encompassing, and increasingly integrated into mega-projects. These 'spaces of exception 2.0' have morphed into exclusive developments, combining service-based SEZs, gated communities, and entertainment functions within a single structure. Real estate conglomerate Megaworld Corporation alone, for example, boasts 21 integrated 'township' developments across the Philippines.

The concept of a self-reliant 'township', according to the assistant manager of a real estate developer, means that: "we need to have everything. Township means you live here, you work here, you play here, so all these institutions we need to have. We have our own hospital, own schools, we are building our own church, just so that we are complete." (Interview, April 2013). One problem with this model of self-contained enclaves, however, is that it is limited by the mismatch of expensive housing and workers' salaries. "The people who live here should ideally work here. But not everyone who works here can afford to live here, because it is really expensive. That's why we are trying to purchase more and more busses" (ibid.). Although the so-called 'township projects' are marketed as environmentally-conscious alternatives to living in enclaves and gated communities in the suburbs, due to reduced carbon footprints as a result of densification, in reality, the urban enclaves in Metro Manila are far from self-sufficient; and commuter flows to, from and between these 'cities within the city' have increased. In the following, three cases of mixed-use enclave development, or "spaces of exception", are presented.

Eastwood City is the first 'township' development in the Philippines that, following the Asian financial crisis, became a SEZ for IT-BPO services in 1997. Developed by Megaworld Corporation as a 'live, work, play community', it constitutes a globally oriented 24-hour enclave space from where offshore services are delivered, largely to North American clients. The 17 hectare mixed-use urban enclave provides office space for more than 100 firms, from call centers to back-offices of international banks. In addition, entertainment, shopping, and residential spaces have been constructed. The privately owned township reflects an Americanized model of modernity, and is simultaneously integrated into US service provision (through call centers) and US service consumption (through McDonalds, Starbucks, and other high-priced food outlets). Eastwood City is a 'globalized' urban enclave, integrated into transnational flows and constitutes a node in multiple global flows of value extraction, which cannot be understood through an analysis of locally-bound processes alone (Kleibert and Kippers, 2016).

Access to Eastwood City is controlled by security guards and, as a private development, several activities possible in public spaces, such as street vending, begging, or demonstrating, are prohibited. A private security force, called *Megaforce*, and plain-clothed investigators are patrolling the enclave to prevent any unwanted behavior or occurrences: "Because at the end of the day, this is still a private property [...]. If people want to have a rally, if they want to protest, they cannot do that here. Because we will stop them at the entrance" (Interview, Property Developer, March 2013). The roads are only open to private cars and taxis; public transportation (e.g. jeepneys, tricycles and busses) have to let their passengers disembark in front of the gate. Allowed to enter are a fleet of private shuttle-busses that connect Eastwood City to other enclaves operated by the same real estate developer, for example to Resorts World, an entertainment and casino enclave close to the airport. Simultaneously, the SEZ remains disconnected and virtually inaccessible for poor communities located in direct geographic proximity across the river.

Entertainment City is a land reclamation and waterfront redevelopment project at Manila bay that has acquired many different names, including *Bagong Nayong Pilipino* (Filipino New Town), Bay City, and Entertainment City. The origins of this development date back to state-led land reclamation plans under the Marcos regime. The 120 hectare Las Vegas-style integrated casino development by the Philippine gaming corporation PAGCOR is currently under development in Parañaque City. Delays were brought about by financial troubles following the Asian crisis, but today a number of projects have been realized, and several more are expected to open in the near future. In total, the 'city' consists of five resorts (City Dreams Manila, Solaire Resort and Casino, Resorts World Bayshore, Manila Bay Resorts, and Westside City), located adjacent to each other. All encompass relatively similar features, with casinos and gambling infrastructure forming the central anchor. Equipped moreover with luxurious hotels, shopping malls, bars and nightclubs, they are intended as 'one-stop-shop' places for international (gambling) tourism.

The developments are clearly modeled on similar resorts in Macao, Singapore and Malaysia. The enclave spaces are, given foreign-ownership restrictions, operated as joint ventures between Filipino real estate conglomerates and foreign investors (Resorts World, for example, by Alliance Global Group and Genting Hong Kong). The entire Entertainment City area is classified as a tourism-SEZ. Over the next four years an estimated 15,000 new hotel rooms will be added in Metro Manila, half of these in Entertainment City's hotels along Manila bay (Colliers International, 2012).

Bonifacio Global City (BGC) is situated on a territory of a former military enclave; the Fort William McKinley base of the US military. After the Second World War, the base was returned to the Philippines and renamed Fort Bonifacio (after the Filipino revolutionary) and subsequently privatized through what was "considered the biggest real estate deal in Asia in 1995" (Casanova, 2011: 110). In a spectacular bidding process, Metro Pacific Group acquired the land for PHP 39 billion. Soon after, land prices dropped due to the Asian crisis, forcing the winner to sell the land again. The 55 per cent privately-owned part of BGC was acquired in equal shares by two Filipino conglomerates, Ayala Land Incorporated and Evergreen Holdings.

In order to establish its image as the premier central business district in the Philippines, the move of the stock exchange from Makati and Ortigas, the two formerly most important central business districts, to BGC is an important step. Moreover, luxury hotel developments are planned and construction is ongoing, including a Grand Hyatt and the 63-floor Shangri-La (intended to become the tallest building in the country). One of the newest developments in BGC is a 62-floor construction by Ayala Land Premier: "The studio units are 25 million peso. The most expensive units, the penthouse unit with your own pool is 150 million peso[2]! It was sold out in four days. And people are wondering: 'Are you really a poor country?' [laughs] 'Cause yeah, we have all these developments" (Interview with business development manager, April 2013).

In order to vacate land for these large-scale developments, the urban poor are often forced to leave and resettle outside the city's boundaries with fewer opportunities for income generation. According to data by the Urban Poor Associates, an estimated 10,000 slum dwellers have been evicted to vacate the land for the BGC development (in Shaktin, 2008: 395). Informal settlers tend to be relocated to distant social housing projects at the fringes of the city, far away from employment opportunities. The construction of these new 'world-class' exclusive developments in Manila is therefore only possible through a simultaneous dispossession and exclusion of population groups based on class and race, exacerbating existing socio-spatial inequalities (Bello et al., 2014; Choi, 2016; Ortega, 2016).

BGC lies on the border of two of Metro Manila's local government units: Taguig and Makati. Both have been involved in a long dispute over the ownership of the country's most expensive central business district, with Taguig *de facto* controlling it (the 'I love Taguig' slogan can be found on many lampposts throughout BGC), although Makati upholds its claim. The stakes are high given the rather large potential source for local tax revenue. This dispute serves to highlight how difficult collaboration on a Metro-wide scale is and shows that rivalries between different political actors inhibit infrastructure and city planning that goes beyond the borders of individual enclave spaces, presenting in particular problems for addressing issues such as traffic, water and

---

2   Approximately US $3m. In November 2016 US $1 converted to around PHP 50 (oanda.com).

waste-management (Urban Land Institute, 2013). Despite the fact that the primarily privately developed and operated enclaves aspire to stay aloof and disconnected from the rest of the city, they are still territorially grounded on land belonging to different public administrations and are imbricated in existing political structures.

The future does not seem to hold any alternatives to this urban development model. Instead, we can observe a further intensification and a spread of the enclave model to second-tier cities. The newest strategy of the most powerful real estate developers is to interconnect their individual private exclusive developments, leading to an intensified form of 'implant-bypass urbanism' (Shatkin, 2008). In a focus group discussion, respondents note that:

> These big real estate developers [...] are creating centers everywhere. We have seen the push to the North, there is definitely presence in the South [of Metro Manila], so now the big groups are starting to stitch these centers together. [...] They are defining their territories, in a way almost like little fiefdoms (November 2016).

10   Exclusive Development(s) and Urban Real Estate

The Philippines, in 2011, manifested the highest income disparities in Asia, as the 40 richest families together accounted for 76 per cent of GDP growth (Agence France Presse, 2013). In 2012, a further concentration of wealth occurred, with an increase of 12 per cent in total wealth recorded among the richest 50 families over the previous year, bringing their collective wealth to $74 billion (Forbes, 2014). This wealth is primarily amassed in a range of sectors that are largely protected from foreign competition and can be classified as rent-seeking[3]. Filipino business conglomerates have diversified into rent-generating sectors, above all real estate (Bello et al., 2014; Gutierrez and Rodriguez, 2013).

In recent years, the real estate sector has been one of the fastest growing sectors in the Philippines and generated PHP 423 billion income in 2013, while receiving PHP 970 million subsidies (Philippine Statistics Authority, 2016).

---

3 *The Economist* (2014) developed a 'crony-index' that simplistically measures the share of a country's billionaires' wealth active in ten industries, selected for their monopolistic tendencies and their dependency on close government connections and favorable policies (e.g. licensing), as a ratio to GDP. The selected sectors include extractive industries, real estate, utilities and telecommunications, and casinos.

Ortega (2016: 3) argues that, "real estate has emerged as an effective circuit of accumulation by political-economic elites, created and sustained by strategic alliances between the state and market forces and among old and new taipan elite families". The extreme profitability for three prominent real estate developers that engaging both in commercial and residential real estate is illustrated by the following figures (based on respective company's 2015 annual reports): Ayala Land Inc. reported a net income of PHP 17.6 billion (increase of 13 %), SM Prime Holdings Inc. PHP 20.9 billion (increase of 14 %) and Megaworld Corp. PHP 10.5 billion (increase of 11 %). Although data by *The Economist* (2016) reveal a recent decrease in crony-sector wealth globally, the Philippines moved up to become the third-highest country on the index, based on a high ratio (more than 10 % in 2016) of crony-sector derived billionaire wealth.

In particular, urban real estate, has become a new profit opportunity eagerly embraced the existing oligarchic elite of the Philippines, who have access to land, sufficient financial resources, and the necessary political connections and insider's knowledge to be able to develop the land. In interviews, real estate developers' narratives usually attribute their success to their 'vision' for and inside knowledge of a particular place. The city has become the epicenter for island spaces of privatized luxury enclaves in different constellations. Whereas previously SEZs were erected on the semi-urban fringes outside of Metro Manila, nowadays, service-based SEZs are found in the heart of the financial district of the capital city. Gated communities are no longer sub-urban low-rise housing 'villages' but are increasingly vertical gated communities in the form of high-rise condominium towers. Also, new SEZs for casino and health tourism are increasingly found in urban areas.

Urban commercial and residential real estate development (and speculation) is intertwined with national economic development strategies involving the creation of sites of exceptions, such as SEZs and technoparks. Speculative and transnational capital is playing an increasing role in contemporary real estate developments in the Philippines. The real estate sector in Manila is increasingly shifting from being an enabler of economic development to a driver of capital accumulation, corroborating Smith's argument that urban real estate is becoming "the centerpiece of the city's productive economy, an end in itself, justified by appeals to jobs, taxes and tourism" (Smith, 2002: 443). Whereas previously the creation of SEZs were seen as a means to an end, aiming to ultimately result in economic growth through the attraction of foreign investments and employment generation, the game today has changed profoundly and the transformation of rural or devalued urban land into 'spaces of exception' itself has become a key driver of economic growth. Goldman (2011) has shown the transformation of the metropolitan region of Bangalore into speculative real estate markets as part of a 'global city' strategy. Both in India and the Philippines, accumulation by dispossession is argued to be constitutive of the creation of enclave spaces, including SEZs and gated communities (Goldman, 2011; Levien, 2013; Ortega, 2016).

11 Conclusion: From Spaces of Exception to Exclusive Development

The above discussion has shown how Philippines state has been carving out 'spaces of exception' for export-production, for segregated residences, and for urban mixed-use developments. The current political-economic moment signals not a deviation from but an intensification of earlier processes. The development of exceptional and exclusive spaces is a continuation of earlier national strategies by the Philippine government. Already during the Marcos era, mega-projects to increase status of the regime with the international community were prioritized over the delivery of basic services to the city's inhabitants. Exclusive enclave development policies thus follow long-term government strategies to hide poverty and the urban poor (e.g. resettlement at the fringes of the city, walling of squatter settlements) instead of focusing on eradicating poverty (Michel, 2010). The attraction of foreign flows capital, the gains of which remain unevenly shared in the current political-economy of the Philippines, is seen as the ultimate goal to judge the country on, whereas concerns about reducing poverty and improving livelihoods are side-lined. Recent economic growth (5.8% GDP growth in 2015) fuelled by real estate and other services sectors have helped the Philippines to shed their image as the 'sick man of Asia'. The major credit rating agencies, moreover, gave the country 'investment grade' in 2015, the highest rating in the country's history. However, as unemployment and poverty figures remain very high, economic growth has been far from inclusive. As the Philippine Development Plan 2011–2016 states, inclusive development remains:

> An ideal which the country has perennially fallen short of, and this failure has had the most far-reaching consequences, from mass misery and marginalization, to an overseas exodus of skill and talent, to political disaffection and alienation, leading finally to threats to the constitution of the state itself.
>
> NEDA, n.d.: 1

The Philippines' history of 'anti-developmentalism' presents a contrasting case to Ong's reviewed 'zones of exceptions' deployed for developmental purposes.

The case may, however, not be unique as other countries are experiencing gentrification and similarly engage in the development of new cities, townships, and mega-projects, driven by a finance-real estate nexus. The Philippines' enclave strategy to economic development is peculiar in that hinges both on the creation of exceptional spaces for production (expanded to include almost all export activities), and for urban living (with a proliferation of gated communities and condominiums), and their integration into mixed-use super-enclaves, which promise a 'live, work, play' environment that minimize engagement with the 'non-exceptional' spaces outside of the enclave - and their inhabitants. The study reveals a convergence of residential and production zones to amalgamate into 'exclusive developments' for elites, reflecting a shift from an enclave strategy based on spaces of exception to one based on spaces of exclusion. In almost ironic contrast to the international development paradigm of 'inclusive development', the Philippines today follows an 'exclusive development' strategy. The fault-line of inclusion and exclusion runs between, on the one hand, existing privileged classes and those individuals plugged into global capital flows (either through participation in the remittance economy or as virtual migrants working night-shifts in call centers servicing overseas clients) and, on the other hand, the 'disposable' rest of the population (see also Ortega, 2016).

While the luxury island-like structures of wealth were conceptualized in this chapter as 'spaces of exception', new 'spaces of exception' closer to Agamben's initial formulation have emerged in the Philippines. In September 2016, Philippine President Rodrigo Duterte declared a 'state of emergency' further advancing the powers of police and armed forces in the so-called 'war against drugs', a thinly-veiled war against the poor. Human rights groups have counted several thousand extrajudicial killings of suspected drug users and dealers since the beginning of Duterte's presidency, many of whom have been killed in the poorest neighborhoods of Metro Manila. In these spaces beyond the high-end luxurious archipelago, areas of suspended laws have been created, whose residents face less than 'bare life'.

References

Abinales, PN and DJ Amoroso (2005) *State and Society in the Philippines*. Lanham, MD: Rowman & Littlefield Publishers.

Acemoğlu, D, & JA Robinson (2012) Why Nations Fail: The Origins of Power, Prosperity and Poverty. New York: Crown.

Agamben, G (1998) Homo sacer: Sovereign power and bare life. Stanford University Press.

Agence France Presse (2013) Philippines elite swallow country's new wealth. *Philippine Daily Inquirer*, 2 March: http://business.inquirer.net/110413/philippines-elite-swallow-countrys-new-wealth (accessed on 10 July 2015).

Amsden, AH (1989) *Asia's Next Giant: South Korea and Late Industrialization*. New York, NY: Oxford University Press.

Anderson, B (1988) Cacique democracy in the Philippines: Origins and dreams. *New Left Review* 169(3): 3–31.

Arnold, D (2012) Spatial practices and border SEZs in Mekong Southeast Asia. *Geography Compass* 6(12): 740–751.

Bach, J (2011) Modernity and the urban imagination in economic zones. *Theory, Culture & Society* 28(5): 98–122.

Balisacan, AM and H Hill (2003) *The Philippine Economy*. Oxford: Oxford University Press.

Bello, W (2009) *The Anti-Development State: The Political Economy of Permanent Crisis in the Philippines*. Pasig City: Anvil Publishing.

Bello, W, K Cardenas, JP Cruz, A Fabros, MA Manahan, C Militante, J Purugganan and JJ Chavez (2014) *State of Fragmentation: The Philippines in Transition*. Focus on the Global South and Friedrich Ebert Stiftung: Quezon City.

Brenner, N and N Theodore (2002) Cities and the geographies of "actually existing neoliberalism" *Antipode* 34(3): 349–379.

Caldeira, TPR (1996) Fortified enclaves: The new urban segregation. *Public Culture* 8 (2): 303–328.

Cardenas, K (2011) Globalization, housing markets, and the transformation of a South City: The case of 21st century Manila. Paper presented at the International RC21 conference, Amsterdam, 7–9 July.

Casanova, AP (2011) Special economic zones and freeports: Challenges and opportunities in the bases conversion and development experience in the Philippines. In: C Carter and A Harding (eds.) *Special Economic Zones in Asian Market Economies*. Abingdon: Routledge, pp. 108–123.

Choi, N (2016) Metro Manila through the gentrification lens: Disparities in urban planning and displacement risks. *Urban Studies* 53(3): 577–592.

Colliers International. (2012) 4Q 2012. Philippine real estate market overview. Research and forecast report. Makati City: Colliers International.

Colliers International (2016) Philippine Property Market 2Q 2016. Makati City: Colliers International.

Connell, J (1999) Beyond Manila: walls, malls and private spaces. *Environment and Planning A* 31(3): 417–439.

Dela Peña, ZB (2015) Philippines on verge of a casino boom. *The Philippine Star*, 13 April: http://www.philstar.com/business/2015/04/13/1443060/philippines-verge-casino-boom (accessed on 2 December 2016).

Diokno, MS (2011) 'Benevolent assimilation' and Filipino responses. In: McFerson HM (ed.) *Mixed Blessing: The Impact of the American Colonial Experience on Politics and Society in the Philippines*. University of the Philippines Press: Quezon City, pp. 90–106.

Doucette, J and S-O Lee (2015) Experimental territoriality: Assembling the Kaesong industrial complex in North Korea. *Political Geography* 47: 53–63.

Douglass, M, B Wissink and R Van Kempen (2012) Enclave urbanism in China: Consequences and interpretations. *Urban Geography* 33(2): 167–182.

Easterling, K (2014) *Extrastatecraft: The Power of Infrastructure Space*. Verso Books.

Farole, T and G Akinci (2011) *Special Economic Zones: Progress, Emerging Challenges and Future Directions*. Washington, DC: The World Bank.

Forbes. (2014) Wealth of Philippines' 50 richest on Forbes list rises to US$74 billion. *Forbes*, 28 August: http://www.forbes.com/sites/forbespr/2014/09/02/wealth-of-philippines -50-richest-on-forbes-list-rises-to-us74-billion/ (accessed on 10 July 2015).

Goldman, M (2011) Speculative urbanism and the making of the next world city. *International Journal of Urban and Regional Research* 35(3): 555–581.

Gutierrez, BPB and RA Rodriguez (2013) Diversification strategies of large business groups in the Philippines. *Philippine Management Review* 20: 65–82.

Hannigan, J (2007) Casino Cities. *Geography Compass* 1(4): 959–975.

Hedman, E-LE and JT Sidel (eds.) (2000). *Philippine Politics and Society in the Twentieth Century*. London: Routledge.

Hogan, T, T Bunnell, CP Pow, E Permanasari and S Morshidi (2012) Asian urbanisms and the privatization of cities *Cities* 29(1): 59–63.

Hsu J-Y (2018) Hsinchu Technopolis: A socio-technical imaginary of modernity in Taiwan? *Critical Sociology*. 44(3): 487–501.

Hutchcroft, PD (1998) *Booty Capitalism: The Politics of the Philippines*. Ithaca, NY: Cornell University Press.

Kacho, KO (2013) Megaworld invites retirees. In: The Mactan New Town Megaworld: http://themactannewtownmegaworld.blogspot.de/2013/10/megaworld-invites -retirees.html (accessed on 8 December 2016).

Kang, DC (2002) Crony Capitalism: Corruption and Development in South Korea and the Philippines. Cambridge: Cambridge University Press.

Kelly, PF (1998) The politics of urban-rural relations: Land use conversion in the Philippines. *Environment and Urbanization* 10(1): 35–54.

King, EB (2007) Making sense of the failure of rapid industrialization in the Philippines. *Technology in Society* 29(3): 295–306.

Kleibert, JM (2015) Islands of globalization: offshore services and the changing spatial divisions of labor. *Environment and Planning A* 47(4): 884–902.

Kleibert, JM and L Kippers (2016) Living the good life? The rise of urban mixed-use enclaves in Metro Manila. *Urban Geography* 31(3): 373–395.

Krinks, P (2002) *The Economy of the Philippines: Elites, Inequalities, and Economic Restructuring*. London: Routledge.

Lees, L, HB Shin and E López-Morales (2016) *Planetary Gentrification*. Cambridge, UK & Malden, MA: John Wiley & Sons.

Leitner, H and E Sheppard (2018) From Kampungs to Condos? Contested accumulations through displacement in Jakarta. *Environment and Planning A*, 50(2): 437–456.

Levien, M (2013) Regimes of dispossession: From steel towns to special economic zones. *Development and Change* 44(2): 381–407.

Manasan, RG (2013) *Export Processing Zones, Special Economic Zones: Do We Really Need to Have More of Them?* Makati City: Philippine Institute for Development Studies.

McCoy, AW (1994) *An Anarchy of Families: State and Family in the Philippines*. Quezon City: Ateneo de Manila University Press.

McKay, SC (2006) *Satanic Mills or Silicon Islands? The Politics of High-Tech Production in the Philippines*. New York, NY: Cornell University Press.

Medalla, EM, GR Tecson, RM Bautista and JH Power (1995) *Catching up with Asia's Tigers*. Makati City: Philippine Institute for Development Studies.

Michel, B (2010) *Global City als Projekt: Neoliberale Urbanisierung und Politiken der Exklusion in Metro Manila*. Bielefeld: Transcript Verlag.

Murphy, P and T Hogan (2012) Discordant order: Manila's neo-patrimonial urbanism. *Thesis Eleven* 112(1): 10–34.

Murray, MJ (2017) *The Urbanism of Exception: The Dynamics of Global City Building in the Twenty-First Century*. Cambridge University Press.

National Economic Development Authority (NEDA) (n.d.). *Philippine Development Plan 2011–2016: In Pursuit of Inclusive Growth*. NEDA: http://devplan.neda.gov.ph/about-the-plan.php (accessed on 12 December 2016).

Neveling, P (2015) Free trade zones, export processing zones, special economic zones and global imperial formations 200 BCE to 2015 CE. In: I Ness and Z Cope (eds.) *The Palgrave Encyclopedia of Imperialism and Anti-Imperialism*. Basingstoke: Palgrave Macmillan, pp. 1007–1016.

Ong, A (2006) *Neoliberalism as Exception: Mutations in Citizenship and Sovereignty*. Durham and London: Duke University Press.

Ortega, AA (2016) *Neoliberalizing Spaces in the Philippines: Suburbanization, Transnational Migration, and Dispossession*. Lanham, MD: Rowman & Littlefield.

Padojinog, WCB and CLS Rodolfo (2004) Developing the Japanese market for Philippine tourism and retirement services: Prospects and impediments. Discussion Paper Series No. 2004-31, Philippine Institute for Development Studies: Makati City.

PEZA (2016) List of operating economic zones, on 31 July, 2016. http://www.peza.gov.ph/index.php/economic-zones/list-of-economic-zones (accessed on 8 December 2016).

Philippine Daily Inquirer (2016) Casino tourism' driving more hotels to be built in PH'. *Philippine Daily Inquirer*, 12 March: www.business.inquirer.net/208484/casiono -tourism-driving-more-hotels-to-be-built-in-ph (accessed on 8 December 2016).

Philippine Retirement Authority (PRA) (n.d.). About PRA. http://www.pra.gov.ph/ main/about_pra (accessed on 10 December 2016).

Philippine Statistics Authority (2016) 2013 Annual Survey of Philippine Business and Industry (ASPBI)—Real Estate Activities: Final Results. Philippine Statistics Authority.

Pow, C-P (2011) Living it up: Super-rich enclave and transnational elite urbanism in Singapore. *Geoforum* 42: 382–393.

Raquiza, AR (2011) *State Structure, Policy Formation, and Economic Development in Southeast Asia. The Political Economy of Thailand and the Philippines*. London & New York, NY: Routledge.

Rodriguez, RM (2010) *Migrants for Export. How the Philippines State Brokers Labour to the World*. Minneapolis, MN & London: University of Minnesota Press.

Rosen, G and A Walks (2015) Castles in Toronto's sky: condo-ism as urban transformation. *Journal of Urban Affairs* 37(3): 289–310.

Schmid, H (2006) Economy of fascination: Dubai and Las Vegas as examples of themed urban landscapes. *Erdkunde* 60: 346–361.

Schmitt, C (1985) *Political Theology: Four chapters on the Concept of Sovereignty*. Chicago, IL: University of Chicago Press.

Shatkin, G (2008) The city and the bottom line: urban megaprojects and the privatization of planning in Southeast Asia. *Environment and Planning A* 40(2): 383–401.

Shatkin, G (2011) Planning privatopolis: Representation and contestation in the development of urban integrated mega-projects. In: A Roy and A Ong (eds.) *Worlding Cities: Asian Experiments and the Art of being Global*. Malden, MA & Oxford: Blackwell Publishing, pp. 77–97.

Smith, N (2002) New globalism, new urbanism: Gentrification as global urban strategy. *Antipode* 34(3): 427–450.

Sidel, JT (1999) *Capital, Coercion and Crime: Bossism in the Philippines*. Stanford, CA: Stanford University Press.

Studwell, J (2014) *How Asia Works: Success and Failure in the World's Most Dynamic Region*. London: Profile Books.

The Economist (2014) Planet Plutocrat. *The Economist*, 15 March 15: http://www .economist.com/news/international/21599041-countries-where-politically -connected-businessmen-are-most-likely-prosper-planet (accessed on 8 December 2016).

The Economist (2015) Special economic zones: Not so special. *The Economist*, 1 April: https://www.economist.com/leaders/2015/04/04/not-so-special (accessed on 26 October 2016).

The Economist (2016) The Party Winds down. *The Economist*, 7 May: http://www
.economist.com/news/international/21698239-across-world-politically-connected
-tycoons-are-feeling-squeeze-party-winds (accessed on 8 December 2016).

United Nations Industrial Development Organisation (UNIDO) (1971) Industrial free-
zones as incentives to promote export-oriented industries. UNIDO: Geneva.

Urban Land Institute (2013). Ten Principles for Sustainable Development of Metro Manila's New Urban Core. Washington, DC: Urban Land Institute.

Van den Muizenberg, O and T Van Naerssen (2005) Metro Manila: Designers or directors of urban development? In: PJM Nas (ed.) *Directors of Urban Change in Asia*.
London & New York, NY: Routledge, pp. 142–165.

Van Helvoirt, B (2009) *Regions, institutions and development in a global economy: Divergent regional business systems in the Philippines*. PhD thesis, Utrecht University,
The Netherlands.

Wade, R (1990) *Governing the Market: Economic Theory and the Role of Government in
East Asian Industrialization*. Princeton, NJ: Princeton University Press.

Wissink, B, R van Kempen, Y Fang and S-M Li (2012) Introduction: Living in Chinese
enclave cities. *Urban Geography* 33(2): 161–166.

Woo-Cumings, M (ed.) (1999) *The Developmental State*. Ithaca, NY: Cornell University
Press.

Wu, S-T and Y-S Chen (2015) The social, economic, and environmental impacts of casino gambling on the residents of Macau and Singapore. *Tourism Management* 48:
285–298.

Zoomers, A (2010) Globalisation and the foreignisation of space: seven processes driving the current global land grab. *The Journal of Peasant Studies* 37(2): 429–447.

CHAPTER 7

The Gangnam-ization of Korean Urban Ideology

Bae-Gyoon Park and Jin-bum Jang

1   Introduction

If there is one key word that could characterize contemporary Korean cities, it would be 'apartments'.[1] Single-unit housing was a dominant mode of residence in Korea before the 1980s, but the construction of apartments and multi-unit homes has rapidly increased since then. In particular, the development of massive new towns in the Seoul Metropolitan Area from 1989 onward has triggered a flood in the supply of apartments, ushering in a transition to apartment life for most Koreans. Reflecting on this transformation, Gelézeau (2007) dubs Korea the "apartment republic." Other scholars have also noted how the sudden apartmentization of the country has shaped middle class cultural life (Park H., 2013) and has led to the virtual destruction of previously existing urban communities (Park C., 2013). A second key word that characterizes Korea's urban transformations is 'new town'. Through the 1980 Housing Site Development Promotion Act, the Korean state supported the construction of several new towns around the country, including Bundang and Ilsan in the Seoul Metropolitan Area. Facing rapid urbanization and a sharp increase in housing demand in some cities, the central government sought to quickly develop a large supply of affordable housing. In 1981, it designated and developed eleven new town sites through the Housing Site Development Promotion Act. By December 2016, a total of 617 new towns had been developed through the act, accounting for a total of 2.5% of the country's total land area and 24.4% of its urban housing. These two key phenomena — high-rise apartments and new town construction — have profoundly shaped Korea's urbanization process since the 1980s.

The model for much of this urban development was Gangnam, a new town south of the Han River in Seoul that was developed in the 1970s. It occupies the

---

1   This chapter is a revised version of an article entitled "Gangnam-ization and Korean Urban Ideology" (in Korean), that first appeared in 2016 in the *Journal of Korean Organization of Regional Geographical Research* 22(2): 287–306. The authors wish to thank Yoonai Han, Bridget Martin and Jamie Doucette for assistance with the translation, proofreading, and editing of this chapter.

dominant model of what a city is for the urban developments that followed it and to this day it continues to serve as an aspirational template for cities around the country. Through the development of physical urban spaces like apartment complexes, new cities, and residential areas, planners and developers do not simply replicate Gangnam as a physical space, however. The urban is not only comprised of the visible built environment—high-rise buildings, apartment, wide roads, and rectangular street networks—but also of various embedded meanings and institutions that are related to lifestyles, modes of thinking, and patterns of social relations. The urban is comprised of these many different elements: its visible shape, its living environment, and its discursive representations. All of these shape how we understand what urban life is and carry with them normative ideals that perform their own implicit ideological work.

In the context of Korean urbanization, 'Gangman' functions as a signifier for a distinct way of life and set of desires. Ji (2016) shows that with Gangnam as its emblematic example, Korean urbanity is marked by aspiration for landscapes of luxury high-rise apartments surrounded by glamorous entertainment and cultural facilities. These apartments are treated as a form of housing preferred by the upper-middle class as well as strategic investment assets for capital accumulation in a society governed by the logic of competitiveness. Additionally, the resources needed to achieve social status and success in Gangnam-ized urban spaces, such as private education, requires the concentration of human, social, and cultural capital. In Korea, the name Gangnam signifies cultural and social superiority and the clustering of activities needed to achieve it. In this sense, Gangnam is an important touchstone for understanding Korean urbanism, its aspirations, wish-images, and ideologies, beyond simply its physical urban form. Gangnam is more than a district of Seoul. It circulates as an urban ideal that encapsulates the dreams and aspirations of Korea's middle classes. New towns purporting to be Gangnam-style are sprouting up around the country, such as the Gangnam of Daegu, the Gangnam of Busan, and the Gangnam of Jinju.

In this chapter, we use the term 'Gangnam-ization' to refer to this proliferation of Gangnam-style urban spaces. Not only are Gangnam's urban spaces copied in plans and reconstructed by planners and policy-makers, but ordinary people and urban residents in Korea have defined and imagined what the urban *is* on the basis of the Gangnam-like urban spaces and Gangnam ways of living. This process, we suggest, now dominates Korea's entire urbanization landscape. Moreover, Gangnam-ization unfolds in two processes that we call 'Gangnam-making' and 'Gangnam-following'. The 'Gangnam-making' process involves the physical construction and discursive representation of

Gangnam, while 'Gangnam-following' involves the replication of Gangnam-style urban spaces elsewhere. These processes are based on an urban ideology structured by institutional forces as well as the space of Gangnam itself. While we divide these two processes for conceptual clarity, they are of course closely intermeshed, mutually constructing each other through actual processes of urbanization. While 'Gangnam-following' involves reproducing Gangnam's urban space, what is referenced and copied is in fact not Gangnam itself, but an imagined, aspirational, and recreated version of Gangnam. The meaning of Gangnam itself is not only transformed through spatial practices of people who live there, but also by the practices of imagining, aspiring, and representing the type of Gangnam deemed necessary for Gangnam-ization elsewhere. 'Gangnam-making' and 'Gangnam-following' are therefore mutually constitutive processes orienting Korean urbanization processes in a specific direction.

Korean cities today face a range of problems. Speculative urban development and rising rents are deepening the country's housing crisis, and the commodification of urban space means eviction and displacement for vulnerable urban dwellers. In this chapter, we use results from interview-based research to show how Gangnam-ization has contributed to these urban problems. On top of the idea that large-scale apartment complexes and new towns are ideal spaces for living, Gangnam-ization means that these living spaces are also objects for speculative gain and key sites through which social and cultural assets such as private education and social distinction can be procured and performed. In other words, Gangnam is shorthand for the Korean dream of upward mobility under Korean developmental capitalism. It is an instantiation of urban developmentalism that has helped to build a system of speculation-oriented urban development in Korea not only through apartment-ization, but also through the figuration of the Korean middle class as speculative consumers of real estate. Therefore, we hope that this chapter on Gangnam-ization contributes to the critical study of urban ideology and Korea's urban issues (see also chapters by Hae and Shin and Kim, this volume), and, by extension, can help to carve out political alternatives for the future.

2   What is a City?

Scholars have traditionally understood cities based on the premise of a dichotomy between the urban and the rural. Urban ecologists from the Chicago school such as Louis Wirth, and other early 20th century social scientists such as Ferdinand Tönnies, Emile Durkheim, Georg Simmel, profoundly shaped scholarly thinking about urban space by contrasting the rural and the urban in social and cultural terms. Recently, however, scholars have questioned this divide. Brenner and Schmid (2014: 747), for example, argue that urbanization has become a planetary phenomenon, not only in city centers but also in urban peripheries and in semi-urban areas. They argue that the epistemology of the urban-rural dichotomy is losing its logical ground. Their criticisms have been inspired in part by Henri Lefebvre's concept of planetary urbanization. According to Schmid (2012: 45), while traditional urban theories based on the West regarded the city as a clearly discernible social object and a spatial unit that provided for a particular way of life, Lefebvre conceived of the city in a more fluid way. Focusing on urbanization processes rather than its forms, and studying these processes over long durations of time, he theorized urbanization as a spatial extension of capitalist industrialization.

Lefebvre emphasized that urbanization and industrialization are an inseparable, interconnected process. According to Lefebvre, the process of industrialization signaled an expansion of industrial logic to the overall society. Consequently, industrialization and urbanization became entangled with each other in mutually constitutive, but also contradictory ways (Schmid 2012, 46). Industrial production sparked the urbanization of society. And, as the city grew, it in turn created the conditions for more industrialization. Industrial contradictions became urban contradictions (Merrifield, 2013: 911). Colonized by industrial capitalist logics, both the traditional city and the countryside underwent fundamental transformations. For Lefebvre (2013), the process of planetary urbanization was an effect of the gradual, deepening process of capitalist development. Planetary urbanization is marked by spreading out and blurring of boundaries of the traditional city, which was previously a regional center and space of concentrated living. The durable, concrete city stopped existing as a material object and became a flexible entity. For Lefebvre (2013), "urban society" emerged out of the ruins of the traditional city, which no longer exists as a social object, but as a relic. For Lefebvre, the idea that the city retained its social meaning is a kind of falsehood. Following this line of thought, indeed, what is a city? Or is the concept of the city no longer even valid?

3   City as Ideology

Even as scholars raise the theoretical question of whether the city actually exists as a social object, or if we even need the city as a concept, popular usage of the term 'city' indicates it still carries some relevance. For example, media, government reports, and textbooks deploy the terms 'world city', 'innovation city', 'creative city', and 'smart city'. Lefebvre (2003: 57) argued that although it is correct to say that the city is no longer a distinct social object, it nonetheless has a historical existence that cannot be ignored. As historical, or traditional, cities started to disappear—colonized and subsumed by the logics of the industrial city—the historical memory of traditional Western cities continued to serve as a basis upon which a number of small cities were imagined and constructed, generating its own set of ideologies for urbanist projects (Lefebvre, 2003: 57). In this sense, the city does not only exist as a material object, but it lives on as a social object shaped by ideologies.

Building on Lefebvre, Wachsmuth (2013) has suggested that the city should be viewed as an ideology. According to Wachsmuth (2013: 4), uncovering the complex processes of urbanization requires moving beyond analyzing the experience of city spaces. What we experience in the city is the manifestation of a totality, but we cannot grasp the processes that come together to shape this totality through an examination of immediate experience alone. Studying representations—viewing the city as a "thought object" rather than as a "real object" (Wachsmuth 2013: 4)—is one way of bringing the seemingly intractable complexities of a social reality into the realm of conceivability. In this way, Wachsmuth (2013: 3–4) proposes putting the city into a "category of practice", not into a "category of analysis." While the use of the city as a category of analysis would presume that the city exists as an objective reality whose ontological characteristics could be explained and analyzed, the use of a practice-based approach would problematize this presumption. Planetary urbanization refuses the idea of the city as an objective reality. According to Wachsmuth (2013: 13), the concept of the 'city' continues to survive and thrive because it circulates through ideological practices. In this sense, the term 'city' is not a neutral description, but an ideological term that favors the interests of certain social forces and groups.

Wachsmuth provides several examples of how the city works as an ideology, including the ideological divide between the urban and the rural mentioned above. The city-country opposition has manifested itself through 1) the spatial division of industry and agricultural spaces, starting with enclosures; 2) a hypothesis that 'the urban' is a spatial container for society and 'the rural' is a spatial container for nature; and 3) the generation of images that show contrasting modes of life in the city and in the countryside. Even though the impacts of this dualistic thinking at the theoretical level have been weakened with the increasing complexity of urban processes, dichotomous ways of understanding the city persist, mainly due to their ideological functions. According to Wachsmuth (2013: 7–8), for example, American public perceptions of cities and suburbs tend to locate the rural at one end and the city at the other end of a dichotomous framing. This framing is historically informed by the American experience of suburbanization, in which public discourses promoted intense housing development as "escape from the city, the icon of sin" and the "re-claiming of traditional countryside values" (Wachsmuth 2013: 8). At the same time, the city center development projects that triggered gentrification place an ideological emphasis on high-tech urban life. These are two examples of how the ideological urban-rural divide circulates as a strategy and system of power for capital accumulation.

As the above examples indicate, the city is not simply a category of analysis, a fixed object available for objective explanation. Rather, as an expression of ideology representing particular interests and power structures, it is a category of practice. The ideological nature of the city, however, functions in relation to different conditions and places. Abstract, academic theories of the world city and the creative city, for example, are rooted within certain epistemological communities that allow ideologies to circulate on a global scale. At the same time, other urban ideologies dominate individual states, societies, or localities. The detached homes, well kempt lawns, and daily commutes of those residing in American suburbs are a case in point. The well-managed high-rise apart-ments of Korea's new towns are another.

Diverse, concrete spaces give rise to a diversity of ways for urban ideologies to manifest. First, ruling elites at the local and national levels can produce and reproduce certain discourses and images—an urban landmark; a narrative of urban history; the economic and political identity of a city—in order to serve either their own interests or the interests of a larger hegemonic power structure. Urban ideologies are also reproduced through the common sense understand-ings of ordinary people in everyday space. The ideology of urban elites and the ideology of ordinary people work together to produce a particular idea of common sense, which is in fact a hegemonic urban ideology: a prevalent way of understanding society, acquiring knowledge, participating in discourse, and feeling emotion. This ideology influences the preferences, desires, and value systems of a city's inhabitants. It also helps to shape the feel of the city along with its spatial forms, which in turn play a pivotal role in sustaining a preexisting capitalist political, economic, and cultural order and the hegemony of the state.

4   Gangnam and Korean Urban Ideology: 'Gangnam-making' and 'Gangnam-following'

How do we understand the city in the Korean context? And what ideological role do urban discourses play? This chapter seeks to understand Korea's urban ideology in relation to Gangnam as a symbolic place. Gangnam is at once a district of Seoul and a powerful urban discourse in Korea. As mentioned above, modern urbanization processes in Korea are marked by high-rise apartment buildings and new town developments. Korea's urbanization is also marked by a set of ideologies distinct from the West, including, in particular, middle class preference for apartment living and new towns. Certain ideal images and aspirations of urban life project themselves through this image. In contrasting Korean housing preferences to Western preferences, it is clear that housing preferences are *socially* produced. In-depth analysis of Gangnam can thus provide a crucial clue to understanding Korea's urban ideology. Gangnam, with its signature high-rise apartment complexes, has a symbolic status as Korea's emblematic 'new town.' The district is an important case for understanding how the accumulation of property assets came to be seen as the key to upward middle-class mobility for many people. Although Gangnam's housing prices and consumer culture surpass what average Seoullites can afford, in popular discourse Gangnam is still described as a space for the urban middle class. This disconnect stems from the historical relationship between how notions of urban life and property accumulation in Gangnam have shaped middle class desires.

In light of the issues and theoretical debates discussed above, this chapter thus aims to investigate the nature of modern Korean urbanization as it relates to the city as an ideology. Specifically, the research views Gangnam not just as a residential area in Seoul but as a dominant urban discourse through which we can make sense of the broader problem of Korean urban ideology. While *elite* ideological propagation is a particularly important issue in Korea given that the state has initiated new town projects and attempted to associate them with modern urban life in general as part of the urbanization of developmentalist ideology, this chapter mainly focuses on the formation of urban ideology by the people who are the principle *consumers* of urban space—how they shape and share their knowledge, discourse, and sensibility of the city.[2] To this end, we conducted life history interviews with urban residents in three particularly 'Gangnam-ized' areas: Gangnam of Seoul, Haeundae of Busan, and Bundang of

---

2 Using a snowballing method, we interviewed six Gangnam residents; seven Haeundae residents; eight Bundang residents; and one resident of Yongin in Gyeonggi Province between July 2015 and January 2016. Eighteen of the participants were women, while four of them were men. This imbalance reflects strong female influence within families on housing migration choice. Residents in their 50s comprised the largest age-range group, reflecting the baby boomer generation's position as core participants of urban middle class formation processes. Our interview questions were created in such a way that the interviewees' feelings and desires would be the focal point of our discussions.

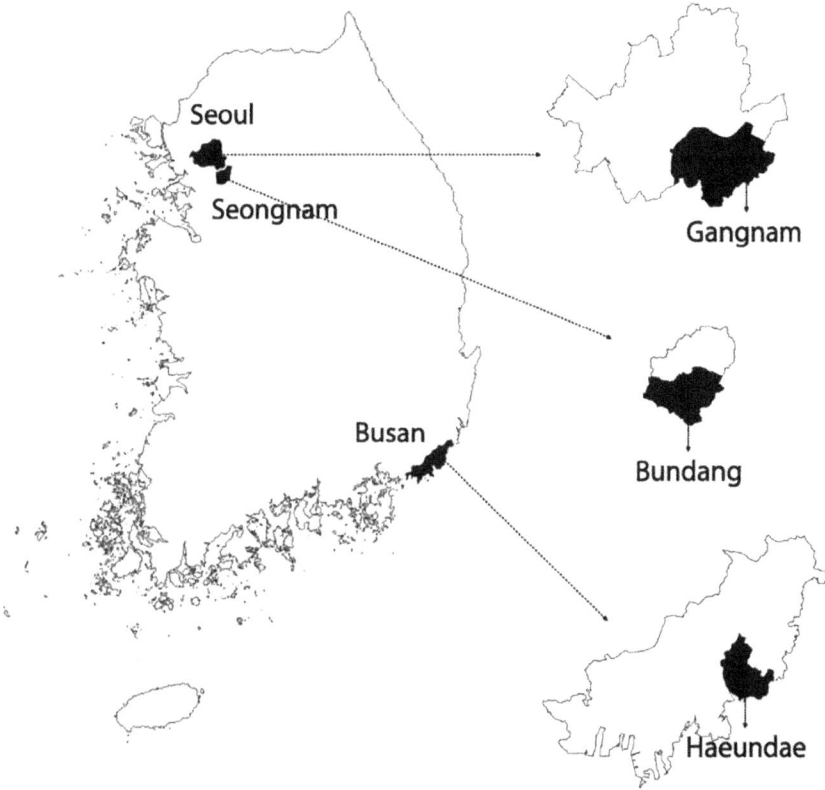

FIGURE 7.1   Locations of Gangnam, Bundang and Haeundae
SOURCE: DRAWN BY YOONAI HAN UNDER THE SUPPORT FROM THE AUTHORS.

Seongnam (see Figure 7.1).[3] In what follows, we examine their own representations of Gangnam as both a physical space and an imaginary.

5   The Representation of Gangnam as an Ideal New Town

1)   *A Well-ordered Space*

In interviews, respondents commonly referred to Gangnam as a well-ordered space. For them, a well-ordered space was defined by long, straight roads (in contrast to curved roads); planned spaces (in contrast to unplanned spaces); and highly visible and tidy streets (in contrast to disorderly streets). These

---

3   Bundang is an administrative unit in Seongnam, as Haeundae is in Busan or as Gangnam is
   in Seoul. One characteristic shared in common by Gangnam, Haeundae, and Bundang is the
   concentration of high-rise apartment complex, the ideal destination for local middle class.

aspects of well-ordered space are accompanied by value judgments that lead to a preference for a Gangnam-style landscape. For example, one interviewee living in Gangnam since the 1990s pointed out that Gangnam's well-ordered spaces seem to correlate with a certain attitude of its residents:

> Actually when I walk the streets of Junggye-dong [in northern Seoul] and Daechi-dong [in Gangnam], I can feel the difference.[4] Like when I visited Bucheon in the Gyeonggi province, it almost felt like China. (...) In Gangnam's case, all the roads are straight and paved straightforward, and the bus stations are neat and tidy, just like the roadside trees are, and also the signboards. (...) designed in the same color. (...) clearly. Think about the fonts on the signboards—they are tidy. And what students wear is so different. (...) they don't stick out. Even though they wear designer brands in Gangnam, it doesn't look too tacky. It actually all goes together really well. But why on earth do kids in Junggye-dong or Bucheon wear that kitschy make-up, that lipstick, with their school uniforms altered on purpose—I mean, in a ridiculous way? Even the way they wear backpacks is different. On their backs, their backpacks are so tightly hanging, right in the middle [laughs]. Those are the differences. And what else? (...) On top of that, it's about the people in Gangnam. I might be biased, but it seems to me that they are all very well ordered even without needing to dress up.
>
> Interview, female Gangnam resident in her 50s, September 2015

Interviewees living in Bundang and Haeundae expressed an almost identical preference for 'well-ordered space'. One interviewee who lived in an older new town development in the city of Seongnam, called Jungwon-gu, later moved to Bundang, another new town development in Seongnam in the early 2000s. Comparing the two developments, she noted that they have a "big gap in terms of their [building] heights." While to her Jungwon-gu was "extremely dense" and gave her "a feeling of instability," Bundang was "organized", "everything you need in life is set up", with an "urban feeling", "calm" and "providing for a relaxed mindset". One interviewee whose migration history includes Busan, Masan (South Gyeongsang Province), Bucheon (Gyeonggi Province), and Mapo-gu and Gwanak-gu of Seoul, described how Centum City in Haeundae felt distinct from other places "across the river" where there was not even anywhere to park. "The whole city", she said, was built "in the middle of nowhere". To her,

---

4 Daechi-dong is a sub-administrative unit of Gangnam-gu, Seoul. The reputation of Daechi-dong for its top quality private education constantly attracts middle class family, despite its relatively outskirt location in Gangnam.

the city fit into the ideal of a "uniform", "clean", and "good-looking" urbanized, [and] with segmented, divided spaces. Using similar language, a number of interviewees repeated a similar preference for "well-ordered space" that they identified as a Gangnam-style landscape.

Two interviewees who shared the same migration history of moving from an older section of Seongnam to the new town of Bundang also used the term 'segmented' (*kongganchok bunwha,* which also translates as *spatially differentiated*) to explain what they meant by well-ordered space. Explaining further, they both related this impression to concerns about safety:

> Residential areas [in Seongnam] are a little different. (...) When my kids would drop by my shop before going home after school, the footpath was like, not too long. (...) It was an unclean area. It was a place where adults would come to hang out—bars, cinemas, places with girls, if you know what I mean. Just not suitable for kids. (...) Compared to Bundang, it was not the best in terms of educational environment. Even the school zone had a line of motels right across the street.
>
> Interview, Bundang resident in her 50s, December 2015

Another interviewee in Busan used nearly identical language in comparing Marine City and Centum City.

> Centum City is different from Marine City. (...) Marine City was good for nightlife, but not so much for residential life. Here, we just have apartments, schools, and offices, and some IT industry. (...) For nightlife we just have restaurants, not, like, adult bars. That's actually what we like the most about where we're living now. (...) Actually that's why I decided to move here in the first place. I was thinking about the issue of safety. When my kids walk to and from school, they are really safe. (...)
>
> Interview, Haeundae resident in her 40s, September 2015

For these respondents, well-ordered space is where spaces with different uses, for example a residential area and a night life area are not intermixed. They are adequately segmented, and segmented space means safe space. In other words, the intermixing of spaces with different functions sparks feelings of unease and uncleanness among interviewees. The above interview from the Bundang resident clearly expressed these connections. Her use of the term "unclean" echoes anthropologist Mary Douglas' (1966) observation that "dirt is matter out of place". This leads us to the conclusion that the most important dimension of the Gangnam-style landscape and its associated new town projects would be the existence of public and private powers that enable planned calculation, regulation, and the management of order and population, and their proper functioning as order, segmentation, and safety.

2)   *A Self-sufficient World of High-end Apartment Complexes*

Another key characteristic of the Gangnam-style city landscape as represented by those who have lived in Gangnam is the notion of a self-sufficient world of large, high-end apartments clustered in large complexes. Two interviewees who lived in Apgujeong-dong and Garak-dong, both of which are in Gangnam, in late 1980s and mid 1990s conveyed their impressions of those places:

> In the end, it was all about accessibility. (…) Unlike a detached house, an apartment complex had everything right there. (…) My apartment complex had a department store right out front. (…) It was very convenient. Anyway, I liked it a lot that I could get anything I needed in the complex, whenever I wanted. (…) I could go to the gym there to exercise, for example. What used to be a hassle had become so easy there.
>
> Interview, Bundang resident in her 50s, January 2016

> When I lived in the Olympic Family apartment complex. (…) [The number of apartment units] was astonishing. (…) There were a lot of shops as well. So imagine, the complex has huge buildings filled with shops and there are also so many little shops here and there. Those little shops were all quite unique. For example, this one was good for one thing, and another one had really nice stir-fried rice cakes, another one delicious fresh juice. They all had distinct characters of their own. That's what the shops in the complex were like.
>
> Interview, Bundang resident in her 40s, January 2016

To summarize, a self-sufficient world manifests not only with the "department store right in front", but also with unique shops in and around the complex. This new, high-end urban space, which was invented in Gangnam, became the key component of Gangnam and its copies in new towns built afterwards.

For instance, one interviewee who moved from Haeundae New Town apartment to Centum City of Busan,[5] followed by another who is currently living in Marine City, said the following:

---

5   Three major new towns in Busan are mentioned by the interviewees. Haeundae New Town, built in the late 1990s, was the prototype Gangnam-style apartment complex. When Centum City was constructed in the early to mid 2000s, sections of Haeundae New Town's population

Well, Centum Park—I had regretted it at the beginning. And the [Haeun-dae] new town as well, it was basically vacant land at the beginning (...) they said it's not livable land, and the land is so muddy. But in the end it turned out to be no more than a rumor (...). Having lived there, after all (...), everything was possible. The environment was created, I mean the new town was created. It is located at a far end of Busan, you see. So it takes quite some time to come from the main part of town, to get to other places. (...) But inside, the town was born to have everything I needed: markets, and private education for kids, and whatever else.

Interview, Haeundae resident in her 40s, September 2015

What I liked about it here is that it's nice to spend time here during the day. We have a swimming pool in front of the house. And on top of the swimming pool, the first ice skating rink in Busan came right here, right beside the apartment. Not to speak of the good kindergarten and the schools nearby (...) They are located in the apartment complex itself, for example really nice kindergartens are there, just across the street. (...) I mean the living condition is just perfect. Also the shops here are quite well equipped. This is what is nice and convenient about living here.

Interview, Haeundae resident in her 50s, December 2015

One of the critical mechanisms that made large, high-end apartment complexes (*danji*) seem like self-sufficient worlds is their economies of scale. The demand-side of these economies of scale is elaborated in the following statement made by one interviewee who moved from Ilwon-dong, Gangnam-gu to Dogok-dong, Gangnam-gu to send her kid to an English-speaking kindergarten in the early 2000s:

The difference is the scale of the demand. Because Ilwon-dong is quite far from the kindergartens we like, if my kid was not that young, I would have just taken my kid to and from the shuttle bus. But he is so young. In Dogok-dong, there are heaps of apartments, and all the mothers gather there. (...) It's all apartments. The four famous ones are all located in Do-gok-dong and Gaepo-dong, because there are just so many kids around there.

Interview, Bundang resident in the age of the 50s, female, January 2016

---

migrated to Centum City. Marine City is the latest high-end apartment complex built in mid 2000s, absorbing a part of its population from Centum City and Haeundae New Town.

In other words, the large, high-end apartment complex (*danji*), the unit of which was invented in Gangnam and exported to other new towns, became the physical basis for large-scale and high-end complexes elsewhere. In turn, these demand-led economies of scale helped to generate the so-called self-sufficient world. As is evident from the interview excerpts above, the Korean urban middle class is attracted to large-scale, high-end apartment complexes, not only because of the convenience to residents of easily obtaining what they need, but also because of the spatial exceptionality that makes the urban life they had dreamed become a reality without the need to interact with anyone outside the apartment complex. If they can afford to live inside the exceptional space of the self-sufficient high-end apartment complex, residents are less subject to political, social, economic, and cultural conditions outside. We can conclude that the spatial exceptionality provided by apartment complexes, the self-sufficient world prepared just for the urban middle class, and a reliance on property exchange value have directed the urban middle-class toward the desire for private profit maximization over common development or maturing of the general society.

3)   Old *New Towns and* New *New Towns*

One of the most dominant representations of Gangnam is that it is the first 'new town' in Korea. In this representation, Gangnam is a metonym for a new, modern life and an urban landscape with neatly ordered boulevards, skyscrapers, and colossal apartment complexes with all the trappings of modern living. Paradoxically, this very representation of Gangnam can provoke people to desire a more-Gangnam-than-Gangnam environment. One self-proclaimed "Gangnam kid" who came to Gangnam in the 1970s and moved to Bundang with his family in 2000 explained his changing feelings toward Gangnam:

> When I took the subway at Gangnam station, it was really clean, and there were not that many people. (...) I could even lie down on the green seats of Line 2 on the subway. (...) Then it started to change. (...) I would think that the train symbolized my sense of the clean new city at that time. Yet that shiny, tidy feeling faded away. After time, when I commuted to my university, the subway conditions got really bad. Getting on and off of the subway felt difficult. Taking the subway was fun when I was in 3rd or 4th grade. (...) it was clean, there weren't many people, and everything was nice. And twenty or twenty-five years passed. Now the subway feels dirty as hell. The green seats from when I was young used to smell like a new sofa, and now it smells filthy ... For me that's how Gangnam is. (...)

> People started to move to Bundang and Ilsan.(...) Bundang felt somewhat cleaner, and the living conditions seemed way better, and even somewhat hip. (...) [In Gangnam] it felt older and older. So it made me think, like, Bundang will be the new Gangnam, you know? And Gangnam might soon be the new Gangbuk, degraded long ago. (...) People we knew also moved [to Bundang]. (...) So we moved, thinking, like, we are finally going to become actual new town citizens, you know? That's how it is. (...) That said, I was actually dreaming of living a more laid-back, easy-going style of life, but (...) Bundang was actually not the case, it was a sheer fantasy. (...) In the end, Bundang was another city anyway. Maybe one difference was that there were enough parking lots at the beginning, but now, even finding parking has become tough, and illegal parking is fined right away.
>
> Interview, Bundang resident in his 40s, August 2015

All new things get old, and Gangnam, the first new town, is no exception. If the source of Gangnam's aspirational pull lies in its status as a 'new' town, it sounds natural that the representation of Bundang as the cleaner, more relaxed, new Gangnam provoked a certain degree of disgust for Gangnam and perpetuates desires for a new-new town. The "relaxed, laid-back" image of the new-new town, however, is indeed a "fantasy", as cited in the above interview. Nevertheless, whether it is fantasy or not does not change the fact itself that this representation is now a powerful emotional propagator of new town, new-new town, and new-new-new town development (e.g. replications of Bundang, itself a replication of Gangnam). It is confirmed by the following responses of two interviewees, one of who migrated to what at the time was the most luxurious apartment in Busan (a new-new town), and recently to Marine City (a new-new-new town), and another who shows a similar migration trajectory.

> I used to live in a large complex (...) As far as I know, it was the biggest apartment complex in the country that time. The complex had 7,800 units. (...) Having lived there for 18 years, we felt the house was getting quite old. And we had to fix it up a bit. We chose what we liked best when we originally got the place, but later we began to feel pulled by better ones. (...) So the people living in this part of the city moved to that better one, like the German migrations of late antiquity. I also followed them, and moved to a bigger and newer unit. (...)
>
> Interview, Haeundae resident in her 50s, December 2015

Then they constructed Centum Park. It was the first apartment of that height in Busan at that time. In 2006, a fifty-something-floor apartment was quite something, you know? So the stereotypical strategy would be to have lived here first and then to move there. Busan residents would move from Haeundae New Town to Centum Park, and then again to Marine City [laughs]. That's what people do, and that's what I did. I moved to I Park[6] in Marine City.

Interview, Haeundae resident in her 60s, December 2015

6   Gangnam "Rejuvenated" and Gangnam as "the National Forefront"

As examined in above interviewees' representations of Gangnam, it works as an archetypical reference point for urban ideology. The representation of Gangnam as the embodiment of the new town itself, however, can lead to a disgust for Gangnam itself, when the desire for Gangnam-ized lifestyle is transplanted to other new towns. In other words, as described above, the desire for a Gangnam life can cause a 'Great German Migration' from Gangnam to emerging new-new towns. In reality, however, this is not exactly what has happened: Gangnam itself began to undergo a "rejuvenation" (as termed by a Bundang resident, who used to live in Gangnam), bringing back population and capital to Gangnam after the 2000s. The "rejuvenation" of Gangnam is not explainable by the idea that Gangnam is the ideal new town. What, then, can offer a sufficient explanation for the "rejuvenation" of Gangnam?

1)   *Representations of Gangnam as Korea's Economic Center*
In order to understand Gangnam's rejuvenation, we need to note the different ways in which interviewees discuss the landmarks of where they live. When referring to Gangnam, they mostly brought up landmarks of economic importance, namely, "Trade Center at Samseong Station", "Kyobo Tower", and "Tehran Street" (one of the biggest clusters of IT industries, venture capitals, and financial activities in Korea). Regarding new town cities other than Gangnam, they referred mostly to green spaces and to spaces of consumption: parks, department stores, shopping centers, high-rise apartments, branded coffee

---

6   'I Park' is the name of an apartment in Marine City, Busan. When its price peaked, it competed with the top five expensive apartments in Seoul, demonstrating its popularity among the middle class population, given that there have been almost no competing apartments built outside Seoul.

shops, and so on. In sum, they represent Gangnam as a space of economic significance, which cannot be conveniently reduced to, or identified with average residential towns or more strictly residential spaces.

> The Trade Center near Samseong Station is (...) tall. (...) But, more importantly, I believe, it is the backbone of the Korean economy. (...) It hosts all the important conferences and meetings year round. So for me, practically that is the center of Gangnam and of Korea, in terms of trade and economy. (...) KEPCO [Korea Electric Power Corporation] will soon build some hundred-story building there. So it will only be growing bigger. It is certainly the most powerful economic engine of the country.
>
> Interview, Gangnam resident in his 70s, July 2015.

These representations by the interviewee, who came to Gangnam in 1978, imply that as long as the Trade Center is the "backbone of Koran economy" with large firms and industries moving in, Gangnam will be where the center is located. It "will only prosper". The expectation for Gangnam to "grow bigger" produces a strong emotional power to "rejuvenate" Gangnam.

2)   *Representations of Gangnam as "the National Forefront"*

We can trace the irreducible "gap" between Gangnam and other new towns by looking at private education opportunities. One interviewee who moved from Ilwon-dong to Dogok-dong,[7] and whose children studied at private academies in Gangnam even when her family was living in Bundang, said that while Bundang only serves Bundang, Gangnam serves all of Korea:

> My kid was talented in math and science, so I wanted to give her more opportunities. But in Bundang, there weren't many things I could do for her. (...) When I lived in Bundang. (...) it was not easy to gather talented kids together. Instead, they all gathered in Gangnam, especially in Daechi-dong, from everywhere across the river and so on. I had no choice but to go there, because there wasn't enough demand for private education for talented kids. All the top private academies were in Gangnam. Even when the same teachers come to teach in Bundang, the quality of their lectures is different. (...) Like I said before, Gangnam serves all of Korea,

---

7   Both Ilwon-dong and Dogok-dong are located in Gangnam, but Ilwon-dong is on the outskirts of Gangnam, far from the clusters of private education services.

and Bundang is for just Bundang. (...) I mean, Gangnam is the place
where the really good ones go. (...) It is specialized.

Interview, Bundang resident in her 50s, January 2016

Two interviewees from Marine City, Busan, also said they have actually witnessed parents sending their kids to Daechi-dong, Gangnam, during vaca-
tions.[8] An interviewee from Centum City, Busan, noted in interviews that there
was "an enormous gap" between Gangnam and her current residence "in an educational sense", which often made her want to "move to a city with abundant
private education opportunities". Together, these representations help us detect a kind of core-periphery structure in the private education market. In the
structure, Gangnam functions as an invincible core with economies of scale,
generated by a large number of middle class families living in apartment complexes where distinctly "specialized" private education products are available.
Human and material resource concentration at such a scale, in turn, makes the
core even stronger.

Indications of a core-periphery structure within the private education
market bolsters the representation that the unique opportunities given in
Gangnam, the "heart of Korea", cannot be replaced by anything else. This representation, we can conclude, has made those living in other new towns outside Gangnam constantly yearn for the life style in Gangnam. The material and
symbolic relationship between Gangnam and other cities is extended fluidly
over the geographic boundary and rendered solid by the representation examined above. In sum, the representation of "Gangnam, the national forefront"
became another key dimension of the drive to "rejuvenate" Gangnam.

7   The City as Property and Gangnam as "Worry-free Stock"

The representation of Gangnam as an economic core, and as a space of rejuvenation, in turn, are linked to the ideas of Gangnam as exchange value, or
Gangnam as asset, which have their own force as representations. In the following interview with a resident who arrived in the 1980s and purchased an
apartment in the 2000s, the respondent refers to Gangnam as "a worry free,
steady-selling stock":

It was my stubborn idea to buy an apartment in Gangnam. (...) My parents and my wife's parents did not agree. (...) They did not understand

---

8   It takes about 3-hour train ride from Marine City, Busan to Daechi-dong, Gangnam.

why on earth I wanted to buy something Gangnam at the very time when the price was peaking, because with that same budget, we could have actually gone somewhere else and lived in a much bigger apartment. (...) But I was stubborn and bought it anyway. (...) I was into the stock market back then because of my work. You have probably heard of the stocks that are strong, promising ones, steady-sellers that never go down. They never fall, but when they do, it means the whole market is declining. They are the worry-free stocks, so to speak. So, I made this analogy between the apartment market and the stock market. Gangnam is the worry-free one that never fails. I would not be able to afford the price with my own budget though. So I thought carefully, discussed it with my wife, and decided to buy. Our calculation was, like, buy first, tighten our belt, and if it seems like it isn't working, we'll resell it. It was a sort of adventure and a wild investment for us. It was still not easy to afford. We bought it with our parents' help and using our life savings. We had hard time meeting the payment. (...) We took out loans.

Interview, Gangnam resident in his 40s, July 2015

That they chose to buy the apartment in Gangnam despite the fact that they had other options to live in a bigger apartment elsewhere within the same budget, and the fact that they also faced parental disagreement, implies that use value or the living condition itself was not their biggest concern. The interviewee represented the housing market as analogous with the stock market, and viewed housing from an investment perspective. Most of all, we can imply that he made an economically rational decision. With their parents' help, he and his wife cautiously invested all their savings and took out loans to purchase worry-free stock.

Another interviewee from Bundang articulated a similar view of residential property as analogous to the purchase of stock.

I mean Gangnam and Bundang are the promising stocks. Even with the economy in recovery, and with apartment prices doubling elsewhere, those in Gangnam increase by three times. So that is quite a difference. (...) One would certainly invest [in Gangnam] if given a choice. I would also choose to do so, if I wanted to own a property for profit. If I imagine myself becoming a millionaire, and buying valuable buildings, I would definitely go for Gangnam, which sounds contradictory, considering that I would not actually choose to live there.

Interview, Bundang resident in his 40s, August 2015

Among the above two interviews, the interviewee from Gangnam prioritized exchange value compared to use value. But his property choices for residential purpose and investment purpose all rested in Gangnam, anyway. In contrast to the former, the latter interviewee clearly differentiated where to live from where to buy. In other words, for him, "rejuvenated Gangnam" would be an attractive, steady investment option, in terms of its exchange value. However, in considering its use value, he would not choose to live there. Thus, he is self-aware in his own contradictory view of Gangnam.

Interviewees in other new towns expressed similar contradictions. One interviewee from Bundang, who moved from an apartment in Bundang to a detached house, reported the following:

> Now living in a detached house, every time we walk into our house, we asked ourselves, 'how could we live in such a dense place? Doesn't that look like a series of matchboxes sitting in line?' There are so many people living in one block of apartments, going up and down on every floor. We realized this only (…) after we moved into a detached house. (…) But actually now, I would prefer moving back to apartment if I could. (…) Detached houses and villas [multi-unit low-rise buildings] are not easy to resell. We did not have to wait too long to find the next person who wanted to buy our property when we were in an apartment. (…) But once we began to own a detached house, it was not that easy. (…) If I only had to take into consideration the living conditions, I would prefer to live in this kind of detached house. But in reality, I prefer to live in apartment for its exchangeability.
>
> Interview, Bundang resident in her 50s, January 2016

From the above interview, we can imply that this resident prioritized exchange value over use value in her choice of residence. She sharply contrasted the value of a detached house or villa with that of apartment based on their different degrees of exchangeability.

We aim to understand how the interviewees, most of who belong to the urban middle class, tend to frame their housing, and the city in general, not only in terms of use value but also in terms of exchange value. Common sense understandings of Gangnam as "steady-selling stock" is connected to a set of deep emotions and aspirations for the urban middle class. Driven by emotional forces, the urban middle class is attracted to Gangnam and other promising new towns. As a result, new town property values increase, centering on Gangnam. One interviewee shared her satisfaction with her property investment in Gangnam and other new towns:

So, when I was buying the apartment [in Gangnam for my son], I thought it was not big enough as he already had two kids. (...) My son said his colleagues were surprised or quite jealous of how he could afford to have two kids and an apartment. He told me, at his age, it is not that common or easy to own a house right after getting married. (...) Still, I worried that his apartment was too small, but he was sort of proud of his set-up, which was much better than his peers. He told me that friends, and even some of his senior colleagues, could not even get married because of housing issues.

Interview, Resident of Yongin[9] in her 70s, August 2015

In this case, the resident owned and invested in multiple properties, which contrasts with other cases in which residents could only afford one property. For them, awareness of cases of multiple property ownership could provoke feelings of frustration and the sense that there is a barrier to entry for certain property markets. In addition to feeling a sense of relative deprivation, they felt they could one day be displaced from the city and its social and cultural networks:

The [recent] redevelopment gave a whole new life to Gangnam. Watching that, I could not help but think about how the barriers for entry seem higher and stronger than before. It's true, it is hard for me to sell my Bundang apartment and afford one in Gangnam. It has already become quite a fortress.

Interview, Bundang resident in his 40s, August 2015

Times have changed. Men used to be able to afford to get married, make a living, and buy a house. But recently it seems like that is no longer the case. (...) In my opinion, I thought my kid would be able to do the same [as we did]. (...) But the housing prices, and the rises in rent, have been extreme. (...) That is the difference between those who are the haves and those who are the have-nots. (...) In my case, I wasn't wealthy, so I am just not used to the idea of handing down an apartment to the next generation. I found that my neighbors in Bundang thought differently. (...) If their kids face barriers to marriage due to housing costs, they will just buy housing for their kids. I would also like to be able to do the same thing.

---

9   Yongin is a city in Gyeonggi Province, adjacent to Bundang.

I do want my kids to be able to make their own way, to make a good living. At the same time, it is kind of sad and embarrassing to talk about that, because there are so many parents who can simply afford to help their kids out. (...) This situation creates a dilemma for me, because on the one hand I should do everything I can for my kids, but on the other, I wonder, what if I give everything away to them and I become a miserable mom? (...) I could fall out of the middle class and become poor. (...) There are so many rich people around here these days, and I wouldn't dare to say I'm really one of them—maybe I'm just not poor. I don't receive any kind of government help, but I'm not really middle class. There are too many rich people around. That's why I felt relatively deprived when I was living in Bundang, because it was a new town full of rich people.

Interview, Resident of Jungwon-gu in Seongnam in her 50s, January 2016

In addition, interviewees also expressed the sentiment that older new towns such as Gangnam and Bundang had transformed from being a space for the urban middle class to a space for the urban upper class, thereby changing the social status of those living in new towns from one's own merit and achievement to an ascriptive, or inherited one, obtainable only by 'gold spoon'[10] inheritance.

So, young people living in both Bundang and Gangnam, in most cases they obviously inherited what they have from their parents. I've got the impression that such populations are growing even bigger. (...) Growing bigger in Bundang, too. Apparently, young people cannot afford to live there by themselves. (...) Most young people begin with their parents' support. I recently noticed that there were a lot of young people like that. (...) Here in Bundang, we could get in because we won a kind of [government-sponsored] lottery to be able to purchase an affordable home, so we could move in at low price at that time. (...) We often imagine we will be the last generation as we cannot hand over our own apartments to our kids. (...) Before, new towns were good because they were affordable. But now it is fortified, after just one generation. After the first generation, new towns will no longer be places where the have-nots can move in without support from older generations.

Interview, Bundang resident in her 50s, January 2016

10 The expression 'gold spoon' emerged in mid-2010s in Korean society as a critique of a society in which some inherited wealth while others remain in a state of relative deprivation.

> I thought that what Gangnam meant was that a person is not troubled by work, money, or time constraints. They could go to a hotel to take a rest every weekend. I thought that was what Gangnam people did. Gangnam was a winner's badge. But in my case, I lived in Gangnam for a long time but I struggled to catch up with others. (...) Those currently coming in, they already have their wealth in front of them, not like the old days when we could come into Gangnam on a tight budget. (...) Even the smallest apartment in Gangnam has a huge rental deposit [*jeonsae*], like four million won [around US $400,000]. Whether they're young or old, those coming into Gangnam are already set up with their wealth.
>
> Interview, Gangnam resident in her 50s, September 2015

This interview captures a key paradox of the Korean middle class. Being middle class meant living in the city, becoming its owner; yet just as they acted upon on their desires and reached their achievement, they faced displacement. This shows how the urban middle class, acting on the logic of "steady-selling stock", and treating the city as an asset, would finally reach its dead-end.

8   Summary of Interviews and Theoretical Implications

Based on the interviews collected by our research team, the self-understanding of the Korean middle class can be summarized with three observations. First, middle class residents convey Gangnam as an ideal new town, and express a preference for the way of living it makes possible. They reference Gangnam as an archetypal well-ordered space and a high-end big apartment complex, an ideal urban landscape. They express strong preferences for the self-sufficient world of the high-end, large-scale apartment complex and see its spatial exceptionality as creating the conditions for the kind of life they had dreamed of, without any need to related to people living outside of their fortress. This idea became an archetype, and spread out of Gangnam into other new town developments. Second, in the way it is imagined, Gangnam occupies the top position in the country's urban hierarchy, or a central position in a core-periphery arrangement. This hierarchy bleeds out into a series of stratifications. While people who do not live in Gangnam feel a sense of inferiority in relation to Gangnam, they may also feel a sense of superiority in relation to people living in other cities. The Korean middle class carries with it the Gangnam versus non-Gangnam distinction, embodying its grammar and reproducing the hierarchical differentiation of space on smaller and smaller scales. Third, the

Korean urban middle class's perceptions of housing and of the city are informed more by exchange value than use value. The logic of exchange value
alone is enough to situate Gangnam at the top of the new town hierarchy. Re-
fracting outward, fixation on exchange value yields a cycle of aspiration and
temptation for newer new towns while at the same time perpetuating anxieties of eventual displacement. This chain reproduces a set of powerful relations,
not only serving but also legitimizing the material interests of powerful actors. In reproducing speculative engagement with the housing market, and the
broad set of desires associated with housing, it serves the interest of property
owners and developers and justifies an overall developmentalist perspective
of the city. The space of the city is at once a commodity and also an emotion-
ally loaded space, as part of its appeal is the way in which it taps into peoples'
senses of hope, desire, pleasure, and sorrow.

   How the Korean middle class perceives cities not only shapes how Korean urbanization processes play out, but also serves to reproduce preexisting
orders of capitalism and the state. Based on strong authoritarian rule and
economic nationalism around the idea of 'modernization of the motherland'[11],
the Korean developmental state helped to spark rapid economic growth during the 1960s and 1970s. It promoted export-led industrialization on the basis of
intensive mobilization of capital and labor. However, deepening internal
contradictions brought political crisis to the developmental regime in the late
1960s and early 1970s. To overcome the crisis, the authoritarian regime announced the Yushin constitution[12] and strengthened its political repression
of opposition groups. The strengthening of authoritarian rule alone, however,
could not stifle the political crisis. The state thereby promoted multiple hegemonic projects to appease the opposition and to maintain political legitimacy.
Addressing complaints from underdeveloped provinces that grew in force
in the 1960s, the state began to pursue balanced regional development
from the 1970s onward, starting with its first Comprehensive National Development Plan.

   Gangnam's development can thus be understood as a hegemonic project. Its
construction was a state response to the contradictions caused by Seoul-centric

---

11   This slogan is political propaganda that was widely used by the Park Jung-Hee administra-
     tion as a way of mobilizing people for export-led industrialization.
12   Yushin constitution was declared by the authoritarian government of Korea in 1972. The
     major amendment made to the constitution was controversial, as it granted the President
     to remain in office for more than two terms.

state development policies, which drew populations into the Seoul Metropolitan Area and caused problems such as severe congestion and housing shortages. In order to mitigate these problems, and to bolster its own political legitimacy in a time of visible crisis, the state supported Gangnam's construction in the 1970s, thus drawing the population toward a peripheral part of the city. In this context, the development of Gangnam, the model new town, was a visible manifestation of the seemingly abstract slogan of 'modernizing motherland', successfully achieved not only by export-led industrialization but also by wide and straight boulevards, cutting-edge urban infrastructure, and high-rise modern apartment complexes. In short, Gangnam was a tangible signifier of successful economic development led by the state. Gangnam's ideological influence, however, went well beyond its geographical boundary to achieve a universal, symbolic image of the ideal city that the Korean urban middle class had imagined. Therefore, the ideological preference for Gangnam-style urban space was easily connected to supporting of the developmental project promoted by state and capital. New towns, including the late 1980s drive to construct two million houses within a matter of a few years, multiplied Gangnam-style urban space throughout the wider metropolitan area. Through this process, the urban middle class, who shared and internalized the Gangnam-ization ideology, grew bigger as well. In turn, tacit public support for Korean capitalism and the developmental state, symbolized by Gangnam-style urbanization, also spread out and was popularized.

In addition, through this process, the ideology of the Korean middle class and the Korean dream were realized. The key components of Korean dream, based on Gangnam, are 1) owing property and 2) a desire for property value increase. Apartment complex development in Gangnam produced a new urban middle class through property price increases. This experience was then repeated through new town construction processes throughout the metropolitan area. Property-based urban development turned the urban middle class into financialized subjects reliant on property value increase. Simultaneously, underdevelopment of social welfare obstructed other channels to enter into the middle class other than relying on property value increase, making the Korean urban middle class even more obsessed with property value. Growing urban middle class desire for property value increases thus meant internalization of a tendency to support political and economic systems that help protect property values. This historically-contructed path has been strengthening the state and capitalism's orientation toward constructionism and developmentalism in Korea.

9   Conclusion: Looking for an Alternative Urban Ideology

Urban ideology is not necessarily constructed by attempts to secure the interests of the state and capital and the existing power structure. Rather, it can be
produced through counter-hegemonic practices that resist the existing hegemonic order. As one example of an alternative urban ideology, Lefebvre and
Merrifield's suggestion to see a city as a place of encounter deserves our attention. In particular, Andy Merrifield (2013) largely accepts Lefebvre's criticism
of the urban-rural dichotomy, and further proposes to re-theorize the city by
focusing on 'the urban' rather than on the traditional concept of city. What
Merrifield suggests is a shift in focus from a 'city' as a fixed entity to 'the urban'
in order to understand the latter as a kind of living organism that is shaped
and energetically transformed by meetings and encounters with commodities,
capital, money, humans, and information in, and throughout city. Citing Lefebvre's (2003: 118) remark that "the signs of the urban are signs of assembly",
Merrifield (2013: 915), highlights the idea that the city does not create anything,
serve any purpose, or have any reality by itself, outside of exchanges, unions,
assemblies, mixtures, concentrations and encounters of humans. Following
Lefebvre (2003) and Merrifield (2013), the city brings together all beings, allowing for their simultaneous existence and encounter. Capital, resources, people,
information, activities, conflicts, and cooperation gather in this 'urban' context, generating changes to gathered subjects. That is to say, while the city is a
place for gathering and encounter, it is not a passive space, or a stage, where
the results of encounters are merely taken in. Urban proximity nurtures unexpected encounters and gives a sense of vibrancy, pivotal elements in defining
the urban. It is through these encounters that people produce urban spaces,
and paradoxically, become 'urban people'. The city is a living organism (Merrifield 2013).

   Considering the realities of the modern capitalist city, Merrifield's suggestion to view the city as a place for meeting and encounter may sound odd.
However if we only define a city by its capitalist urbanization logics, in which
urbanization is seen mainly as a spatial fix to the crisis of over-accumulation,
we would unintentionally internalize dominant, capital-centric understandings of the city. Reflecting on this, we can approach Merrified's suggestion as
an alternative ideological practice that seeks to overcome dominant urban discourses. Drawing on this idea, we can use it to recognize that specific groups'
attempts to monopolize surplus values by tearing down and privatizing urban
spaces have been an important barrier for the collective activities of people
meeting and encountering each other in cities, i.e. for their ability to generate

urban commons. The meaning of the city in this sense is best thought of as a place of encounters. In defining the city in this way, and in exercising an alternative ideological practice, Merrifield and Lefebvre provide a path forward for overcoming the blinding and disorienting effects of the appropriation, destruction, and privatization of urban common spaces.

This approach also holds potential for overcoming Gangnam-ization as the mainstream Korean urban ideology. If the preexisting urban system of Korea is the structural source of urban problems in Korean cities, and if the examined urban ideology of Gangnam-ization composes one dimension upholding the structure, then one of the political efforts to decisively break with the current condition would be building an alternative urban ideology for a different urban system. Gangnam-ization and its reproduction in new towns around the country—including recently expanding gentrification (see Hae and Shin and Kim, this volume) and a new generation of new 'new towns' in Seoul[13]— embody the hegemony of current urban ideology. Building a new alternative city beyond today's limits requires theoretical and ideological practices that think, speak of, and experiment with an urban(ity) beyond that which we already have. Particularly needed are the material and conceptual practices to see city as a place for meeting and encounter, and ultimately to nurture diverse and vibrant encounters in Korean cities.

In this context, it is inspiring to witness the recently emerging practices that open up new imaginations on city. Various experiments of 'maeul-mandeulgi' (literally, meaning 'village-making'),[14] initiated by the Seongmisan community, mark a symbolic example of alternative city-making that accommodates different ways of meeting and encountering each other. Housing cooperative experiments are recently drawing attentions as the housing rent and deposit (*jeonsae*) crisis deepens, galvanizing practices for allowing alternative encounters. These experiments signal alternative urban movements, refusing the encounters mediated by 'Gangnam-ization' and championing encounters informed more by collective cooperation and commons than by exchange

---

13   The newest generation of the 'new town' was promoted by former Seoul mayor Lee Myung-bak in the early 2000's. The authors view these new towns as attempt to 'Gangnam-ize' 'Gangbuk', neighborhoods North of the Han River in Seoul, which contrasts sharply with Gangnam, south of the Han River.

14   The literal meaning of maeul-mandeulgi is village-making. It was promoted as a city policy under city of Seoul mayor Park Won-soon, but also exists as a grass-roots movement. The basic idea of maeul-mandeulgi is to empower local inhabitants at a smaller scale to exercise democratic control on the village they live in. 'Seongmisan' located in Mapo-gu, Seoul, marks a symbolic success of the movement.

values. Small initiatives such as Mapo People's House, for instance, have been experimenting with a more radical form of urban commoning practice. Mapo People's House shares open access to its high priced office space with local grass-root organizations in Mapo, thereby creating a place for meeting and encounter full of liberty and liberation.

Of course, these experiments and practices certainly contain limits and risks partially because of their localist nature. Notwithstanding the limitations and constraints the experiments currently bear, the authors believe they carry fundamental roots for practicing alternative urban ideologies going beyond 'Gangnam-ization.' Emerging experiments, which refuse to live in the closed, exclusive spaces of apartments built on speculative interests and aspirations, instead focus on producing relationships of heterogeneity, the commons of the village and the city, and sharing responsibility and outcomes. This widens the ideological ground for revolutionary discourses and alternative urbanization models. In particular, the recent rise of experiments hold promise insofar as they offer an empirical basis for recognizing the city as a collectively produced and used commons, not a mere sum of private property. We hope that this view eventually contributes to formulating the theoretical basis for resisting the speculative urbanization of a seemingly unfailing market for private ownership.

References

Brenner, N and C Schmid (2014) The 'urban age' in question. *International Journal of Urban and Regional Research* 38(3): 731–755.

Douglas, M (1966) *Purity and Danger: An Analysis of Concepts of Pollution and Taboo.* London: Routledge.

Gelézeau, V (2007) *The Republic of Apartments* (in Korean). Seoul: Humanitas.

Ji, J-H (2016) The Development of Gangnam and the Formation of Gangnam-style Urbanism: On the Spatial Selectivity of the Anti-Communist Authoritarian Developmental State (in Korean). *Journal of the Korean Regional Geographical Society* 22(2): 307–330.

Lefebvre, H (2003) *The Urban Revolution,* Minneapolis: Minnesota University Press.

Merrifield, A (2013) The urban question under planetary urbanization. *International Journal of Urban and Regional Research* 37(3): 909–922.

Park, C (2013) *Apartment: Society of Public Cynicism and Private Passion* (in Korean). Seoul: Mati.

Park, H (2013) *APT Game: How They Became Middle Class* (in Korean). Seoul: Humanist.

Schmid, C (2012) "Henri Lefebvre, the Right to the City and the New Metropolitan Mainstream." in N. Brenner, P. Marcuse and M. Mayer (eds.). Cities for People, Not for Profit: *Critical Urban Theory and the Right to the City.* Routledge, pp. 42–62.

Wachsmuth, D (2013) City as ideology: reconciling the explosion of the city form with the tenacity of the city concept. *Environment and Planning D: Society and Space* 31: 1–16.

CHAPTER 8

Volatile Territorialities: North Korea's Special Economic Zones and the Geopolitical Economy of Urban Developmentalism

Jamie Doucette and Seung-Ook Lee

The Kaesong Industrial Complex is developing everyday. Across the Demilitarized Zone, the embodiment of 60 years of division, roads have been built, electricity wires laid and communication links connected. And every single day, commuter buses make the trip to Kaesong from Seoul. Today, Kaesong Industrial Complex produces not just goods, [but] the basis for peace on the Korean peninsula.

Kaesong Industrial District Management Committee (2007, 30)

The axis of sovereignty and security is not delimited by national borders but increasingly relies on the production of a linked geography of technoindustrial nodes that can circumvent political obstacles and bridge politically divided entities.

AIHWA ONG (2006, 118)

1 Introduction

Over the last decade, there has been a growing body of literature on urbanization in East Asia that critically interrogates how interactions between and mutations of sovereignty, territory, and political economy shape the urban.[1] This literature has focused on the contestation, reconstruction, and rescaling of sovereign territoriality and state capacity (Hsu 2009; Park, Hill, & Saito 2012) in general, and on emergent sites of capitalist investment such as free economic zones, special administrative zones, technology hubs and clusters, enclave factories, and elite residential zones in particular. The latter are sites

---

1 This is a revised, updated, and extended version of an article that first appeared in Political Geography (Doucette and Lee 2015). Thanks to Graham Bowden for help updating the map.

where nation-states and other actors have used targeted, spatially selective strategies to pursue integration in global markets (Ong 2004, 2006; Sidaway 2007a, 2007b) and where, by extension, "intensified processes and patterns of uneven development are increasingly expressed" (Sidaway 2007b, 332). The Kaesong Industrial Complex (KIC) is one such site. Located just south of the city of Kaesong, North Korea and north of the Korean De-Militarized Zone (DMZ) near Seoul, the KIC was until recently home to 124 light manufacturing companies that employed approximately 54,000 workers from the Democratic People's Republic of Korea (DPRK)—who worked for a small fraction of the cost of South Korean workers—and 820 from Republic of Korea (ROK) according to Kaesong Industrial District Management Committee. A joint South-North Committee managed the zone, making it one of the few inter-Korean projects with significant daily interaction between citizens of both North and South Korea. Despite the continuing legacy of Cold War politics on the Korean peninsula, or, rather, because of it, the case of the KIC demonstrated how the re-territorialization of sovereign power can be used to create new sites through which to experiment with practices that are not yet possible to replicate at other scales.

For Aihwa Ong (2006, 98; 204), new jurisdictions such as the KIC—like the export-processing and free economic zones that have preceded them—serve as important spaces of contemporary political-economic experimentation in Asian contexts, where they have often been used to circumvent political obstacles and bridge politically divided entities. Ong, in particular, has examined how the Chinese government has used various "zoning technologies" such as special administrative regions and special economic zones to re-spatialize national territory and realign mainland enclaves with various Chinese-dominated political entities overseas in order to develop sites of capitalist growth and assuage geopolitical anxieties surrounding the transfer of sovereignty over Hong Kong and Macau. Special zones have proliferated along the developed coast and, increasingly, newer zones have begun to appear further inland as the Chinese government has attempted to expand economic development and balance regional interests.

Ong is not the only observer to note the transformative role zones have played promoting capital accumulation and reworking state and urban form (Palan 2003; Bach 2011; Cross 2014; Easterling 2014; Murray 2017). The globally mobile consultants who have promoted the development of export processing zones and similar entities share a similar albeit more affirmative perspective. For instance, Jean-Paul Gauthier, Secretary-General of the World Export Processing Zone Association, writes in that organization's mission statement that "zones will always have a function as a testing-ground and pilot for beneficial reforms that are not yet politically possible on a national, regional, or international level" (Gauthier, n.d).

Although we should be cautious of regarding them as autonomously governed or strictly neoliberal entities (see Cartier this volume), it is true that special economic zones have long been used to intensively territorialize capital accumulation in Northeast Asia (Hsu et al. 2018). They have become such a standard part of the story of East Asian export-led growth that they have even recently been promoted as part of Official Development Assistance programs among East Asian donors. South Korea's Knowledge Sharing Program (Doucette and Muller 2016) is one such example. While it has expressed some caution about the problems associated with contemporary zones on the Korean peninsula (such as unsold apartments due to real estate speculation and lack of regulation—see Hsu this volume for a comparison), the KSP regards Korea an "exemplary state" that has "utilized SEZs at the early stage of industrialization and economic breakthrough" (Jeong and Pek 2016, 16).

But there are more than geoeconomic reasons for promoting zones. As Ong (2006, 98–99) argues, the use of zoning practices can also help ease some of the geopolitical tensions on the Korean peninsula and stimulate new forms of economic and political interactions. She argues that through special economic zones and other sites of experimentation,

> North Koreans can interact with South Koreans and other foreigners to develop access to external sources of capital, skills, and knowledge. These zones are places where notions of an eventual national reunification can be practically broached and tested, thus eventually creating an alternative imagining of biopolitical governing for the rest of North Korea, as well as suggesting a way to the eventual reunification of the two Koreas.
>
> *Ibid.*, 117

The implication here is that the creation of new geoeconomic practices, material infrastructures, and sites of exchange has the potential to redefine the organization of sovereignty and security on the divided Korean peninsula; in this sense, the creation of such new juridical spaces can help circumvent the political obstacles of Cold War antagonism and division (*Ibid.*, 118).

In this chapter, we take Ong's productive suggestion that territorial experimentation through such zoning technology might help ease geopolitical tensions on the Korean peninsula as a point of departure for our examination of North Korea's zoning strategies and, in particular, the KIC. We argue that the KIC represents an experimental but volatile form of territoriality, one that has provided a unique urban-industrial space for inter-Korean engagement and global market integration despite periodic conflicts between the diverse range of actors, interests, and ideologies that the project has been assembled across. Nonetheless, efforts to pursue geopolitical containment of North Korea and concerns surrounding the practices carried out in the zone have threatened the duration of the project, marking it as an unstable experiment, and, indeed, one that has been indefinitely put on hold for the time being since February 2016. By extension, we also argue for the benefits of a geopolitical economic approach (Glassman 2018; Lee, Wainwright & Glassman 2018) to such zoning policies, one that situates them within dense networks and relations that are multi-scalar in nature and that involve multiple state and non-state actors.

While acknowledging the potential for the KIC to promote new interactions among the two Koreas, we conclude that this form of territoriality remains *volatile* in the sense that the flows of people, resources, and goods that maintain the zone have been liable to change rapidly and unpredictably due to its location at a site of intense geopolitical attention and antagonism and the potential this brings for conflict among the actors that condition it. Against the dominant representation of North Korea as a rogue state, we want to be clear at the outset that such volatility cannot solely be reduced to the structure of the North Korean regime but is related to two important factors. The first is the continuation of a Cold War framework of enmity by actors on both sides of the Korean peninsula, including US policymakers. The second is the ethical and political conundrums raised by the situation of workers in the zone, which can be attributed to the largely capitalist nature of the KIC. Both factors introduce uncertainty into the duration of the zone even while they help produce it as a novel urban site of geopolitical and economic experimentation.

This paper is organized as follows: the next section examines recent literature on territoriality that we feel are useful for addressing the relations that have produced the KIC as an *experimental* and *volatile* form of territoriality. The following section then charts the emergence of the project from former South Korean President Kim Dae Jung's Sunshine Policy and his policy of economic cooperation or *Kyounghyup*. It then situates the KIC within competing geopolitical and geoeconomic representations of a wide network of actors that have contested or supported the project, including South Korean social movements, conservative politicians, and international actors such as the United States government. We then examine the configuration of the KIC from the perspective of North Korea's own changing territorial policies and international relations, including its embrace of special economic zones along its border with China and smaller development zones across the national territory. In the third section, we scrutinize the role that labor plays in shaping the zone as a project of market integration and discuss some of the questions that the KIC's labor policies raise for a variety of mediating actors. Finally, we examine the recent closures and reopenings of the zone to suggest geopolitical volatility will continue to inflect zoning strategies for the time being in a manner that creates challenges for peaceful engagement on the peninsula.

The research for this chapter is the product of two intersecting research programs: one on the social-spatial restructuring of the Korean developmental state and the role of Korean social movements in that process and another on the transformation of the territorial politics of North Korea in the context of Northeast Asian political economy. As such, both authors have been tracing the development of the KIC since it opened in 2005, using a variety of methods that include both textual analysis of key documents and semi-structured interviews. The analysis we provide below is based on mixed methods that involve scrutinizing media and policy reports in South Korea, North Korea, China, and the United States in order to grasp some of the different ways in which the KIC project has been represented by the strategic actors involved in assembling or contesting it. We also briefly draw on prior, semi-structured interviews conducted with South Korean officials and civic activists. These participants were selected on the basis of their involvement in documenting the development of the KIC and/or their participation in organizations involved in shaping inter-Korean relations. We also carried out complementary expert-oriented interviews involving Chinese and North Korean scholars with specialist knowledge of North Korea's territorial policies. In addition, one of the authors was able to visit to the KIC on a promotional tour organized by South Korea's Ministry of Unification for a foreign chamber of commerce in the spring of 2007, before such tours were largely suspended.

2   Volatile Territorialities

Before examining the KIC as a novel form of territoriality, it is important to first review some of the critical literature that can help us situate special economic zones and their role in shaping the geography of urban development in East Asia and beyond. There has been a growing literature on the nature of sovereignty and territoriality in recent years that we feel can help account for the significance of zones as a spatial form. Scholars have debated the degree to which such special economic zones of various types can be regarded as exceptional, neoliberal spaces in terms of the degree of legal and institutional autonomy and market liberalization they embrace (see Cartier, this volume). Likewise, Korean scholars have pointed out that the border-order nexus idealized by the Westphalian system was never fixed in the East Asian context, and thus zones should not be seen as purely exceptional spaces to the territorial contexts in which East Asian states have developed nor always instances of neoliberal governance. Park et al. (2017) note that diverse forms of special zones have thrived in East Asia. They suggest that three different forms of special zones have developed in East Asia—neoliberal zones, developmental zones, and transitional zones.[2] The latter two types demonstrate that East Asian zones cannot be fully elucidated by neoliberal exceptionalism.

One thing that is clear from the literature is that because of the distributed sovereignty that shapes many zonal strategies, analysis of the KIC and other zones requires a move away from methodologically nationalist or "territorially trapped" approaches to the linkages between sovereignty and territory and, by extension, to the Northeast Asian region's geographical political economy (Agnew 2010; Park 2013). Traditional approaches to statecraft within international relations and institutional political economy (particularly rational choice and game-theoretic perspectives but also neo-Weberian approaches such as developmental state theory) tend to depict national states as the sole cohesive actor with authority over national territory. There is a tendency in this literature to identify the state with political society to the neglect of hegemonic struggles that permeate both state and civil society and thus shape state policy.

In contrast, recent literature on East Asian urban development within geography and cognate disciplines have paid much more attention to geographically expansive relations that shape developmental trajectories, such as the role of transnational networks, strategic and spatially-selective state rescaling, and inter-scalar and inter-class relations (Glassman 2004; Gimm 2013; Park 2005; Sonn 2010). Instead of replicating homogenous and bounded notions of national space that focus on elite national bureaucracies, the focus here is on a wider assemblage of diverse political actors. This shift of focus away from traditional understandings of national sovereignty is not unique to studies of East Asian political economy but also resonates with recent interventions that theorize political-economic geographies as spatially variegated (Peck & Theodore 2007), sovereignty as a networked and distributed phenomenon (Agnew 2005; Antonsich 2009), and the urban as assembled through a variety of mobile policies and ideas along with their mutations (McCann & Ward 2012). As we discuss below, such geographically expansive and relational understandings of territory, sovereignty, and the urban are valuable for understanding the KIC as an experimental and volatile form of territoriality: one that involves a diverse mix of actors, interests and infrastructures.

---

2   The KIC is classified as a transitional zone here.

Following Raffestin (2012, 121), in this chapter we move away from the notion of territory as a naturalized, physical container dominated by a single organizational authority but, instead, draw attention to *territoriality*—the condition or status of a territory—as a relational construct that is "simultaneously a system of relations with [multiple] material and immaterial realities as well as a set of representations of these realities". Raffestin's emphasis on the role of labor (conceived not only as work but broadly as units of energy and information) as vital for the production of territory—not to mention the role of 'mediators' such as money and other factors that facilitate the process—is particularly useful when it comes to the study of a special economic zone that has been designed to take advantage of large pools of relatively low-cost North Korean labor. Moreover, Raffestin's understanding that territories are produced by other territories in a highly selective "process of a reshuffling or abandonment of certain (territorial) constructs to permit the insertion of other activities linked to new or transformed relations" (Raffestin 2012, 130) is also insightful in the context of the KIC which is extremely contingent on wider territorial interests and representations of actors on the Korean peninsula and beyond.

While there is a temptation to depict zones as a free-floating or mobile 'software' (Easterling 2014; Ong 2006), we feel that these important contextual dimensions should not be neglected. In her chapter in this volume, Carolyn Cartier makes a cognate point about the existing structure of districting in contemporary China and cautions against seeing the zone as a decontextualized 'analog' for neoliberalism. Neveling (2015) makes a similar point in his work on zones as sites of class consolidation and imperial formation. Like the enclave spaces described by Sidaway (2007b, 332), the KIC depends on a range of distinct legal norms and exceptions as well as an array of formal and informal practices that cut across specific territorial boundaries whose contexts should not be elided. While the physical infrastructure of the KIC resembles the modular industrial parks common to export processing zones, the transversal sets of rights, regulations, and legal exceptions that condition it speak to a unique convergence of geopolitical and geoeconomic interests that are contingent to the context and thus distinguish the KIC from many other zoning projects.

Finally, Raffestin's insight that territories are often limited in duration and extension and can be strategically turned on and off (Sack 1986) is essential for our argument that the KIC and other inter-Korean engagement projects constitute experimental and hence volatile forms of territoriality—in the sense that they are liable to change rapidly. Of course, Raffestin is not the only author to advocate a more relational examination of territoriality within human geography and cognate social sciences. A number of contemporary authors have advocated for perspectives that are sensitive to tensions between the topographical and topological (seen as inter-related rather than opposed) not to mention material and immaterial dimensions of territory (Martin and Secor 2014). For example, Painter (2010) calls for sensitivity to how a variety of networks, ideas, and practices co-produce territory as a construct that is "necessarily porous, historical, mutable, uneven and perishable" (1094). "Territory is not the timeless and solid geographical foundation it sometimes seems" argues Painter, "but a porous, provisional, labor-intensive and ultimately perishable and non-material product of networked social-technical practices" (2010, 1116; cf. Elden 2013). Likewise, Sassen (2013) describes territory as a mix of regimes with a variable contents, locations, and institutions. As such, she argues that the physical space of a territory as well as the practices that go on in it is shaped by geographically expansive flows of capital, information, and professionals that are enrolled into the project, as well as by material flows of commodities, water, and energy that combine to give a sense of permanence to a particular place, even though territories remain, in Sassen's terms, transversally bordered spaces (cf. Passi 1999).

The KIC, in part, depended on a similar interplay of material and immaterial elements and consisted of an assortment of institutional regimes and flows of labor, resources, and expertise. For instance, the water and energy that powered the zone were largely supplied by the South. The construction and infrastructure expertise of Hyundai Asan, a subsidiary of South Korean conglomerate Hyundai, was enrolled to produce the physical infrastructure of the KIC and the now-suspended Mt. Kumgang resort area. More importantly, the flow of North Korean workers into the KIC was a significant factor that conditioned the zone. Here North Korean labor interacted with South Korean capital and product design in a labor process jointly controlled by managers from both Koreas, working side by side. Like a Möbius strip, the *topography* of the KIC was one of a distinctly bounded surface; its boundaries were highly controlled and constituted a fenced-off zone within North Korea. The DMZ bordered the KIC to the south. To the north lay a few small villages, outer-suburbs of the city of Kaesong, where entry and exit were tightly controlled. On a tour of the zone in 2007 attended by one of the authors, participants were invited to lunch at a restaurant on the outskirts of the village that was included within the territory of the zone but physically fenced off from the rest of the village. During the temporary shutdown of the zone in 2013, there were reports of local village youth crossing the fences and exploring the zone at night, though there was no reported theft, damage or vandalism. More recently, however, when hope of restarting the zone has ebbed to its lowest point after its closure in February 2016, North Korea has taken steps to utilize the factories and plant in the zone. In October 2017, Radio Free Asia reported that North Korea secretly operated 19 clothing factories without notifying South Korea (RFA 2017). South Korea's Ministry of Unification announced, "The government takes the basic stance that North Korea should not infringe on South Korean firms' property rights. We've made clear that factories and machinery at the zone belong to the South's companies" (Yonhap News 2017, no page). However, North Korea claimed, "it is nobody's business what we do in an industrial complex where our nation's sovereignty is exercised" (Reuters 2017, no page).

While the zone itself was territorially confined, the recent South-North controversy between the property rights and sovereignty demonstrates that the workers and the products they made occupied a more indistinct and ambiguous *topological* space: juridically speaking, for them the KIC was neither fully inside nor fully outside the territorial jurisdictions of North and South Korea. While North Korean workers were governed under North Korean labor law, the goods that they produced were given product designation status as made in South Korea. To do so, South Korea effectively *reterritorialized* goods made in the KIC as produced in South Korean territory by including goods made in the KIC in its free-trade agreements. For example, Singapore, the European Free Trade Association (EFTA), and the Association of South East Asian Nations (ASEAN) all have provisions in their FTAS with South Korea that recognize goods made in the KIC as South Korean, providing they are exported from South Korea. China also recognizes KIC goods as made in South Korea (Knudsen and Moon 2010, 253). The South Korean government also tried to include KIC goods in the Korea-US FTA, but put this issue aside for further discussion because the US did not formally recognize trade with North Korea under America's International Emergency Economic Powers Act (Haggard & Noland 2009).[3]

The overlapping territorial jurisdictions not to mention juridical ambiguities and exceptions that have been used to produce the KIC also make it an unstable and unpredictable space inasmuch as these exceptions and ambiguities

---

3   Knudsen & Moon (2010, 254) point out that while inclusion of KIC goods in South Korea's foreign trade as South Korean means that some goods produced in North Korea are treated *de facto* as those from a state with most-favoured-nation status, it would be difficult to formally recognize KIC products under Article 11 of the WTO's 1994 Agreement on Rules of Origin. This is because goods made in the KIC are not "wholly obtained" in South Korea, nor have they undergone "substantial transformation" in South Korea. While some countries used special rules in FTAs such as integrated sourcing initiatives, outward processing, and qualifying industrial zones to recognize extra-territorially produced goods, organizations like the WTO are reticent to recognize goods made in the KIC as South Korean due to the geopolitical tension surrounding trade with North Korea (*Ibid.*, 254–255).

can easily become contested by a variety of actors involved in operating and configuring the zone. The site itself becomes, at times, a key space for working out geopolitical conflict: a site where demands are made for not only further investment or guarantees surrounding operations of the site but also for broader geopolitical demands, such as cessation of joint US-SK military drills and North Korea's nuclear and missile programs. Therefore, the KIC is extremely sensitive to changes that occur in the wider geopolitical environment, such as North Korea's nuclear tests or even internal changes to governments of North Korea, South Korea, or the United States. During these times of tension, access to the zone became restricted; flows of labor, resources, and expertise held back; and commitments over wages or prior promises to expand the zone have been subject to renegotiation. This makes the zone a rather volatile place in as much as it can easily be shuttered and suspended. Thus, to ensure support for the zone, it has been marketed not only as an important *capitalist* experiment but also as a key site of cooperative geopolitical and geoeconomic engagement. Even the labor of North Korean workers is often represented not simply as wage labor but as work that collectively nurtures peace and reunification. As we discuss below, such representations appeal not only to capital but also to political forces that have long sought engagement between the two Koreas. At the same time, conservative discourses of geopolitical containment and Cold War antagonism have threatened and even, for the moment, suspended the viability of the zone. In this sense, as Lussault (2007, 113 cited in Painter 2010, 1102) argues, the production of territory often depends less on the material aspects of space (though, in our opinion, these still remain significant) than on the system of ideas that frame the space in question.

3   From Reunification to *Kyeonghyeop*

The ideas and ideologies that shape territoriality are not confined to state actors alone, but also include, as Agnew (2010, 781) argues, critical ideas about territory espoused by social movements, and the use of these ideas by politicians, help create alternative geographical imaginaries of territory. These ideas have the capacity to reshape state power and legitimation. In the South Korean context, the KIC emerged from the wider geographical imaginary of national reunification, a long-held goal of the democracy movements of the 70's and 80's. Especially after the Kwangju Uprising of 1980, the politics of national liberation, peaceful coexistence, and reunification as means to work toward the dissolution of the division system became amplified in the counter-hegemonic discourse of South Korean democracy movements (Koo 2001; Lee 2007; Shin

2002). The transition to democracy in 1987, however, did not bring sudden re-unification, and the Korean peninsula remained divided. While strong student movements for reunification remained active throughout the early 1990s, pub-lic support for reunification began to waver due to fears about the enormous costs that sudden reunification might bring, as witnessed by the travails of Ger-man reunification and North Korea's severe economic problems since the mid-1990s. As an alternative to the high costs that would be associated with sudden integration, the opening of experimental zones of engagement was proposed. Instead of reunification, the idea of *Kyeonghyeop*, or 'economic cooperation' became popular, and was quickly institutionalized after the inauguration of President Kim Dae Jung in February 1998.

The KIC project was embraced as one such experimental zone by former South Korean President and Nobel Prize-winner Kim Dae Jung. Kim rose to fame as a key oppositional politician from the Korean democracy movement; he was elected in December 1997 and served as President of the Republic of Korea during 1998–2003. The KIC and the (currently closed) Mt. Kumgang tourist resort were two flagship programs of Kim's Sunshine Policy which also included a series of initiatives designed to increase inter-Korean cooperation at multiple ministerial levels such as aid and knowledge exchanges, family re-unions, and the hosting of joint cultural events. While generally supported by a wide variety of popular political forces associated with the Korean democracy movement, many liberal-left political forces saw the largely capitalist charac-ter and spatially selective nature of Kim's engagement projects as insufficient, if not problematic. Their original demands for reunification included more plural and egalitarian forms of cooperation between North and South Korea. As (H.O Park 2009, 109) suggests, the 1980s democracy movement considered unification as a task "immanent to other democratic and national objectives". However, in the post-Cold War era, "the politics of unification has been infused with a transnational market expansion". For Park, this turn is problematic in that it removed the "binding ties of unification with the tasks of decoloniza-tion, critique of capitalist domination, and social justice" (*Ibid.*, 110).

Park argues that underlying *Kyeonghyeop* is a renewed developmentalism that has been partly induced by the 1997 financial crisis and the failure of eco-nomic liberalization to deliver on its 'long-promised' re-distribution of wealth (2009, 115). While she is correct in pointing out that *Kyeonghyeop* resembles past developmentalism in that the state has been a powerful actor involved in creating hegemony for the power of capital, it may be more appropriate to treat projects like the KIC as representing something closer to what Park and Lepawsky (2012) term 'developmental neoliberalism'. The project is not cen-tered around industrial upgrading or rapid industrialization at the national scale as much as it is oriented towards creating a special, light-manufacturing zone exclusively for small and mid-sized Korean businesses. Projects such as the KIC thus represent a process by which the infrastructural capacities of the older 'developmental state' and emergent neoliberal restructuring projects aimed at attracting footloose capital are enabled or brought into existence through a "deliberately selective process of sociospatial segmentation of state territory and populations" (*Ibid.*, 118; Park 2005, 865–867). Though the KIC shares much of the rhetoric of using capitalist development as a nation-building project, it targets a more selective site for intervention than past industrial policies and is more in line with the new forms of fragmented spatial policy and strategic use of zoning technologies to create spaces of political-economic experimentation as highlighted by Ong (2006) and others than a full-blown nation-building form of developmentalism *per se*.

While in the wake of the 1997 financial crisis, the KIC became seen as a potential solution for the declining profitability of the country's small and mid-sized enterprises, we should not reduce the creation of the KIC to simple capitalist desires. Rather we must situate it within the complex interplay of a variety of political interests. Importantly, continued support for the KIC and other economic cooperation projects hinge partially on South Korean reformers and activist groups that emerged from the democracy movement. Engagement with the North is supported by a wide variety of social and civic movements and politicians and not simply those movements with an explicitly left-nationalist orientation such as those activists that participated in the nationalist student movement of the 1980s and the 1990s (M. Park 2009). Even those with what are described as fairly non-nationalistic, radical, egalitarian tendencies within social movements seem to conditionally endorse the project or are at least muted in their concerns about it. Many on the liberal-left see the zone as, at minimum, a form of 'capitalist peace' that is facilitated through increased trade and market integration (Chung 2013, 98). Furthermore, many South Korean liberal-left reformers are reticent about publicly criticizing the project due to the fact that discourse around North Korean human rights has frequently been used by conservative forces to obstruct peace and reconciliation efforts (Hong 2013). Nevertheless, there exist some voices inside left-egalitarian groups that criticize the low wages of the North Korean workers at the KIC. For instance, Chung (2009) claims that the greedy pursuit of profit by the companies at the KIC has been obscured in the name of promoting the national economy.

The largely quiet response to the politics of *Kyeonghyeop* and the KIC in particular on the left was complemented by a tacit endorsement of the project by several prominent conservative politicians in South Korea during the administration of President Lee Myung-bak. However, not all conservatives supported the zone and many remained opposed to it, raising questions about long-term support—especially after the conservative government Lee Myung-bak quickly moved to suspend the Mt. Kumgang resort area (an important site for family reunions between divided families) after a South Korean tourist was shot to death there in 2008. Many conservatives initially saw the KIC and Mt. Kumgang projects as examples of *peojugi*—unconditional giving without return or "the most generous aid to North Korea" (Kim et al. 2009, 456)—a "violation of the principle of economic exchange" (H.O. Park 2009, 112)—and some criticized the government for promoting the KIC without seeking a 'people's agreement' (Hankook Ilbo 2006; Shin 2003). Even some conservative commenters such as Cho Gab-je argued that South Korean workers at the KIC could become hostages when inter-Korean military conflicts would break out (See Lee 2016a for conflicts of various geopolitical visions and imaginations around the KIC in South Korean politics). Traditional conservatives have painted the liberal-left and their efforts at engagement as being 'slavish' to North Korean interests against South Korean ones, and many have persistently labeled supporters of the Sunshine Policy as 'chongbuk chwap'a': a term translated as 'Pro-North Leftists.'

This rhetoric makes it difficult for conservatives to endorse engagement projects. Instead, they tend to criticize the Sunshine Policy as a threat to Korea's territorial integrity (Doucette 2013; Doucette and Koo 2013; Doucette and Koo 2016) and argue that money from inter-Korean economic projects supports North Korea's missile and nuclear programs (Lee 2015, 698).[4] The irony here is that while the creation of an internal, communist enemy has often enabled South Korean conservatives to maintain a state of exception over South Korean citizens and workers' civil and human rights in a way that has promoted capitalist development (Lee *et al.*, 2013), the same rhetoric obstructs many conservatives from throwing their support behind the KIC even though

---

4 This discourse served as a justification for the closure of the KIC in February 2016: "To date, the total amount of cash that flowed into North Korea through the Gaeseong Industrial Complex is 616 billion won (560 million dollars), with 132 billion won (120 million dollars) in cash having flowed into North Korea last year alone, and the Government and the private sector have invested a total of 1.019 trillion won. It appears that such funds have not been used to pave the way to peace as the international community had hoped, but rather to upgrade its nuclear weapons and long-range missiles ... Today, in order to stop funds of the Gaeseong Industrial Complex from being used to support the development of North Korea's nuclear and missile capabilities, and to prevent our businesses from suffering, the Government has decided to completely shut down the Gaeseong Industrial Complex" (Ministry of Unification 2016). This statement's linking of the money from the KIC to nuclear and missile development has been criticized for lacking sufficient evidence.

it aims to expand capitalist social relations into the North. Traditional conservatives have found the project hard to support because it is not framed in strong anti-communist rhetoric and/or because of the possibility that interaction with North Koreans has the potential to invoke rival discourses of peace and engagement that undermine the production of a North Korea as a territorial threat.

Nonetheless, and despite this antagonism toward the liberal-left, some prominent hard-line conservatives have eventually lent support to the project. For instance, after his inauguration in 2008, conservative President Lee Myung-bak appointed hardliner Moo-Hong Moon, the former director of unification policy under the conservative Kim Young Sam regime, to the position of President of the KIC's joint North-South Management Committee (KIDMAC). Moon had initially opposed both the Sunshine Policy and the KIC project, but he came to regard it as an effective vehicle for changing North Koreans' attitudes towards capitalism and markets (Stanton 2007; Stanton 2009). In the fall of 2010, Lee Myung-bak's Minister of Unification Woo-Ik Yoo announced that South Korea would spend more on infrastructure at Kaesong, and prominent conservatives who visited the KIC such as then-Chairman of President Lee's Grand National Party, Joon-pyo Hong, publicly declared that they supported increased economic activity at the KIC (Cronin 2012, 17), though he later altered his stance which we will explicate below. This was a novel phenomenon because conservatives have traditionally tended to emphasize geopolitical containment of North Korea over geoeconomic engagement (Lee 2015). Perhaps some conservatives, while still embracing geopolitical goals of containing North Korean power, moved towards tentatively embracing geoeconomic engagement. Others were simply willing to use the KIC as a temporary experiment given the 'policy fatigue' with North Korea that is prevalent in diplomatic circles.

The support of politicians such as Moon, however, does not mean that traditional anti-communist ideology ceased to animate their concerns, but rather that they re-articulated their stance from one of simple opposition to conditional support of the KIC as a 'Trojan horse' for introducing capitalism to the North. As Christine Hong (2013, 533) points out, this rhetoric of warfare and enmity, largely related to the irresolution of the Korean War, renders North Korea largely as a target with the aim of shattering its territorial power from within through the construction of a proxy or virtual space, in this case the KIC. While certainly this is not the dominant representation of the project, it is one that resonates with previous conservative frames and was used to generate support among more hard-line conservatives. However, if the rhetoric of enmity is pushed too far, it can easily make interaction between the two Koreas dysfunctional and thus contribute to the volatility of the zone, in as much as it departs from the initial vision of a project as one of peaceful engagement. Such was the case surrounding the closure of the zone in 2016 amidst North Korea's nuclear tests. In particular, more recently, skepticism toward the KIC increasingly resonates with serious youth unemployment in the South and concerns about the erosion of the standard employment relation (Doucette 2015; Doucette and Kang 2017). To take advantage of this, Joon-pyo Hong, after he became a presidential candidate in 2017, criticized the KIC not just for violating UN sanctions but also for taking jobs from South Korea and giving them to young people in North Korea (Kang 2017). In order words, the highly touted geoeconomic potential of the KIC, its capacity to effectively enjoy North Korea's cheap labor power and low land rent, has been further questioned under the contemporary economic conditions in the South.

This ambivalent tension between geopolitical containment and geoeconomic engagement at the national level is also reflected in the configuration of international support for the project. For instance, some US policy experts have looked at the project as a site of potential engagement with North Korea, one that might allow for a reconfiguration of previous strategies that, to date, have been centered around denuclearization and disarmament as a pre-condition for economic engagement. For instance, the Center for a New American Security's Patrick Cronin (2012, 31–32) has argued that US policy has been hostage to the notions that North Korea can be easily coerced to give up its nuclear weapons and that China will somehow prioritize denuclearization in its economic cooperation with North Korea. Rather, Cronin claims, economic cooperation between the US and North Korea through projects such as the KIC might provide opportunities not only for lessening North Korea's economic dependence on China but also provide the US with an opportunity for contact with North Korea's fledgling leadership under Kim Jong-un. Nonetheless, United States policy towards the North remains predominantly animated by containment, particularly in light of continuing nuclear and missile tests. The United States continues to limit trade with North Korea as part of its non-proliferation policies and tends to view the KIC as "a source of cash subsidies" to the Kim family (Niksch 2006, 1). Because of this concern, the South Korean government, as a US ally, maintained strict controls over shipment to the KIC, restricting complex machinery, electronics, laser-related equipment, chemical product facilities, and other sophisticated high-technology equipment. Personal computers, commonly available in the South, were restricted and kept under lock and key in the KIC, and tracking devices were used for items with technology that could be used for proliferation (*Ibid.*, 18). Since 2010 South Korea also sought to limit cash payments to North Korea under the May

24 Measures, that ban most inter-Korean economic cooperation and trade, enacted following the alleged sinking of a South Korean corvette by a North Korean torpedo. Instead, it promoted payment in kind, such as instant noodles and other foodstuffs, as we discuss further below.

4   The Dynamics of North Korea's Territorial Politics

North Korea's policy towards the KIC is also shaped by competing geopolitical and geoeconomic logics that cannot be reduced to the imperatives of either South Korea or the United States. North Korea has fostered spatially selective policies that reterritorialize national space in order to facilitate political-economic experimentation and market integration for some time even though it is often portrayed as the most isolated and closed country in the world. Inspired by China's reforms in the 1980s, North Korea's first zonal experiment, the Rajin-Sonbong (or Rason) free trade zone in the northeastern corner of its territory, began in 1991. In general, outside watchers have considered North Korea's introduction of this spatial experiment as an inevitable economic choice and argued that it compromised North Korea's unique *juche* [self-reliance] economic system. However, as Lee (2014a) argues, North Korea's territorial imperative of 'security first, economy next' has shaped these territorial strategies. The North's zoning policies were introduced only after it felt that its security concerns were addressed and not simply because of economic collapse. Many researchers overlook these territorial dynamics, accepting instead the dominant explanation that North Korea has been compelled to open its territory due to economic crises (Chung 2004; Noland & Flake 1997). While it is correct that growing economic difficulty, especially after the collapse of the Soviet bloc and the pragmatic turn of the Chinese Communist Party, led the North to modify its longstanding territorial imaginary of itself as "an impregnable fortress" (Gray and Lee, 2017; Lee 2014a; Smith 2005, 225–226), economic explanations alone cannot account for its embrace of zonal policies.

   Since the early 1990s when the North first applied zoning technology, ongoing tensions between national security and economic development have substantially affected its territorial strategies (see more in Lee, 2014a). For instance, Kim Jong Il's response to President Roh's suggestion to expand the KIC into Haeju, one of the major port cities in the western coast—only 75km from Kaesong, 20km from Incheon, and 100km from Seoul—reveals this anxiety:

> Concerning establishment of new industrial complexes, our territory is small, unlike China or the Russian Far East. Under this condition, to fully

convert the territory into industrial complexes will destroy the national self-sufficient economy that we have built up, entangle it in the market economy, and bring about a mental calamity that negates the *juche* ideology.[5]

Kim emphasized that the North had already made a huge concession in geostrategic and military terms in the case of the KIC. According to the transcript of the inter-Korean summit meeting in 2007, Kim Jong Il mentioned that Kaesong was the third choice for the inter-Korean SEZ behind Sinuiju and Haeju, which are located in less militarily strategic locations (also see Richardson & Bae 2009, 72). Military strategists have pointed out that the KIC can serve as a buffer zone for the South to restrain a sudden attack by North Korea and to hinder troop movements and deployments (Kim 2004). Likewise, Hwang (2004) points out that the development of the KIC substantially moves the truce line northward about 10-15km, weakening North Korea's military defense. Kim Jong Il's promotion of the KIC was thus seen as a "brave step" that was taken despite strong opposition from the military elite (Chosun Ilbo 2013a, no page).

During the summit meeting, Kim also complained of slow development of the KIC when South Korean President Roh suggested to develop more inter-Korean SEZs such as Haeju. The original plan of the KIC was to develop the complex through three stages: the first stage to develop 3.3 km² in industrial zone (2002–2007); the second to develop 5 km² industrial zone and 3.3 km² for a supporting zone (2006–2009); and the third to establish 11.6 km² of industrial zone and 6.6 km² of a supporting zone (2008–2012) (Im 2005, 41). However, the first stage has yet to be completed. From the North's perspective, it had committed a geo-strategically important area for the project, but the South was trying to create other new joint industrial complexes without fulfilling its promises to fully develop the KIC first.

What we should note here is that the working of the KIC has been swayed not only by political dynamics within South Korea and the U.S. but also by internal political tensions inside the North Korean regime. Though specific features of North Korean politics remain obscure to outside observers, we can glimpse the conflicting visions of the KIC between the military and the cabinet. In regard to South Korean President Roh's suggestion of a Haeju SEZ, Kim Jong Il replied that the military would oppose such a project, and he reproached his

---

5 On 24 June 2013, the National Intelligence Service released the transcript of the 2007 inter-Korean summit meeting between Roh Moo-hyun and Kim Jong Il (Pressian 2013, our translation).

cabinet and economic bureaucrats, questioning how he could allow them to develop Haeju SEZ in light of the sluggish progress of the KIC. After the death of Kim Jong Il in December 2011, the tensions around the KIC seem more pronounced. *The China Post*, a Taiwanese newspaper, ran a story under the headline "North Korean leaders divided over Kaesong industrial enclave". While cabinet members view the KIC as an important income source and defend its legitimacy as "a legacy project left by our late great general (Kim Jong Il) that we cannot give up", the military regard it as a "strategic liability" (*The China Post* 2013, no page). Ironically, this opposition mirrors the conflicts over the KIC between South Korean conservatives and liberals-progressives described above.

This conflict between security and development intensified again when the North temporarily suspended operations of the KIC in response to joint U.S.-South Korean military drills on 9 April 2013. Even before the closure of the KIC, the North Korean government threatened the South that it would transform the Complex back into its original use as a military base. North Korea's state-run Chosun Central TV stressed with aggressive rhetoric that this restoration would lead to the reoccupation of the KIC as a strategic military zone, with a new, wide-open road on which to advance into South Korea (requoted from Kim 2013). Yet after the KIC shutdown, Yang Gon Kim, the secretary of the Central Committee of the Workers' Party of Korea and director of United Front Department, told Sang-kwon Park, CEO of Pyeonghwa Motors, "I had no intention of closing the Kaesong Industrial Complex, but it ultimately suspended operation due to military authorities" (Dong-A Ilbo 2013, no page). Another report quoted a military spokesman that "it is senseless for hundreds of South Koreans and vehicles to cross the border every day when the North wages a full-scale war against the South" (YJ. Lee 2013, no page; cf. Chosun Ilbo 2013b). While some consider this discourse to be typical political maneuvering by North Korea, it does not preclude the existence of political frictions inside the North Korean regime and their effect on the operation of the KIC as well as North Korea's wider territorial policies. For instance, in an interview carried out by one of the authors in Pyongyang in November 2011, a researcher from the Research Institute of Unification confirmed that there had been strong opposition from the military against the decision to set up the KIC in the first place.

Finally, despite this internal power struggle and the escalating inter-Korean tensions that led to the closure of the KIC for about five months between April to September 2013, and indefinitely since February 2016, the North Korean government expanded its trans-border economic projects with China (Lee 2014b; Yoon and Lee 2013) and announced the 14 new zones across the country in

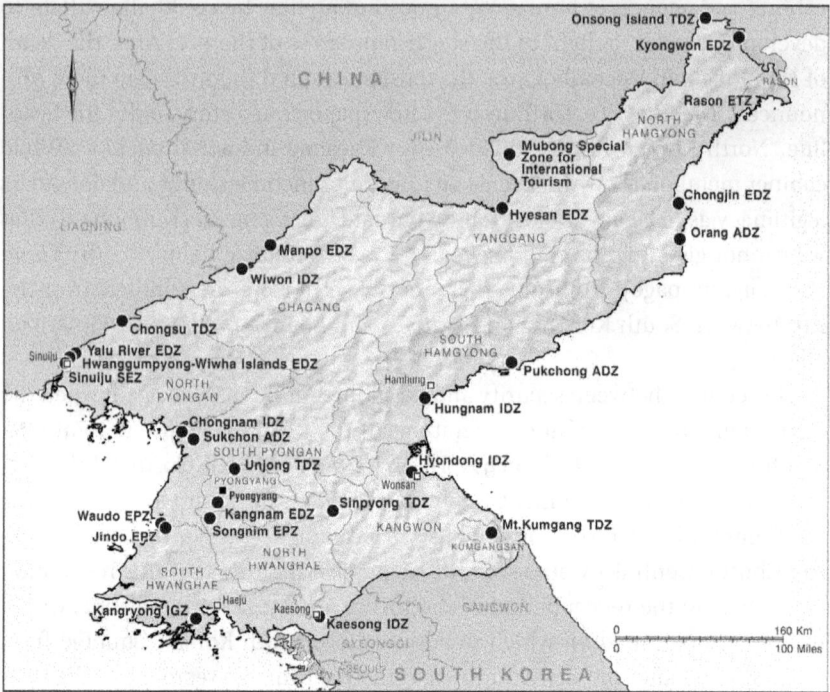

FIGURE 8.1   North Korea's Special Economic Zones
        Note: Acronyms: ADZ (Agricultural Development Zone); EDZ (Economic
        Development Zone); EPZ (Export Processing Zone); IDZ (Industrial
        Development Zone); and TDZ (Tourism Development Zone).
        SOURCE: MAP DRAWN BY THE AUTHORS BASED ON VARIOUS REPORTS AND
        PRESS ARTICLES DOCUMENTING NORTH KOREA'S ZONAL DEVELOPMENT

November 2013 (Sinuiju SEZ as the national-level and 13 other smaller development zones as the local-level) and six more local-scale development zones
in July 2014. Three more zones were designated—two in the border region
with China in April and October 2015 and one near Pyongyang in December
2017. Figure 8.1 shows that six zones were set up along the border region with
China, which was expected to further facilitate Sino-North Korean economic
cooperation along with the two existing SEZs that have been jointly developed
since 2011—the Rason Economic and Trade Zone and the Hwanggumphyong-
Wihwa Islands Economic Zone.[6] The axis of zoning practices shifted from

---

6   In an interview with one of the authors in May 2011, Xiao Yu, director of the Center for North-
    east Asia Studies at Jilin University, described the dynamics of North Korea's zoning policy

the southern border (with South Korea) to the northern border (with China). Many of the regulations surrounding taxation and the enforcement of by-laws developed to govern the KIC have been transplanted in order to help govern North Korea's other SEZS (J. Lee 2018).

5   Labor, Gender, Territoriality

The contingent support for the KIC within both Koreas, as well as the Cold War logics that have led to its repeated closure, are not the only factors that contributed to the zone's status as a volatile urban-industrial experiment. This status extends down to and is affected by the everyday practices of the very subjects who work in the zone and whose labor is central to the viability of the KIC as a largely capitalist project. In other words, it is not simply the production of support for the zone through discourses of engagement, geopolitical strategy, and reunification among an ensemble of state and non-state actors that has authorized its construction and enabled its relative coherence as an experimental form of territoriality. The control of labor is also a key factor in enabling the production of the KIC as a capitalist space. As Peck (1992) pointed out long ago, labor control (and resistance) plays a central role in the construction of urban economies and their territorial coherence. In the case of the KIC, the uncertainties and lack of clarification surrounding the effective rights, labor standards, and wage payment of workers helped produce it as an urban-industrial site for appropriating surplus value. At the same time, the ambiguity that surrounds labor rights there has also contributed to the KIC's volatile status because of the ethical and political questions that the conditions of these workers raise.

At its peak in 2013, the KIC employed close to 55,000 North Korean workers. These workers are predominantly female and most are from either the city of Kaesong itself, which the zone borders upon, or from the capital, Pyongyang.[7] Their employment is governed under a labor law drafted by the North Korean government after consulting with the Hyundai Asan Corporation and then adopted by the Standing Committee of the (North Korean) Supreme People's Assembly (Human Rights Watch 2006b, 7). The Kaesong Industrial District

---

as: "Since 2000, when the KIC worked well, North Korea downplayed Rason SEZ. Yet as the development of the KIC has slowed down, the North has drawn more attention to the Rason. Nevertheless, North Korea's view of the KIC is fundamentally different from that of the Rason. While it regards the former as intra-national cooperation towards reconciliation and reunification, the latter targets not only China but the world".

7   Author interview 2007, South Korean official involved in the KIC project.

Management Committee (KIDMAC) was in charge of enforcing the KIC law, monitoring compliance, and punishing violators, under the supervision of North Korea's Central Special District General Bureau for Kaesong Industrial Complex (*Ibid.*, 4). In 2012, the minimum wage cost of labor in the zone was roughly US$67 a month (although with other incentives North Korean workers could make up to US$120 a month), working 6 days, 48 hours a week.[8] North Korean workers were not paid in South Korean won, however, but in a cash equivalent of North Korean won the value of which is difficult to independently verify, though in practice KIC companies have their NK staff sign a payroll form that lists their rate of pay (Human Rights Watch 2006a, 2006b). Human rights groups have expressed misgivings about the lack of enforcement and formal clarification surrounding worker's rights, including workers' understanding of their existing rights. For instance, Human Rights Watch has raised concerns over the fact that the North Korean government, and not the workers themselves, selects workers' representatives subject to the approval of the South Korean companies operating at the KIC: a violation of international norms on state interference in the organization, operation, and functioning of workers' organizations (2006b, 12–13).

Moreover, concerns about labor exploitation in the zone also serves as grounds for conservatives in both South Korea and the U.S. to criticize and contest the KIC project. For example, Jay Lefkowitz, U.S. President Bush's Special Envoy for Human Rights in North Korea, has strongly criticized the labor conditions at the KIC. In the Opinion section of *The Wall Street Journal*, he asserted that

> [t]he world knows little about what actually goes on at Kaesong, and given North Korea's track record, there is ample cause for concern about worker exploitation. The South Korean companies apparently pay less than $2 a day per worker, and there is no guarantee that the workers see even this small amount.
>
> LEFKOWITZ, 2006, no page.

The $2 a day figure quoted above was calculated based on black market exchange rates for North Korean Won and earned a quick rebuttal from the South Korean government that this figure is speculative and misleading. In contrast,

---

8 Article 32 of the KIC Labor Law stipulates that South Korean companies shall pay wages to North Korean workers directly in cash. However, on North Korea's demand, South Korean companies remit worker salaries to the North Korean government (Human Rights Watch, 2006b, 7–8).

TABLE 8.1   The amount of Choco Pies shipped into the Kaesong Industrial Complex (KIC)

Year	2008	2009	2010	2011	2012
Amount ($1,000)	80	260	1,920	1,870	1,980

SOURCE: SHIN (2013, 265, retrieved from the Ministry of Unification)

others have speculated that the *de facto* wages and benefits that workers enjoyed at the KIC are considerably higher than the formal wage of state sector workers in North Korea in general (H. Lee 2018). Nonetheless, the uncertainly surrounding the actual wages of workers in the zone allowed South Korean conservative media to reproduce this narrative in order to criticize the KIC as an engagement project (Lee 2006; Lee and Kim 2006). In contrast, North Korean scholars also note that the wages of workers in the zone were on average lower than in Chinese-invested zones in North Korea. However, they argue that this was a special concession granted to South Korea in order to support the wider, intra-national, territorial project of inter-Korean engagement on the peninsula. Researchers from North Korea's Economic Institute at the Academy of Social Sciences claimed that the KIC was out of generosity to South Korean businesses to suffer from growing lack of international competitiveness, especially against China.[9]

Besides the low wages, or wage equivalents that they receive, KIC workers are additionally reimbursed through gifts in kind, especially with a popular South Korean snack cake (see Table 8.1) named 'Choco Pie.' As the companies at the KIC are not allowed to pay more than the regular wage, they provided six Choco Pies as a perquisite for nighttime shifts or overtime work. Consequently, the cakes became a common, alternative token of exchange at private markets called *Jangmadang* in the North and a popular status symbol (Ha 2013). According to Park *et al.* (2014), a box of these small sweet treats can be traded for a value of $10, which is considerably more than the alleged black market value of KIC wages in North Korean won. The treats became one of the most popular gifts for North Korean families at the recent family reunions between the two Koreas (Yi 2014). For South Korean intellectuals who hope that the KIC will become a site where North Korean people can learn and adopt the basic principles of a market economy (e.g., the concept of profit), the popularization of this small chocolate snack was seen as having had a positive and dramatic

9 Author interview, November 2009.

effect. The Choco Pie was even touted as a symbolic and powerful catalyst for transforming the North Korean system and even for freeing the North Korean people: "[Through Choco Pie] It was clear that the workers had gotten at least some idea of capitalism and that it wasn't all bad" (Park *et al.* 2014, no page); "Choco Pies are an important mind-changing instrument" (Branigan 2013, no page). A journalist from *Chosun Ilbo*, a major conservative newspaper in South Korea, extols this small snack as a 'window of freedom' through which North Korean people will open their eyes to the outside world (Chi 2013), and perhaps even function as the Trojan Horse conservatives were looking for. As such, it constitutes an important but contentious object in the wider assemblage of actors that constitute the zone. Moreover, as "the pies are viewed by some in the North as dangerous symbols of capitalism" (S. Kim 2011, no page), the North Korean state attempted to regulate the number of Choco Pies distributed to workers or to demand the companies pay with cash. Many companies even replaced Choco Pies with cup noodles (Park *et al.* 2014).[10]

Finally, the production of the KIC as a site for appropriating North Korean women workers' labor power was not simply a matter of wage rates and payment in kind but also involved the representation of North Korean workers as a diligent work force working not only for capital but also for the greater political project of reunification. After the KIC was formally launched in 2005, KIDMAC ran bilingual flash ads in a number of newspapers to advertise the project. The adverts consisted of factory scenes of female assembly workers assembling garments. The text running over the images read: "At their diligent fingertips a hopeful future is being molded" (see Figure 8.2). The message was that the labor of these workers is seen not simply as wage labor but as emotional labor that *nurtures* the economy for the wider project of peace and reunification. But why have low-paid workers in an industrial zone been assigned this task? How is it, exactly, that simple assembly line work is supposed to perform the labor of unification? Why is it that such work was seen something to be done for low wages, payment in kind, and in the site of a factory complex? This is not to say that workers should not be involved in the work of engagement and unification, but why was unification being imagined in this way?

---

10   One North Korean scholar whom the authors interviewed argued that it seemed that South Korea had intentionally intended to affect North Korean people through its exchanges in kind at the KIC in order to feed and spread fantasies about capitalism and the market economy. The scholar, claimed, however, that because North Korea people had lived under the benefit of the socialist system for a long time, they would not be seduced by a few Choco Pies (Author interview of a scholar from the Research Institute of Unification on 14 November 2011).

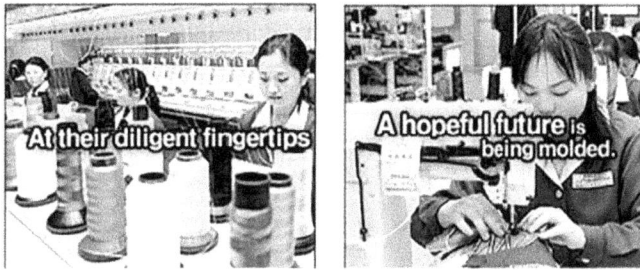

FIGURE 8.2 At their diligent fingertips... A hopeful future is being molded
         SOURCE: KIDMAC

Similar to discourses of 'nimble fingers' that have been documented by feminist scholars examining the gendering of light manufacturing work, such language attempts to naturalize the KIC's labor conditions by representing North
Korean women workers as producing not just goods, but also "the basis for
peace on the Korean peninsula" (Caraway 2007; KIDMAC 2007, 30; Ong 1987).
As Ong (1991, 291) points out, such discourses that fixate on physical qualities
of gendered labor tend to "disassemble" the female worker into "eyes and fingers adapted to assembly work"—or in this case to the labor of reunification—
in a way that provides justification for low wages and long work hours (Elson &
Pearson 1981). Furthermore, as Mills (2005, 177) argues, the implicit corollary to
stereotypes of docile workers with nimble fingers is "the belief that such nov-
ice female wage earners are largely unsusceptible to the appeals of labor organizing" or, in this case, of directing participating—in more ways than simply
wage labor—in the political work of inter-Korean engagement. Such discourse
tends to depoliticize the agency of women workers because it forestalls inquiry
into the actual labor conditions they face. During a tour of the zone in 2007,
managers and ministry officials promoting the zone used a similar language of
gender stereotyping. Conversing with a few visitors on the tour from a foreign
chamber of commerce, one of the managers exclaimed: "You see, the North
Koreans, they possess very special finger skills, much better than the Chinese
or Malaysians or Filipinos..."

   While it is beyond the scope of this paper to look more fully into the labor
process at KIC, it is possible to argue that the symbolic production of the KIC
as a site of 'docile' labor—not to mention the commodification of North Korea
women workers' labor power and the ambiguity surrounding their labor rights
and proper payment for their work—has helped facilitate the zone's viability
as a capitalist experiment but also its volatility. The absence of independent
organization among North Korean workers, and the lack of involvement in the

project by South Korean labor unions, helps maintain a relatively demobilized, low-wage, labor force. At the same time, the labor conditions experienced by these workers also raises ethical questions that have the potential to undermine support for the project. The situation of workers in the zone raises doubts that zones like the KIC might be able to create conditions for workers leading to "life, freedom, and new political openings" (Ong 2006, 117) and suggests that a more egalitarian re-imagining of the zone—one that might involve the participation of independent labor organizations, for instance—is desirable. To return to Ong's suggestion above that zoning technologies might create an alternative form of governing compared to the rest of North Korea, it seems that a great deal of work remains to be done to properly qualify the assertion that the benefits that accrue to workers who labored in the zone are the *inverse* of the suspension of rights and the reduction to bare life that Ong describes as governing the majority of the North Korean population. In contrast, uncertainties about these workers' labor conditions, compensation, and rights— combined with the geopolitical representations described above—are likely to continue to be used to criticize and/or limit the scope of projects like the KIC, marking it as a form (or volatility) of territoriality whose future duration is deeply uncertain.

6   Conclusion

We have argued that the KIC can be considered as a novel experiment in urban-industrial territoriality, one that has been facilitated by a wide network of actors and practices that have helped assemble the project by developing the zone, creating market access, laboring in its factories, and facilitating international support. Without this larger network, it would be difficult to effectively realize surplus value from the labor of KIC workers, whose work facilitates an uneasy and problematic capitalist peace. Nonetheless, the convergence of these actors at such an intense node of geopolitical antagonism, as well as concerns surrounding the labor practices within the zone, make it a particularly unpredictable project. The degree to which the KIC and other inter-Korean zonal projects will produce alternative imaginaries of governance on the peninsula thus seems uncertain given their recent closure. The other flagship economic engagement project, the Kumgang Mountain Resort, also developed by Hyundai Asan, was shut down after nearly ten years of operation. Besides the present closure of the zone and its five-month shutdown in the spring and summer of 2013, the KIC has faced various slowdowns and restrictions on entry and exit of goods and people during inter-Korean tensions at other times in the past. The 2013 closure of the zone came at a point of transition in both Koreas with the ascendency of Kim Jong Un after the death of his father, Kim Jong Il, as well as the inauguration of conservative South Korean President Park Geun Hye, daughter of the former dictator Park Chung Hee. Both fledging administrations had a stake in demonstrating a firm stance towards each other. While the zone was reopened in September 2013, the five-month shutdown affected a number of firms' economic performances, with some clients switching suppliers for fear that inter-Korean instability would affect their ability to receive products on time. Some firms pulled out or sold their company assets to pay back debts incurred by the shutdown. For some analysts, the closure underlined the fact that the KIC remains "hostage to volatile relations," a problem they attribute to the conditions on the peninsula at large (Dawney cited in Salmon, 2013).

While the recent thaw in Korean relations following the election of liberal President Moon Jae-in raises hope that the Koreas might experiment with further engagement through zonal policy, it is thus difficult to tell what the future has in store for the KIC.[11] South Korean anxiety over North Korea's nuclear ambitions and continued missile tests continue to affect the project. Even during periods of relative détente, efforts to normalize the KIC through greater internationalization have been met with obstacles. The five-point accord agreed by both Koreas in 2013 to reopen the zone promised to expand capacity and increase its internationalization, potentially opening the zone as a site attractive to global capital as a way of addressing the often volatile relations between North and South. The agreement included a clause that committed both Koreas to "actively promote the introduction of investment from foreign businesses," by holding "joint investment relations sessions abroad" and seeking preferential tariffs for Kaesong products exported to third countries. The accord also promised to work towards raising the "labor affairs, tax, wage and insurance" of the zone to global standards (Carter 2013, no page). However, these incentives failed to further internationalize the KIC or quarantine it from geopolitical tensions. Foreign firms had previously been eligible to invest in firms that operate in the KIC, but many had not done so out of concerns over the stability of their investments, not to mention reputational risk. Moreover, the internationalization of the KIC clashed with legislative efforts in U.S. Congress to expand the sanctions against North Korea, such as H.R. 1771, the North Korea Sanctions Enforcement Act (Manyin et al. 2014, 2). While the impeachment of President

---

11   In his first new-year press conference, President Moon acknowledged that reopening of the KIC and Mt. Kumgang Resort should be considered "within the framework of the international sanctions imposed by the UN Security Council" (Ser 2018).

Park Geun-hye in 2017 raised hopes for a renewal of engagement (Doucette 2017), the tension between geopolitical containment and geoeconomic engagement seem likely to continue to shape the zone.

Nevertheless, while the future use of zoning technologies for alternative, inter-Korean relations is difficult to predict, it seems that zonal experiments will continue to reshape North Korea's economic landscape. Its Rason Zone has already become the second richest city in North Korea and North Korean government continues to set up various types of zones across the territory, regardless of tighter international economic sanctions. This seemingly contradictory move, we argue, demonstrates that North Korea's own territory dynamics "security first, economy next" still pervade its zoning strategy even during the Kim Jong Un era (Lee 2016b). In other words, North Korea's successful nuclear and missile tests are ironically expected to widen the space for its geoeconomic strategy. Despite the uncertainty surrounding the KIC's unstable territoriality, zoning technologies continue to reshape the nexus between sovereignty, territoriality, and political economy on the Korean peninsula.

References

Agnew, J (2005) Sovereignty regimes: territoriality and state authority in contemporary world politics. *Annals of the Association of American Geographers* 95(2): 437–461.

Agnew, J (2010) Still trapped in territory? *Geopolitics* 15(4): 779–784.

Antonsich, M (2009) On territory, the nation-state and the crisis of the hyphen. *Progress in Human Geography* 33(6): 789–806.

Bach, J (2011) Modernity and the urban imagination in economic zones. *Theory, Culture and Society* 28(5): 99–122.

Branigan, T (2013, 1 May) Choco Pies offer North Koreans a taste of the other side. *The Guardian*, http://www.theguardian.com/world/2013/may/01/choco-pies-north-koreans Accessed 22.02.2014.

Caraway T (2007) *Assembling Women: The Feminization of Global Manufacturing*. Ithaca: Cornell University Press.

Carter, AF (2013) Kaesong goes international: You cannot be serious? *Wall Street Journal: Korea Realtime*. http://blogs.wsj.com/korearealtime/2013/09/12/foster-carter-kaesong-goes-international-you-cannot-be-serious/ Accessed 21.02 2014.

Chi, H (지해범) (2013, 6 May) Choco Pie at the KIC (개성공단 초코파이). *NK Chosun* (NK 조선). http://nk.chosun.com/news/articleView.html?idxno=148896 Accessed 22.02.2014. (In Korean).

Chosun Ilbo (2013a, 9 April) N. Korea pulls workers out of Kaesong Complex. http://
english.chosun.com/site/data/html_dir/2013/04/09/2013040900517.html Accessed
26.12.2013.

Chosun Ilbo (조선일보) (2013b, 1 June) The North's military determined to shut down
the Kaesong Industrial Complex from the beginning of the year (北군부, 연초
부터 개성공단 폐쇄로 작심하고 몰고갔다) http://news.chosun.com/site/data/
html_dir/2013/06/01/2013060100265.html Accessed 20.01.2014. (In Korean).

Chung, BH (정병호) (2009, 23 May) How should the progressive camp view the KIC
issue? (진보진영은 개성공단 문제를 어떻게 봐야 하는가?) *Left 21*, http://left21
.com/article/6528 Accessed 19.02.2014. (In Korean).

Chung, MI (2013) Thoughts on a peace-regime to end the Korean War. *Global Asia*
8(3): 92–98.

Chung, YC (2004) North Korean reform and opening: dual strategy and '*silli* (practical)
socialism'. *Pacific Affairs* 77(2): 283–304.

Cronin, P (2012) *Vital Venture: Economic Engagement of North Korea and the Kaesong
Industrial Complex*. Washington: Center for a New American Security.

Cross, J (2014) *Dream Zones: Anticipating Capitalism and Development in India*. London: Pluto Press.

Dong-A Ilbo (2013) "A messanger [sic] for Kaesong Industrial Complex," 13 August, http://english.donga.com/srv/service.php3?biid=2013081366088 Accessed
19.01.2014.

Doucette, J (2013) The Korean Thermidor: on political space and conservative reac-
tions. *Transactions of the Institute of British Geographers* 38(2): 299–310.

Doucette, J (2015) Debating Economic Democracy in South Korea: The Costs of Commensurability. *Critical Asian Studies* 47(3): 388–413.

Doucette, J. 2017 The Occult of Personality: Korea's Candlelight Protests and the Impeachment of Park Geun-hye. *Journal of Asian Studies* 76(4): 851–860.

Doucette, J, & SW Koo (2013) Distorting democracy: politics by public security in contemporary South Korea. *The Asia-Pacific Journal* 11(48/4).

Doucette, J, and S-O Lee (2015) Experimental territoriality: Assembling the Kaesong
industrial complex in North Korea. *Political Geography* 47: 53–63.

Doucette, J, and S Kang (2017) Legal geographies of labour and postdemocracy: Reinforcing non-standard work in South Korea. *Transactions of the Institute of British
Geographers*. Doi: 10.1111/tran.12216.

Doucette, J, & SW Koo (2016) "Pursuing Post-democratization: The Resilience of Politics by Public Security in Contemporary South Korea." *Journal of Contemporary
Asia* 46(2) 198–221.

Doucette, J and AR Müller (2016) Exporting the *Saemaul* spirit: South Korea's Knowledge Sharing Program and the 'rendering technical' of Korean development. *Geoforum* 75: 29–39.

Easterling K (2014) *Extrastatecraft: The power of infrastructural space.* London: Verso.

Elden, S (2013) *The Birth of Territory.* Chicago: University of Chicago Press.

Elson, D & R Pearson (1981) 'Nimble Fingers Make Cheap Workers': An analysis of women's employment in Third World export manufacturing. *Feminist Review 7*: 87–107.

Gauthier, JP (no date) Mission. *World Export Processing Zone Association. http://www .wepza.org/mission/* (accessed 12 January 2015).

Gimm, DW (2013) Fracturing hegemony: regionalism and state rescaling in South Korea, 1961–71. *International Journal of Urban and Regional Research 37*(4): 1147–1167.

Glassman, J (2004) *Thailand at the Margins: The Internationalization of the State and the Transformation of Labour.* Oxford: Oxford University Press.

Glassman, J 2018 Geopolitical economies of development and democratization in East Asia: Themes, concepts, and geographies. *Environment and Planning A 50*(2): 407–415. 10.1177/0308518X17737170.

Gray, K and JW Lee (2017) Following in China's footsteps? The political economy of North Korean reform. *The Pacific Review 30*(1): 51–73.

Ha, TW (2013, 29 May) Merit-based bonus for workers in N. Korea. *The Dong-A Ilbo.* http://english.donga.com/srv/service.php3?biid=2013052967518 Accessed 22.02.2014.

Haggard, S & M Noland (2009) A security and peace mechanism for Northeast Asia: the economic dimension. *The Pacific Review 22*(2): 119–137.

Hankook Ilbo (한국일보) (2006, 11 May) The people's agreement is necessary for 'concessions to North Korea' ('대북 양보'에는 국민 동의가 필수). http://news.hankooki .com/lpage/opinion/200605/h2006051019401723920.html Accessed 5.01.2014. (In Korean).

Hong, C (2013) The mirror of North Korean human rights: technologies of liberation, technologies of war. *Critical Asian Studies 45*(4): 561–592.

Hsu, JH (2009) The spatial encounter between neoliberalism and populism in Taiwan: regional restructuring under the DPP regime in the new millenium. *Political Geography 28*: 296–308.

Human Rights Watch (2006a) North Korea: Workers' Rights at the Kaesong Industrial Complex. South Korean Companies Violate Labor Law. http://www.hrw.org/en/ news/2006/10/01/north-korea-labor-rights-risk-joint-industrial-complex Accessed 1.07.2013.

Human Rights Watch (2006b) Briefing Paper: North Korea: Workers' Rights at the Kaesong Industrial Complex. http://www.hrw.org/legacy/backgrounder/asia/ korea1006/korea1006web.pdf Accessed 1.07.2013.

Hsu, J-y D-W Gimm, and J Glassman (2018) A tale of two industrial zones: A geopolitical economy of differential development in Ulsan, South Korea, and Kaohsiung, Taiwan. *Environment and Planning A 50*(2): 457–473.

Hwang, I D (황일도) (2004) The development of the KIC substantially moves the truce line northward (개성공단 개발로 휴전선 사실상 北上). *Shin Dong-A* (신동아), 532, 228–234. (In Korean).

Im, E (임을출) (2005) *Welcome to Kaesong Industrial Complex* (웰컴투 개성공단). Seoul: Haenam. (In Korean).

Jeong, HG and JH Pek (2016) *Special Economic Zones: What Can Developing Countries Learn from the Korean Experience?* Seoul: Ministry of Strategy and Finance, Republic of Korea.

Kaesong Industrial District Management Committee (2007) *Welcome to the Kaesong Industrial Complex.* Seoul: KIDMAC.

Kang, J (강주희) (2017, 28 April) Hong Joon-Pyo 'Reopening the KIC is a violation of UN sanctions'. Moon Jae-In, 'Reopening after conversation' (홍준표 '개성공단 재개는 유엔제재 위반', 문재인 '대화후 재개'). *Views & News* http://www.viewsnnews.com/article?q=144573 Accessed 10 February 2018.

Kim, MJ (2004) The military implications of the Kaesong Industrial Complex Project. *Northeast Asia Strategic Analysis*, April, 1–4.

Kim, S (2011, 21 November) Kaesong lets Choco Pie fever get out of control. *Korea Joongang Daily.* http://koreajoongangdaily.joins.com/news/article/article.aspx?aid =2944430 Accessed 28 March 2014.

MK Kim (김문경) (2013, 28 April) 'The Kaesong Industrial Complex' back into a key military base? North Korea's comments attract attention ('개성공단', 다시 군사요충지로?…北 언급 주목돼). *YTN.* http://www.ytn.co.kr/_ln/ 0101_201304281748006750_001 Accessed 18.01.2014. (In Korean).

Kim, B, J Kim, and K Ryu (김병철, 김재준, 류근관) (2009) Power of a Word in Media Politics: An Analysis of 'Peojugi,' the Most Generous Aid to North Korea. [미디어 유행어와 여론의 그랜저 인과관계] *Korean Journal of Journalism & Communication Studies 53*(1): 412–438. (In Korean).

Knudsen, DJ, & WJ Moon (2010) North Korea and the politics of international trade law: the Kaesong Industrial Complex and WTO rules of origin. *Yale Journal of International Law 35*(1): 251–256.

Koo, H (2001) *Korean Workers: The Culture and Politics of Class Formation.* Ithaca: Cornell University Press.

Lee, JT (이종태) (2018, 16 January) 개성공단은 자본주의를 어떻게 가르쳤나 [How did KIC teach Capitalism?] *SisaIn* (시사인) 539, http://www.sisain.co.kr/?mod=news &act=articleView&idxno=31026 Accessed 20 January 2018.

Lee, H (이하늬) (2018, 6 February) '임금이 달러박스란 주장은 거짓' ['The claim that the wage is a dollar box is false] *Weekly Kyunghyang* (주간경향) 1264. http:// weekly.khan.co.kr/khnm.html?mode=view&artid=201801301331181&code=113 Accessed 10 February 2018.

Lee, M-G, and S-R Kim (2006, 1 May) Are Gaesong workers being exploited? *The Dong-A Ilbo.* http://english.donga.com/srv/service.php3?biid=2006050139698 Accessed 20.02.2014.

Lee, N (2007) *The Making of the Minjung: Democracy and the Politics of Representation in South Korea*. Ithaca: Cornell University Press.

Lee, S-O (2014a) The production of territory in North Korea: 'Security First, Economy Next'. *Geopolitics 19*(1): 206–226.

Lee, S-O (2014b) China's new territorial strategies towards North Korea: security, development, and inter-scalar politics. *Eurasian Geography and Economics 55*(2): 175–200.

Lee, S-O (2015) A geoeconomic object or an object of geopolitical absorption? Competing visions of North Korea in South Korean politics. *Journal of Contemporary Asia 45*(4): 693–714.

Lee, S-O (이승욱) (2016a) Geopolitics of the Kaesong Industrial Complex: Space of exception, universal space or hostage space? (개성공단의 지정학: 예외공간, 보편공간 또는 인질공간?) *Space and Society* (공간과 사회) *26*(2): 132–163.

Lee, S-O (이승욱) (2016b). North Korea's special economic zones strategy in the Kim Jong-Un era: Territorialization, decentralization, and Chinese-style reform and opening? (김정은 시대 북한의 경제특구전략: 영역화, 분권화, 그리고 중국식 개혁개방? *Journal of the Economic Geographical Society of Korea* (한국경제지리 학회지) *19*(1): 122–142.

Lee, S-O, N Jan, and J Wainwright (2013). Agamben, postcoloniality and sovereignty in South Korea. *Antipode 46*(3): 650–668.

Lee, S-O, J Wainwright, and J Glassman (2018) Geopolitical economy and the production of territory: The case of US–China geopolitical-economic competition in Asia. *Environment and Planning A 50*(2): 416–436.

Lee, YJ (이영종) (2006, 30 April) U.S. Special Envoy for Human Rights in North Korea, 'labor exploitation at the KIC' (미국 북 인권특사 '개성공단 노동 착취'). *Joongang Ilbo* (중앙일보). http://nk.joins.com/news/view.asp?aid=2717317 Accessed 20.02.2014. (In Korean).

Lee, YJ (이영종) (2013) The threat from the military to close the Kaesong Industrial Complex (군부가 주동한 개성공단 폐쇄 협박). *Sisa Journal* (시사저널), 1225, http://www.sisapress.com/news/articleView.html?idxno=60226 Accessed 20.01.2014. (In Korean).

Lefkowitz, J (2006, 28 April) Freedom for all Koreans. *The Wall Street Journal*. http://eng.unikorea.go.kr/board/view.do?boardId=BOoooooooo90&menuCd= DOM_oooooo201002oooooo&startPage=42&dataSid=219998 Accessed 20.02. 2014.

Lussault, M (2007) *L'homme spatial: La construction sociale de l'espace humain*. Paris: Seuil.

Manyin, ME, E Chanlett-Avery, I.E. Rinehart, M.B. Nikitin, & W.H. Cooper (2014) *U.S.-South Korea Relations*. Congressional Research Service R41481.

Martin, L, and A Secor (2014) Towards a post-mathematical topology. *Progress in Human Geography 38*(3): 420–438.

McCann, E, and K Ward. (2012) Assembling urbanism: following policies and 'studying through' the sites and situations of policy making. *Environment and Planning A 44*: 42–51.

Mills, MB (2005) From nimble fingers to raised fists: women and labor activism in globalizing Thailand. *Signs 31*(1): 117–144.

Ministry of Unification (2016, 10 February) Government statement regarding the complete shutdown of the Gaeseong Industrial Complex. http://www.unikorea.go.kr/eng_unikorea/news/releases/?boardId=bbs_0000000000000034&mode=view&cntId=44417&category=&pageIdx=5 Accessed 11.02.2018.

Murray, MJ, 2017 *The Urbanism of Exception*. Cambridge UK: Cambridge University Press.

Neveling, P (2015) Free trade zones, export processing zones, special economic zones and global imperial formations 200 BCE to 2015 CE. In I. Ness & Z. Cope (eds.),*The Palgrave Encyclopedia of Imperialism and Anti-Imperialism* (pp. 1007–1016). Basingstok: Palgrave Macmillan.

Niksch, L (2006) The troubled R.O.K.-U.S. military alliance: revitalization, downgrading, or dissolution? Paper for a Conference on U.S.-Korean Relations by The Center for International Strategy, Technology, and Policy, Georgia Institute of Technology, 1–2 November.

Noland, M, and G Flake (1997) Opening attempt: North Korea and the Rajin-Sonbong Free Trade and Economic Zone. *Journal of Asian Business 13*(2): 99–116.

Ong, A (1987) *Spirits of Resistance and Capitalist Discipline: Factory Women in Malaysia*. Albany, State University of New York Press.

Ong, A (1991) The gender and labor politics of postmodernity. *Annual Review of Anthropology 20*: 279–309.

Ong, A (2004) The Chinese axis: zoning technologies and variegated sovereignty.*Journal of East Asian Studies 4*: 69–96.

Ong, A (2006) *Neoliberalism as Exception*. Chapel Hill: Duke University Press.

Painter, J (2010) Rethinking territory. *Antipode 42*(5): 1090–1118.

Palan, R (2003) *The Offshore World: Sovereign Markets, Virtual Places, and Nomad Millionaires*. Ithaca: Cornell University Press.

Park, B-G (2005) Spatially selective liberalization and graduated sovereignty: politics of neo-liberalism and 'special economic zones' in South Korea. *Political Geography 24*(7): 850–873.

Park, B-G (2013) Looking for more space-sensitive Korean studies. *Korean Social Science Review 3*(2): 157–193.

Park, B-G, RC Hill, & A Saito (eds.) (2012) *Locating Neoliberalism in East Asia: Neoliberalizing Spaces in Developmental States*. Chichester: Wiley-Blackwell.

Park, B-G, S-O Lee and S Cho (박배균, 이승욱, 조성찬) (eds.) (2017) *Spaces of Exception in East Asia* [특구: 국가의 영토성과 동아시아의 예외공간]. Seoul: ALT.

Park, B-G, and J Lepawsky (2012) Spatially selective liberalization in South Korea and Malaysia: neoliberalization in Asian Developmental States. In B-G. Park, R.C. Hill, & A. Saito (eds.), *Locating Neoliberalism in East Asia: Neoliberalizing Spaces in Developmental States* (pp. 114–147). Chichester: Wiley-Blackwell.

Park, H.O (2009) The politics of unification and neoliberal democracy: economic cooperation and North Korean human rights." In S. Ryang (ed.), *North Korea: Towards a Better Understanding* (pp. 109–128). Plymouth, UK: Lexington Books.

Park, M (2009) Framing free trade agreements: the politics of nationalism in the anti-neoliberal globalization movement in South Korea. *Globalizations 6*(4): 451–466.

Park, M, F Cha, and E Contreras (2014, 27 January) How Choco Pie infiltrated North Korea's sweet booth. *CNN.* http://edition.cnn.com/2014/01/27/world/asia/choco-pie-koreas/ Accessed 22.02.2014.

Passi, A (1999) Boundaries as social processes: territoriality in a world of flows. In D. Newman (ed.), *Boundaries, Territory and Postmodernity* (pp. 69–88). London: Grank Cass.

Peck, J, (1992) Labor and agglomeration: Control and flexibility in local labor markets. *Economic geography 68*(4): 325–347.

Peck, J, and N Theodore (2007) Variegated capitalism. *Progress in Human Geography 31*(6): 731–772.

Pressian (프레시안) (2013, 25 June) The full text of the transcript of the 2007 inter-Korean summit meeting: a dialogue record for 246 minutes ([2007 남북정상회담 대화록 전문] 246 분의 대화 기록). http://www.pressian.com/news/article.html?no=107979 Accessed 13.01.2014. (In Korean).

Raffestin, C (2012) Space, territory, and territoriality. *Environment and Planning D: Society and Space 30*: 121–141.

Reuters (2017, 10 October) North Korean workers operating in closed, South-invested factory zone. https://uk.reuters.com/article/us-northkorea-kaesong-southkorea/north-korean-workers-operating-in-closed-south-invested-factory-zone-idUKKBN1CB0VR Accessed 10 February 2018.

RFA (2017, 6 October) North Korea secretly making clothing in Kaesong Industrial Park with South's equipment. https://www.rfa.org/english/news/korea/korea-kaesong-10062017180901.html Accessed 10 February 2018.

Richardson, HW, & C. C-H Bae (2009) Options for the capital of a reunified Korea. *SAIS Review of International Affairs 29*(1): 67–77.

Sack, RD (1986) *Human Territoriality: Its Theory and History.* Cambridge: Cambridge University Press.

Salmon, A (2013, 24 December) Inside North Korea: could the Kaesong complex give hope for the future? *The Telegraph.* http://www.telegraph.co.uk/news/worldnews/asia/northkorea/10535828/Inside-North-Korea-Could-the-Kaesong-complex-give-hope-for-the-future.html Accessed 22.01.2014.

Sassen, S (2013) When territory deborders territoriality. *Territory, Politics, Governance* *1*(1): 21–45.

Ser, M-J (2018, 10 January) Moon stands firm on sanctions on North in New Year's press conference. *Korea Joonang Daily*. http://koreajoongangdaily.joins.com/news/article/article.aspx?aid=3043136 Accessed 11.02.2018.

Shin, G-W (2002) Marxism, anti-Americanism, and democracy in South Korea: an examination of nationalist discourse. In T. Barlow (ed.), *New Asian Marxisms* (pp. 359–384). Durham: Duke University Press.

Shin, JH (신지호) (2003, 5 August). The tragedy from unscrupulous inter-Korean economic cooperation (무원칙經協이부른비극). *The Donga Ilbo* (동아일보). http://news.donga.com/List/Series_70040100000040/3/70040100000040/20030805/7970851/1 Accessed 5.01.2014. (In Korean).

Sidaway, JD. (2007a) Spaces of postdevelopment. *Progress in Human Geography 31*(3): 345–361.

Sidaway, JD (2007b) Enclave space: a new metageography of development. *Area 39*(3): 331–339.

Smith, H (2005) *Hungry for Peace: International Security, Humanitarian Assistance, and Social Change in North Korea*. Washington, DC: United States Institute of Peace.

Sonn, JW (2010) Contesting state rescaling: an analysis of the South Korean state's discursive strategy against devolution. *Antipode 42*(5): 1200–1224.

Stanton (2007) Kaesong Industrial Complex: the inter-Korean project to watch. Wikileaks Cable 07SEOUL2144 Accessed June 2013.

Stanton (2009) ROK's Kaesong manager: DPRK trying to shake ROK politics. Wikileaks Cable 09SEOUL808 Accessed June 2013.

The China Post (2013, 5 April) North Korean leaders divided over Kaesong industrial enclave. https://www.chinapost.com.tw/asia/korea/2013/04/05/375175/North-Korean.htm Accessed 18.01 2014.

Yi, J-s (2014, 21 February) Most popular gift for North Korean families was 'Choco Pie'. *The Kyunghyang Shinmun*. http://english.khan.co.kr/khan_art_view.html?artid=201402211908127&code=710100 Accessed 23.02.2014.

Yonhap News (2017, 10 October) N.K.'s resumption of Kaesong complex violates property rights. http://english.yonhapnews.co.kr/news/2017/10/10/0200000000AEN2017101004700315.html Accessed 10 February 2018.

Yoon, S-H, and S-O Lee (2013) From old comrades to new partnerships: dynamic development of economic relations between China and North Korea. *The Geographical Journal 179*(1): 19–31.

CHAPTER 9

From 'Special Zones' to Cities and City-regions in China

Carolyn Cartier

1   Introduction[1]

The idea of state developmentalism in East Asia, in the reach of Cold War history, internalizes uneven political-economic geographies. In 1949, the People's Republic of China (PRC) became the region's primary geopolitical pivot and an ally of the Democratic People's Republic of North Korea. In response, the U.S. government supported postwar industrial development in the 'non-communist' economies of the region. South Korea and Taiwan, writes Bruce Cumings (1987: 67–68), "were enmeshed in a system of American hegemony that brought them economic and military aid on an unheard-of scale." From 1955–1978, South Korea and Taiwan together received US$9.05 billion in U.S. assistance (compared to US$3.2 billion for Africa and Latin America combined). With Hong Kong and Singapore, South Korea and Taiwan became 'economic miracles'—signifying export-oriented industrialization, rapidity of socio-economic transformation, and new understandings about the role of the state. Challenged by these 'newly industrialized economies' (NIEs) on its regional doorstep, and on an uncertain course, the Chinese Communist Party (CCP) took the decision, in December 1978, to open to the world economy.

The CCP had a new model in mind. In November 1978, Party leadership, geopolitically limited from visiting Taiwan or Hong Kong, traveled to Southeast Asia to learn about Singapore's 25-year transformation from colony to industrial economy and city-state; China's leader, Deng Xiaoping, compared the size of Singapore's area and population. He reportedly said, "If I had only Shanghai, I too might be able to develop Shanghai as quickly. But I have the whole of China!" (in Lye, 2016: 107). Within three years, the PRC would declare itself open to foreign investment and trade in four 'special economic zones' on the south China coast. Called an experiment, they were located as far away from the capital, Beijing, as possible. The first one, Shenzhen, located strategically

---

1   Research for this work has been supported by the Australian Research Council Discovery Projects (DP120101901; DP170100871).

on the Hong Kong boundary, landmarked China's opening to global capitalism after prolonged isolation during the Mao era (1949–1976).

Yet before Shenzhen was declared a special economic zone, it was established within the Chinese system of administrative divisions as a new 'sub-provincial-level city'. Its specially designated economic function amplified its ontological status in the subnational governing system. In an interrelated process of urban-economic transformation, new domestic and international investment in the 'zone' jump-started development of the large city that Shenzhen would become. Shenzhen was not an economic zone carved out of a port or an industrial area or a rust-belt region. Its area was a historic agricultural frontier or 'greenfield' site on the boundary of an Asian NIE. The idea of the special economic zone was the seed of the city-region north of Hong Kong. In response to these historical conditions, and the project of urban developmentalism in East Asia, this chapter critically evaluates the idea of 'zone' and how zone has traveled, as a word and a concept, and the political-economic context in China where special economic zones are also normal jurisdictions within the administrative-territorial system.

2   Zone: An Expansive Idea?

The significance of the idea of zones is inseparable from Asian regional development and the NIEs. Export-oriented industrialization in the NIEs, in the 1960s and 1970s, modeled export-processing zones (EPZs) for a next wave of developing Asian states in China, India, and beyond. Taiwan opened the first one in the region, at Kaohsiung, in 1965. In the 1980s, with special economic zones, China appeared to have continued reliance on zone-based industrial development. Then in the 2000s India sought to follow suit. In 2007 the Department of Commerce of India explained, in 'Special Economic Zones are the dream projects of the Government', how zones were "launched by the Government of India, with great fanfare, on the model of the Special Economic Zones in China, in the fond hope that they would help India replicate the Chinese success story of rapid industrialization" (Parliament of India, 2007: para. 6.1). In this virtually utopian discourse, zones would be keys to economic desire and actual material results. As the idea proliferated, zones became an economic space, a policy approach, and a set of assumptions or geographical imagination about rapid economic growth.

In the scholarship, work on zones has adopted a range of approaches, ranging from transition theory to Marxist political economy and interdisciplinary development theory, to variations in poststructuralist theory (cf. Deyo, 1987;

Farole and Akinci, 2011; Litwack and Qian, 1998; Nee, 1992; Ong, 2004, 2006; Yeung et al., 2009). The dependent development literature demonstrates how strong states matter in Asia, and places EPZ activity in local, 'national' and global arenas. In this stream, *The Political Economy of the New Asian Industrialism*, edited by Frederic Deyo (1987), remains the baseline treatment in historical perspective. It finds economic contributions of EPZs to have been underestimated and overstated, underestimated because their economic role has been more substantial than international subcontracting (dominant only in Singapore), yet overstated because their role declined by the 1970s in relation to the expansion of national economies (Haggard and Cheng, 1987). The latter condition especially characterizes China.

The poststructural approaches, confronting rigidities of Fordism and methodological nationalism, and recognizing variegated capitalisms, seek to explain processes of transformation and transboundary flows. Approaches infused by postcolonial theory often appear in spatial inquiry through widespread 'mapping', 'representing' and 'situating' of local conditions and power relations. In this arena the leading poststructural scholarship, by Aihwa Ong (2004, 2006), has sought to lend greater insight into ontological conditions of zones. By articulating zone in the present participle, Ong suggests how 'zoning' generates not only mobility of labor and capital but also, as context and concept, 'spaces of political and economic exception' where sovereign power exercises regulatory networks for new political economic potential (2004: 70; cf. 2006: *passim.*). This apparent capacity, in which 'zones' exist in relation to and simultaneously as 'exceptional' from state territory, generates 'zoning technologies' that would mark out and govern their differences.

Where historical work on East Asian developmentalism tends to emphasize the role of the state and path dependence, and poststructural approaches find transboundary economies generated through mobility of labor and capital in 'exceptional' spaces, recent contributions extend the idea of 'zone' through generalization of globalizing conditions. Their ideational aesthetics incorporate impulses of flexibility associated with urban neoliberalization. In architectural commentary on urbanism, for example, the idea of zone predictably circulates to reproduce architecture's historical core conceits—form and function. Keller Easterling's (2012) architectural treatment of 'the phenomenon of the free zone' energizes circulation through play of neoliberal valences and biological metaphors, describing zones as 'highly contagious' and 'breeding'. Notions that "the world has dominant software for making urban space: the free zone—the formula that generates Shenzhens and Dubais all around the world" and "zone is now the germ of a city-building epidemic that reproduces glittering mimics of Dubai, Singapore, and Hong Kong" (Easterling, 2014: 15, 26) extend the zone analog to world cities. A Shenzhen global model is simply fantastic. The curious element in this treatment is a political postmodernity that conflates significantly different territories, political economies, and state institutions.

The idea of zone is also merging with 'enclaves'. In political geography an enclave is a territory fully surrounded by another state, but this has given way to an array of 'enclave spaces' in categorical terms, e.g. ethnic enclaves, tourist enclaves and so on. Export-processing zones also appear in James Sidaway's (2007a, 2007b) summary of enclaves as 'development and postdevelopment spaces'. The trend continues in work that treats zones as essential contexts of urban development. Martin Murray (2017), extending Ong's terminology, pursues 'urbanism of exception' through 'assemblage of enclaves', including 'autonomous zones', as if proliferating and diversifying into a range of 'promiscuous and powerful extraterritorial global forms' (207). Their 'accelerated unbundling of sovereign territoriality' (215) construes how such spaces of capital would deterritorialize from national landscapes.

Yet what is it that is deterritorializing? If 'zoning' addresses zone ontology and 'zoning technologies' accounts for zone formation, then such concepts should contribute to resolving the fixed space problem, i.e. the notion that zones exist as abstract economic spaces apart from dynamics of the territorial state. On the other hand, if 'zoning' marks the appearance and form of spaces called zones, effectively representing explanation through replication, then we are compelled to ask why research on zones falls back on repetitious ontology. What theoretical and methodological critiques can we draw on to clarify this problem? Can the conceptual history of analog models, with roots in the history of postwar spatial science, shed light on the issue?

The next section introduces analog circulation of research paradigms and the longer history of analog models in postwar spatial science. The second section reframes 'zoning technologies', 'spaces of exception' and 'sovereignty' through state and market perspectives to make evident how neoliberal emphasis on zones contributes to narrowing inquiry into the role of the state and state territorial dynamics. It develops a state–market problematic to examine how 'zone' and 'zoning technologies' reproduce notional space of neoliberal marketization even where state capitalism defines regional economies through state territorial strategies.

The third section responds to the problem through the assessment of subnational territory and the development of 'territorial economies' in China through changes to administrative territory.

3   Analog Circulation

The problem of analog circulation in research design is not new and yet it is not an obvious tool in the critical theoretical kit. In recent self-reflections, Giorgio Agamben (2009) takes up the problem of analog circulation through Thomas Kuhn's (1962) *The Structure of Scientific Revolutions*. Its core thesis, about how paradigms 'function' in research design and the mutually constitutive process of knowledge formation and formation of knowledge communities, has made sociological study a precondition for understanding the history of science. Less well known is how Kuhn's response to criticisms—the paradigm concept required differentiation—embeds analog thought. Kuhn (1970) subsequently defined 'exemplars' and the 'disciplinary matrix', two main paradigms, in which exemplars circulate as analog models whereas the matrix constitutes the broader knowledge of the community.

The problem at stake is the exemplar: how its analog circulation risks increasingly internalizing limits whose conditions become paradoxically inconspicuous through circulation or spread and acceptance. Problems and limitations embed in analog thought as 'scientists model one problem solution on another' (Kuhn, 1977: 470). In analysis of Kuhn's dialog, Andrew Mair (1986: 351) identifies how the 'exemplar method', transmuting 'a *pedagogic* as well as a *heuristic* role' uses 'solutions to past problems in order to account for new situations'. Such analog circulation takes uncharted flight through models 'without recourse to explicit correspondence rules or even empirical generalizations' (ibid.). Analog circulation thus also reproduces through mere identification and selection of analogic conditions, i.e., only presumably 'like' conditions that resemble those of the preexisting model.

The problem of the analog thus emerges as a cautionary methodological issue for comparative research. This is particularly the case in geographical research design since, as Mair (360) observes, "a subset of analogical arguments is uniquely geographic; the application of analyses derived in one place to new situations in other places." Thus, the idea of zone—as a geographical artifact of concentrated economic activity under late capitalism—circulates imbued with these potentials.

Differences in analog models demonstrate particular problems of the exemplar for social science research. Outstanding in physical geography are large-scale models of river and estuary systems built by the U.S. Army Corps of Engineers. In Sausalito, California, a 1.5-acre-plus building houses a working scale model of the San Francisco Bay. The Corps built 'The Bay Model' of the San Francisco and Sacramento-San Joaquin River Delta System in the 1950s and 1960s to test potential changes to hydraulic flow. A scaled-down version of the world at its feet, The Bay Model is an analog in fluvial geomorphology. It models mechanics of the physical world in a laboratory setting. The Bay Model is a model of what it seeks to model.

In contrast, the exemplar, as analog, circulates to model different places and 'other things'. Analog models circulate to frame research whose constitutive conditions demonstrate similar order—similar forms, patterns, structures, and internal arrangements. Thus, analog modeling of space, at the meta-scale, concerns apparent *a priori* similarities of spatial form and structure, which facilitate the replication of analog concepts. Consider how analog models in postwar spatial science on 'systems' found analog properties in the pattern and structure of spatial hierarchy:

> Spatial systems may be organized hierarchically so that large high order areas in a system may collect flows from, or deliver flows to small low order areas in the system. Examples at a geographical spatial scale are rivers, alpine glaciers and central place systems. Examples in the organic realm are at a much smaller scale, i.e. trees, blood vessels, airways, bile ducts and even the microscopic branching of the Purkinje cell in the brain.
>
> WOLDENBERG, 1979: 429

Called 'persistent geometric progressions', "these spatial hierarchies all exhibit certain mathematical regularities which lead one to speculate about a common generating model" (Woldenberg, 1979: 429).

The analog logic on display is one in which similar patterns are held to be explicable by mathematical generalization. Michael Woldenberg's interrelated work with urban geographer Brian Berry pursued the idea of rivers and central places as 'analogous systems'. Woldenberg and Berry (1967: 129) observed, "In recent years geomorphologists have conceived of rivers as open systems, and urban geographers and others have applied the term system to cities or sets of cities." But self-evident problems—great leaps among domains or topic areas and subjects characterized by widely different conditions—confirm the character of analog as method. Mair (1986: 360) writes "Woldenberg and Berry (1967) even attempted to compare river systems and central place systems," an effort judged to be 'actually stillborn' and 'rapidly recognized as having little positive content'. Such logical flaws characterized spatial science in the postwar period.

A related field, called 'social physics', was an interdisciplinary arena in which 'laws of physics', such as diffusion of gases, were applied to social change. The emblematic 'law' of social physics was 'the gravity model', in which 'the analogy with Newton's law of gravitation assumed that humans interact over space as heavenly bodies do in the celestial system' (Barnes 1994: 567). The idea that total human diffusion in space can be predicted using physical laws demonstrates fundamental problems of the analog between different and incommensurable systems. While we are tempted by 'outer space' jokes, no similarities are to be found between the orbits of planetary bodies and processes of social and cultural change and human mobility. (In the era the neoliberal university, famous professors might be referred to as 'stars', around whom students might gather or 'orbit', but this is a metaphorical elocution.) The paradigm as analog works by bracketing the conditions of the system on which the model is based, turning its conditions, including people and places, into generalized, interlinked elements.

In recent tangles with analog effects, Agamben observes how scholarly use of paradigms compares unfavorably with the degree to which they face analysis. Agamben (2009: 9) scrutinizes his own development of paradigms (*Homo sacer*, the state of exception, the concentration camp) from historic phenomena and acknowledges that his "approach has generated a few misunderstandings, especially for those who thought...that my intention was to offer merely historiographical theses or reconstructions." He evaluates critical claims in various works, from those of Aristotle to Foucault and Kuhn, to parse the meaning and function of paradigms. He concludes their circulation does not inform dialectical reasoning between the general and the particular, but that it works on the logic of the analog. Instead of working to inform deductive and inductive reasoning between the nomothetic and ideographic, for theory building, the analog form is a singularity that fixes paradigmatic meaning. The paradigm as analog represents its subject through repetition of a systematic case. Regular analog exposition of the paradigm, model, or 'truth' is what significantly constitutes its intelligibility.

In a lecture on the subject at the European Graduate School, Agamben (2002: 4) discusses paradigms in relation to Aristotelian thought and does so because "philosophy very rarely refers to the problems of paradigm and analogy." "Aristotle says," continues Agamben, "that the paradigm, the example, does not concern a part with respect to the whole, nor the whole with respect to the part, it concerns a part with respect to the part." This is significant: in part-to-part reasoning, the analog operates in the absence of synecdoche, articulation of theory and empirics, and induction and deduction. *The analog thus internalizes the capacity to operate in the absence of history.*

Building on this critique, let us continue the discussion of 'zones' as a problem of analog circulation. In the international academy and in the context of the post-Fordist era of late capitalism, 'zone' is a context and concept on multiple continents. Following Mair, 'zone' is one among geographic analogs whose conditions, derived from one or more places, apply to new situations. Drawing on the Aristotelian insight—analog as 'a part with respect to the part'—we should encounter zone comparisons through like forms, patterns, structures, and internal arrangements, in which similarity and transferability contribute to analog potential. The links to global capitalism also predict 'negative space' or blanked-out national space beyond zones through reductionism, i.e., 'zones' in 'China' or China's 'zones' and so on—the subject of zones entertains neither domestic geography nor territorial geography beyond zones except zone flows, linkages, and connections. The analog model will be confirmed especially if 'zone' exists territorially trapped, i.e. with assumptions about a fixed area or boundary and lacking integration with state territory in general.

4   The State–market Problematic

The PRC's decision to open to the world economy, in 1978, gripped the trending edge of late capitalism. China earned a 'global bonus' by opening to the world economy with the evolving neoliberal economic policy regime that would pro-pel another round of rapid growth and accumulation. Meanwhile the decade of the 2000s witnessed a profusion of monograph literature on neoliberalism. Where the classic idea of the state–market dichotomy transmits the view that states and markets are distinct or opposed, I use the state–market problematic to indicate the interrelationality of the state and marketization in the PRC, and the nature of evolving understanding about state capitalism in China, i.e. not a particular problem or a condition with resolute parameters but rather a meta-view from which it is possible to formulate entry points and critical questions whose answers may open up new research possibilities.

Leslie Sklair's (2001) *The Transnational Capitalist Class* spoke directly to neo-liberal policy earlier than the main wave of scholarship, which appeared in the decade from 2004 to 2014. (In 2004 'neoliberalism' appeared in the title of some 50 monographs, over two times the count of the previous year; in 2014 the number of monographs featuring the keyword reached an all-time peak of nearly 120 titles.) Where Sklair's (2001: 25–26) title did not signal the epony-mous market in monographs, his class analysis defines a core condition of "the neoliberal globalizing solution": "market-driven increases in the size of the cake to be redistributed" witnessing "the enrichment of many combined with the impoverishment of many more in rich and poor countries alike." Between the market and the state, globalizing neoliberalization, through extending markets and rolling back state redistributive measures, has contributed to intensified research focus on the market and the role of the state in extending markets.

5 'Zoning Technologies'

In this stream of scholarship, Aihwa Ong's *Neoliberalism as Exception: Mutations in Citizenship and Sovereignty* appeared in 2006. Its page one states, "Asian governments have selectively adopted neoliberal forms in creating economic zones and imposing market criteria on citizenship." 'Zoning' first appears as 'zoning technologies', which "have carved special spaces in order to achieve strategic goals of regulating groups in relation to market forces" (7). The book's Chapter Four, "Zoning technologies in East Asia," reprises, with various editorial changes, her essay, "The Chinese axis: zoning technologies and variegated sovereignty," which provides an account of "Greater China as a distinctive kind of regional space" through "zoning technologies for integrating distinct political entities such as Hong Kong and Macao, and even Taiwan and Singapore, into an emerging Chinese axis" (2004, 70; cf. 2006, 98–99). Here, 'zones' exist in relation to China's economic and political interests in the Asian NIES. How do they come into existence and proliferate? EPZs are 'created by an act of exception, the free trade or export-processing zone "is like a country within a country"' (2004: 75; 2006: 103). These representations are emblematic:

> Learning from economic zones elsewhere in Asia, China has developed zoning technologies that are distinctive in creating the forms for the alignment of the mainland with overseas Chinese-dominated polities in an archipelago of variegated sovereignty.
>
> 2004: 76; cf. 2006: 104

> This Chinese axis came about through the building of overlapping economic and political zones that are marked off from conditions prevailing in the centrally planned socialist environment. In the opening to the global economy, the Chinese state invoked the logic of exception to create the system of Special Economic Zones in the late 1970s.
>
> 2004: 76; cf. 2006: 104–105

> SEZs were initially modeled on EPZs in Taiwan and South Korea.
>
> 2004: 77; cf. 2006: 103–106

In these passages SEZs are 'modeled' on EPZs. Not the same, they are a version, with like functions and characteristics. They are 'distinctive' 'forms', 'marked off from conditions of the socialist planned environment'. As the analog operates through similitude, transfer and separation, 'marked off' represents boundary and fixed area, lacking integration with state territory in general—because 'the system' of 'zones' is 'exceptional', characterized by 'variegated sovereignty'.

The only systematic empirics in the work are two short tables, which cite Wikipedia. The article and the book's chapter include "Table 1 Major Forms of Zoning in China", for which Wikipedia is the source; the book's identical table omits the source. "Table 2 Powers of Autonomy and Regulations in Economic and Political Zones" (2004: 82; 2006: 109) states "Economic Zones" have "Autonomy in all economic and administrative matters"; the only source noted in the article is Wikipedia, where the book version cites a PRC website on Hong Kong. The main text summarizes, "In short, the coastal zone authorities and open cities are spaces of exception to the centrally planned socialist economy. They enjoy autonomy in all economic and administrative matters" (2004: 81; 2006: 108). If only it were so simple.

Their brevity proves particularly consequential because the stated notion of autonomy is false. Special economic zones in China do not have autonomy let alone in 'all economic and administrative matters'. Like 'post-truth' politics, the false statement emerges like a parallax vision for a free-market economy. It sounds right, in a way—because it confirms 'our own' ideology—to ignore the untruth. But like 'post-truth' politics, we have to explicitly identify it, and as an item in particular need of correction. A theoretical weight must be lifted from the market side of the state–market problematic and placed on the side of the state. 'Special zones' in the PRC are territorial governing areas under the jurisdiction of and directly governed by the party–state in which the CCP maintains authority over the government. Every subnational territory is governed by a hierarchical combination of Party committee and government offices and each maintains a series of five-year plans. By definition, none has autonomy.

When the PRC established 'special zones', it decentralized the planned economy and continued governing authority. In the PRC, only Hong Kong and Macao, as Special Administrative Regions, have political and economic autonomy to make and approve laws and policy, but the PRC central government retains the authority to return legislation that contradicts or infringes on national law. Even so, the CCP governs indirectly in Hong Kong and Macao though the Liaison Office of the Central People's Government. Thus, if the sign value of 'special zones' transmits 'market', analog circulation of zones has the effect of de-historicizing and mis-characterizing forms of sovereignty, while re-contextualizing and generalizing ideas about neoliberalizing economy.

Analog reasoning hobbles potential for comparative research. Not concerned with the general and the particular, or theory and empirics, but rather, in Agamben's (2002: 4) terms, existing as 'depolar and not dichotomic', 'tensional and not oppositional', analog circulation is iteratively simple—borrowing and transferring—and alternately complex—de-historicizing and re-contextualizing. Such conditions, Agamben (2002: 4) reflects, "contribute to how the analog 'produces a field of polar tensions which tend to form a zone of undecidability which neutralizes every rigid opposition." (For Agamben, 'zone' is a metaphor.) Capacity to neutralize impedes and thwarts critique. Ong refers to a "low-flying" approach that "stays close to discursive and nondiscursive practices" for "mid-range theorizing" "in a space of betwixt and between that is the site of the problem and of its resolution" (2006: 13). Maintaining observations that are neither empirically grounded nor theoretical stable contributes to conceptual tension and factual strain, apparently the polar analogy that Agamben predicts.

6   Greater China

The critique of zone analog points to questions about the space and territory of zones (Cartier, 2017). Where Ong finds zoning constitutes "creative respatialization of national territory," she holds that it does not reproduce "the container model of national sovereignty" or "some formulaic or container view of sovereignty"; it rests on "the term 'graduated sovereignty' to identify the rescaling of state power across the national landscape and the differential scales of regulation on diverse groups of citizens and foreigners" (Ong, 2006: 98, 100; 2004: 71–72). This approach to sovereignty continues to appear in the literature and thus invites attention. Ong introduces it in the following terms. "Neoliberalism as exception refines the study of state sovereignty, long conceptualized as a political singularity," in how "market-driven strategies of spatial fragmentation respond to demands of global capital for diverse categories of human capital, thus engendering a pattern of noncontiguous, differently administered spaces of 'graduated' or 'variegated sovereignty'" (2006: 7). The concern, at this juncture, is what spatial imagination it represents.

For Ong, variegated or graduated sovereignty usefully frames "China's opening" and its "production of new spaces of exception with border-crossing powers" (2006: 102). The spatial imagination, i.e. 'new spaces' 'with border-crossing powers', enlivens 'the Chinese axis', but this phrase is uncommon in the literature. We turn to the 2004 article for its formulation:

> Flexible state practices, I argue, deploy zoning technologies for integrating distinct political entities such as Hong Kong and Macao, and even Taiwan and Singapore, into an emerging Chinese axis. Furthermore, although zoning technologies are ostensibly about increasing foreign investments and economic activities, they create the spaces and conditions of variegated sovereignty aligned on an axis of trade, industrialization and gradual political integration. Thus this Chinese-dominated archipelago challenges widespread assumptions that economic and political forms of integration develop in different spheres. Greater China, I argue, is a state-driven strategy to economically integrate disarticulated political entities as a detour toward eventual political integration.
>
> ONG, 2004: 70; cf. 2006: 98

Thus Greater China is the outcome of China's 'flexible state practices' through 'zoning technologies' related to Hong Kong, Macao, Taiwan and Singapore, producing a 'Chinese axis of common economic interests' (Ong, 2006: 115).

This 'Chinese-dominated archipelago' (Ong, 2004: 70) encompasses the historic NIES (minus South Korea, plus Macao) in a metaphorical elocution. The archipelagic imaginary works to form a cultural-economic group while eliding political realities of an independent Singapore and political sovereignty on Taiwan. Ong then extends the axis: "the Chinese axis is also an imaginary line of cultural sovereignty" which "runs along an ideological plane of the graduated political field" (2006: 115). Yet a spatiality of differentiated state powers, whether in the PRC or a 'Greater China', remains undefined. Nevertheless, the formulation for both Greater China and zones arguably depends on the idea of sovereign exception.

A meta-view on sovereignty forms its own subject of inquiry, and critical questions about it are at hand. Ronald Jennings, writing "A genealogy of Agamben's critique of sovereignty" in *Anthropological Theory*, implores what was the question to which sovereignty was the answer? Calling sovereignty "the concept of our moment," the trouble is its "remarkably under-theorized paradigm shift" (Jennings, 2011: 24). The question was, how does sovereignty reflect neoliberal triumphalism and its discontents, in relation to which all other subjects, in 'centers' of critical thought production, are situated. In Ong's terms, graduated or variegated, "sovereignty is manifested in multiple, often contradictory strategies that encounter diverse claims and contestations, and produce diverse and contingent outcomes" (2006: 7). Here, the debt to Foucault and governmentality would be apparent. For example, "techniques of government" have "a graduating effect on sovereignty" (2006: 77).

Jennings's (46) line of inquiry travels ultimately to Agamben's formulation of the relationship between sovereignty and modernity in which "modernity, sovereignty, and the exception are essentially synonymous." Jennings reads this logic of extremes as a postmodern one whose "same kind of totalizing movement" also appears in "Agamben's very particular invocation of Foucault" which calls for "correction," specifically, that the modern biopolitical must be imbricated with sovereignty. If sovereignty is theoretically operational with modernity and exception, then Ong must resituate exception to separate 'zones' from 'China' at large to achieve the formulation for Greater China.

But Greater China represents a knowledge formation that has waned since the turn of the century. Analysis of the NIEs stimulated research on diaspora, Asian business networks, and transnationalism (cf. Ash and Kueh, 1993; Harding, 1993; Shambaugh, 1995; So and Chiu, 1995; Ma and Cartier, 2003; Ong and Nonini, 1997; Seagrave, 1995). The era's emblematic books, *Lords of the Rim* (Seagrave, 1995) and *Ungrounded Empires* (Ong and Nonini, 1997), found in Greater China cultural transnationalism and an overseas Chinese capitalist class. As Ong repeats, Greater China, an economic region of the new Pacific Century, "is very different from Western discourses of regionalism such as the 'Pacific Rim'" (2006: 115). But the rise of China has not sustained the subject of Greater China in the literature.

Greater China as a regional idea gained momentum as a counterpoint to the broader Pacific Rim scholarship, inviting interest in networked activity between Chinese diasporic populations in Southeast Asia and the Asia Pacific at large. Hong Kong, the PRC's *de facto* international financial center, grounded Greater China and Chinese transnationalism at the geo-economic pivot of China and Southeast Asia. The idea of Greater China has worked to usefully group places—China, Hong Kong, Taiwan—and processes in a transboundary regional economy with incommensurable sovereign power.

But narratives of Greater China and the Pacific Rim already peaked in scholarship in the mid-1990s. 'Greater China' peaks in 1996, just before Hong Kong returns to the PRC (see Figure 9.1). The trajectory of these terms paced capital flows into Shenzhen and the Pearl River delta beyond: Hong Kong was the essential bridge between 1980, when Shenzhen opened, and 1997, when Hong Kong became a special administrative region of the PRC. The worldview of Greater China envisioned border-crossing mobilities from the 'Chinese axis' via Hong Kong. It did not have a position within the PRC from which to see the future of Chinese state capitalism as the architect of urban and regional

FIGURE 9.1   Ngram (0) of Pacific Rim and Greater China, 1980–2008
SOURCE: GOOGLE NGRAM VIEWER (HTTPS://BOOKS.GOOGLE.COM/NGRAMS)

change. Ideas about 'Greater China' especially did not grasp how the PRC would maintain centralized political authority through the next half-century (Huang 2008). Like an incoming typhoon, Chinese transnationalism stalled on the south China coast. A 'Chinese axis' moved onshore.

7   Locating the State

Governmentalizing to form 'zoning' and 'zoning technologies' discursively constructs state interest in marking out space for market economy, and leaves 'the rest' as if fixed under central planning. For instance, Ong periodically contrasts 'zones' with 'socialist central planning' and 'centrally planned socialist environment'. These phrases would appear to narrate the PRC's general economy outside zones, and thus separate subnational territory into two separately governed economic categories. By treating areas outside 'zones' as if under 'central planning', the zone analog sequesters the zone as if unintegrated with state territory in general.

In interest to situate the PRC's watershed decision to open China to the world economy, Ong writes "In 1972, the Chinese state spectacularly invoked an exception to the normativity of socialist central planning" (2006: 103). In fact, socialist central planning existed in 1972. The year 1978–1979 is mistakenly identified as 1972, a time during the Cultural Revolution (1966–1976). Since 'centrally planned' was the condition to which '1978' was the answer, what part of the argument depends on existence of Mao-era socialist conditions? Indeed, the reality of centrally planned production ended unevenly and in some places well before 1978 (White, 1998a, 1998b). The apparent answer—holding the state economy and the national territory constant, and allowing 'zones' to exist as spaces of marketization—serves the neoliberalism as exception argument. Its effect brackets realities of widespread economic decentralization in general, i.e. outside 'zones' (e.g. Landry, 2008; Lin and Liu, 2000). By the mid-1990s not only was the coastal region at large open to the world economy, hundreds of cities in China nationwide had named thousands of 'zones' after they gained control of urban land to develop real estate (Cartier, 2001a, 2001b).

Work drawing on zoning technologies finds potential to inform political economic questions in transborder contexts. Another important one where political differences prevail is the case of the Kaesong Industrial Complex in North Korea, an economic area that was jointly operated by North Korea and South Korea. Analysis of the Kaesong complex by Jaime Doucette and Seung-Oak Lee (2015, see also this volume) reveals the complex geopolitical landscape in which South Korea attempted to support the zone in the face of periodic threats by the North Korean government to close the factories and return the area to its original use as a military base. In 2016, after a series of militarized provocations, South Korea recalled its workers and the zone folded. Where Ong found 'zoning mechanisms' to be 'an economic detour leading to broader political integration' (2006: 116), this projection has not eventuated on the Korean peninsula or across the Taiwan Strait. Beijing's relations with Hong Kong became strained in the 2010s, and Taiwan became increasingly distant from Beijing after the 2016 general election that returned the Democratic Progressive Party to power. 'Zoning' has not won China smooth geopolitical integration through marketization.

But there is a more fundamental discursive problem that returns 'zone' to the state. The word zone is a selected English-language translation of diverse types of administrative territories in China. All subnational territory in the PRC is one or another type of zone. This state–market problematic emerges in the rendering of *qu* 区 whose multiple meanings are area, district, region, and zone. The character 区 is the third character in *xingzheng quhua* 行政区划, the administrative divisions, in which all subnational territory is some type of *qu*. An urban district or *chengqu* 城区 is an administrative subdivision of a city. The compound *diqu* 地区 means prefecture, the level of government between the province and the county. The meaning of *qu* 区 enfolds different territories at different levels of government. Among tens of thousands of designated economic areas in China all are territorial administrative areas directly governed by the Party and government offices. A *jingji tequ* 经济特区, literally 'economic special district', is what in English has been termed 'special economic zone', as a consequence of the legibility of 'zones' in Asia, i.e. SEZs in China were specifically named after the EPZs in Asia. In light of these realities in the PRC, the expansion of 'zone' demonstrates, borrowing Sklair's terms, how the transnational capitalist class narrates the world economy.

Shanghai's 'globalizing' precinct for special economic development, a finance and trade district of super-tall buildings, is the Pudong New Area 浦东新区. It includes that same word, *qu*, but Pudong's official English-language translation is 'new area'. Pudong is also an administrative division, an urban district 城市区 of Shanghai. Party history attributes its territorial-administrative category, 'new area', to Deng Xiaoping, Jiang Zemin and Li Peng, in which they compared and aimed to distinguish Pudong from special economic zones, especially Shenzhen (Xie, 2013). Pudong would develop services industries and high-technology manufacturing under central government leadership, not standard manufacturing industries like Shenzhen. That the PRC's ranking leadership parses and differentiates among such would-be simple terms underscores the general condition of administrative territories, their functional specificity, and their place in party-state governance. By early 2017 the central government designated 17 'new areas' (which has a Wikipedia page).

Research on China and India, in pursuit of the zone phenomenon, identifies limits of the paradigm as exemplar. Before turning to territorial economies in China, let us conclude this section on the state–market problematic in India. Based on fieldwork in Andhra Pradesh, which has more economic zones than any other Indian state, Jamie Cross (2010, 2015) finds zones to be highly unexceptional spaces that demonstrate structural continuities with the economic landscape at large. Cross (2010: 358) writes: "India's zones are better theorized as unexceptional spaces that make legible, legitimate and visible the conditions of informality and precariousness under which most economic activity already takes place in South Asia." Cross's analysis finds the economic conditions of zones not special to them but rather sites of the reproduction of otherwise existing economic conditions. In the 1990s 'zone fever' broke out in China as thousands of economic zones proliferated discursively—informally or illegally—for expedient real estate developments (Cartier, 2001b).

8 Territorial Economies

In the 1980s, in the face of unknown unfolding complexities, international analysis of economic reform in China lit on special economic zones for their capacity to bundle explanation of location, marketization, and transition. "Tellingly," explains the economist Barry Naughton (2009a: 3), "the single economic reform most closely associated with Deng personally [Deng Xiaoping] were the Special Economic Zones, which had an important element of international reassurance and signaling." This 'international reassurance and signaling' debuted Shenzhen for capital investment from Hong Kong and the world economy.

But the problem of the SEZ as analog conflated zones with areas on the scale of entire cities and regions, and the Chinese central government's project of building new cities, among which Shenzhen is only one. Naughton poses the question: "What Chinese institutions can we recommend for adoption by other developing or transitional economies?" "None," he replies, and yet "we must deal with one apparent exception. Hasn't the Chinese policy of Special Economic Zones (SEZs) been replicated around the world?" Here Naughton (2009b: 8–9) identifies the analog model: "what is most innovative about Chinese SEZs is size, multi-functional use as a laboratory of multiple types of reforms, and openness to the domestic economy"—which makes them "not a good candidate for replication." The SEZ is not a good candidate for replication because it is instantiated within the domestic territorial system and an organized political entity. One SEZ was an island province, Hainan, nearly the size of Taiwan. When India sought to establish 'SEZs', after an era of lacklustre EPZs, it confronted the problem and realized the size of the Chinese SEZs could not be matched (SEZs: how will they perform? 2001; Sharma, 2015). The process of establishing large-scale development areas in China released massive tracts of state land for industrial development. The circulation of land capital itself contributed significantly to accumulation.

Over-determination of 'zone' occludes general processes of territorializing new cities and regions in China. Historically, Chinese rural territories at the meso-scale, called prefectures and counties, were largely rural. In the 1980s, to entrain the urban process, the Chinese government began reterritorializing prefectures and counties as cities to accumulate rural land for urban development. Consistent with party–state authority, now every city in the PRC is a territorial jurisdiction at one of three ranks of government: province-level city (*zhixia shi* 直辖市); prefecture-level city (*diji shi* 地级市); or county-level city (*xianji shi* 县级市). Their hierarchical ranks establish power relations among the administrative divisions and ranks of Party and government officials appointed to govern them (Cartier, 2016; Landry, 2008). But the international literature commonly disregards these conditions and their implications for state power and economic development, and, consequently, comparative theorization.

Does a scholarship of 'zones' exist in the Chinese academy? Liu Junde, founding director of the Center for Research on Administrative Divisions in China, formulates 'administrative area economy' or 'administrative district economy' (*xingzhengqu jingji* 行政区经济) to assess the relationship between the mandate to govern and the interrelated conditions of territory, boundary, land, economy and population (Liu, 1996, 2002). This territorial economy approach conceptualizes the role of the state in conceiving, reterritorializing, and developing administrative territory. Operational as an applied method, it assesses interrelated administrative divisions—'zones'—for potential adjustment because the state frequently merges, expands, or rescales the rank of an area to propel new rounds of economic growth (Cartier, 2015, 2016; Martinez and Cartier, 2017). The Pudong New Area of Shanghai emerged only when the Shanghai Planning Bureau mapped it across a triangle of land on the eastern bank of the Huangpu River, combining three districts, one county and a township. In 2009 it merged an adjacent county and doubled its size. These territorial adjustments are frequent yet missing from 'zone analog'.

9   Coda

Marking achievements from Shenzhen to Shanghai Pudong and beyond, the twenty-first century Chinese state continues targeted development through new city-regions (Cartier, 2018). On 1 April 2017 the CCP Central Committee and the State Council announced the establishment of Xiongan New Area in southern Hebei province on the historic periphery of the Beijing capital region. The future Xiongan combines three historic counties for a new economic territory that will be governed by Hebei province and the central state. This is first time that a 'new area' has been officially aligned with the Party Central Committee, heightening its political importance and financial transfers.

Xiongan is the focus of a long-term plan to redistribute the population, economy, and government services and institutions including enterprises, hospitals, and universities, from Beijing. The state plan for the capital region decrees that 'non-capital functions' unrelated to Beijing's status of national capital must be relocated outside the city—Xiongan is the main destination. (The equivalent in Australia would be if Canberra, the capital, was the size of Brisbane, Melbourne, and Sydney combined, grew beyond its resource limits, and then the federal government responded by building an 'overflow' city in an adjacent state, subject to direct oversight by federal parliament.) Located in the region of Beijing, but not in Beijing, Xiongan is a new city for Beijing. In the state-market problematic, it raises new interests in the powers of the state.

In the 1980s, after the 'miracle' years of the NIES, special economic zones in China surged topologically into the world economy as if extending another round of zone-based development. Other countries, including India, sought to harness the SEZ model. The scale and scope of the SEZs, from Shenzhen to the Pearl River delta and beyond, anchored new cities and city-region development. But the notion that SEZs fire connections to global capital contributes to bracketing state territorial conditions as subnational territories. In state territorialization of the urbanizing economy, SEZs in China are among a larger range of development strategies.

Ideas about zoning technologies reflect the 1990s era of networks, between mainland China, Hong Kong, and Taiwan, in a meso-scale view that accommodates the anthropological *emic* i.e. 'in my field site things are different' variety of argument. Its theoretical resonance, in late 20th-century south China, embeds in a particular time and place. In this 'Chinese axis', zones of neoliberalism as exception lent contextualization, in absence of common sovereignty, to the transboundary regional economy in formation. It did not have a position within the PRC from which to see the future of Chinese state capitalism as the architect of urban and regional change. With the rise of China at large, the idea of 'Greater China' has become comparatively less important in the scholarship.

Yet formulations derived from neoliberalism as exception in Greater China have continued. In the absence of critical methodology, its analog circulation risks detaching zones from contingent realities. Generalization of the zone idea would ideally churn theoretical capacity and provide comparative approach, yet the effervescent analog reproduces 'hovering spaces', i.e. instead of dynamic territorialization, the zone is a site 'over' and 'into' which labor and capital 'flow' or 'cross'—allowing 'zone' to literally stand in for territorial complexities. In the state-market dichotomy, this zone mis/leads to assumptions about 'zones' as if places where state-driven rules are replaced by market conditions and diminished sovereignty, limiting local histories, societies, and economies. For postcolonial scholarship, with its commitments to worldviews 'from below', and whose ethics represent deconstruction of knowledge–power, this is surely a paradoxical outcome.

A new strain of work hyper-circulates 'zone' to encompass world-city spaces defined by intensive concentration of spectacular built forms. This notion of zone, shedding historical context, predictably travels analogically to 'glittering' enclaves for another round of spectacle effect. It signifies that which it cannot reproduce while lighting on new forms, fracturing empirics of actual geographical history. Such a predictable form-and-function approach is internally contradicted: a parallax vision for territorial change whose realities it works to occlude and compress.

Despite the inherent spatiality of 'zone', zone analog skates over their processes of formation. Zone analog acutely brackets actual conditions of state-designated urban-economic areas and their territorial formation. Economic treatments describe locations, sizes, and functional areas in fixed spaces, but want for inquiry into institutional conditions and territorial dynamics. Poststructural treatments, represented through exception and variegation, generate permeable sites where labor and capital jostle for product and accumulation—flexible production meets flexible citizenship, yet what is the zone and the space of the zone remain curiously backgrounded. In China, urbanization since the 1980s has been based on establishing new cities, and city-region development, through complex, state-directed territorial changes. Changes to the administrative divisions in China at the meso-scale, including Shenzhen, have widely reterritorialized rural areas as administrative 'cities' in advance of urbanization. These 'zones' are special because they are so much more than 'zones'.

References

Agamben, G (2002) Giorgio Agamben: What is a paradigm? Lecture at the European Graduate School. Transcript of a lecture. Available (consulted 1 October 2016) at: http://www.maxvanmanen.com/files/2014/03/Agamben-What-is-a-paradigm1.pdf.

Agamben, G (trans. by L D'Isanto with K Attell) (2009) *The Signature of All Things: On Method.* New York: Zone Books.

Ash, RF and YY Kueh (1993) Economic integration within Greater China: Trade and investment flows between China, Hong Kong and Taiwan. *The China Quarterly* 136(Dec.): 711–745.

Barnes, TJ (1994) Social physics. In: RJ Johnston, D Gregory and DM Smith (eds.) *The Dictionary of Human Geography,* 3rd ed. Oxford: Blackwell, 567.

Cartier, C (2001a) *Globalizing South China.* Oxford: Blackwell.

Cartier, C (2001b) Zone fever, the arable land debate and real estate speculation: China's evolving land use regime and its geographical contradictions. *Journal of Contemporary China* 10(28): 445–469.

Cartier, C (2015) Territorial urbanization and the party-state in China. *Territory, Politics, Governance* 3(3): 294–320.

Cartier, C (2016) A political economy of rank: The territorial administrative hierarchy and leadership mobility in urban China. *Journal of Contemporary China* 25(100): 529–546.

Cartier, C (2017) Zone analog: The state-market problematic and territorial economies in China. *Critical Sociology* DOI: 10.1177/0896920517712367.

Cartier, C (2018) Magic cities, future dreams—urban contradictions. In: J Golley and L Jaivin (eds.) *The Chinastory Yearbook 2017: Prosperity*. Canberra: The Australian National University Press, 46–61.

Cross, J (2010) Neoliberalism as unexceptional: Economic zones and the everyday precariousness of working life in South India. *Critique of Anthropology* 30(4): 355–373.

Cross, J (2015) The economy of anticipation: Hope, infrastructure, and economic zones in South India. *Comparative Studies of South Asia, Africa and the Middle East* 35(3): 424–437.

Cumings, B (1987) The origins and development of the Northeast Asian political economy: Industrial sectors, product cycles, and political consequences. In: FC Deyo (ed.) *The Political Economy of the New Asian Industrialism*. Ithaca, NY: Cornell University Press, 44–83.

Deyo, FC (ed) (1987) *The Political Economy of the New Asian Industrialism*. Ithaca, NY: Cornell University Press.

Doucette, J and S-L Lee (2015) Experimental territoriality: Assembling the Kaesong Industrial Complex in North Korea. *Political Geography* 47(July): 53–63.

Easterling, K (2012) Zone: The spatial softwares of extrastatecraft. *Places Journal*. Available (consulted 1 February 2017) at: https://placesjournal.org/article/zone-the -spatial-softwares-of-extrastatecraft/

Easterling, K (2014) *Extrastatecraft: The Power of Infrastructure Space* (London: Verso).

Farole, T and G Akinci (eds.) (2011) *Special Economic Zones: Progress, Emerging Challenges, and Future Directions*. Washington, DC: The World Bank.

Haggard, S and T-J Cheng (1987) State and foreign capital in the East Asian NICs. In: FC Deyo (ed.) *The Political Economy of the New Asian Industrialism*. Ithaca, NY: Cornell University Press, 84–129.

Harding, H (1993) The concept of "Greater China": Themes, variations and reservations. *The China Quarterly* 136(Dec.): 660–686.

Huang, Y (2008) *Capitalism with Chinese Characteristics: Entrepreneurship and the State*. Cambridge: Cambridge University Press.

Jennings, RC (2011) Sovereignty and political modernity: A genealogy of Agamben's critique of sovereignty. *Anthropological Theory* 11(1): 23–61.

Kuhn, TS (1962) *The Structure of Scientific Revolutions*. Chicago: Chicago University Press.

Kuhn, TS (1970) *The Structure of Scientific Revolutions,* 2nd ed. Chicago: Chicago University Press.

Kuhn, TS (1977) *The Essential Tension: Selected Studies in Scientific Tradition and Change*. Chicago: Chicago University Press.

Landry, PF (2008) *Decentralized Authoritarianism in China*. New York: Cambridge University Press.

Lin, JY and Z Liu (2000) Fiscal decentralization and economic growth in China. *Economic Development and Cultural Change* 49(1): 1–21.

Litwack, JM and Y Qian (1998) Balanced or unbalanced development: special economic zones as catalysts for transition. *Journal of Comparative Economics* 26(1): 117–141.

Liu, J (1996) 中国行政区划的理论与实践 (*China's Administrative Divisions in Theory and Practice*). Shanghai: East China Normal University Press.

Liu, J (2002) 中外行政区划比较研究 (*A Comparative Study of Chinese and Foreign Administrative Divisions*). Shanghai: East China Normal University Press.

Lye, LF (2016) Suzhou Industrial Park: More than just a commercial undertaking. In: YN Zheng and LF Lye (eds.) *Singapore-China Relations: 50 Years*. Singapore: World Scientific, 105–130.

Ma, LJC and C Cartier (eds.) (2003) *The Chinese Diaspora: Space, Place, Mobility, and Identity*. Lanham, MD: Rowman & Littlefield.

Mair, A (1986) Thomas Kuhn and understanding geography. *Progress in Human Geography* 10(3): 345–369.

Martinez, MH and C Cartier (2017) City as province in China: The territorial urbanization of Chongqing. *Eurasian Geography and Economics*. Available at: http://dx.doi.org/10.1080/15387216.2017.1312474

Murray, MJ (2017) *The Urbanism of Exception: The Dynamics of Global City Building in the Twenty-First Century*. Cambridge: Cambridge University Press.

Naughton, B (2009a) China: Economic transformation before and after 1989. Paper presented at '1989: Twenty Years After', University of California, Irvine, 6–7 November 2009. Available (consulted 1 July 2016) at: https://pdfs.semanticscholar.org/02e5/b77c98d6afef55a5cc1b7f0cf0425a1c44a0.pdf

Naughton, B (2009b) Singularity and replicability in China's developmental experience. *China Analysis* 68(Jan.): 1–22.

Nee, V (1992) Organizational dynamics of market transition: Hybrid forms, property rights, and mixed economy in China. *Administrative Science Quarterly*, 1–27.

Ong, A (2004) The Chinese axis: zoning technologies and variegated sovereignty. *Journal of East Asian Studies* 4(1): 69–96.

Ong, A (2006) *Neoliberalism as Exception: Mutations in Citizenship and Sovereignty*. Durham, NC: Duke University Press.

Ong, A and DM Nonini (eds.) (1997) *Ungrounded Empires: The Cultural Politics of Modern Chinese Transnationalism*. New York: Routledge.

Parliament of India (2007) Parliamentary Standing Committee on Commerce, Parliament of India, Eighty Third Report on the Function of Special Economic Zones. Available (consulted 15 October 2016) at: http://164.100.47.5/newcommittee/reports/EnglishCommittees/Committee%20on%20Commerce/Report%20SEZ1.htm.

Seagrave, S (1995) *Lords of the Rim*. New York: Putnam's Sons.

SEZs: how will they perform? (2011) *The Hindu*, Aug. 16. Available (consulted 1 August 2016) at: http://www.thehindu.com/2001/08/16/stories/0616000l.htm

Shambaugh, DL (ed) (1995) *Greater China: The Next Superpower?* New York: Oxford University Press.

Sharma, M (2015) *Restart: The Last Chance for the Indian Economy.* Gurgaon, Haryana: Random House India.

Sidaway, JD (2007a) Enclave space: a new metageography of development? *Area* 39(3): 323–330.

Sidaway, JD (2007b) Spaces of postdevelopment. *Progress in Human Geography* 31(3): 345–361.

Sklair, L (2001) *The Transnational Capitalist Class.* Oxford: Blackwell.

So, A and S Chiu (1995) *East Asia and the World Economy.* Thousand Oaks, CA: Sage.

White, LT III (1998a) *Unstately Power: Volume I, Local Causes of China's Economic Reforms.* Armonk, NY: M.E. Sharpe.

White, LT III (1998b) *Unstately Power: Volume II, Local Causes of China's Intellectual, Legal and Government Reforms.* Armonk, NY: M.E. Sharpe.

Woldenberg, MJ (1979) A periodic table of spatial hierarchies. In S Gale and G Olsson (eds.) *Philosophy in Geography.* Dordrecht: Springer Netherlands, 429–456.

Woldenberg, MJ and BJ Berry (1967) Rivers and central places: analogous systems? *Journal of Regional Science* 7(2): 129–139.

Xie, G (2013) 浦东为何不叫特区叫新区 (Why Pudong is called a new area and not a special zone), *Pudong Development* 6: 59–60.

Yeung, YM, J Lee, and G Kee (2009) China's special economic zones at 30. *Eurasian Geography and Economics* 50(2): 222–240.

CHAPTER 10

Waiting and Remembering: Economy of Anticipation and Materiality of Aspiration in Dandong, China

Christina Kim Chilcote

1   Introduction

Facing the North Korean city of Sinuiju across the Yalu River, the Chinese border city of Dandong in Liaoning Province has recently taken on large urban developmental projects as part of a plan to build the wider city as the new economic hub of East Asia.[1] This plan began to take shape when Dandong was included in the "Five Points One Line" development strategy in 2009, which envisioned well-connected industrial zones along the northeast coast of China. With major highway and road constructions, linking Dandong to large nearby cities of Dalian and Shenyang, the city began building a new district south of the current metropolitan center. This new district, according to the local government, is expected to house 400,000 new residents, and become "the modern administrative, technological, commercial, residential centers of the future Dandong" (Dandong Municipal Committees of Communist Party of China 2010). The following year, construction for a new bridge connecting the new district to North Korea began with domestic and foreign investment. The then mayor announced that this new Yalu Bridge is expected to "become a major link between the two countries" and to play a vital role in the city's economic future (China Daily 2010). At the same time, North Korea and China announced plans to build two new Special Economic Zones (SEZs) on two North Korean islands, Hwanggeumpyong and Wihwa, located on the Yalu River between Dandong and Sinuiju. These new urban development projects – the

---

1   A plan to build an economic hub in Dandong began during Kim Jong-Il's unofficial visit to Beijing in January 2001 to meet with Jiang Zemin, the General Secretary of the Communist Party at the time. Through ensuing meetings, China and North Korea agreed to jointly develop the Dandong-Sinuiju area as an economic passageway and future distribution center for East Asia.

district, the bridge and the two sEZs – make up the plan to build Dandong as an economic hub of East Asia.

While construction projects in and around Dandong are still underway, hopes for what they may bring are high. During an interview with Daily China, an official from the city's Foreign Economic and Trade Bureau boasted the new district's potential:

> With two high-speed railways, four expressways, a seaport and an airport, Dandong has become one of the region's hubs of transportation and logistics. Its economic hinterland covers Liaoning, Jilin, Heilongjiang and Inner Mongolia and even extends to all of Northeast Asia, including the DPRK, South Korea, Russia, Mongolia and Japan.
>
> ZHU and LIU 2012

Here, what distinguishes Dandong from other Chinese cities connected by these railways, expressways and water and air routes is its close tie, historically and geographically, to North Korea. Its former mayor Chen Tiexin (March 2004 – February 2008) specifically pointed this out when he said that "[Dandong's] unique geographic positions means we can explore international shipping routes and develop border trade with the Democratic People's Republic of Korea" (China Daily 2009). As this chapter will demonstrate, it is Dandong's ties to North Korea through its neighboring city Sinuiju that is fueling the borderland's development toward a future based on livelier cross border trades.

Currently connected to Sinuiju by the Friendship Bridge, Dandong is already home to approximately 20,000 North Korean laborers working in factories in and near the city and to agents representing various companies and factories in North Korea.[2] Dandong hosts 70% of Sino-North Korean trade traffic, the majority of which are filtered to other larger cities around China, and many local residents rely on some type of trans-border activities.[3] In Dandong, the familiar characterization of North Korea as behind the times and economically isolated from the world – characterizations that anticipate its eventual collapse – transform into lucrative business opportunities. Entrepreneurs from China, South Korea, Japan, the United States and other nations have gathered

---

2   Today, there are over 150,000 North Korean visitors to Dandong annually. Approximately 70% are business or work related (Jung 2014). See Kim and Kang (2015) for more on North Korean laborers in Dandong.

3   This percentage generally fluctuates from 40% to 70% depending on what is included in the statistic. The lower percentage excludes trade traffic that merely passes through the city while the higher number includes all trade traffic. See Seung Ho Jung (2014: 6–7) for more analysis on this statistic.

here to trade with and manufacture goods through agents and laborers from North Korea both licitly and illicitly. Amidst these ongoing trans-border activities, the new urban developments point to a future of a more vibrant economic interaction across the Sino-Korean border and to a growing economy based on such future.

This chapter is about the new urban developmental projects in Dandong and what they produce and reveal about regional geopolitical dynamics as well as the symbolic, temporal and affective work that goes into sustaining them. Urban developments as aspirational and future oriented are not a new phenomenon. Similar to other cities around the world, the city-wide efforts to build for a more prosperous future in which it will play a role as a major economic hub is defining Dandong's present as a time of building and hard labor as it *waits* for the actualization of its urban development projects. I see such *waiting time* as the overriding temporal mode of Dandong's current economy. In other words, the idea that the region will become East Asia's economic hub has fueled an *economy of anticipation* oriented toward realizing that idea. While 70% of Sino-Korean trade passes through the city as mentioned, border trade does not make up the city's largest revenue, and the city lacks industrial infrastructure to attract large corporations and foreign investment. Yet, the citywide physical transformation in the last decade portrays Dandong as a trade-based hub. The current economy built around this idea is, therefore, anticipatory in the sense that Dandong is not yet considered a major hub for larger corporations or foreign investors.

Based on fourteen months of fieldwork in Dandong from July 2013 to August 2014, this chapter observes how Dandong's economy of anticipation illustrates an almost hopeful path toward prosperous economic engagement in a region where North Korea plays a significant role as a *capitalist frontier:* an imagination of the future that departs from media coverage of the region as a ticking time bomb. I explore Dandong's developmental projects as well as the larger urban-scape that makeup this economy of anticipation, paying attention to its material and discursive constellation and effects. Through this examination I argue that Dandong's recent urban development simultaneously deploys a politics of waiting and a politics of memory to inscribe its central role in East Asia's future as an economic hub while also promoting the idea that capitalist relationships lead to peace.

2   Economy of Anticipation

Scholars have studied anticipation as a powerful temporal and affective component of contemporary political economy. These studies examine how hopes for a better life in the future transform into anticipatory pursuits in the present, pursuits that are marked into urban spaces, policies, bodies and psyches (Appadurai 2013; Adams 2013; Cross 2010; Taussig 2004; Fuller and Benei 2001; Redfield 2000; Holston 1989; Kwon 2015). Adams, Murphy, and Clarke (2009) write that anticipation is a state of "thinking and living towards the future," in which the future – bright or gloomy – "sets the conditions of possibility for action in the present" (2009: 246, 249). This state of living in anticipation is replete with disappointments, uncertainties, and risks as what constitutes a better life is constantly updated with new information, technology and challenges. Anticipation is, therefore, affective and expansive.

The anticipation in Dandong's economy also embodies these characteristics. It operationalizes a future in which the continuation of North Korea's current authoritarian state, framed as a security threat, is impractical. As such, North Korea is framed as a *developing* nation within this future vision for the region. As North Korea is transformed from a *failing* nation into a *developing* nation, the anticipatory state is filled with discourses about hopes for peace in the region. More specifically, the expectation is that through economic development, the people of North Korea will gain agency, choice and eventually human rights (Glaser, Snyder, and Park 2008), and that the people of Dandong will gain prosperity. This expansive logic, however, excludes some *from* the process of speculative actions. For example, rural migrant workers in Dandong are not seen as major players in the future economic hub, even though they are part of the new district as bricklayers. Rather, wealthy investors, innovative entrepreneurs, and local factory workers are envisioned as the beneficiaries of this future economic hub. Dandong's waiting time is, therefore, also a period of classification and hierarchization as it excludes those who lack the ability to participate in this future economy. This temporal orientation is a political one. As Arjun Appadurai (2004) writes of the capacity to aspire as an observational site for inequality, the temporal orientation of anticipation is also a site of differentiation.

The phrase "economy of anticipation" has been used to describe certain market sectors, especially those related to 1. financial markets (stock, bond, futures, derivatives, commodities, futures, and foreign exchange); 2. risk management (insurance, security, and crisis intervention); and 3. Special Economic Zones. In studies of financial markets, anticipation is discussed as a built-in feature of the financial market. It involves trading securities and commodities based on a calculated prediction about a particular market in future time (Appadurai 2012; Miyazaki 2006; Zaloom 2008). Economic practices that I examine are similar to these practices in that they include forms of investment based on predictions of future events and conditions. The difference lies in what is considered in the calculation of risks and awards for an investment. If the calculations for financial markets are based on market analysis of existing economic sectors, what I discuss concerns calculating any and all means of profit-making based on predictions of a market based on the idea of North Korea as a capitalist frontier that is yet to exist. Some of these include investments in the form of small businesses in Dandong aimed at creating local business networks for more direct investment in North Korea in the future. Participating in businesses ranging from cafes to trade offices, entrepreneurs I interviewed described their participation in the local market as part of a longer and broader investment for the future.

In the second sector, risk management, anticipation is produced as future disasters become knowable through security regimes (Collier and Lakoff 2008; Evans and Reid 2014, Lakoff 2007). These regimes are built on knowing and assessing possible (political, economic or natural) threats and preparing for a state of emergency. These include preventative practices such as putting together insurance packages and also preparatory ones such as building and strengthening national security. The core aim of the economy of anticipation I refer to is similar in that it produces North Korea as a disaster factor in need of intervention. Nonetheless, it is different, as the nature of the disaster is not based on an event but on the regime itself. Thus, this economy is not built around preparing for a disaster or averting a state of emergency. While contingency plans in the event of North Korea's collapse by internal revolt or mass defection exist within relevant government offices, the kinds of economic activities that occur in Dandong with and through North Korea are not characteristic of preparing for such emergency. Rather, it is about appropriating the present moment that defines North Korea's current disastrous regime as coming to an end for immediate or future profit. For example, during my fieldwork, the execution of Kim Jong-un's uncle Jang Song Thaek on December 12, 2013 brought about speculations about regime collapse owing to its weakening political elites as well as various doomsday scenarios (Metz 2013; Demick and Choi 2013). In Dandong, there were rumors about people losing money who had associations with Jang. The streets, especially near the Custom House where many doing business with North Korean counterparts visit to send or receive merchandise, and restaurants popular among North Koreans were empty for the rest of December as some were called back for questioning and others stayed low-key. However, the execution and rumors about who might be next did not halt the local border economy. In fact, those who were not associated with Jang's business network became more active in their attempts to expand their businesses to fill the void created in the wake of the execution.

The third economic sector that is characteristic of an economy of anticipation is made up of SEZs. Jamie Cross (2010) has *specifically* used this term to describe and analyze India's SEZ projects. Cross writes that zones make promises of a better future, and that they themselves become the "vehicles" for achieving that future (2010: 13). According to Cross, economy of anticipation is what allowed India's recent infrastructural projects. However, competing voices in the process of building these projects and the zones' failures to deliver what they promised rendered the zones "politically charged spaces of anticipation" (Cross 2010: 13). Similar to what Cross has examined, China's expansionist economic and urban development policies make up Dandong's economy of anticipation, and it, too, is politically charged (see also Cartier, this volume). These state-centered aspirations have manifested locally in developmental projects and other market activities that aim to boost the local economy and hope to generate more profit in the future. But unlike what Cross examined in India, the developmental projects in Dandong are not limited to SEZs but cover the entire metropolitan city and beyond. Memories of failed zones also do not dictate the terms of anticipation in Dandong. Rather the failures of other states reinforce the need for more development locally and nationally, as discussed below.

3   New District and the New Bridge

The most visible manifestations of Dandong's economy of anticipation are the new district and the new bridge (Figure 10.1). These are efforts by the local government and planners to set up concrete infrastructure in anticipation of a more vibrant border exchange. The new bridge began constructions in late 2011 after an agreement between China and North Korea in 2010. The news of its construction was welcomed in Dandong, as the only functioning bridge (the Sino-Korean Friendship Bridge) is old and narrow by today's standards. With a single lane for automobiles and a single parallel railway track, the Sino-Korean Friendship Bridge operates by alternating the direction of traffic once a day. In the morning, trucks, vans and sedans line up in front of the Custom House in Dandong to ensure that they cross the bridge into Sinuiju before the afternoon shift of traffic. In the afternoon, people gather around the Custom House for visitors and deliveries from North Korea. If for some reason a truck could not cross before the bridge closed for the night, it would have to wait in Sinuiju until the next afternoon.

The new Yalu Bridge, when it finally opens, promises a faster, smoother and more efficient connection between Dandong, Sinuiju and Pyongyang.

FIGURE 10.1   Photo of the new bridge under construction in October 2013
Note: To the right of the photo is Dandong's new district and to the
left is Sinuiju. The field north of the bridge is also North Korean
territory
SOURCE: PHOTO BY AUTHOR

Featuring four lanes (two lanes each direction), it will also alleviate the traffic woes of the old bridge. With connection to the wider transportation infrastructures, which reached Dandong in the last decade, the new bridge will be
connected to the newly paved highways to Shenyang, Dalian and beyond. In a
brochure made by the city for foreign investors, the bridge is also envisioned
to connect Dandong not only to Sinuiju and Pyongyang but also to Seoul and
Japan and eventually to the Trans-Siberian Railway (Dandong Municipal Committees of Communist Party of China 2010). Hopes for the role of the bridge
remain high and optimistic, and it was initially expected to be in operation by
July 2014 (Zhu and Liu 2012). For now, however, its new structure spans awe-
somely over the river to an open dirt field, reminding the spectator that North
Korea may not be quite ready to be part of the economic hub.

Despite North Korea's unpreparedness, Dandong's local government continues to make efforts to vitalize the new district. In 2011, the local government
relocated the City Hall to the new district, providing a shuttle for the employees from the current metropolitan center several times a day. Dandong's most
prestigious high school (Dandong Er Zhong) also relocated to the new district.
A satellite campus of a local university has been built and an international
boarding school (Eaglebridge International School) began accepting students
in 2014. In addition to new parks, performance center, library, hospital and stadium, the new district is also home to residential, commercial and industrial

projects by domestic and international corporations. And in 2015, the city released a statement that it will establish a trade zone (Guomenwan) which will be open for local residents living within 20 kilometers (approximately 12.5 miles) of the Sino-North Korean border. Based on an agreement with North Korea to boost local border trade, those in the zone "will be able to exchange commodities with people from North Korea on a duty-free basis, of up to 8,000 yuan ($1,288) a day" (Martina 2015). Despite these efforts to designate the new city as Dandong's new metropolitan center, the local government has not yet succeeded in attracting enough local businesses and residents largely due to the lack of a working service sector, public transportation, local markets, and a public school system, to name a few.

Once a year, however, the city attracts local Dandong residents as well as tourists and investors during the highly publicized "China-DPRK Economic, Trade, Culture and Tourism Expo" (trade expo hereinafter). During my field-work, I attended the second trade expo in October 2013 with South Korean entrepreneurs who were invited to the event as business leaders of the South Korean community and again with Chinese entrepreneurs who attended as the general public. Weeks before the event, posters and banners advertising the expo were placed throughout the city. And during it, the city provided shuttle buses from the current city center to the new district several times a day. There were various events including public performances, and private speeches and meetings (Figure 10.2) as well as stalls outside and inside the main exhibition hall. These stalls (Figure 10.3) sold all kinds of items such as food (honey, medicinal roots, dried fruit and vegetables), souvenirs (key chains, coin purses, figurines, and pins) and oil paintings (of animals, sceneries, and famous buildings) from North Korea but also handmade leather bags and embroidery from Turkey, woodwork from Africa, carved stones from Central Asia and more.

The trade expo started in 2012 to connect potential businesses primarily between China and North Korea but also other countries to North Korea through Dandong. For the local entrepreneurs that I accompanied, however, the 2013 expo did not translate into immediate sales opportunities or provide new information or contacts. For those already familiar with doing business with North Korean agents, it was seen largely as a promotional event for the city.[4] Nonetheless, it is through such events that the city's future as the economic hub are discursively reproduced and distributed. In an interview with China Daily regarding the expo, the Party chief of Liaoning province, Wang

---

4   During informal conversations after the 2013 Expo, many local businessmen in attending complained that it was a publicity stunt by the city to attract news reporters.

FIGURE 10.2   Private briefing at the trade expo
               SOURCE: PHOTO BY AUTHOR

FIGURE 10.3   Indoor stalls at the trade expo
               SOURCE: PHOTO BY AUTHOR

Min, said "Dandong should seize the opportunity and encourage more private companies to play roles in the development of the region, which can inject vitality to local economy" (Zhu and Liu 2012). In the same article, a researcher at the Liaoning Academy of Social Sciences is quoted about Dandong's future economic role in the region:

In fact, 2012 has been a difficult year for China's international trade. However, thanks to Liaoning's coastal economic belt development strategy, the construction of the new Yalu River Bridge linking China and the Democratic People's Republic of Korea and the joint development of DPRK's Hwanggumpyong Island, Dandong is offered great opportunities for further opening-up (ibid).

South Korean media reports featured similar responses to the event. According to South Korean news coverage, investors and buyers from Hong Kong, Taiwan, India, Russia, Malaysia and Pakistan attended the expo held in 2013 and "signed 93 preliminary deals worth US$1.6 billion" (Yonhap News 2014). In sum, media reports from China and South Korea about the expo since its inception in 2012 stress the role of Dandong as "the most vital link in Sino-DPRK trade and business cooperation" (Zhu and Liu 2012), painting an optimistic future of the region.

These high hopes and optimism, officially supported by the local government, however, have caused financial loss for some entrepreneurs. Predicting that the new city's development will expand beyond the current perimeter, the former mayor (of 2009–2010 who was enthusiastic about the new district) made an unofficial announcement to factory owners nearby to get ready to sell their property.[5] Among them were a garment factory owned by a South Korean businessman. Upon hearing the news, the owner made plans to transfer his business elsewhere and stopped all production. He repainted and repaired the factory and got it ready for a sale. But months passed without any word from the city causing him financial loss. He eventually sold it to a Chinese businessman at a loss and opened another factory in Southeast Asia. Today, the new city's development has not expanded as the former mayor had predicted and the future of these older factory sites remains uncertain.

When I asked about the lack of activity in the new district, local entrepreneurs and residents did not seem particularly concerned. One local Chinese entrepreneur explained that it takes time to vitalize new cities. Pointing to other newly built cities across China, he assured me that the new district will be booming with people and businesses in "ten years."[6] Those doing business with North Korea had similar responses. For them, the increasing number of North Korean laborers in Dandong and the state of North Korea's economy as desperately needing foreign investment and capital were sure signs of Dandong's inevitable economic growth and of the new district's prosperous future.

---

5 From personal interview with a local South Korean entrepreneur in November 2013.
6 From personal interview in March 2014.

Unlike foreign investors who might get tired of waiting and leave, I did not detect a sense of urgency in vitalizing this new space among the local residents. The local residents, especially those who invested in its real estate, seemed fine with waiting as property values increased over time, and as they predicted that the new district will flourish after the SEZs on two North Korean islands are completed. Their frustrations were rather directed toward sanctions and the larger geopolitical tensions that had immediate effects on their cross-border business transactions. Spatially separated from the everyday life of Dandong residents, it was as if the new district and the new bridge were also temporally separated and occupying a future time of peaceful economic and geopolitical relationships.

4   Special Economic Zones on North Korean Islands

The sites of two SEZs represent another large sector of Dandong's economy of anticipation. In 2011, around the time North Korea began to export workers in large numbers to China, the two countries agreed to build special economic zones on two North Korean islands, Hwanggeumpyong and Wihwa.[7] Since the groundbreaking ceremony on September 15, 2012, barbed wire demarcating the larger island of Hwanggeumpyong had been set up and basic infrastructural construction begun. Wihwa Island also showed signs of being cleared in preparation for development. Unlike the expectations of the original plan, however, development on these islands has been slow. Experts analyzed that the slow development is due to difficulties in getting investors especially when there are "gaps in laws and contracts" that regulate the zone (Abrahamian and See 21: 2014).[8]

Despite their slow development, these SEZs and others are expected to play an important role in North Korea's economic future (Hong 2002; Weaver 2002; Man 2012; Abrahamian and See 2014; Snyder 2015). China's SEZs are especially seen as providing a roadmap for North Korea's economic reform (Yoon and Lee 2012; Gill 2011; Wu 2005; Duchâtel and Schell 2013), despite growing concerns over class disparity; issues of public health, housing and access to basic

---

7   The larger Hwanggeumpyong island is located adjacent to the new district and Wihwa island is located more north by the current metropolitan center of Dandong.

8   North Korea's experimentation began earlier in the 1990s with the Rajin-Sonbong SEZ, now called the Rason SEZ. For more on this and North Korea's other experiments, such as the Kaesong Industrial District with South Korea which began in 2003, see John Kim and Andray Abrahamian (2011); Frank Ruediger (2014); Andray Abrahamian and GK See (2014); and Jamie Doucette and Seung-Ook Lee (2015).

services for the floating population; and issues of labor and gender rights (Hsu 2006; Hanser 2008; Ong 2014; Rofel 1999; Ngai 2013; Osburg 2013). However, as Jamie Doucette and Seung-Ook Lee (2015) argue, SEZs are not "a free-floating or mobile 'software'" that can be applied anywhere (Easterling 2014; Ong 2006). And as I will show, the SEZs and the new zonal-like urban projects in Dandong rely on locally specific histories and symbolic work.

There are aspirations embedded in these projects that represent the future role of Dandong as an economic strategic node in East Asia and of China's capitalist influence in North Korea. China's involvement in building the two SEZs, however, is different from its earlier SEZs. Similar to what it is doing in Africa (Davies et al. 2008; Braütigam and Xiaoyang 2011), the two SEZs near Dandong are part of China's foreign expansion policy rather than domestic strengthening project. This aspiration for expansion, temporally and spatially, highlights the positive role China hopes to play in the region while strengthening its economic and political position. Scholars of the region have cited China's and North Korea's long-standing diplomatic relation and China's undeniable role in North Korea's foreign trade as serving the basis of such future and demand more attention (Haggard and Noland 2007; Park 2009; Glaser, Snyder, and Park 2008). Many South Korean scholars have also analyzed the economic relationship of the two states as building the foundations for further economic cooperation in the region that will eventually bring about peace in the region while others argue for more South Korean participation drawing on national re-unification narratives (Incheon-Dandong-Hankyoreh International Forum 2012). These observations conceive of economy and politics as separate realms and equate the development of the economy with the development of peace. As zones of economic engagement, the SEZs and the imagined economic hub are given precedence over other spaces (for example un- or under- development spaces, military spaces and liminal spaces where licit and illicit exchanges occur) in these accounts. However, as I will demonstrate below, they are entangled in the wider politics, history and aspirations.[9]

5   Teeth and Lips

China's efforts to develop its close economic ties to North Korea through the new urban development projects are enhanced by the memorialization of

---

9   Jamie Doucette and Seung-Ook Lee (2015) make similar efforts to position North Korea within the wider geopolitics in their examination of the Kaesong Industrial Complex.

FIGURE 10.4   Statute of the People's Liberation Army by the Yalu River
SOURCE: PHOTO BY AUTHOR

historical sites throughout the city that stress their close historical and political relationship. Along the Yalu River are statues of young soldiers waving
to three villagers as they are about to cross the river (see Figure 10.4). These
soldiers are portrayals of the People's Liberation Army (PLA) on their way to
aid North Korea during the Korean War. It is rumored that one of the soldiers,
positioned in the center, is modeled after Mao Zedong's most beloved first son
Mao Anying who was killed in action shortly after he was stationed in North
Korea. Next to the soldiers are villagers too old to join the army and a child
offering three hardboiled eggs to the soldiers. According to an elder Dandong
resident, a hardboiled egg in the 1950s was a rarity that was only consumed on
very special occasions and hard to obtain for ordinary peasants. The offering
of the eggs to the soldiers in the statute, thus, symbolizes the official narrative
that the people supported North Korea in Korea's civil war despite the poor
economic state of China post-civil war.

Commemorating the Korean War and China's assistance, the central government also built "The Commemorative Museum of War to Resist U.S. Aggression and Aid North Korea" in 1958. In 1993, the museum reopened with
renovations and expansion in remembrance of the 40th anniversary of the
Armistice Agreement (signed by delegates from China, North Korea and the

FIGURE 10.5   The obelisk at the Commemorative Museum of War to Resist U.S. Aggression
              and Aid North Korea
SOURCE: PHOTO BY AUTHOR

United States) that temporarily suspended the Korean War in 1953.[10] The museum is located in the center of the city on top of a hill and features four new statues of Chinese soldiers in battle around a tall marble obelisk (see Figure 10.5) that can be seen from the main thoroughfare of the city. The height of the obelisk, 53 meters, represents the year that the Armistice Agreement was signed (Zhang and Zhang 2000). High CCP officials, including the future President Hu Jintao, attended the opening ceremony for the renovated museum (Song 2012).

Since the reopening, the museum has been named one of China's historical educational tour site and students on fieldtrips frequent the museum (Kang 2012). At the entrance of the museum are giant bronze statues of Mao Zedong and Peng Dehuai, the commander of the CCP during the Korean War, shaking hands. And behind them, etched into another large bronze plaque, are the following words in Chinese and English:

> The War to Resist U.S. Aggression and Aid Korea is a just war... In October
> 1950 when the Korean people were in a very difficult position and the

---

10   Representative from South Korea was not present during the signing. See Bruce Cumings
      (1981) for more on this history.

security of China was threatened seriously, the Party Central Commit-tee and Chairman Mao Zedong... made a decision to 'Resist U.S. aggres-sion and aid Korea as well as protect home and nation' ... After fighting a bloody war ... the Korean and Chinese people's army defeated the 'UNC' ... Ceasefire in Korea was realized. The victory of the war to resist U.S. aggression and aid Korea defended the security of the DPRK and China, safeguarded the peace in the Far East and the world and exerted a far-reaching effect upon the international situation.

The positioning of the United States and the absence of South Korea in this plaque reveals prevailing Cold War bipolar politics that highlight China and North Korea's close historical and political relationship that is as close as "lips and teeth" (Armstrong 2004). By evoking bipolar politics in which the United States is seen as *the* enemy of China and North Korea, this narrative offers a his-torical background to current economic relationship between the two states.[11] Such conjuring of historical memories that rationalize and legitimize current economic relationships with North Korea, however, is not merely limited to those etched into historical sites and relics.[12] In 2010, then Vice President Xi Jinping gave a speech for the 60th anniversary of the Korean War reminding the PLA audience of China's participation in the "great anti-American Korean War" that restored "peace and forestalled invasion" (Halpin 2015).[13] And in 2011, during Hu Jintao's visit to the White House, the famous Chinese pianist Lang Lang performed a popular song from a film about the Korean War that de-picted the PLA soldiers fighting the American "wolves" (ibid).

These controversial occasions, though infrequent, illustrate North Korea's importance in China's hope for expansion of influence within the region and beyond. While China and the United States have pursued closer economic rela-tionship, China has an agenda to position itself within Asia as the super power. And its strategy for the Korean peninsula, I argue, calls upon the *past* (memory politics) as well as the *future* prospect of the region (politics of waiting).

---

11   This frame of bipolar politics fails to narrate the intertwined history of socialism and capi-talism. Heonik Kwon (2010), in his study of Cold War discourses, writes that socialism and capitalism were not simple oppositions. Rather socialism was "an integral part of general social struggles to counter the injustices and contradictions of a colonial political order and to achieve a politically independent and economically prosperous nation-state in its stead" (Kwon 2010: 51).

12   The use of memory in politics has been examined by numerous scholars. For more per-taining to East Asia see (Koga 2008; Kim 2010; Suh 2010; Gong 2001).

13   Xi also asserted that the United States started the war condemning Harry Truman, a point of contention among historians. See Halpin (2015) for more on his speech and Cumings (1981) for a discussion of this controversy.

By evoking their common history and of China's aid during the war, its memory politics calls upon North Korea to follow China as it defines the future. Accordingly many studies that focus on the growing economic relations between China and North Korea highlight this earlier "bond" based on communist ideologies (Yoon and Lee 2012; Glaser, Snyder, and Park 2008; Snyder 2003; Haggard and Noland 2007; Park 2002). At the same time, South Korea and China is able to set aside their historical conflicts by sharing the common future goal of economic prosperity and solidarity in East Asia.[14] While China is pursuing economic cooperation with North Korea by calling upon the past, it is pursuing one with South Korea by calling upon their common future. In Dandong, this layering of discourses symbolizing the common history and future of China and the Korean peninsula coexist in its historical sites and in its new urban development projects.

6   Materiality of Ambition

Dandong, similar to other border cities, is a frontier city. In its modern history, many wars have been fought here including the Sino-Japanese War (1894–1895), Russo-Japanese War (1904–1905) and the Korean War (1950–1953). These violent wars and their deep-seated expansionist agendas have marked Dandong's cityscape, the materiality of which remains as the city's spectacle at night. The central government has appropriated these "debris" of past aspiration to support its current agenda in the region (Stoler 2013). To uphold and maintain the spirits around Dandong's anticipated future, it is not enough to merely re-assert utopic visions of the future based on urban and economic developments. Symbolic and ideological work of situating the debris with their violent history is equally significant and necessary.

Like the widely circulated satellite image of the Korean peninsula at dusk, Sinuiju at night from Dandong is dark with occasional faint glimmers of light in the distance. While restaurants, cafes, souvenir shops and hotels along the Yalu River in Dandong emanate kaleidoscopic neon lights that pierce into the night sky, Sinuiju, with a cityscape indistinguishable from Dandong's by day,

---

14   Scott Snyder (2009) argues that what used to be organized around ideology has been replaced with economic interests in the region and examines how the signing of a diplomatic relationship between China and South Korea in 1992 and the end of the Cold War signaled this shift. Park (2002) also highlights the significance of the year 1992 in China's economic policy toward both South and North Korea.

disappears into an abyss of darkness.[15] Spanning this uncanny, imbalanced nightscape are two bridges, so vividly lit that they reflect a mirror image of their structures into the Yalu River. Both were built by the Japanese army in the first half of the twentieth century. The Friendship Bridge (completed in 1943 during the Second Sino-Japanese War) connects the two cities while the Broken Bridge (completed in 1911 after the First Sino-Japanese War and the Russo-Japanese War) abruptly disappears half way across the river from Dandong. During the Korean War (officially referred to as "the War to Resist U.S. Aggression and Aid Korea" in China), both bridges were targeted by the United States to prevent Chinese aid from reaching North Korean soldiers and to devastate Sinuiju with incendiary bombs (Kang 2013).[16] The newer Sino-Korea Friendship Bridge was repaired during the wartime. However, the older bridge was left unattended to until it was preserved and named as a historical site by the State Council of China and opened for tourists in 1993. Today, the Sino-Korean Friendship Bridge (renamed in 1990 from the Yalu Bridge) is the only land transportation infrastructure in use connecting the two cities (see Figure 10.6).

The two iron bridges of Dandong are failed projects by the Japanese empire of the early 20th century. While Russia initiated the building of the Manchurian railway network, it became part of Japan's ambitious project of expanding its empire into China in the early 1900s. The idea was to connect the Japanese archipelago via railways to China, Russia and beyond. China's current trope of connectivity, prosperity and utopic visions of development bears familiarity to Japan's past project. This resemblance of Japan's past aspirations and China's current ones is important in understanding the region's changing political landscape; in historicizing the conditions of the city; and in reflecting upon the non-linear temporality of progress and development (Ferguson 1999; Buck Morss 2002; Park 2015, and more).[17]

---

15   There are nights when lights can be seen in Sinuiju along the river or in the city proper couple miles inland. However, Sinuiju at night, during my fieldwork between 2013–2014, remained mostly dark. Lack of electricity is a well-documented issue in North Korea (Hotham, 2015; Lankov, 2013) and some of Sinuiju's electricity is provided by China through Dandong.

16   Sinuiju, North Korea is a light industry city developed during the Japanese colonization period from 1910 to 1945. During an intense two-day attack on November 5 and 8, 1950 under General Douglas MacArthur, 65% of transportation system, military installation, factories and government buildings were destroyed and more than five thousand, mostly civilians, were killed by more than 500 tons of incendiary bombs (See Thompson and Nalty 1997).

17   Colonial modernity as an analytic helps historicize China's vision for itself and for the region. It allows a comparison of China's progressive aspirations to that of Japan's in the past, materiality of which are still visibly erect in Dandong. I rely on the analytic of

FIGURE 10.6   Photo of the Friendship Bridge and the Broken Bridge from Dandong
SOURCE: PHOTO BY AUTHOR

The old iron bridges were part of a violent imperial expansion plan. Japan's lasting colonial policy and ensuing wars in the region have been well documented
and theorized by many scholars (Koga 2013; Koga 2008; McNamara 1990; Robinson and Shin 1999; Gries et al. 2009; Kohli 1994; Kim 2010). In Dandong, these
two bridges have since colonial times been re-appropriated to represent and
narrate the story of China and North Korea's close relationship. The old bridges
had to become something other than a representation of its colonial history
and of Japan's imperial aspiration for China. Today, one is a remnant of "American atrocities" that stress China's "leadership and bravery," and the other a
symbol of China and North Korea's "friendship" that will bring about economic changes (Zhang and Zhang 2000). The sense of the relationship between
China and North Korea in Dandong is very different from popular depiction of
China as a parent and North Korea as a "petulant" child (Economist 2013), or
an "unruly neighbor" (Glaser, Snyder, and Park 2008) in media and scholarly

---

colonial modernity to think together modernity, capitalism and colonialism. As a framework, it is useful for a historical investigation that is trying to "locate the origin of capitalist development in the colonial era, implicating the origin of Korean modernity in what
was called Western modernity, which Japan simultaneously sought to imitate and overcome in its metropole and colonies" (Shin and Robinson 2001). However, my project is
not about historically tracing the relationship between modernity and capitalism in the
colonial era (although that would be an interesting project). Rather, the colonial modernity analytic allows me to compare and reflect upon the resemblance of aspirations and
ambitions embedded in the three bridges.

reports. Rather, the relationship that is stressed through these bridges symboli-cally celebrates their common history and trajectory, which is utilized as the basis of Dandong's strategic location as an economic hub.

7   Conclusion

Embedded in Dandong's economy of anticipation is the ambitious plan to build an economic hub. I call this ambitious because it envisions a seamlessly connected world in which the market will solve problems of security and pov-erty within the region and beyond into North Korea. With more economic co-operation and capital investment, the plan is expected to create more jobs for all, leading to better financial and social security and eventually to "peace" in the region. The market fundamentalist idea that the "unfettered market" will solve social, political and economic problems, however, has not been success-ful (Stiglitz 2007). As Naomi (Klein 2008) writes in *The Shock Doctrine,* neolib-eral market policies exploit disaster situations through a misrepresentation of the economic as bringing political freedom. Accordingly, Dandong's capitalist future, while bright and aspirational, designates North Korea as a disaster fac-tor in need of market interventions and reproduces it as a capitalist frontier for the wider region. And Dandong's economy of anticipation ensuing from its future as an economic hub elicits economic responses from the present by producing "projected needs" and "creating markets" to solve the North Korean problem (Adams, Murphy, and Clarke 2009: 250–252). Through this process, as Adams, Murphy, and Clarke observe, "promissory capital speculation and development logics render some places as backward in time, needing antici-patory investment, while other places are deemed already at the cusp of the 'new' future, marked by the virtue of rapid change... Promissory market log-ics not only find new sites of investment, but produce them as problematized domains" (2009: 251).[18] To put it simply, North Korea is relegated as needing economic investment and intervention through China's plan of building the economic hub. The problem that I am identifying with this speculative logic is not only in its reproduction of classes and hierarchy based on capital, but also in how it recognizes foreseeable problems arising out of implementing such developmental policies without consideration for local dynamics and existing concerns, including labor exploitation, uneven urban development, resource extraction and income inequality.

---

18   Also see Kim Fortun (2001) and Sunder Rajan (2006).

The question I propose to ask is: what led to the problematization of North Korea and the wide circulation and acceptance of economic cooperation as the solution for peace in the region? Economic development and regional stability have been China's national priority since Deng Xiaoping's economic reform in 1978. This economic reform policy reached Dandong in the 1990s and influenced its foreign policy toward North Korea (Glaser, Snyder, and Park 2008). At the same time, a shift in South Korea's economic development policy in the late 1990s, which included a policy to economically engage North Korea, coincided with China's economically friendly policy toward North Korea (Park 2015). In her critique of South Korea's unification policy, Hyun Ok Park (2015) argues that while South Korea's economically friendly shift towards North Korea stems from "visions of a new capitalist order in Asia during the post-Cold War years," "beneath the surface of cooperation and reconciliation, the policy of economic engagement with North Korea entails an intense struggle between the two Koreas for hegemony" (2015: 203–204). Accordingly, concerns for the security of the people and peace for the region are secondary to the nation state's vision to maintain its position within the regional hierarchy.[19] In the end, Park writes, "The economic engagement policy does not guarantee resolution of social antagonisms sown during and after the Cold War in South and North Korea" (2015: 211).

Despite oppositional voices from academics and activists, China and South Korea's economic interest in North Korea continue in market fundamentalist form.[20] The irony here is that while North Korea and its perseverance pose a problem, its persistence is also what makes it into an economic frontier and an untapped resource. For these precise reasons, economic interest in North Korea persists, producing waiting time that suspends a space for critical engagement and questions about the effects of pursuing utopic visions of modernity and progress for the region. Anticipating the future, Dandong reproduces the all too familiar narrative of urban development as the pathway to peaceful relationships: a vision that sustains speculation in the present but does so at the cost of forestalling important questions about the nature of such development itself. As this chapter demonstrated, the urban development projects are situated in wider politics, history and aspirations; and the future of Dandong's

---

19   She writes, "Economic engagement with North Korea was to strengthen the South Korean economy and consequently secure its leadership position in Asia. Here, cooperation with China was considered imperative. Anticipating that China would become a global economic superpower, South Korea planned to link itself with China through its economic network with North Korea... South Korea feared that China, Japan and even the United States would dominate investment in the North" (Park, 2015: 203).

20   For more see Park (2015:192), Kim et al. (2007) and Incheon-Dandong-Hankyoreh International Forum (2012).

urban development as well as North Korea's role as a capitalist frontier require more locally specific examination.

References

Abrahamian, A and GK See (2014) The ABCs of North Korea's SEZs. *A US–Korea Institute at SAIS Report:* 7–36.

Adams, V (2013) *Markets of Sorrow, Labors of Faith: New Orleans in the Wake of Katrina.* Durham, NC: Duke University Press.

Adams, V, M Murphy and AE Clarke (2009) Anticipation: Technoscience, Life, Affect, Temporality. *Subjectivity* 28(1): 246–265.

Appadurai, A (2004) The Capacity to Aspire: Culture and the Terms of Recognition. In: V Rao and M Walton (eds) *Culture and Public Action.* Palo Alto, CA: Stanford University Press, 59–84.

Appadurai, A (2012) The Spirit of Calculation. *Cambridge Anthropology* 30(1): 3–17.

Appadurai, A (2013) *The Future as Cultural Fact: Essays on the Global Condition.* London: Verso Books.

Armstrong, CK (2004) *The North Korean Revolution, 1945–1950.* Ithaca, NY, NY: Cornell University Press.

Bräutigam, D and T Xiaoyang (2011) African Shenzhen: China's Special Economic Zones in Africa. *The Journal of Modern African Studies* 49(01): 27–54.

Buck-Morss, S (2002) *Dreamworld and Catastrophe: The Passing of Mass Utopia in East and West.* Boston, MA: The MIT Press.

China Daily (2009) Dandong City Bordering DPRK. *China Daily,* 14 July. Available (consulted 10 December 2015) at: http://www.chinadaily.com.cn/china/2009-07/14/content_8423440_4.htm

China Daily (2010) Another Bridge to Link DPRK. *China Daily,* 8 March. Available (consulted 10 December 2015) at: http://www.chinadaily.com.cn/m/liaoning/2010-03/08/content_9553798.htm

Collier, S and A Lakoff (2008) The Problem of Securing Health. In: S Collier and A Lakoff (eds.) *Biosecurity Interventions: Global Health and Security in Question.* New York, NY: Columbia University Press, 7–32.

Cross, J (2010) Neoliberalism as Unexceptional: Economic Zones and the Everyday Precariousness of Working Life in South India. *Critique of Anthropology* 30(4): 355–373.

Cumings, B (1981) *The Origins of the Korean War: Liberation and the Emergence of Separate Regimes, 1945–1947.* Princeton, NJ: Princeton University Press.

Davies, M, H Edinger, N Tay and S Naidu (2008) How China Delivers Development Assistance to Africa. *Stellenbosch: Centre for Chinese Studies.* Available (consulted 15 January 2013) at: http://www.ccs.org.za/downloads/DFID_FA_Final.pdf

Demick, B and JY Choi (2013) North Korea's Youth Revolution Stirs Unease.

Doucette, J and SO Lee (2015) Experimental Territoriality: Assembling the Kaesong Industrial Complex in North Korea. *Political Geography* 47(July): 53–63.

Duchâtel, M and P Schell (2013) China's Policy on North Korea: Economic Engagement and Nuclear Disarmament. *SIPRI Policy Paper*, 40. Solna: Stockholm. Peace Research Institute.

Easterling, K (2014) *Extrastatecraft: The Power of Infrastructure Space*. New York, NY: Verso Books.

Economist (2013) China Continues to Fret over Its Troublesome Neighbour. *Economist*, February 2. Available (consulted 10 December 2015) at: http://www.economist.com/news/china/21571196-china-continues-fret-over-its-troublesome-neighbour-naughty-step

Evans, B and J Reid (2014) *Resilient Life: The Art of Living Dangerously*. Malden, MA: Polity Press.

Ferguson, J (1999) *Expectations of Modernity: Myths and Meanings of Urban Life on the Zambian Copperbelt*. Berkeley, CA: University of California Press.

Fortun, K (2001) *Advocacy after Bhopal: Environmentalism, Disaster, New Global Orders*. Chicago, IL: Chicago University Press.

Fuller, CJ V Benei (eds.) (2001) *The Everyday State and Society in Modern India*. London: C Hurst & Co Publishers Ltd.

Gill, B (2011) *China's North Korea Policy: Assessing Interests and Influences*. Washington, DC, US Institute of Peace.

Glaser, B, S Snyder, and JS Park (2008) *Keeping an Eye on an Unruly Neighbor: Chinese Views of Economic Reform and Stability in North Korea.* Available (consulted 14 December 2012) at: http://www.usip.org/files/resources/Jan2008.pdf

Gong, GW (2001) The Beginning of History: Remembering and Forgetting as Strategic Issues. *Washington Quarterly* 24(2): 45–57.

Gries, PH, Q Zhang, Y Masui, et al. (2009) Historical Beliefs and the Perception of Threat in Northeast Asia: Colonialism, the Tributary System, and China–Japan–Korea Relations in the Twenty-First Century. *International Relations of the Asia-Pacific* 9(2): 245–265.

Haggard, S and M Noland (2007) *North Korea's External Economic Relations. Peterson Institute for International Economics Working Paper* (07–7). Available (consulted 22 October 2013) at: http://papers.ssrn.com/sol3/papers.cfm?abstract_id=1008902.

Halpin, DP (2015) The Other History Controversy: China and the Korean War. *North Korea News,* 8 July. Available (consulted 14 December 2015) at: http://www.nknews.org/2015/07/the-other-history-controversy-china-and-the-korean-war/

Hanser, A (2008) *Service Encounters: Class, Gender, and the Market for Social Distinction in Urban China*. Stanford, CA: Stanford University Press.

Holston, J (1989) *The Modernist City: An Anthropological Critique of Brasilia*. Chicago, IL: University of Chicago Press.

Hong, IP (2002) A Shift toward Capitalism? Recent Economic Reforms in North Korea. *East Asian Review* 14(4): 93–106.

Hotham, O (2015) Lights out in Pyongyang? North Korea's energy crisis. *NK News*, 22 May. Available (consulted 10 April 2017) at https://www.nknews.org/2015/05/lights-out-in-pyongyang-north-koreas-energy-crisis/

Hsu, CL (2006) Cadres, Getihu, And Good Businesspeople: Making Sense Of Entrepreneurs In Early Post-Socialist China. *Urban Anthropology and Studies of Cultural Systems and World Economic Development* 35(1): 1–38.

Incheon-Dandong-Hankyoreh International Forum (2012) *Incheon-Dandong-Hankyoreh Internatoinal Forum.* Seoul: The Hankyoreh Foundation for Unification and Culture.

Jung, SH (2014) North Korea's Trade with China: Aggregate and Firm-Level Analysis. Unpublished doctoral thesis, Seoul National University, Seoul.

Kang, JW (2012) An Ethnography of the Border City Dandong between China and North Korea: Through the Relations of North Koreans, Overseas Chinese in North Korea, Joseonjok, and South Koreans. Unpublished doctoral thesis, Seoul National University, Seoul. (In Korean).

Kang, JW (2013) *Making and breaking borders: Cultural anthropological guide to reading Dandong.* Paju: Kŭl Hangari. (In Korean).

Kim, DC (2010) The Long Road Toward Truth and Reconciliation. *Critical Asian Studies* 42(4): 525–552.

Kim, J and A Abrahamian (2011) Why World Should Watch Rason." *The Diplomat*, 22 December. Available (consulted 15 November 2012) at: http://thediplomat.com/2011/12/why-world-should-watch-rason/

Kim, KR, HB Cho, S Lee and JA Cho (2007) *Measures for Vitalizing North-South Economic Cooperation Governance.* Seoul, Korea: Ministry of Unification. (In Korean).

Klein, N (2008) *The Shock Doctrine.* New York, NY: Penguin Books.

Koga, Y (2008) The Double Inheritance: The Afterlife of Colonial Modernity in the Cities of Former "Manchuria." Unpublished doctoral thesis, Columbia University, New York, New York.

Koga, Y (2013) Accounting for Silence: Inheritance, Debt, and the Moral Economy of Legal Redress in China and Japan: Accounting for Silence. *American Ethnologist* 40(3): 494–507.

Kohli, A (1994) Where Do High Growth Political Economies Come From? The Japanese Lineage of Korea's "Developmental State." *World Development* 22(9): 1269–1293.

Kwon, H (2010) *The Other Cold War.* New York, NY: Columbia University Press.

Kwon, J (2015) The Work of Waiting: Love and Money in Korean Chinese Transnational Migration. *Cultural Anthropology* 30(3): 477–500.

Lakoff, A (2007) Preparing for the Next Emergency. *Public Culture* 19(2): 247–71.

Lankov, A (2013) The Real North Korea: Life and Politics in the Failed Stalinist Utopia. Oxford, United Kingdom: Oxford University Press.

Los Angelels Times, 14 December. Available (consulted 3 January 2016) at: http://www
.latimes.com/world/la-fg-north-korea-youth-20131214-story.html#axzz2nSm6iIwL.

Man, H (2012) The significance of defining Sino–North Korean relationship: For the future of China and North Korea economic cooperation. *KDI North Korean Economic
Review* 2: 59–76. (In Korean).

Martina, M (2015) China, North Korea to Open Border Trade Zone – Media. *Reuters UK,* 13 July. Available (consulted 5 October 2015) at: http://uk.reuters.com/
article/2015/07/13/uk-china-northkorea-trade-idUKKCN0PN1C820150713

McNamara, DL (1990) *The Colonial Origins of Korean Enterprise: 1910–1945.* Cambridge:
Cambridge University Press.

Metz, S (2013) Strategic Horizons: When North Korea Collapses, U.S. Must Be
Ready. World Politics Review. *World Politics Review,* 18 December. Available (consulted 3 January 2016) at: http://www.worldpoliticsreview.com/articles/13450/
strategic-horizons-when-north-korea-collapses-u-s-must-be-ready

Miyazaki, H (2006) Economy of Dreams: Hope in Global Capitalism and Its Critiques.
Cultural Anthropology 21(2): 147–172.

Ngai, P (2013) Subsumption or Consumption? The Phantom of Consumer Revolution
in "Globalizing" China. *Cultural Anthropology* 18(4): 469–495.

Ong, A (2006) *Neoliberalism as Exception: Mutations in Citizenship and Sovereignty.*
Duke, NC: Duke University Press.

Ong, LH (2014) State-Led Urbanization in China: Skyscrapers, Land Revenue and "Concentrated Villages." *The China Quarterly* 217: 162–179.

Osburg, J (2013) *Anxious Wealth: Money and Morality Among China's New Rich.* Stanford, CA: Stanford University Press.

Park, DB (2002) Sino-Korean Relations since 1992: Achievements and Prospects. *East
Asian Review* 14(1): 3–20.

Park, HO (2015) *The Capitalist Unconscious: From Korean Unification to Transnational
Korea.* New York, NY: Columbia University Press.

Park, JS (2009) *North Korea, Inc: Gaining Insights Into North Korean Regime Stability from Recent Commercial Activities.* Available (consulted 14 December 2012) at
http://www.usip.org/publications/north-korea-inc-gaining-insights-north-korean-
regime-stability-recent-commercial

Rajan, KS (2006) *Biocapital: The Constitution of Post-Genomic Life.* Duke, NC, Duke University Press.

Redfield, P (2000) *Space in the Tropics: From Convicts to Rockets in French Guiana.*
Berkeley, CA: University of California Press.

Robinson, ME and GW Shin (eds.) (1999) *Colonial Modernity in Korea.* Boston, MA:
Harvard University Asia Center.

Rofel, L (1999) *Other Modernities: Gendered Yearnings in China After Socialism.* Berkeley, CA: University of California Press.

Ruediger, F (2014) Rason Special Economic Zone: North Korea as It Could Be. *38 North: Informed Analysis of North Korea*, 16 December. Available (consulted 20 December 2014) at: http://38north.org/2014/12/rfrank121614/

Shin, GW and M Robinson (2001) *Colonial Modernity in Korea*. Boston, MA: Harvard University Asia Center.

Snyder, S (2003) Sino-Korean Relations and the Future of the US-ROK Alliance. *NBR ANALYSIS* 14(1): 51–72.

Snyder, S (2009) *China's Rise and the Two Koreas: Politics, Economics, Security*. Boulder, CO: Lynne Rienner Publishers.

Snyder, S (2015) North Korea's Latest Export: Labor. *Forbes*, 22 May. Available (consulted 20 October 2015) at: http://www.forbes.com/sites/scottasnyder/2015/05/22/north-koreas-latest-export-labor/

Song, C (2012) Commemorative Museum of War to Resist U.S. Aggression and Aid North Korea. *ChinaHighlights*. Available (consulted 15 October 2015) at: http://www.chinahighlights.com/dandong/attraction/commemorative-museum-of-the-war-to-resist-u.s.-aggression-and-aid-north-korea.htm

Stiglitz, J (2007) Beppe Grillo's Blog: The Pact with the Devil by Joseph E. Stiglitz. *Beppe Grillo's Blog*. Available (consulted 20 January 2013) at: http://www.beppegrillo.it/eng/2007/01/stiglitz.html

Stoler, AL (ed) (2013) *Imperial Debris: On Ruins and Ruination*. Durham, NC: Duke University Press Books.

Suh, JJ (2010) Truth and Reconciliation in South Korea: Confronting War, Colonialism, and Intervention in the Asia Pacific. *Critical Asian Studies* Vol 42 (4): 503–524.

Taussig, M (2004) *My Cocaine Museum*. Chicago, IL: University of Chicago Press.

Thompson, W and BC Nalty (1997) *Within Limits: The U.S. Air Force and the Korean War*. Honolulu, HI: University Press of the Pacific.

Weaver, LR (2002) China Tycoon Charged with Corruption. CNN, 27 November. Available (consulted 10 February 2016) at: http://edition.cnn.com/2002/WORLD/asiapcf/east/11/27/china.tycoon/index.html

Wu, A (2005) What China Whispers to North Korea. *The Washington Quarterly* 28(2): 35–48.

Yonhap News (2014) N. Korea, China to Hold Annual Trade Fair in Oct. *Yonhap News*, 16 June. Available (consulted 18 October 2015) at: http://english.yonhapnews.co.kr/northkorea/2014/06/16/1/0401000000AEN20140616007700315F.html

Yoon, SH and SO Lee (2012) From Old Comrades to New Partnerships: Dynamic Development of Economic Relations between China and North Korea. *The Geographical Journal* 179(1): 19–31.

Zaloom, C (2008) The Productive Life of Risk. *Cultural Anthropology* 19(3): 365–391.

Zhang, H and Z Zhang (2000) *Solidification of the historical moment: commemorating the 50th Anniversary of the Chinese People's Volunteers' War to Resist US Aggression and Aid Korea*. Liaoning: Liaoning People's Publishing House. (In Mandarin).

Zhu, C and C Liu (2012) Largest Border City Poised for Trade Boom. *China Daily*, 7 November. Available (consulted 19 November 2015) at: http://www.chinadaily.com .cn/m/liaoning/dandong/2012-11/07/content_15887471.htm

The Developmental State, Speculative Urbanization and the Politics of Displacement in Gentrifying Seoul

Hyun Bang Shin and Soo-Hyun Kim

1   Introduction

This chapter is a case study of the city of Seoul, South Korea (hereafter Korea) that discusses how gentrification plays out in an economy that is heavily shaped and nurtured by strong state intervention.[1] In part, we attempt to expand the existing gentrification debates by including a case that goes beyond the usual suspects in the global North (Lees, 2012; Lees et al., 2015). The condensed urbanization and industrialization led by the Korean developmental state fundamentally changed the country's cityscape from the 1960s. After having gone through a trial-and-error period of eradicating widespread substandard, illegal settlements, the Korean developmental state implemented an urban redevelopment program in 1983, which relied heavily on the joint collaboration between real estate businesses and property owners. The program fundamentally fed upon Seoul's highly speculative real estate market (Shin, 2009), promoting 'vertical accumulation' (Shin, 2011) that tried to maximize accumulation through high-density construction and has become the main feature of Korea's urbanization in recent decades. While the redevelopment projects from the 1980s might have contributed to the provision of much more improved physical conditions of living than what dilapidated neighborhoods used to provide, these projects incurred a life of huge socio-economic hardship for most local residents due to displacement and relocation (Davis, 2011; Shin, 2008). Homes affordable for poor families were subject to 'domicide' (Porteous and Smith, 2001), destroyed to make way for new infrastructure and commercial housing, and to cater for the needs of the country's middle classes and addressing the state aspiration of beautification and modernization. Embedded in this urban

---

1   This chapter is a revised version of an article that originally appeared as Shin, H.B. and Kim, S-H. (2016) The Developmental State, Speculative Urbanization and the Politics of Displacement in Gentrifying Seoul. *Urban Studies* 53(3): 540–559.

context, a case study of Seoul is a useful means by which to inform the existing literature on gentrification investigating non-Western empirics.

For our discussions, we prescribe to a broader definition of gentrification, which emphasizes capital (re-)investment, commodification of space and (various forms of) displacement (Clark, 2005; Lees et al., 2008). We therefore keep a distance from a narrow conceptualization that associates gentrification only with incremental upgrading of dwellings or inner-city neighborhoods, and from excessively associating gentrification with the specificities of Anglo-American metropolises only (e.g. Maloutas, 2012). Following Ley and Teo (2014), we also acknowledge that gentrification as a process may emerge and exist even if the concept itself is not sufficiently circulated in a society. In Korea, gentrification has only gained its academic currency in recent years (e.g. Kim et al., 2010). Redevelopment (*jaegaebal* in Korean) and demolition (*cheolgeo*) are the terms that have been more widely circulated as popular, academic and policy expressions. To some extent, this is an outcome of confining gentrification to its classic form of inner-city residential upgrading. With few exceptions (e.g. Lee and Joo, 2008; Shin, 2009), gentrification has been regarded as being inapplicable to neighborhood transformation through wholesale demolition and redevelopment (e.g. Kim and Nam, 1998).

By examining Seoul's experience of urban redevelopment during the last 30 years, we argue that new-build gentrification is not just an attribute of the cities in the global North ruled by neoliberal 'roll-out' states (Davidson and Lees, 2010). In other words, new-build gentrification is an endogenous process embedded in Korea's speculative urban development processes. However, Seoul's new-build gentrification is not simply a replication of new-build gentrification in the global North, but a process that reveals distinctive characteristics due to the influence of the strong developmental (and later (neo-)liberalizing) state. By adopting an evolutionary approach and making use of local historical archives, government records and authors' first-hand research, this chapter attempts to deliver a more in-depth, nuanced interpretation of Seoul's history of urban development and gentrification.

The rest of the chapter consists of four sections. Firstly, we provide an analytical framework that brings together the importance of real estate (as part of the secondary circuit of capital accumulation) and the role of the developmental state, and discuss their relevance for gentrification. Secondly, we examine the history of Seoul's urban redevelopment during the last 30 years, examining how the developmental (and later (neo-)liberalizing) state has shaped urban redevelopment practices that exhibit the key characteristics of new-build gentrification. This is followed by a section that discusses how the state and large businesses took an upper hand in promoting redevelopment, and how resistance to this was rendered ineffective despite the colossal consequences for local residents. The final section brings together the main findings and makes a set of conclusions.

2   Real Estate, the Developmental State and Gentrification

In discussing urban accumulation crises and the emergence of increasingly deregulated capitalism in the 1960s, Henri Lefebvre highlighted the possibility of real estate's rise as a second sector of accumulation to address the inherent risks of falling rates of profits and heightened competition that capitalism faces in perpetuity. He argued that,

> As the principal circuit – current industrial production and the movable property that results – begins to slow down, capital shifts to the second sector, real estate. It can even happen that real-estate speculation becomes the principal source for the formation of capital, that is, the realization of surplus value. The second circuit supplants the first, becomes essential.
>
> LEFEBVRE, 2003: 160

In line with Lefebvre's argument, David Harvey (1978) put forward the concept of 'capital switching' between different circuits of capital as a fix to (over-) accumulation crises. The secondary circuit of capital accumulation, that is, investment in the built environment (e.g. infrastructure and housing), gains particular importance due to its function of absorbing shocks generated from the primary circuit of industrial production. The shock absorption can occur in several ways. For instance, it may operate as a buffer to absorb low profitability in the production circuit and boost a sluggish economy. Classic examples would include the New Deal in times of the Great Depression in the US and more recently, China's state-led investment in fixed assets as a pre-emptive means to generate economic development and advance urbanization (see Shin, 2014).

The rise of the secondary circuit of capital entails the inevitable ascendancy of 'real estate (speculation, construction) ...a circuit that runs parallel to that of industrial production' (Lefebvre 2003: 159). As capital feels the poisonous seduction of speculative profits from real estate, it is difficult to dismiss the speculative desire, especially in times of global economic ups and downs affecting national economies. The rise of real estate accompanies spatial investment strategies in order to facilitate (re-)valuation of real estate properties, producing speculative urban development (Goldman, 2011; Shin, 2014). Speculation also becomes rampant as obsolescence becomes 'a neoliberal alibi for creative destruction', which concentrates on areas with the highest returns on investment in a market that has been increasingly entwined with the global financial capital (Weber, 2002: 532). To help perpetuate this process, the local state 'operates through decentralized partnerships with real-estate capitalists, and what remains of the local state structure has been refashioned to resemble the private sector, with an emphasis on customer service, speed, and entrepreneurialism' (Weber, 2002: 531).

In this context of the rise of the real estate sector and intensifying state intervention in promoting speculative urbanization, contemporary gentrification in the global North is increasingly characterized by large-scale real estate projects resulting in state-led, new-build gentrification (Lees et al., 2008). Gentrification is no longer confined to its classic process of residential upgrading mostly focused on the dilapidated inner city. Real estate projects that accompany the redevelopment of existing residential, commercial or brownfield sites come to constitute new-build gentrification, which result in either direct or indirect displacement of residents in targeted project sites or in adjacent spaces (Davidson and Lees, 2010).

East Asia, including Japan and tiger economies (Hong Kong, Singapore, South Korea and Taiwan) in particular, saw the heavy intervention of developmental states from the outset of their economic development and condensed urbanization in the second half of the twentieth century. The East Asian developmental path was epitomized by centralized policy-making for economic growth, strong state intervention in investment decision-making, control of finance, export orientation, investment in human capital, the authoritarian control of civil society and close ties with business interests (Castells, 1992; Woo-Cumings, 1999). The state-led investment to produce and expand fixed assets and collective consumption (esp. housing) was phenomenal. Depending on the nature of the state–economy and state–society relations, the particular type of prioritized collective consumption differed across countries. For instance, Singapore focused more on the production of public housing to meet the demand from the coalition between the state and the popular sector, while in Korea, the strong alliance between the state and large conglomerates made public housing investment less of a priority (Park, 1998). The developmental state's legitimacy depended on successfully guaranteeing the economic security of the national populace, co-opted into various state ideologies.

East Asia's condensed economic development and urbanization were accompanied by the state-led, heavy investment in the built environment co-mingled with speculative real estate markets due to their land-scarce environment. As argued by Jang-sup Shin (2007), who emphasizes the importance of the 'stickiness' of mobile assets (or capital) in the age of globalization, improving the quality of the built environment has been one of the main urban accumulation strategies increasingly adopted by the East Asian states. Place promotion, beautification and mega-event promotion also helped East Asian states rewrite their urban landscapes. In Korea, subnational actors (e.g. Seoul municipal government or district governments within Seoul) were all in this together under the directives from the central government during the period of industrialization and urbanization.[2] Government-owned development corporations such as the Korea Land Corporation and Korea National Housing Corporation played key roles in facilitating the state intervention in the built environment, often working with the private sector. While Korea experienced political decentralization from the 1990s, having had the first election to elect district and municipal mayors, provincial governors (in 1995) and local assembly members (in 1991), sub-national actors are still bound by a growth politics that retained investment in the built environment at its core (e.g. Park, 2008).

It is in this context of state-led economic development and urbanization that we aim to contextualize the prominence of state-led, new-build gentrification under the developmental state. Translating economic success into the urban landscape involved the wholesale clearance of dilapidated urban spaces and their replacement by upscale commercial and residential buildings and facilities. In other words, urban spaces seeing widened rent gaps were put into higher and better uses by the state, capitalists and the emergent middle-class populace, who would have shared profits from closing the rent gap (see Smith, 1996 for rent gap discussions). In Korea, this process was particularly pronounced from the early 1980s when the country was seeing the channeling of surplus capital into real estate to accumulate property assets. The 1980s saw declining profit rates in the Korean economy compared to those experienced during the more labor-intensive growth under the developmental state in the 1960s and 1970s (see Shin, 2009). The surplus capital made its way into the secondary circuit, tapping into the speculative property market that had experienced major price increases, thus resulting in the speculative urbanization presiding over industrialization (Shin, 2018: 359–361). For instance, Jung (1998: 136) notes that,

---

2   See Shin (2018: 359–361) for a more detailed discussion of the relationship between industrialization and urbanization in South Korea.

During the past twenty-two years from 1974 to 1996, land prices for all the nation's land increased by 17.6 times, in rural areas by 10.2 times and in smaller cities by 20.2 times. However, land prices in the six largest cities increased by 28.9 times, and in Seoul by 32.9 times.

Korean conglomerates were also heavily engaged in property speculation in the country's real estate markets (Sohn, 2008: 116–117). Not only were they operating major construction firms to reap profits from the state-financed re-structuring of the built environment, but they also heavily acquired real estate holdings.[3] For instance, in 1989, it was reported that these conglomerates were in possession of real estate properties whose total value reached more than a half of their combined equity capital (Sohn, 2008).

3   Urban (Re)development and Emerging New-build Gentrification
         in Seoul

3.1 *The Rise and Containment of Substandard Settlements in the 1960s and 1970s*

Seoul accommodates about one-fifth of the national population. This stands in sharp contrast with the land situation: Seoul's surface area occupies less than 1% of the national territory, therefore producing a very high population density of 17,000 people per square kilometer. Seoul has always experienced a high de-mand for residential land in times of rapid urbanization and economic devel-opment from the 1960s. Migration of cheap labor to Seoul was one of the main drivers of economic development, but Seoul's urban infrastructure, housing in particular, was hardly sufficient to cope with the demand rising from the rapid population increase. Illegal substandard settlements, known as *panjachon* in Korean (translated as 'village of wooden-board framed houses'), sprung up in and around Seoul. Facing no alternatives, the municipality to some extent turned a blind eye to such development. By 1966, according to an official count, there were approximately 136,650 illegal dwellings, more than one-third of the total municipal housing stocks (Seoul Metropolitan Government; SMG, 1973: 185).

Eventually, a series of government attempts took place to control the growth of such illegal settlements. The authoritarian state, headed by a president who led a military coup in 1961, exercised draconian measures to suppress and con-tain the growth of substandard settlements, if not completely eradicate them. For instance, from 1972, Seoul's aerial pictures were taken four times a year

---

3 See Pirie (2008) for his account of the Korean market and firm activities.

and 159 ground surveillance posts were erected in substandard settlements to map any new construction of illegal dwellings. Government officials deployed routine patrols while residents were encouraged to spy on neighbors to report any illegal construction (SMG, 1973: 192).

Restraining the growth of existing substandard settlements was accompanied by the development of large-scale new housing estates (known as *danji* in Korean) as part of the ten-year (1972–1981) housing construction program (see Figure 11.1). This was to accommodate the demand for modern housing from the newly emerging middle class (Lee, 1994). The program aimed at achieving an economy of scale and efficient land use, focusing on the then urban fringes to the south of the River Han where land assembly was relatively cheap and less confrontational due to a much scarcer density of population (Planning and Coordination for the Cabinet Office, 1972: 253–254). Each *danji* was huge in scale, comprising of about 27,000 flats in the case of *Mokdong danji*. New flats produced in the late 1970s became subject to rampant speculation. For instance, the total amount of deposits from applicants attracted to a sales announcement of new housing estates in 1977 by five construction companies amounted to about 4.6% of the national money supply at the time (Mobrand 2008:382). In short, the new housing construction drew an intense degree of

FIGURE 11.1 View of Banpo medium-rise apartment *danji*, completed in the 1970s
    SOURCE: PHOTOGRAPH FROM SEOUL HISTORY COMPILATION COMMITTEE
    2008

interest from both homebuyers and speculators, which in turn led to the emergence of housing redevelopment targeting substandard settlements in Seoul's more central areas to exploit the developmental potential.

3.2   *Property-led Redevelopment Since the 1980s*

One of the pilot redevelopment programs experimented in the 1970s was called 'consignment redevelopment'. It required owner-occupiers in substandard settlements to form a steering committee and consign to a private builder the clearance of dwellings and construction of new flats or multi-household units. In situ upgrading without demolition was not favored by the municipality who preferred to establish a 'modern' facade of the city (Kim et al., 1996: 95–101; SMG, 1983: 335–336). The municipality was to recommend credible builders and conduct supervision. Each project was small-scale, requiring 20–30 households to join hands so that about 1000-square-metre housing lot could be assembled (Kim et al., 1996: 96). Eventually, the program was not successful: only 2253 dwellings in 12 project areas were redeveloped in this way (Kim et al., 1996). Major constraints were the large costs of reconstruction and temporary relocation, which burdened the participating owner-occupiers.

Having learnt from the 1970s, the municipal government introduced a revised policy in 1983 (The KyungHyang Shinmun, 1984), which became the model for subsequent redevelopment programs in following decades. The program, known as the 'Joint Redevelopment Programme' (hereafter JRP), largely depended on the use of joint contributions from local property owners (mostly dwelling owners but not necessarily owner occupiers) and builders that supplied development finance and carried out construction and marketing (Ha, 2001; Shin, 2009). Unlike the 1970s, the JRP was to substantially increase the scale of reconstruction, facilitated by the growing popularity of high-rise apartments among the emerging middle classes for the purpose of both consumption and investment (see Figure 11.2).

In substandard settlements subject to the JRP, the majority of dwellings were without de jure property ownership, as they had no land titles (SMG, 1998: 20–21). As the 1973 Temporary Act prohibited any upgrading of existing dwellings to prevent the spread and expansion of such settlements, owner-occupiers in these settlements faced unfavorable conditions in terms of investment in their own properties. This condition also prevented the arrival of middle class households as individual gentrifiers, and in turn discouraged the rise of 'first-wave' gentrification (Hackworth and Smith, 2001). The suppression of development however created a massive rent gap (Shin, 2009), thus opportunities for reaping profits once these settlements became subject to commercial redevelopment and closure of the rent gap.

(a) Before redevelopment

(b) After redevelopment

FIGURE 11.2 Ogsu neighbourhood before and after redevelopment (project period: November 1984–October 1990)
SOURCE: PHOTOGRAPHS PROVIDED THROUGH THE COURTESY OF THE SEOUL INSTITUTE

The introduction of the JRP as a redevelopment model can be understood more as the gradual evolution of endogenous policies. While it is not possible to verify if the national or municipal government imported or consulted a particular overseas policy due to limited availability of interviewees or official archives, the combination of state assistance, corporate interests and commercial redevelopment targeting large-scale substandard and illegal settlements would be considered as a highly unprecedented urban policy in the global

South at the time. The summary of ad hoc communications with a former housing official who served in the municipality between 1992 and 1997 also testifies that the JRP introduction was embedded in Seoul's particular urban contexts:

> The JRP was an eye-opening idea. Seoul at the time was facing the hosting of the 1986 Asian Games and the 1988 Summer Olympic Games, and was in need of redeveloping panjachon. But, this was going to be impossible if previous methods were used, given local residents' economic hardship and the government's financial capacity. Construction firms were in need of projects, and if they were to provide money and take the responsibility, the government would not have to worry any more. At first, it was just a trial, but it quickly spread to cover the entire city, testifying the formidable power of the combination of local residents and capital, thus joint redevelopment. Development profits were the main impetus of the JRP promotion. (Meeting on 30 September 2013 and telephone communication on 1 November 2013)

Seoul's housing market, especially the emergent high-rise apartment sector, was seeing a speculative boom throughout the 1980s and 1990s. This meant that construction firms were able to reap profits by selling commercial new-build flats in the new housing market (after deducting flats to be sold to participating property owners at construction costs). High-density construction was therefore crucial (Shin, 2011). Government data examining 65 JRP districts between 1990 and 1996 suggest that the number of dwellings experienced a 303% increase after redevelopment, while the number of residents witnessed a 32% increase (SMG 1998: 32). In other words, redevelopment resulted in the construction of more spacious single-family units in neighborhoods that used to experience house-sharing and overcrowded conditions. The floor-to-area ratio (hereafter FAR; the ratio of gross floor space to the land surface area that a building occupies) of redeveloped districts during this period often reached 300% or higher. The high-density redevelopment was supported by various government incentives to help property owners lessen their burden of paying for construction and guaranteeing a certain amount of profits for builders. If poorer property owners opted out of a project, they sold the right (to buy a redeveloped flat at construction costs) to speculators or first-time homebuyers at a price that was determined somewhere between the price of existing dwellings (before the arrival of redevelopment) and the subsidized price of new flats they were originally entitled to pay as a member of property owners' association called the redevelopment association. This would have resulted in what López-Morales (2011) referred to as 'ground rent dispossession', a situation in which property owners were disadvantaged in fully appropriating potential ground rent. The dispossession of this nature also becomes the basis for the rise of speculative activities by absentee landlords and developers (see Shin, 2009).

3.3   *Densification of Old Residential Units in the 1990s*

The redevelopment of substandard settlements was accompanied by the densification of existing low-rise detached houses in formal, established neighborhoods. House owners rebuilt their one- or two-storey detached dwellings to convert them into multi-household units that were usually three- to four-stories high excluding the basement (see Figure 11.3). The municipal government contributed to this process by relaxing planning regulations (e.g. easing the requirements for a minimum distance between dwellings or the provision of parking spaces). Small-scale builders were naturally the main participants in this segment of the housing market.

Each densified multi-household dwelling was subdivided to be rented out. Usually a detached dwelling for one family was densified and then subdivided to provide living space for five households. The authors' own estimation from the municipal government data suggests that about 750,000 multi-household units were produced between 1990 and 2001, accounting for about 66% of all housing units produced in Seoul in this period. Approximately 150,000 detached dwellings are estimated to have been demolished in this process. These

FIGURE 11.3 Neighbourhood with a concentration of multi-household dwellings
SOURCE: PHOTOGRAPH BY HYUN BANG SHIN IN 2002

multi-household dwellings contributed to the expansion of more affordable housing stocks with flexible tenure for low-income urban residents (Shin, 2008), but as a neighborhood, what prevailed were worsening living conditions due to inadequate provision of parking spaces, narrow streets and the absence of green or recreational spaces.

3.4   Reconstruction of Medium-rise Apartments between the Mid-1990s and 2000s

From the mid-1990s, Seoul saw the expansion of urban redevelopment targeting extant medium-rise estates to a higher density. This process was initially concentrated in south Seoul where large-scale danji estates were previously constructed. The redevelopment of medium-rise housing estates is often referred to as 'reconstruction' or *jaegeonchug* in Korean to differentiate it from the redevelopment of substandard settlements classified as *jaegaebal*. The reconstruction adopted the JRP model. Each project was to be initiated by the property owners' association (known as reconstruction association, again to differentiate it from redevelopment association for substandard settlement redevelopment), which would also include a construction firm or a consortium of firms. The increase in building density and in the number of flats as a result of reconstruction allowed the reconstruction committee (consisted of flat owners and collaborating construction firms) to sell additional commercial flats on the new housing market. The sales revenues would help lower the overall construction costs for existing owners and ensure a certain level of profits and speculative gains for both owners and construction firms. Only members of reconstruction association were to reap the benefits, as was the case in the previous JRP structure.

The reconstruction of existing apartment complexes became popular between 1998 and 2007, in particular when Korea was recovering from the aftermath of the 1997–1998 Asian financial crisis. According to the *2008 Housing Handbook* from the Ministry of Land, Transport and Maritime Affairs, 94,492 flats were demolished during the ten-year period, followed by the reconstruction of about 180,562 flats. These accounted for about 14% of all apartment units in Seoul as of 2007. Given the large-scale nature of projects that required a huge amount of upfront financial input, reconstruction projects were mostly led by large construction firms (as was the case in JRP projects). The popularity of construction firms and their housing brand became an important factor that determined the price of reconstructed flats. Major firms associated with the largest conglomerates such as Hyundai, Samsung and Daewoo became the most sought-after brand names among flat owners in this regard.

3.5   Redevelopment of High-density Low-rise Residential Areas in the 2000s

From 2002, Seoul's urban redevelopment expanded to address high-density low-rise residential areas where multi-household dwellings were concentrated. This was promoted under the label of 'New Town Programme' (NTP). As the then mayor indicated at the opening ceremony of a pilot project site in March 2004, "the project aims to create another city within a city" (SMG, 2004). As of July 2010, 35 mega-districts were designated, which included 372 subdistricts (SMG, 2010). This covered a total area of 27.34 square kilometers, about 6% of Seoul's surface area. As of September 2008, 350,000 households (850,000 people or 8% of the municipal population) were subject to the NTP (Jang and Yang, 2008). Of these, 69% or 230,000 households were tenants, and the municipal planning aimed to reduce the share of tenant households to 19.2% upon program completion (Jang and Yang, 2008).

The NTP was led by the municipal government from its birth, which was also heavily politicized due to the then Seoul mayor who had an aspiration to secure national presidency. This situation was further exacerbated as the NTP also responded to the speculative aspiration held by those property owners who did not benefit from the previous rounds of JRP. Major builders also welcomed the policy as it promised the emergence of another market for their operation. To ensure the success of the pilot projects at the NTP outset, the municipality was put "in charge of building public facilities" and the municipal development corporation "responsible for implementing housing development work" (Korea Herald, 2002).

The NTP aimed at scaling up redevelopment projects so that a number of outdated residential neighborhoods and urban facilities would come together to form a mega- district. Like in JRP projects, demolition and reconstruction were perceived as the norm. After piloting, private builders took more initiatives for housing development at the subdistrict scale, adopting either a JRP-style redevelopment model or the 1990s' reconstruction model. Nevertheless, the municipal government made comprehensive efforts to ensure the success of the NTP, including the establishment of a separate division to oversee the progress, publishing regular progress newsletters for publicity.

However, the NTP caused a substantial reduction in affordable housing stocks for low-income residents who were concentrated in multi-household dwellings, especially after the demise of panjachon settlements. The interim evaluation suggested that about 80% of original residents were leaving project sites due to rising housing costs. In comparison with JRP projects, dwelling owners were more likely to lose out due to the increase in financial contributions (Kim, 2010). Neighborhoods with multi-household dwelling concentration were experiencing already fairly high FAR of 200%, and there was a higher share of tenants' households whose demand for compensation (both in-kind and in-cash) would place additional constraints upon financial outlook of each NTP project. Under these circumstances, the weakening real estate market resulting from the 2008 global financial crisis also made it financially difficult for property owners and construction firms in particular, who became more wary of the uncertain business outlook (Ha, 2010).

3.6   A Summary of Seoul's Redevelopment History

Urban redevelopment through the demolition of substandard settlements and existing medium-rise apartment complexes brought about profound changes to Seoul's landscape. Seoul's urban transformation therefore shows a strong resemblance with new-build gentrification, incurring the displacement of the majority of low-income owner-occupiers and tenants from their original neighborhoods. While there are no data showing the scale of displacement since the implementation of the JRP, reports suggest that about 0.72 million residents faced eviction between 1983 and 1988, which amounted to 8;9% of the then municipal population (ACHR, 1989). Reports also suggest that JRP projects saw nearly four-fifths of original residents displaced permanently (Ha, 2004). Official municipal records for JRP projects completed between 1993 and 1996 indicated that 84% of tenants and 55% of dwelling owners were permanently displaced (Kim et al., 1996: 221). The situation has been replicated in NTP projects (Jang and Yang, 2008). Table 11.1 summarizes the scale of redevelopment over the years. The table also includes a summary of key events in South Korea.

The involvement of large construction companies with a strong capacity to mobilize financial resources was important especially because of the immense scale of each redevelopment project. The largest neighborhoods subject to redevelopment could accommodate as many as 5738 households (Kim et al., 1996). According to the data from the municipal government, the average number of demolished dwellings from 211 redevelopment projects (completed by the end of 2010) turned out to be 379 units, while the average number of newly constructed flats reached 977 units.

4   Speculative Desire and the Politics of Displacement

Gentrification is not an automated process and socio-political struggles matter (Smith 1996). These struggles are of crucial importance especially for poor owner-occupiers and tenants who bear the brunt of redevelopment in the form of involuntary displacement. From the early 1980s Seoul's redevelopment resorted to the collective mobilization of property owners whose shared material interests brought them together. The material interests here largely refer to the increased exchange value of their properties (therefore, development gains) overshadowing enhanced use value (improved living conditions). Studies, however, find that existing property owners were replaced by speculative absentee landlords as projects progressed (Shin, 2009). By the time demolition took place the share of owner-occupiers in the total number of property owners tended to be in the range of 20;30% only. This imbalance becomes the source of a redevelopment association being influenced by outsiders' interests rather than those of local residents. Ironically, this would translate into a more financially sound project from the perspective of the capital.

Absentee landlords tend to take the side of construction firms as they share common objectives: to displace existing tenants quickly and demolish dwellings to shorten the project schedule and prevent the unnecessary rise in overall costs. This becomes one of the major reasons behind the frequent use of violent measures to remove physical and human barriers to redevelopment. The compensation provision is also meant to affect only the officially recognized last-remaining residents subject to displacement, disregarding other forms such as chain displacement that occur before last-resident displacement (Marcuse, 1985). Property owners and builders often strive to reduce the number of last-remaining eligible tenants to minimize the official costs of compensation, especially the costly provision of redevelopment rental flats.[4]

Displacement of poor owner-occupiers and tenants has thus been the inevitable outcome of Seoul's urban redevelopment (Kim et al., 1998). The flow of capital into redevelopment areas affected the whole of Seoul with no evident concentration in only inner-city areas (see Figure 11.4). Upon introducing the JRP in 1983, there was no compensation arrangement for tenants. Against the backdrop of heightened democratization movements in the 1980s and the early 1990s, the large-scale displacement of tenants became a major source of discontent (ACHR, 1989). The demolition of the most affordable and flexible means of residence such as panjachon invoked great difficulties for poor tenants in particular (Shin, 2008). Tenants' struggles against forced eviction and

---

4 Chain displacement refers to the displacement of those households who used to occupy a dwelling before the 'last-remaining' household and who were displaced due to the dwelling's physical decline or rent increases. Such households are often hidden from the actual estimation of displaced households even though their displacement might have occurred during the entire process of neighborhood decline (see Marcuse, 1985: 206).

TABLE 11.1 The scale of major redevelopment programmes in Seoul and the summary of key events

Period	Major projects	Scale	Graphic representation	Key events
1960s and 1970s	Substandard settlements, their expansion and clearance	Official estimation of 136,650 illegal dwellings by 1966, more than one-third of the then total municipal housing stocks	Medium-rise flats / Squatters	1961 Military coup and the beginning of the Park Chung-hee regime 1972 Commencement of ten-year Housing Construction programme 1973 Temporary Act to prohibit expansion of substandard neighbourhoods 1979 The end of the Park regime after his assassination, shortly followed by another military coup that led to the beginning of the Chun Doo-hwan regime
1980s to 2000s	Joint redevelopment	Demolition of about 80,000 dwellings in substandard settlements and construction of about 206,000 flats by the end of 2010. Affected about 10% in the 1980s alone, affecting 10% of municipal population	JRP	1983 Implementation of the Joint Redevelopment programme 1986 Seoul Asian Games 1988 Seoul Olympic Games 1989 Formal introduction of rehousing provision for eligible tenants in JRP districts

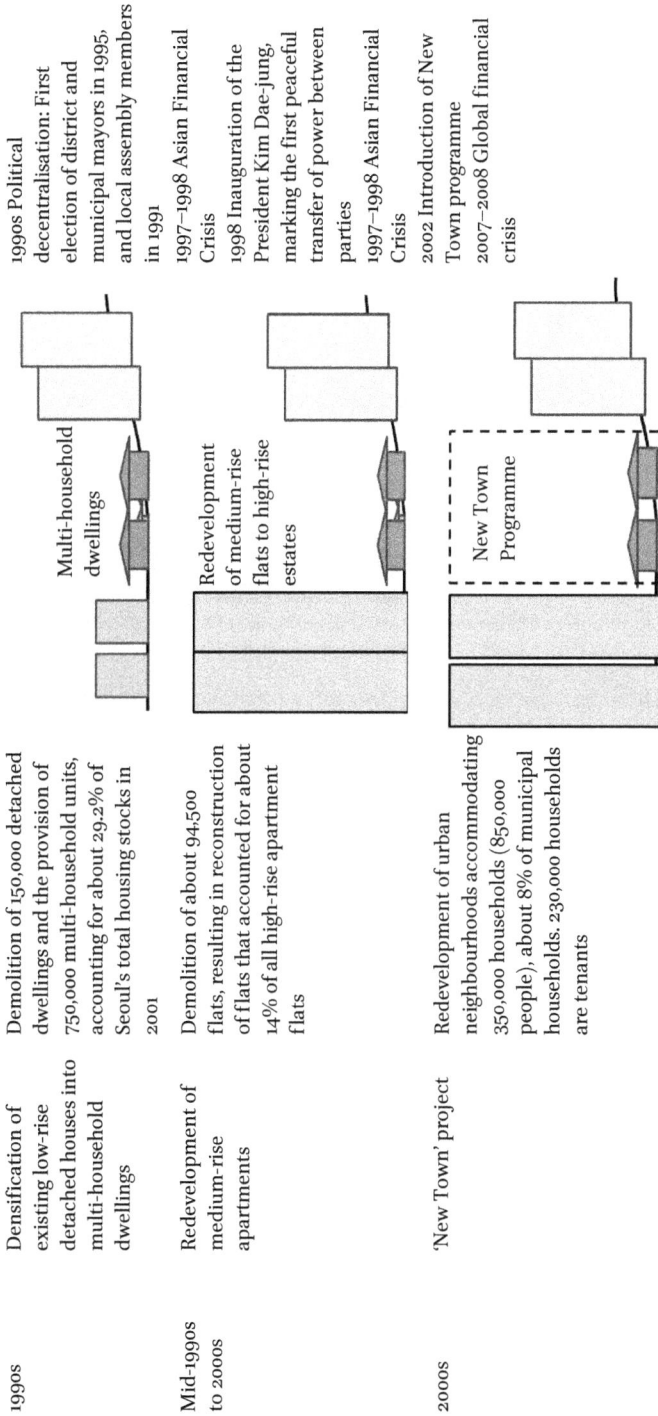

1990s — Densification of existing low-rise detached houses into multi-household dwellings — Demolition of 150,000 detached dwellings and the provision of 750,000 multi-household units, accounting for about 29.2% of Seoul's total housing stocks in 2001

Mid-1990s to 2000s — Redevelopment of medium-rise apartments — Demolition of about 94,500 flats, resulting in reconstruction of flats that accounted for about 14% of all high-rise apartment flats

2000s — 'New Town' project — Redevelopment of urban neighbourhoods accommodating 350,000 households (850,000 people), about 8% of municipal households. 230,000 households are tenants

Multi-household dwellings

Redevelopment of medium-rise flats to high-rise estates

New Town Programme

1990s Political decentralisation: First election of district and municipal mayors in 1995, and local assembly members in 1991

1997–1998 Asian Financial Crisis

1998 Inauguration of the President Kim Dae-jung, marking the first peaceful transfer of power between parties

1997–1998 Asian Financial Crisis

2002 Introduction of New Town programme

2007–2008 Global financial crisis

SOURCE: KIM (2010), JANG AND YANG (2008) AND SEOUL MUNICIPAL GOVERNMENT DATA

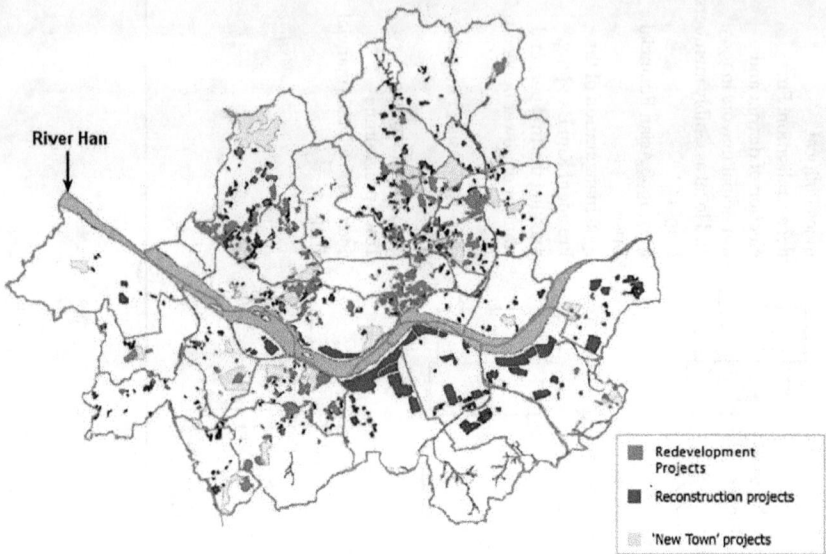

FIGURE 11.4 Locations of areas designated for redevelopment in Seoul
SOURCE: MAP ADOPTED FROM BUREAU OF HOUSING (2008) AND ADJUSTED

their call for housing rights were often undermined by the brutal oppression of the authoritarian state, which prioritized urban beautification and portrayed evictees' protests as threatening national stability (Kim et al., 1998). Protestors were also often stigmatized as being motivated by self-interests for more compensation, pursuing personal interests at the expense of public gains, an experience that is often replicated elsewhere around the world (see Shin, 2013 for China's case).

Eventually, the tenants' struggle, the democratization movement throughout the 1980s, and international concern all placed pressure upon the state, who yielded some concessions for tenants. By mid-1989 these came to be in the forms of cash (equivalent to three months' living costs) and in-kind compensation for eligible tenants. The latter referred to the mandatory requirement to provide public rental flats (known as 'redevelopment rental housing') in the same neighborhood to rehouse willing and eligible tenants (Kim et al., 1996: 109–110). To be eligible, tenants should have been registered residents and have lived there at least three months at the time of the government approval of the redevelopment masterplan. However, the provision of rehousing arrangement legitimized the municipal government to further push forward the complete eradication of substandard settlements throughout the 1990s, and by 2000, practically all panjachon settlements were cleared (Kim, 2011). The provision of rehousing arrangement, prescribed as a response to tenant evictees' outcries for their basic rights notably led to the subsiding of the tenants movement against displacement (see Shin, 2018 for the genealogy of urban rights struggles). When the growth of civil society movements in parallel with the democratization of the country propelled active intervention in policy-making processes, the housing rights movement also gravitated towards legal systems to improve the general housing welfare for the urban poor (e.g. setting up a minimum housing standard) (Lee, 2012) rather than resistance to displacement.

While the provision of redevelopment rental flats could be deemed as progress, this was not hugely popular among tenants, as these rental flats did not fully address tenants' household economies and tenure preferences (Shin, 2008). The lack of provision of temporary relocation measures while the construction took place added further constraints. Tenants, in their post-redevelopment life in rehoused public rental flats have also been known to face social discrimination. Redeveloped neighborhoods see the juxtaposition of luxury commercial flats with public rental flats, showing a social mix of tenure at the neighborhood scale. However, incidents of discrimination by better-off residents against public tenants have become a major source of concern since the 1990s (Ha, 2008). Furthermore, compensation measures only benefited JRP tenants and did not help tenants displaced due to the reconstruction of more established apartment estates – *jaegeonchug*. The primary rationale behind this was the government classification of the former as serving the public interests, while the latter was treated as being exclusively in the private domain. This unequal treatment placed the issue of redevelopment compensation for tenants as if it was part of welfare provision for the urban poor rather than housing rights in general.

Developmental states are known to have co-opted the general population in their pursuit for rapid economic development and societal stability (frequently through authoritarian means) to maximize the mobilization of resources and their productive use (Woo-Cumings, 1999). Despite the suppression of democratic processes and civil society, state legitimacy is often secured through getting things done and raising the living standard. For the emerging middle class, the speculative desire to accumulate property assets often leads to the perception of redevelopment as a societal progress as Tang (2008) noted. Viewed as the 'culture of property' by Ley and Teo (2014), this tendency may impel people to keep distance from denunciating redevelopment projects and displacement. Hsu and Hsu (2013) also refer to the 'political culture of property' in Taiwan, which privileged property ownership and supported close collaboration between real-estate developers and landowners for property-led redevelopment since the 2000s. In such contexts, displacement is taken as an inevitable pre-condition of progress, and the civil society may be discouraged from setting a progressive agenda to fight negative consequences of redevelopment.

In Korea, this mechanism had been undermining popular resistance against eviction, albeit sporadic upheavals, and hindering movements from strengthening until the country's real estate market started to dramatically weaken in recent years. Now, the weakening real estate market is ironically providing a renewed opportunity for critical urban scholars and social movements to produce alternative perspectives and strategies to resist the class re-making of urban space.

5   Conclusion: Gentrification in Seoul as an Endogenous Process

This chapter on the place-specificity of gentrification in Seoul contests the view that gentrification travels from its 'originating center' to 'peripheral cities' (Atkinson and Bridge, 2005). It is shown instead that the emergence of Seoul's gentrification can be regarded as an endogenous process, embedded in Korea's construction of speculative urban development. From its birth, Seoul's gentrification has been a process of socio-spatial restructuring at the municipal scale. Instead of individual upgrading, Seoul's gentrification has been characterized by the demolition of entire neighborhoods to make way for new-build housing estates, catering for the needs of the country's middle-class populace. Displacement is at the core of this transformative process of converting neighborhoods into a 'higher and better' use to close the rent gap (Smith, 1996; Slater 2009). However, Seoul's gentrification is not simply mimicking the new-build gentrification in the global North, as the process is heavily influenced by the strong developmental, and later (neo-)liberalizing, state. Furthermore, despite its potential, displacement has failed to become a major political agenda. This owes partly to the brutal suppression of residents' protests against forced eviction, reflecting the authoritarian nature of developmental states inherent among the newly industrialized economies and partly to the state concession to co-opt those discontented. The provision of public rental housing as part of in-kind compensation for eligible tenants was clearly conforming to the latter strategy.

Seoul's experience of gentrification allows us to expand the gentrification debates on cities outside of the usual suspects of the global North by situating Seoul's 'new-build' gentrification in the context of the speculative and exploitative process of extracting exchange value from the built environment (Harvey, 1978; Lefebvre, 2003). Substandard settlements and other neighborhoods subject to redevelopment became conduits for capital that speculated on the real estate and benefited from increased ground rents (Desai and Loftus, 2013; Goldman, 2011; López-Morales, 2011; Shin, 2009). The role of the Korean developmental state is noteworthy, broadening our understanding of the global geography of gentrification. By employing a critical understanding of the political economy of urban spatial restructuring, the case of the endogenous emergence of gentrification in Seoul shows that the exploitative process of gentrification and displacement is inevitable when central and local states are keen to facilitate urban accumulation via the secondary circuit of the built environment (see also Lees et al., 2015, 2016). Contemporary gentrification researchers often associate the global spread of gentrification with the neoliberal expansion of urban policies. This chapter contends that gentrification transcends the realm of neoliberal 'roll-out' states and is also heavily influenced by the proactive intervention of developmental states in constructing speculative built environments. The process of gentrification in Seoul could not have been consolidated without the presence of those large conglomerates as the major partners of the Korean developmental state. The chapter therefore highlights the importance of investigating and contextualizing the nature and role of real estate capital and its relationship with the state in gentrification debates.

Does the neoliberalization of the Korean developmental state, as argued by some commentators (e.g. Choi, 2012), produce any significant changes to the patterns of gentrification? In answer to this question, we argue that continuity has been the essence of urban redevelopment practices in Korea under both the pre-crisis developmental state and post-crisis (neo-)liberalizing developmental state. The fundamental investment structure and institutional set-up, which shaped the geography of urban redevelopment, witnessed some changes (e.g. a more comprehensive area-based approach in the NTP), but they displayed a certain degree of continuity in terms of policy scope and key emphasis. To the extent that the developmental state placed a heavy emphasis on market orientation and proactive entrepreneurial state intervention in urban redevelopment, it could also be argued that the Korean developmental state befriended neoliberalization. Neoliberal governance emphasizes partnership or coalition with business interests (and sometimes with civil society) to enhance economic competence and ensure market supremacy (Brenner and Theodore, 2002). The emergence of this neoliberal governance was not something alien to the developmental state that was already founded on a strong alliance with business interests and co-opted the national populace while suppressing social movements. The legacy of the developmental state era would prevail, as the state and large conglomerates continued to be important actors in shaping and formulating urban mega-projects and housing construction. To this extent, we concur with the notion of 'hybridity' in urban policy formation, which draws upon the idea that state policies under neoliberalization contain both elements of 'neoliberalism' and 'developmentalism' (Choi, 2012; Park et al., 2012). The concept also emphasizes the persistent manifestation of developmental characteristics in the process of neoliberalization. As far as Seoul's urban redevelopment and gentrification is concerned, state intervention in the built environment has been persistent regardless of Korea's economic liberalization.

So what will be the future of Seoul's gentrification? The future depends largely on the degree of the vibrancy of the real estate market. A particular culture of property prevails, dictating that property investment in redeveloped neighborhoods will produce a certain amount of return on financial input. It is however doubtful if this practice would continue in the future. To some extent, the global financial crisis in 2008 has undermined the confidence of property-based interests in the real estate market (Ha, 2010). Korea also experiences one of the lowest birth rates in the world, leading to the fear of a rapidly ageing society, raising doubts about future housing demand. As the myth of property investment withers away, the state's legitimacy may also be shaken, leading to the rise of discontent in the context of exacerbated uneven development. How all these influence urban redevelopment and gentrification will need to be closely examined in the coming years.

References

ACHR (1989) *Battle for housing rights in Korea. Report of the South Korea Project of the Asian Coalition for Housing Rights.* Bangkok: Asia Coalition for Housing Rights [and] Third World Network.

Atkinson, R and G Bridge (eds.) (2005) *Gentrification in a Global Context: The New Urban Colonialism.* London: Routledge.

Brenner, N and N Theodore (2002) Cities and the geographies of 'actually existing neoliberalism'. *Antipode* 34(3): 349–379.

Bureau of Housing (2008) *Urban renewal projects and Seoul's housing policy.* Seoul: Seoul Municipal Government (in Korean).

Castells, M (1992) Four Asian tigers with a dragon head: A comparative analysis of the state, economy, and society in the Asian Pacific rim. In: R Appelbaum and J Henderson (eds.) *States and Development in the Asian Pacific Rim.* Newbury Park, CA: SAGE, pp. 33–70.

Choi, B-D (2012) Developmental neoliberalism and hybridity of the urban policy of South Korea. In: B-G Park, RC Hill and A Saito (eds.) *Locating Neoliberalism in East Asia: Neoliberalizing Spaces in Developmental States.* Chichester: Wiley Blackwell, pp. 86–113.

Clark, E (2005) The order and simplicity of gentrification – a political challenge. In: R Atkinson and G Bridge (eds.) *Gentrification in a Global Context: The New Urban Colonialism.* London: Routledge, pp. 256–264.

Davidson, M and L Lees (2010) New-build gentrification: Its histories, trajectories, and critical geographies. *Population, Space and Place* 16(5): 395–411.

Davis, LK (2011) International events and mass evictions: A longer view. *International Journal of Urban and Regional Research* 35(3): 582–599.

Desai, V and A Loftus (2013) Speculating on slums: Infrastructural fixes in informal housing in the global South. *Antipode* 45(4): 789–808.

Goldman, M (2011) Speculative urbanism and the making of the next world city. *International Journal of Urban and Regional Research* 35(3): 555–581.

Ha, S-K (2001) Substandard settlements and joint redevelopment projects in Seoul. *Habitat International* 25: 385–397.

Ha, S-K (2004) Housing renewal and neighborhood change as a gentrification process in Seoul. *Cities* 21(5): 381–389.

Ha, S-K (2008) Social housing estates and sustainable community development in South Korea. *Habitat International* 32(3): 349–363.

Ha, S-K (2010) Housing crises and policy transformations in South Korea. *International Journal of Housing Policy* 10(3): 255–272.

Hackworth, J and N Smith (2001) The changing state of gentrification. *Tijdschrift voor Economische en Sociale Geografie* 92(4): 464–477.

Harvey, D (1978) The urban process under capitalism: A framework for analysis. *International Journal of Urban and Regional Research* 2: 101–131.

Hsu, J-y and Y-h Hsu (2013) State transformation, policy learning, and exclusive displacement in the process of urban redevelopment in Taiwan. *Urban Geography* 34(5): 677–698.

Jang, N and J Yang (2008) *Key Issues and Improvements of New Town Project in Seoul.* Seoul: Seoul Development Institute (in Korean).

Jung, H-N (1998) Land prices and land markets in Korea, 1963–1996: Explanations from political economy perspectives. *The Korea Spatial Planning Review* 27: 127–146 (in Korean).

Kim, S-H (2010) Issues of squatters and eviction in Seoul. *City, Culture and Society* 1(3): 135–143.

Kim, S-H (2011) Squatter settlement policies and the role of the state. *Housing Studies Review* 19(1): 35–61 (in Korean).

Kim, S-H, et al. (1998) (eds.) *Eviction from the Perspective of Evictees.* Seoul: Korea Centre for City and Environment Research (in Korean).

Kim, B-W, NA Kwon and J-H Gil (2010) Analysis of the commercial characteristics about the Samcheongdong-gil gentrification. *Journal of the Korean Regional Economics* 15: 83–102 (in Korean).

Kim, KJ, Lee IJ and SH Jeong (1996) *Substandard Housing Redevelopment in Seoul: 1973–1996*. Seoul: Seoul Development Institute (in Korean).

Kim, K and Y-W Nam (1998) Gentrification: Research trends and arguments. *Journal of Korea Planning Association* 33(5): 83–97.

Korea Herald (2002) Development of urban centers in northern Seoul to begin soon. *Korea Herald*, 5 November (in Korean).

Lee, J-W (1994) Industrialization and the formation of the new middle class in Korea. *Korea Journal of Population and Development* 23(1): 77–96 (in Korean).

Lee, W-H (2012) The history of evictees' movement and key agendas. *City and Poverty* 97: 38–57 (in Korean).

Lee, S-Y and K-S Joo (2008) Neighborhood change as a gentrification process in Yongsan redevelopment district. *Journal of the Korean Urban Geographical Society* 11(3): 113–123.

Lees, L (2012) The geography of gentrification: Thinking through comparative urbanism. *Progress in Human Geography* 36(2): 155–171.

Lees, L, HB Shin and E López-Morales (2015) (eds.) *Global Gentrifications: Uneven Development and Displacement*. London: Policy Press.

Lees, L, HB Shin and E López-Morales (2016) *Planetary Gentrification*. Cambridge: Polity Press.

Lees, L, T Slater and E Wyly (2008) *Gentrification*. London: Routledge.

Lefebvre, H (2003) *The Urban Revolution* (trans. R Bononno). Minneapolis: University of Minnesota Press.

Ley, D and SY Teo (2014) Gentrification in Hong Kong? Epistemology vs. ontology. *International Journal of Urban and Regional Research* 38(4): 1286–1303.

López-Morales, E (2011) Gentrification by ground rent dispossession: The shadows cast by large scale urban renewal in Santiago de Chile. *International Journal of Urban and Regional Research* 35(2): 330–357.

Maloutas, T (2012) Contextual diversity in gentrification research. *Critical Sociology* 38(1): 33–48.

Marcuse, P (1985) Gentrification, abandonment and displacement: Connections, causes and policy responses in New York City. *Journal of Urban and Contemporary Law* 28: 195–240.

Mobrand, E (2008) Struggles over unlicensed housing in Seoul, 1960-80. *Urban Studies* 45(2): 367–389.

Park, B-G (1998) Where do tigers sleep at night? The state's role in housing policy in South Korea and Singapore. *Economic Geography* 74(3): 272–288.

Park, B-G (2008) Uneven development, inter-scalar tensions, and the politics of decentralization in South Korea. *International Journal of Urban and Regional Research* 32(1): 40–59.

Park, BG, RC Hill and A Saito (2012) (eds.) *Locating Neoliberalism in East Asia: Neoliberalizing Spaces in Developmental States.* Chichester: Wiley Blackwell.

Pirie, I (2008) *The Korean Developmental State: From Dirigisme to Neoliberalism.* London: Routledge.

Planning and Coordination for the Cabinet Office (1972) *Administration white paper.* Seoul: Government of the Republic of Korea.

Porteous, JD and SE Smith (2001) *Domicide: The Global Destruction of Home.* Montreal: McGill-Queen's University Press.

Seoul History Compilation Committee (2008) *Seoul in photographs Vol.5: Expanding Seoul (1971–1980).* Seoul: Seoul Metropolitan Government (in Korean).

Shin, HB (2008) Living on the edge: Financing post-displacement housing in urban redevelopment projects in Seoul. *Environment and Urbanization* 20(2): 411–426.

Shin, HB (2009) Property-based redevelopment and gentrification: The case of Seoul, South Korea. *Geoforum* 40(5): 906–917.

Shin, HB (2011) Vertical accumulation and accelerated urbanism: The East Asian experience. In: M Gandy (ed.) *Urban Constellations.* Berlin: Jovis, pp. 48–53.

Shin, HB (2013) The right to the city and critical reflections on China's property rights activism. *Antipode* 45(5): 1167–1189.

Shin, HB (2014) Contesting speculative urbanization and strategising discontents. *City* 18(4–5): 509–516.

Shin, HB (2018) Urban movements and the genealogy of urban rights discourses: The case of urban Protesters against redevelopment and displacement in Seoul, South Korea. *Annals of the American Association of Geographers* 108(2): 356–369.

Shin, J-S (ed.) (2007) *Global challenges and local responses: the East Asian experience.* London; New York: Routledge

Slater, T (2009) Missing Marcuse: On gentrification and displacement. *City* 13(2): 292–311.

SMG (1973) Municipal administrative outline. Seoul: SMG.

SMG (1983) *Municipal administration.* Seoul: SMG.

SMG (1998) *Masterplan for the housing redevelopment in Seoul.* Seoul: SMG.

SMG (2004) Seoul embarks on a New Town project. 25 March. Available at: http://english. seoul.go.kr/gtk/news/news_view.php?idx=164 (accessed 20 June 2013).

SMG (2010) New Town project statistics (as of 30 June). Seoul: SMG.

Smith, N (1996) *The New Urban Frontier: Gentrification and the Revanchist City.* London and New York: Routledge.

Sohn, N (2008) *Real Estate Class Society.* Seoul: Humanitas (in Korean).

Tang, W-S (2008) Hong Kong under Chinese sovereignty: Social development and a land (re)development regime. *Eurasian Geography and Economics* 49(3): 341–361.

The KyungHyang Shinmun (1984) Tax incentives for redevelopment apartments. The *KyungHyang Shinmun*, 31 January (in Korean).

Weber, R (2002) Extracting value from the city: Neoliberalism and urban redevelopment. *Antipode* 34(3): 519–540.

Woo-Cumings, M (ed.) (1999) *The Developmental State*. New York: Cornell University Press.

CHAPTER 12

The Fall of the Hong Kong Dream: New Paths of Urban Gentrification in Hong Kong

Iam-chong Ip

1   Introduction

In recent years some scholars (Butler, 2003, 2007; Hamnett, 2003, 2009, 2010) have attempted to portray gentrification as a gradual process of class replacement and post-industrialization.[1] Their view contrasts to the long-standing literature on gentrification concerning about the issues of class displacement and socio-spatial justice (Glass, 1964; Ley, 1996; Rose, 1984; Smith, 1996, 2000, 2002). The proponents of this revisionist take on gentrification decouple the concept of gentrification from class conflict by portraying an evolutionary process – the increasing population of middle class in the cities caused by deindustrialization and the expansion of financial and service sectors. The imperatives to capital accumulation and class inequalities no longer figure in their narratives of gentrification. A handful of East Asian scholars also endorses this attendant capitalist triumphalism. They see urban gentrification in cities such as Shanghai and Singapore as beneficial projects launched and managed by urban states and the private sector for the purpose of improving citizens' quality of life (Hogan et al., 2012; Li and Song, 2009). The rise of the new middle class and proliferation of desires for an elite way of urban life have subsequently shaped a clean-sweep approach to urban redevelopment for urban mega-projects (Wang and Lau, 2009).

Interestingly enough, public opinion in Hong Kong has recently shifted in opposite direction. The economic miracle of Hong Kong, especially before the 2000s, served as a successful case of urban gentrification and fast-growing middle class in East Asia, and provided evidence to support the triumphalist view. Many local people also felt proud of it. However, this is no longer the case over the past decade. Since the year of 2010, after the publication of a bestseller titled *Property Developer Hegemony* in Hong Kong, the Chinese term "Property

1   I would like to thank Jamie Doucette and Bae-Gyoon Park for comments and suggestions. This work has been supported by the Early Career Scheme sponsored by the Research Grants Council of Hong Kong (Project no.: 23600616).

Hegemony" (*dichan baquan*) has become a catchword. According to a survey conducted in 2011, 85% respondents had heard about this term among which 77.9% believed that "Property Hegemony" really exists and 73.3% found it "serious" as a social problem (Hong Kong Institute of Asia-Pacific Studies, 2011). Li Ka Shing, the most successful property developer in Hong Kong, was now portrayed by many protesters as "devil". It is not simply a story of the changing public image of tycoon but also about the dramatic transformation of Hong Kong's *status quo*, i.e. its administration, political machinery, and the path of urban development, in which people have gained, lost, and suffered.

What really matters for understanding these changes is not primarily the economic performance of Hong Kong, but the spatial-economic restructuring triggered by the city's increasing politico-economic integration into China. The expansion of middle class and their housing and investment demand had played a role in the development of a property and finance-led regime of accumulation before the Asian Financial Crisis in 1997. But I argue that, since the early 2000s, urban development of Hong Kong has no longer been managed and regulated by a city-state power with a relatively stable accumulation regime, i.e. a balancing of production, distribution and demand within limits which are compatible with social cohesion (Boyer, 2000). Instead, the city's urban economy has increasingly been subject to diverse state-led neoliberal interventions and political calculations, resulting in destabilization of given social boundaries and coherence. Eventually, a widespread discontent with property developers and their power emerges out the shift in accumulation regime.

This chapter draws on a recent wave of scholarship on the non-western paths and institutional mechanisms of urban development (Lees, Shin and Lopes-Morales, 2016; Park et al., 2012) to offer an account of Hong Kong's urban development. It thus places emphasis on the contested nature of urban space (Brenner, 2009: 198, 204), and offers a historical-systematic analysis of the roles of both the middle class and state actors in urban gentrification. In what follows, I first analyze the uniqueness of Hong Kong's experience, specifically paying attention to the multiple paths of gentrification and its changing forms (Davidson, 2010; Davidson and Lees, 2005; Park, Hill and Saito, 2012; Shin, 2009). I then empirically assess the rise and fall of the middle class and their relevance to urban gentrification in Hong Kong with census data and other statistics and develop a theoretical account for understanding the recent wave of urban redevelopment and other strategies of urban upgrading and the new and diverse roles of the state in this process. Finally I take the case of Wan Chai's serviced apartment as an exemplar of the new path of urban developmentalism oriented towards the capital flows and elite networks enabled by the rise of China as a global and regional capitalist power.

2   Hong Kong: A Property-led Regime

Unlike that of other successful East Asian countries whose late industrialization, post-industrial turn and rapid urban growth under a strong developmental state (Amsden, 1989), the case of Hong Kong is quite unique for its role of entrepôt primarily for the British Empire's pursuit of power and wealth in Far East since the mid-nineteenth century. The colonial elites, instead of being committed to any long term project of nation-building and development, engaged themselves in managing a Crown Colony with relatively stable social order and a business hub, yet hypersensitive to geopolitical changes, especially at a time of China's political turbulence. Hence, the thesis of "developmental states in East Asia" (White, 1988; Chan, Clark and Lam, 2006) is inadequate for capturing the politico-economic nature of Hong Kong's city-state. The term "developmental state" implies a new bunch of states following the model of nation-state that came to dominate the western world after the nineteenth century. However, it overlooks different kinds of state, such as colonial states and city-states, that were viable in history or even at present. The thesis of "developmental state" tends to provide accounts of state-to-state variations and comparisons, rather than understanding of the relations among them (Boyd and Ngo, 2005). In the case of post-war Hong Kong, urban changes feature as less a state-led developmentalist project *per se* than a process of remaking the city state by indigenizing colonial power as a set of governing strategies (Law, 2009: 168) and of an eventual and subsequent subordination of the managerial-capitalist state into China in recent years.

The Cold War period witnessed Hong Kong's industrial take-off, like the stories of other "East Asian Dragons", that occurred in the American-led East Asian liberal hegemonic order and its containment of Communist China and the Soviet Union. What shaped the economic path of Hong Kong in the immediate postwar years was not a state-led project *per se* but capital flight and refugees as source of cheap labor from China. The Hong Kong economy was successfully rebuilt with flexible production and small enterprises in response to the favorable international and regional markets. However, the colonial state did not implement unambiguously *laissez faire* policies as neoliberalists and the local power elites suggested (Friedman, 1981: 54; Rabushka, 1979: 83). Instead, it regulated economic activities and improvised its intervention strategies in a selective and *ad hoc* manner. For example, while it provided mass provision of subsidized housing for low-income groups, it made strategic use of the colonial land system (government control over all land supply) by pursuing collaboration with business groups for facilitating property development and large-scale redevelopment. It even made determined interventions into financial markets during the crisis years (Schiffer, 1991).

In the late 1970s, when the ideological-political conflicts of the Cold War faded away, China began its economic reforms in the post-Mao period. It attracted Hong Kong's manufacturing sector to relocate to the Mainland and this new regional division of labor, in return, contributed to the huge inflow of capital into Hong Kong's financial, property and service sectors (Chiu, 1994; Smart and Lee, 2003: 164). The following two decades witnessed the first wave of Hong Kong's urban gentrification and property boom. In response, the colonial state always adopted neoliberal ideology by pragmatically making rules and actively intervening into economic affairs to serve the power elites' interests. In the last two decades of its colonial rule, it successfully managed a middle-class society characterized by a regime of accumulation that won public consent by delivering economic prosperity to most people and managing a stable political order. In general, it brought upward social mobility to the city in the shift of deindustrialization.

Under this regime, gentrification, usually termed as "urban renewal", referred to a process referring to clean-sweep redevelopment of old tenement houses in favor of building high-rise residential blocks and office towers (Ley and Teo, 2014). From the early 1980s to 1996, the property bubble coincided with the rise of middle class and their purchasing power (Figure 12.1). In this period, the proportion of the middle class ("Managers and administrators", "Professionals" and "Associate professionals") in the total working population increased from 8.7% to 29.2% (Census and Statistics Department, 1992a: 94; Census and Statistics Department, 2002: 23) and their monthly household income in all decile groups increased significantly. The growth rate for the 8th–10th decile groups, the range into which most of the middle class fell, reached more than 10% every five years. (Census and Statistics Department, 2002: 25). Their purchasing power is evidenced by the rapid growth rate of homeownership, from 28% in 1981 to 51% in 2001 (Census and Statistics Department, 1992b: 64; 2002: 70). The theory of class replacement seems to be sustained with regard to the urban gentrification of Hong Kong in these two decades.

Yet, this class replacement process was enabled and structured by state policies. The primary factor was the colonial government's pursuit of a series of large-scale public housing programs, firstly for resettling squatter populations in the 1950s (Castells, 1986) and eventually for helping low-income tenants in the 1970s (Smart, 1992). During 1980s–1990s, it even expanded to subsidized

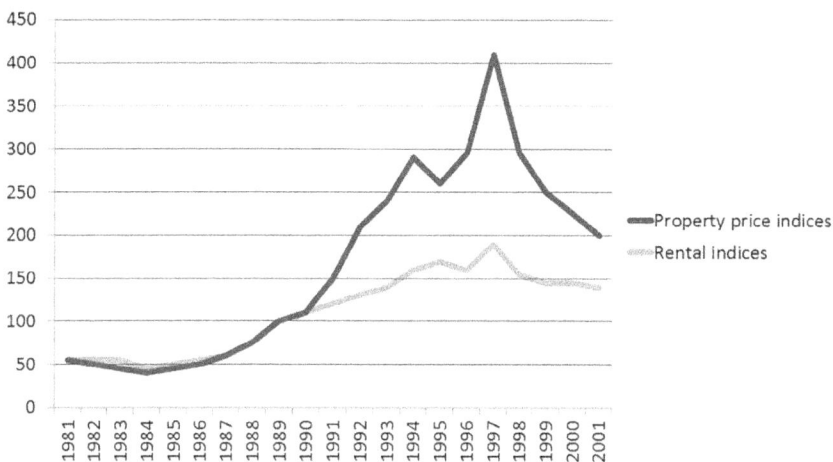

FIGURE 12.1   Rental indices and property price indices in Hong Kong (1981–2001)
SOURCE: RATING AND VALUATION DEPARTMENT (1981–2001) *HONG KONG*
PROPERTY REVIEW, HONG KONG: HONG KONG GOVERNMENT (1989=100)

homeownership for the lower middle class. These programs were run by building high-rise residential blocks accommodating low-income residents and
gradually relocating them to new towns at the outskirts of the city. The success
of these policies ensured social stability and more room for property development. Second, the effect of the rise of middle class and their residential needs
contributed only a small part to the property bubble in Hong Kong, compared
to expectations of capital gains and huge demand from investors (Tse and Ganesan, 1999). For instance, the indices of rental price (largely an indicator of
housing needs) and house price, since the late 1980s, diverged by the former
lagging far behind the latter. In other words, middle class families and other
upper classes engaged themselves as investors rather than simply home buyers
in this process; together with the institutional investors, they fuelled speculation for profit and expected that the rise of property prices will never end
(Smart and Lee, 2003: 160–161).

Behind the property boom lay a finance-based and property-led regime of
accumulation spurring changes in government policy preferences and even
the everyday practices of ordinary residents (Sum, 2002: 74). The aspirations
of achieving social mobility through urban gentrification and property boom
had successfully created a social imaginary and territory on which capitalist
state authority, decision-making and management are seen as binding (Jessop 2016, p. 73). At the time, Hong Kong's property developers expanded their
scope of business to cover service sector, stock market and banking sector and

gradually became an echelon of powerful elites. In the 1990s, most listed Hong Kong companies were property-related and the largest five of them accounted for 70% of the private property market (Tse and Ganesan, 1999: 71; Mitchell and Olds, 2000; Renaud, Pretorius, and Pasadilla, 1997; Haila 2000). Revenues from land sales and other related taxes accounted for over 30% of the total government revenue (Smart and Lee, 2003: 159).

One of the most illustrative examples of this regime of accumulation, with regard to government policy and its neoliberal preferences, was the establishment of Land Development Corporation (LDC, established in 1988), a publicly founded and financed corporation operating according to the "prudent commercial principles". The government desired to actualize urban rent and to share it with property developers. The planning documents and official statements of LDC defined the inner city as a space of urban decay in urgent need of renewal and the corporation was tasked with overcoming the difficulties of assembling land for development due to multiple ownership of the properties to be redeveloped. LDC served as a public body empowered with the ability to request resumption of government's ownership rights to the land (Planning, Environment and Lands Branch, 1996). By doing so, the private interest in redevelopment was made equivalent to "public interest".

Apart from government, individual home buyers, institutional investors, property developers and government shared the profit derived from property speculation and the optimistic expectations that supported it. Few would challenge this property-led regime's "wealth effect," which served as a foundation for Hong Kong's middle-class dream (Ley and Teo, 2014: 1298). Hence, the increasing importance of the middle class in Hong Kong to urban gentrification in the 1990s, rather than a simple factor of market demand, is a hegemonic process of consensus-making and interest-alignment (Gramsci, 1971; Loopmans, 2008).

3 The Interventionist Turn in the Post-1997 Era

Before 1997, the western media portrayed the return of the city to Chinese sovereignty as a political drama. However, it arrived as an economic crisis as the Asian financial crisis shattered the economic miracle of Hong Kong. As a result, a big slump in the property market followed and it was estimated that about 130,000 households (Poon, 2011: 69), mostly middle class, were facing negative equity at the turn of the century. Due to weak investment incentives and the shrinking purchasing power of the local population, after 1997, property prices plunged drastically until 2004 (Figure 12.2), resulting in slowing down

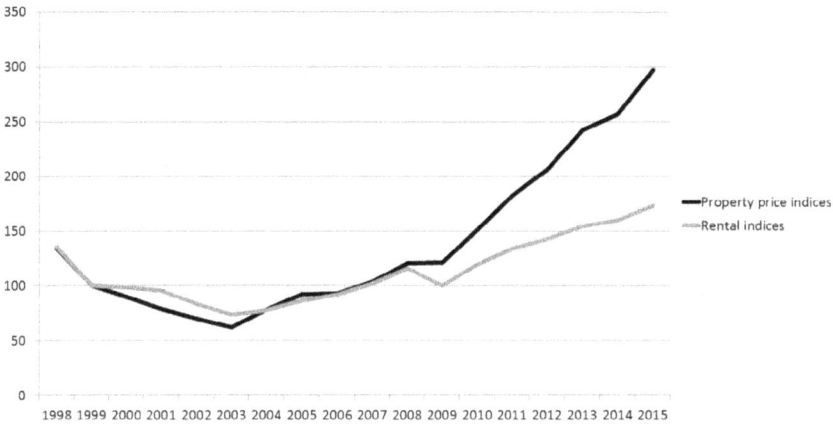

FIGURE 12.2   Rental indices and property price indices in Hong Kong (1998–2016)
SOURCE: RATING AND VALUATION DEPARTMENT (2008–2016) *HONG KONG PROPERTY REVIEW*, HONG KONG: HONG KONG GOVERNMENT (1999=100)

the process of urban gentrification and Hong Kong's economy at large. Despite the post-2003 economic boom and further integration with China's strong economy, Hong Kong could not regain their confidence in Hong Kong's dream for better life and social mobility.

From 2003 to 2015, there was another property boom in Hong Kong. The price index and rental index increased by 362% and 133%, respectively. However, in the meantime, median monthly domestic household income increased by only 25% although the size of middle class grew by about 40% (Census and Statistics Department 2017: 78). Since then, the purchasing power of the medium-income groups remains stagnant and the homeownership rate has reached a record high of 53% in 2006 and then slowed down to in 52.1% in 2011 and 48.5% in 2016, respectively (Census and Statistics Department, 2017: 87). Few people believe that a property boom could benefit the whole society. Socio-economic grievances, along with the popularity of post-materialist values, spur more hatred against the business-dominated and developmentalist regime (Ma, 2011).

One should seek stronger explanation for the new wave of urban gentrification from reasons other than the demand of middle class. On the supply side, the government had tried on interventionist policies in attempt to reactivate the property-led model of development. In the immediate years after 1997, one of the hidden agendas for the post-handover government was to out-perform the previous colonial government in solving social and economic problems (Cheung, 2000: 301). Contrary to other East Asian countries' path of the triumph of neoliberalism over state-led developmentalism in practice and rhetoric in the 2000s (Chang, 1998; Pirie, 2005), the Hong Kong government developed a stronger faith in interventionist measures and stimulus packages for political reasons, overriding its previous pro-market stance. Chief Executive Tung Chee-hwa advocated "new vision" (Tung, 1997: Paragraph 3) and boasted his success in rescuing the stock market and the currency rate from financial crisis in 1998.

Since the financial crisis in 1997, when the gloomy property market situation discouraged private developers from bearing the cost of redevelopment, the Hong Kong government has been planning ahead of the market and has taken the lead to deliver urban renewal more quickly (Planning, Environment and Lands Bureau, 1999a, 1999b: 2). In 2001, the government launched the Urban Renewal Authority (URA) for taking over the task of LDC in a more pro-actively way. The government granted HK$10 billion to the URA as initial fund for starting up its projects. The URA was given a list of planning parameters and financial guidelines, including 225 project plans, redevelopment priorities, and a list of historical buildings to be preserved, among others. Instead of following LDC's "prudent commercial principles" applied to each project, the URA, with a statutory body of "prudent financial principles", was permitted to undertake loss-making projects cross-subsidized by other profitable ones. Apart from clean-sweep approach to redevelopment, it broadened the scope of urban renewal to incorporate other strategies such as "rehabilitation", material incentives to flat owners for carrying out repair work, and "preservation", physical refurbishment and reuse of old buildings. It further introduced a new concept of "revitalization", together with other "Rs" (Redevelopment, "Reservation" and Rehabilitation) to make the slogan of a comprehensive strategy of "4Rs" and to link up the other strategies for urban regeneration.

For boosting urban renewal, the URA is not merely more resourceful than the LDC (Ng, 2002: 145) but characteristic of its power to skip bureaucratic procedures with limited accountability and public engagement. Previously the LDC was required to take "all reasonable steps" to acquire the land before it initiated the power of resumption of government land (a power akin to eminent domain in the USA). Now it is almost entirely within URA's discretion when to apply for land resumption through the Secretary for Planning, Environment and Lands (Secretary for Development after 2007) to the Chief Executive (Ng and Tam, 2000). The setup of URA indicated the government's stronger will to intervene into the urban renewal process more intensively and extensively. It is difficult to assess URA's effect on the recent property bubble. But one may conclude that the path of Hong Kong's urban gentrification is shaped not simply by the local state's new strategies, but also the central state's new intervention-ist measures.

The resumption of China's sovereignty over Hong Kong and its admission to the WTO marked the beginning of the Beijing government's pursuit of further regional integration. The Closer Economic Partnership Agreement (CEPA) is an example. Unlike most free trade agreement, the idea of CEPA was not nego-tiated and carefully studied by equal parties; instead it was firstly proposed by the Hong Kong General Chamber of Commerce and followed up by the Beijing government very quickly. The most immediate political calculation is about shoring up the legitimacy of the first Chief Executive Tung Chee Wah and his government by rescuing local economy from recession. However, CEPA, in-stead of enabling a fundamental change of Hong Kong's economic structure, reinforced the city's role as a financial center and service hub. It brought in an enormous flow of capital and visitors from mainland China and opened its gates to Hong Kong-based capital and professionals. As a result, investment banks, hedge funds, regional headquarters of multi-national companies, high-end producer-services providers such as accounting, auditing and consultancy firms, etc., have expanded their business ties into China through this offshore hub and business center (Meyer, 2008).

The large amount and volatility of capital inflows and outflows, in foreign direct investment (DI) and portfolio investment, have overwhelmed the city in recent years. Mainland China has become Hong Kong's largest recipient and investor region of outward and inward DI respectively. Since 2003, Hong Kong has served as a financial hub for an increasing number of Chinese firms and foreign capital looking for investment opportunities in China and aboard (see Figure 12.3). It is evidenced by the growing number of regional headquarters and local offices in Hong Kong, with an increase of 46% and 143% respectively from 2002 to 2016. The amount of equity funds raised by initial public offerings (IPOs) of H-share companies (companies incorporated in mainland China that are traded on the Hong Kong Stock Exchange) increased by 350% from 2003 to 2015 (Securities and Futures Commission 2016). It is no surprise that the prop-erty price index roughly parallels the increased rate of capital flows (about threefold) rather than domestic housing demand. The overpriced property also destroys the housing ladder of the middle and lower class. In recent years, the property boom in Hong Kong has further attracted mainland institutional investors, mostly state-owned enterprises, so much that the city has become second only to New York as a target for Chinese capital (Tang 2017). In the fol-lowing section, I will take Wan Chai as a case study, with particular attention to the rise of serviced apartment as a new landscape of urban gentrification.

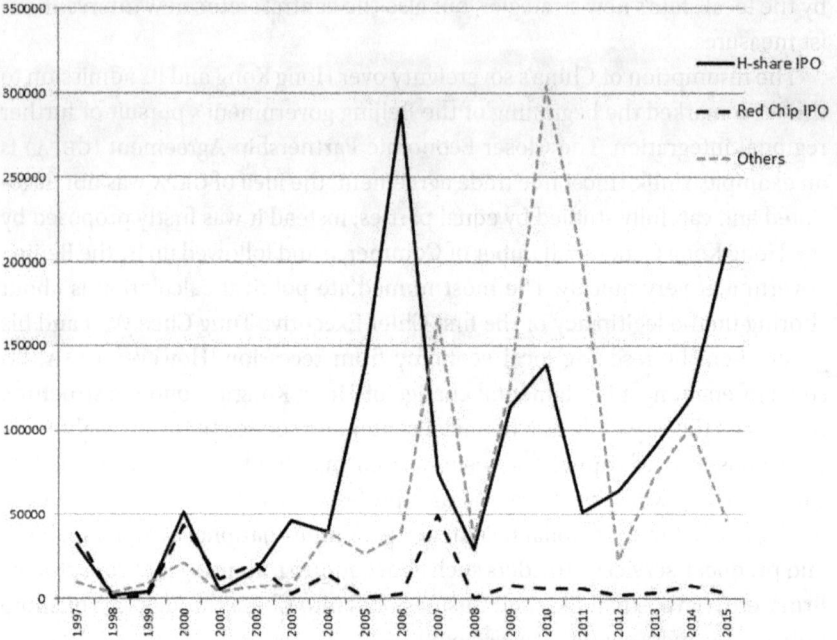

FIGURE 12.3   Equity funds raised directly and indirectly through Hong Kong (1997–2017)
SOURCE: CENSUS AND STATISTICS DEPARTMENT (HKD MILLION)

4   Wan Chai and the Rise of the Serviced Apartment

Wan Chai is one of the earliest Chinese urban settlements on the northern shore of Hong Kong Island in Hong Kong. Due to its proximity to Central, the central business district of Hong Kong (Figure 12.4), the coastline of Wan Chai was extended northward through a series of land reclamation schemes for commercial and residential developments since as early as 1841. A large reclamation area for the North Wan Chai commercial district of skyscrapers and an exhibition center was gradually developed since the 1980s (Figure 4.3). However, the Chinese settlement at the heart of Wan Chai, a neighborhood featuring traditional wet markets, small shops and low-rise tenement houses, underwent a relatively slow process of change and remained immune from large-scale redevelopment until the intervention initiated by the URA in the 2000s.

The Johnston Road project, one of the URA's earliest projects featured a mix of serviced apartments, historic preservation, and high-end dining and shopping landmarks. It is located at the junction of Johnston Road and Ship Street, a site covering 1,970 square meters, and one of the URA's top three priority

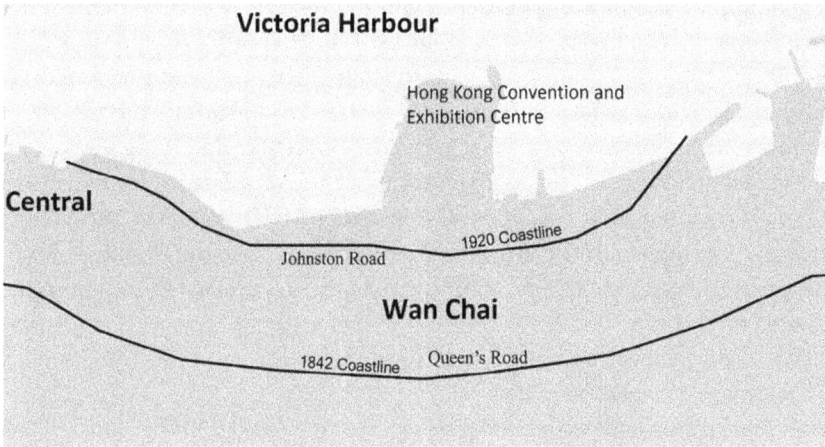

FIGURE 12.4   Wan Chai and Central (HKD million)
                SOURCE: SECURITIES AND FUTURES COMMISSION

projects. It took six months for it to acquire 80% of the ownership in terms of floor area in early 2003. Among the owners who refused to accept the URA's offers, the owner of Woo Cheong Pawn Shop, a small listed company owned by the Law, is the most noteworthy. Law Sau-Yiu, managing director of the company preferred to wait for a better market situation in the near future before selling (Xin, 2002). During a standstill in the negotiations, URA threatened to initiate the procedure of land resumption and all the rest of the owners accepted the offers reluctantly in October 2003. It then announced the tender of development partnership in January 2004. The URA followed the quick procedure of compulsory land resumption and a tight development schedule to override owners who were holding out.

In this case, time compression was enabled primarily by the state who strengthened its capacity of intervention and expanded its scope of power to forcefully take advantage of the rent gap between capitalized ground rent and rent potential (Smith, 1996). The concern for heritage preservation did not compromise the imperative for redevelopment. Indeed, the plot ratio of the preserved building would be transferred to other redevelopment sites (*Sing Tao Daily*, 2000). From the very beginning, this project was made commercially possible, feasible and desirable by the government's policy discretion on plot ratio.

The Authority, with public money, had to bear the cost of acquisition (HK$880m) and the risk of redevelopment (*Oriental Daily*, 2003). The rubric of "holistic strategy", of which historic preservation is a key component, allowed the URA to justify various government subsidies including premium exemption for this project (HK$191m) and 41 other projects (Development Bureau, 2010: 42). As Billy Lam Chung-Lun, the Chief Executive of URA, said, "The key is not about the project *per se*. Instead, it is about how to integrate with projects, whatever redevelopment, resurrection, beautification, revitalization, or historic preservation, as a synergy. It makes Wan Chai and Hong Kong more lively and glamorous" (Lam, 2005). URA made use of the fancy term of "Wan Chai old town" to boost the land value of a place ("old town"). This term refers not to the administrative district, but to the area south to the Hennessy Road, i.e. a new sociospatial configuration in proximity to the relatively new business district on the waterfront and Central (Brenner 2004: 13). In 2007, Chief Executive Donald Tsang also proudly mentioned the revitalization of Wan Chai his *Policy Address* (Tsang, 2007: 24).

This rescaling and zoning strategy seemed to work out in the midst of the rebound of Hong Kong's property market. In 2004, the Johnston Road project was planned as a site with the plot ratio of 1:10 and a 43-storey apartment building (named as "J Residence"), including a 3-storey shopping mall. It was estimated to provide more than 300 apartment units at the price of HK$50,000 per square meters and several ground floor shops at the price of HK$100,000 per square meters (*Hong Kong Economic Times*, 2004). In the same year, it was open to public tender and K. Wah International Holdings Ltd (K. Wah), a local developer won the joint contract with URA who owned 40% of the shopping mall and shared a percentage of the revenue from the sales of apartment. The private developer got 19,510 square meters of area at the cost of HK$600m, around HK$31,000 per square meters. This project, offering 381 studios, including 290 one-bedroom, 87 two-bedroom apartments, and 4 penthouses, targeted at the market of serviced apartment for business visitors and corporate expatriates rather than local families.

This project was quite exceptional in the mainstream property market. By the time when it was launched, no new residential block was built for this purpose in Wan Chai, except several old buildings renovated into serviced apartments. Hong Kong's serviced apartments, a small niche of Hong Kong property market until recently, began with a handful of "hotel-like" projects completed by local developers in the 1980s (Mcmillan 2009). Most serviced apartment projects, including those like the Johnston Road project and conversion of old buildings, emerged out of the decision of the Town Planning Board (TPB) on lifting restrictions by deleting the term "Service Apartment" (SA) and re-categorizing it as a type of residential use in 2000 (Director of Planning, 2005). TPB's deregulation encouraged professional property management chains ventured into the market (Jones Lang LaSalle, 2009: 5, 9–11).

The immediate consequence of the URA's project is the valorization of the development potential of the "Wan Chai old town" at an exponential rate. Before its completion, the developer received an offer of HK$75,000 per square meters (*Sing Tao Daily*, 2006) for six apartment studios from a foreign company for staff accommodation. It was such a big hit in the market that the price of some studios reached as high as HK$100,000 per square meters when it was completed in 2007. K. Wah promoted the complex of historic buildings, a newly built shopping mall and serviced apartment tower as a part of a new zone called "Soho East", east to the current "Soho" and Lan Kwai Fong in Central. In attempt to connect the "Wan Chai old town" with the trendy districts of pubs, cafes, restaurants, and galleries, etc., that surround the central business center, the project triggered the effect of "revitalization" to the whole area of "old town Wan Chai". Less than two years later, the Lung Moon Chinese restaurant, an old building nearby, was sold at the price of HK$250,000 per square meters: almost three times the price of the pawn shop offered to Law by the URA in 2003 (see Figure 12.5).

The success of J Residence and another URA project completed in 2010 stimulated property investors' minds. More property developers have been attracted to new build and renovation projects for serviced apartments, such as Fraser Suites (2007), Garden East (2009), and Chi Residences (2013), etc. With the third largest serviced apartment stock (1,653 units in 2012) in Hong Kong, Wan Chai has become a residential concentration of business visitors. It was estimated that the number of business travellers, overseas residents with employment visas, and local small domestic households, who need serviced apartments, would reach 4.75 million per year, among which almost 4 million are non-local people.

The expansion and daily operation of the financial sector and producers services generate a sizable number of vacancies to be filled by people from overseas, who stay for years, months, or even weeks. The market for serviced apartments is highly responsive to the volatility of financial market. The burst of financial bubble would result in a sudden decline of foreign recruitment and expatriates and their housing needs. According to a survey, while the occupancy rate had been around 90% since 2004, it plunged to 75% abruptly during the Subprime Mortgage Crisis and rebounded back to over 90% in 2010 (Savills Research, 2011a; The Apartment Service Worldwide, 2011, p. 28). It dropped again to about 76.7% in 2016 (Savills World Research, 2016). The movement of rental index of serviced apartment follows the similar pattern (Savills Research, 2011b) and it has achieved a growth rate of 60% from 2003 to 2015, higher than the rental index of property (Savills World Research, 2015).

FIGURE 12.5   J Residence, J Sense and Woo Cheong Pawn Shop
SOURCE: PHOTO TAKEN BY THE AUTHOR

On the supply side, the high rate of yields and steady demand for serviced apartments attract a wide variety of investors, ranging from local property developers, international management chains, individual investors and financial institutions. Despite the small percentage of the local residential market, the gross yield of the industry of serviced apartment reached 8–11%, higher than other sectors of property market (Jones Lang LaSalle, 2009: 11; Savills Research, 2011a; Kush, 2012; Savills (Hong Kong) Limited, 2013). While the major stock of serviced apartments is largely provided by local major developers such as Cheung Kong and Hang Lung, a large group of international and regional operators such as Marriot, Ascott International, Shama, Kush Concept, and Chi International, share the market with local major players such as New World Properties and Hopewell Real Estate. The growing investment opportunities attract individual and institutional investors such as investment banks like Morgan Stanley whose market expectations are largely shaped by the global outlook as well as local fundamentals. Henceforth, compared to the local residential property market, the investment demand for serviced apartments is more institutionally complicated, multi-layered and globally linked. Thus, Wan Chai has been undergoing urban gentrification in a highly globalized way.

Wan Chai remains a magnet for financial and property capital, and related professionals. While local tycoons reluctantly sold their Central office towers, those on the Wan Chai waterfront become the most attractive site for mainland investors. Over the past three years, they ventured into it for record setting en-bloc purchases, such as that of The Centre for HK$40.2 billion in 2017. Indeed, Chinese enterprises, partially encouraged by China government, have aggressively invested in overseas property markets, especially Hong Kong in recent years. They are rarely absent in the tender process for Hong Kong's land sales and always beat the market's expectations. In 2017, more than 70% of Hong Kong's land sites were sold to them in terms of land value (Lands Department 2018).

5   Conclusion

The role of the middle class in urban gentrification, as Lees, Shin and Lopez-Morales suggested, needs to be reconsidered and it is increasingly the creation of the state – local and national (Lees, Shin and Lopez-Morles 2016: Chapter 4). In Hong Kong, the middle class and their housing and investment demand mattered more in the citywide property boom and the rise of gentrified neighborhoods in the 1980s and the 1990s (Smart and Lee, 2003). However, in the past two decades, their housing needs can no longer explain the volatility of the urban changes.

This decoupling process, involving complicated institutional mechanisms deserves further analysis and theorization. The financial crisis and economic recession at the turn of the century seriously weakened the effective demand and purchasing power of the middle class. The change in sovereignty without democratic reform made the government more susceptible to pressure from sectoral interests of key property developers rather than responsive to the demand for greater public accountability (Cheung, 2000: 303). Although corporatist conflict gained momentum and turned into an intense competition for Hong Kong's urban vision from the late 1990s to the years of economic crisis (Jessop and Sum, 2000: 2301–2304), the government preferred to rescue the crumbling property-led regime of accumulation, under which state-led gentrification is one of the most favorable and viable policy options. As a result, stimulating investment in property is prioritized over strengthening effective demand of people for goods and services.

The property-finance-led regime, despite losing its "wealth effect" on the local population in the immediate years after 1997, has created an institutional path in which the local state inclines to seek further financial sources and opportunities from China, rather than launching fundamental transformation. The flow of capital, the concomitant business visitors and relocation of local offices and regional headquarters to the city for capturing Chinese business opportunities are primarily attributed to the global financial bubble as well as the Beijing government's politically intended policies. It triggered another phase of urban gentrification in Hong Kong. Hong Kong's path-dependency is structurally correspondent with China government's political project of eventually incorporating its frontiers, Hong Kong, Macau and Taiwan, into its national state structure and global capitalist power. What I described above is less a state project than a geopolitical process of remaking the post-colonial city-state's relationship with its central state and repositioning the city in global economy.

The rise of serviced apartment, as a niche property market, a type of mobile residence and a globally connected and locally disconnected urban form, is a symptom of Hong Kong's new urban developmentalism characteristic of global capital-human mobility and splintering urbanism (Graham and Marvin, 2001; Soja, 2000: 235). Together with the huge influxes of mainland visitors and the sprouting of shops and malls catering to mass tourism, it constitutes an urban landscape beyond recognition, fuelling popular resentment by local residents. Hong Kong had served as a model for China's economic reform in the 1980s. Now China, in return, gives the city a magic ticket to future prosperity in a more globalized world. But the changes bring Hong Kong people to a dystopia in which they strongly feel alienated from their homeland (Ip, 2015).

References

Amsden, AH (1989) *Asia's Next Giant: South Korea and Late Industrialization*. New York: Oxford University Press.

Boyd, R and TW Ngo (2005) Emancipating the political economy of Asia from the growth paradigm. In: R Boyd and TW Ngo (eds.) *Asian States: Beyond the Developmental Perspective*. London and New York: RoutledgeCurzon, 1–18.

Boyer, R (2000) Is a finance-led growth regime a viable alternative to Fordism? a preliminary analysis. *Economy and Society* 29: 111–145.

Brenner, N (2004) *New State Spaces: Urban Governance and the Rescaling of Statehood*. Oxford: Oxford University Press.

Brenner, N (2009) What is critical urban theory? *City* 13(2–3): 198–207.

Butler, T (2003) Living in the bubble: gentrification and its 'Others' in North London. *Urban Studies* 40: 2469–2486.

Butler, T (2007) For gentrification? *Environment and Planning A* 39: 162–181.

Castells, M (1986) *The Shek Kip Mei Syndrome: Public Housing and Economic Development in Hong Kong*. Hong Kong: Centre of Urban Studies & Urban Planning, University of Hong Kong.

Census and Statistics Department (1992a) *1991 Population Census: Main Report*. Hong Kong: Hong Kong SAR Government.

Census and Statistics Department (1992b) *1991 Population Census: Summary Results*. Hong Kong: Hong Kong SAR Government.

Census and Statistics Department (2002) *2001 Population Census: Summary Results*. Hong Kong: Hong Kong SAR Government.

Census and Statistics Department (2017) *2016 Population By-Census: Summary Results*. Hong Kong: Hong Kong SAR Government.

Chan, S, C Clark and D Lam (2006) *Beyond the Developmental State: East Asia's Political Economies Reconsidered*. London: Macmillan Press.

Chang, HJ (1998) Korea: The misunderstood crisis. *World Development* 26: 155–161.

Cheung, A (2000) New interventionism in the making: interpreting state interventions in Hong Kong after the change of sovereignty. *Journal of Contemporary China* 9(24): 291–308.

Chiu, S (1994) *The politics of laissez-faire: Hong Kong's strategy of industrialization in historical perspective*. Hong Kong: Hong Kong Institute of Asia-Pacific Studies, Chinese University of Hong Kong.

Davidson, M (2010) Love thy neighbour? social mixing in London's gentrification frontiers. *Environment and Planning A* 42(3): 524–544.

Davidson, M and L Lees (2005) New-build 'gentrification' and London's riverside renaissance, *Environment and Planning A* 37(7): 1165–1190.

Development Bureau (2010) *Work of the Urban Renewal Authority*. Document submitted to Legislative Council Panel on Development on 22 June 2010.

Director of Planning (Planning Department) (2005) Practice Note for Professional Persons No. 3/2005: Status of Service Apartment Use in Approved Planning Applications. Available (consulted 29 January 2012) at: http://www.pland.gov.hk/pland_en/tech_doc/pra_note/pn_3_2005.html

Friedman, M (1981) *Free to Choose*. Harmondsworth: Penguin Books.

Glass, R (1964) *London: Aspects of change. Centre for Urban Studies Report No. 3*. London: MacGibbon & Kee.

Graham, S and S Marvin (2001) *Splintering Urbanism: Networked Infrastructure, Technological Mobilities and the Urban Condition*. London: Routledge.

Gramsci, A (1971) Notes on Italian History. In: Q Hoare and GN Smith (eds.) *Selections from Prison Notebooks*. London: Lawrence and Wishart, 52–120.

Haila, A (2000) Real estate in global cities: Singapore and Hong Kong as property states. *Urban Studies* 37(12): 2241–2256.

Hamnett, C (2003) Gentrification and the middle-class remaking of Inner London, 1961–2001. *Urban Studies* 40(12): 2401–2426.

Hamnett, C (2009) The new Mikado? Tom Slater, gentrification and displacement. *City* 13(4): 476–482.

Hamnett, C (2010) On gentrification: 'I am critical. You are mainstream': a response to Slater. *City* 14(1–2): 180–186.

Hogan, T, T Bunnell, CP Pow, E Permanasari and S Morshidi (2012) Asian urbanisms and the privatization of cities. *Cities* 29(1): 59–63.

Hong Kong Institute of Asia-Pacific Studies (2011) *Press Release: A Summary of An Opinion Survey on Hong Kong Residents' Views on "Property Hegemony"*. Accessed on 22 January 2017, https://www.cuhk.edu.hk/hkiaps/tellab/pdf/telepress/11/Press_Release20110810.pdf

Hong Kong Economic Times (2004) [URA opens tender for the HK$700m worth of development project on Johnston Road tomorrow. Intense competition among property developers is expected]. 26 February , D03. (In Chinese).

Ip, IC (2015) Politics of belonging: a study of the campaign against mainland visitors in Hong K. *Inter-Asia Cultural Studies* 16(3): 410–421.

Jessop, B (2016) State Theory. In: C Ansell, and J Torfing (eds.) *Handbook on Theories of Governance*. Cheltenham and Northampton: Edward Elgar Publishing, 71–85.

Jessop, B and N Sum (2000) An entrepreneurial city in action: Hong Kong's emerging strategies in and for (inter)urban competition. *Urban Studies* 37(12): 2287–2313.

Jones Lang LaSalle (2009) *Serviced Apartment: Achieving Suite Success*. Hong Kong: Jones Lang LaSalle.

Kush (2012) Case Study: Kush Serviced Apartments, Hong Kong (Press Release). Accessed on 29 January 2012, http://www.district-15.com/media/D15_casestudy.pdf

Lam, B (2005) [Revitalization, radiation: the URA's theory and practice.]. *Ming Pao Daily News*. 27 June , D06. (In Chinese).

Lands Department (2018) *Land Sale Result 2017/18*. Available: (Access 9 January 2018) http://www.landsd.gov.hk/en/landsale/records/2017-2018.pdf

Law, WS (2009) *Collaborative Colonial Power: The Making of the Hong Kong Chinese*. Hong Kong: Hong Kong University Press.

Lees, L, HB Shin and E Lopes-Morales (2016) *Planetary Gentrification*. Cambridge: Polity.

Ley, D (1996) *The New Middle Class and the Remaking of the Central City*. Oxford: Oxford University Press.

Ley, D and SY Teo (2014) Gentrification in Hong Kong? epistemology vs. ontology. *International Journal of Urban and Regional Research* 38(4): 1286–1303.

Li, SM and YL Song (2009) Redevelopment, displacement, housing conditions, and residential satisfaction: a study of Shanghai. *Environment and Planning A* 41(5): 1090–1108.

Loopmans, M (2008) Relevance, gentrification and the development of a new hegemony on urban policies in Antwerp, Belgium. Urban Studies 45(12): 2499–2519.

Ma, N (2011) Value changes and legitimacy crisis in post-industrial Hong Kong. *Asian Survey* 51(4): 683–712.

Mcmillan, AF (2009) Serviced apartments are starting to pay off for owners. *South China Morning Post* (SCMP), 20 November. Available (consulted 12 December 2012) at: http://www.scmp.com/article/698826/serviced-apartments-are-starting -pay-owners

Meyer, DR (2008) Structural change of Hong Kong economy after 1997. *The China Review* 8(1): 7–29.

Mitchell, K and K Olds (2000) Chinese business networks and the globalization of property markets in the Pacific Rim. In: HWC Yeung and K Olds (eds.) *Globalization of Chinese Business Firms*. Houndmills: Macmillan, 195–215.

Ng, M and C Tam (2000) Urban restructuring and urban renewal: lessons from the Tsuen Wan Town Centre Redevelopment Project. *Planning and Development* 16(1): 9–18.

Ng, M (2002) Property-led urban renewal in Hong Kong: any place for community? *Sustainable Development* 10(3): 140–146.

Oriental Daily (2003) [89% of ownership is acquired for the Johnston Redevelopment Project]. February 6, B15. (In Chinese).

Park, BG, RC Hill and A Saito (eds.) (2012) *Locating Neoliberalism in East Asia: Neoliberalizing Spaces in Developmental States*. Malden: Wiley-Blackwell.

Pirie, I. (2005) The new Korean state. *New Political Economy* 10 (1): 25–42.

Planning, Environment and Lands Branch (1996) *Urban Renewal in Hong Kong*. Hong Kong: Government Printer.

Planning, Environment and Lands Bureau (1999a) Major concerns raised by organizations (As 24 November 1999). Document prepared for the Subcommittee (Legco) to Study the Urban Renewal Authority White Bill.

Planning, Environment and Lands Bureau. (1999b) *Consultation Paper on the Urban Renewal Authority Bill*. Hong Kong: Hong Kong Government.

Poon, A (2011) *Land and the Ruling Class of Hong Kong*. 2nd Edition. Hong Kong: Enrich.

Rabushka, A (1979) *Hong Kong: A Study in Economic Freedom*. Chicago: Chicago University Press.

Renaud, B, F. Pretorius and B Pasadilla (1997) *Markets at Work*. Hong Kong: HKU Press.

Rose, D. (1984) Rethinking gentrification: beyond the uneven development of Marxist urban theory. *Environment and Planning D: Society and Space* 2(1): 47–54.

Savills (Hong Kong) Limited. 2013. *Market Research Report*. Accessed 24 Jan 2017, URL: http://www.hkexnews.hk/reports/prelist/Documents/EHOPEWELL-20130529-19 .pdf

Savills Research (2011a) *Hong Kong: Serviced Apartments*. Hong Kong: Savills.

Savills Research (2011b) *Hong Kong: Residential Leasing*. Hong Kong: Savills.

Savills World Research (2015) *Briefing: Residential Leasing*, November 2015. Hong Kong: Savills.

Savills World Research (2016) *Briefing: Residential Leasing*, November 2016. Hong Kong: Savills.

Schiffer, J (1991) State Policy and Economic Growth: A Comment on the Hong Kong Model. *The International Journal of Urban and Regional Research* 15(2): 188–209.

Securities and Futures Commission (2016) *Table 3: Equity Funds Raised Directly and Indirectly through Hong Kong*. Available (consulted 17 April 2017) at: http://www.sfc .hk/web/EN/files/SOM/MarketStatistics/b03.pdf

Shin, HB (2009) Property-based redevelopment and gentrification: the Case of Seoul, South Korea. *Geoforum* 40: 906–917.

Sing Tao Daily (2000) [Four pre-war buildings in LDC's redevelopment areas are listed as heritage]. 23 October, B19. (In Chinese).

Sing Tao Daily (2006) [A foreign company bids for six units of J Residence]. 30 June, C02. (In Chinese).

Smart, A (1992) *Making Room: Squatter Clearance in Hong Kong*. Hong Kong: University of Hong Kong, Centre of Asian Studies.

Smart, A and J Lee (2003) Financialization and the role of real estate in Hong Kong's regime of accumulation. *Economic Geography* 79(2): 153–171.

Smith, N (1996) *The New Urban Frontier: Gentrification and the Revanchist City*. London: Routledge.

Smith, N (2000) Chapter 4: New globalism, new urbanism: gentrification as global urban strategy. In: N Brenner and N Theodore (eds.) *Spaces of Neoliberalism: Urban Restructuring in North America and Western Europe*. Malden: Blackwell, 80–103.

Smith, N (2002) New globalism, new urbanism: gentrification as global urban strategy. *Antipode* 34(3): 427–450.

Soja, E (2000) *Postmetropolis; Critical Studies of Cities and Regions.* Oxford: Blackwell.

Sum, N (2002) An entrepreneurial city in action: emerging strategies for (inter-)urban competition in Hong Kong. In: J Logan (ed) *The New Chinese City: Globalization and Reform.* Oxford: Blackwell, 74–91.

Tang, Z (2017) Hong Kong Now a Top Destination for Mainalnd Real Estate Investment. *MingTianDi: Asia Real Estate Intelligence.* Available (access 9 January 2018) at: https://www.mingtiandi.com/sponsored/hong-kong-now-a-top-destination-for -mainland-real-estate-investment/

The Apartment Service Worldwide (2011) *The Global Serviced Apartment Industry Report 2011–2012.* London: The Apartment Service.

Tsang, D (2007) *The 2007–08 Policy Address: A New Direction for Hong Kong.* Hong Kong: Government Printer.

Tse, RYC and S Ganesan (1999) Hong Kong. In: J Berry and S McGreal (eds.) *Cities in the Pacific Rim: Planning Systems and Property Markets.* London: Spon Press, 67–88.

Tung, CW (1997) *Policy Address 1997–98: Building Hong Kong for a New Era.* Hong Kong: Government Printer.

Wang, J and S Lau (2009) Gentrification and Shanghai's new middle class. *Cities* 26(2), 57–66.

White, G (ed) (1988) *Developmental States in East Asia.* London: Macmillan.

Xin, PL (2002) [Yu Tai Hing does not sell its ownership of pawnshop to URA]. *Hong Kong Economic Times*, 30 May, A26. (In Chinese).

CHAPTER 13

Planning as Institutionalized Informality: State, Casino Capitalists and the Production of Space in Macau

Kah-Wee Lee

On 30 January 2008, the secretary for transport and public works of the Macau Special Administrative Region (SAR), Ao Man-Long, was convicted of corruption and sentenced to 27 years in prison.[1] The coverage of this case was sensational, detailing every development project under investigation, every one of the 100 accomplices and witnesses, and the personal fortunes of Ao and his family. It revealed many irregularities and indiscretions in land sales and planning processes in the years following Macau's handover to the People's Republic of China (PRC) in 1999 and the subsequent liberalization of the casino industry. Ao had intervened by changing the normal process of "open bidding" for projects to "bidding by invitation" so as to favor specific players or by facilitating the exchange of land parcels and development rights without due process. In the media reports, iconic projects like the Macau East Asian Games Dome, the Starworld Casino-hotel, the Venetian Macau and the Macau International Airport as well as important public works like the sewerage system at Coloane and the Friendship Bridge were all scandalized by association.

Ao's case ignited public and academic debate on the importance of urban planning in disciplining the influx of foreign capital brought about by casino liberalization. Thus, Tieben (2009: 10) argues that "the proliferation of casino clusters together with unregulated and opportunistic property developments began to threaten the city's physical environment and urban heritage". Pinheiro and Wan (2011: 28) argue that, due to the lack of planning oversight, "great swathes of prime public land have been eaten up by real estate and gaming interests". During fieldwork in Macau in 2010, I was constantly reminded of this desire to define the present by discarding the past. When I spoke with Mr. Cheang Kok Keong, President of the Association for Macau Historical and Cultural Heritage Protection, he stressed the values of good planning:

---

1   This chapter is a revised and extended version of an article that was originally published in Environment and Planning A (Lee 2014). The additional research that went into the revision was supported by the MOR AcRF Start up Grant R-295-000-100-133.

透明度, 科學化, 民眾參與.[2] Dr. Jose Chui, brother of the current Chief Executive, published a doctoral dissertation that advocates replacing the current piecemeal model of planning with a centralized and integrated model that can carry out long-term visions (Chui, 2008).

The media spectacle of Ao's punishment and such discourses frame the urban planning and development of Macau in the idiom of a lack, which forecloses deeper understanding of how a planning regime like Macau's is intimately tied to a specific mode of spatial production. It further erects the year of 1999 as an artificial historical marker that valorizes the present by vilifying its past as colonial, corrupt and inefficient. Yet, as Simpson's (2008: 1054) critique shows, post-handover Macau is a "spatiotemporal intersection of the failed projects of Maoist socialism and Portuguese empire as well as the twin dreams of a local phantasmagoric consumer utopia and a Chinese socioeconomic hybrid of 'market socialism'". Rather than interpreting Macau as yet another instance of "neoliberal exception", Simpson (2016) foregrounds the latent forms of governance in Macau's complex history that influenced its contemporary development. The intersections of developmentalist, colonial, socialist and neoliberal ideologies and practices exceed the explanatory power of any single label, demanding instead a more historically inflected analysis that takes into account pathway dependencies at the level of specific governing practices.

In this chapter, I examine specific moments in Macau's urban development before and after the handover in 1999 to show how urban planning has constituted a regime of institutionalized informality in the shaping of Macau. In such a regime, the production of space operates in a state of strategic ambivalence that simultaneously invigorates and undermines the rules of governance. Planning practices function as a medium of negotiation between various interest groups, as well as an index of the changing geopolitics of Macau as it transitioned from Portuguese to Chinese rule. This conceptualization requires us to think counter-intuitively of planning as generating value through disorder, rather than a project that is always antagonistic towards disorder. As urban theorist Ananya Roy (2009) argues, informality is neither a status attached to a specific actor (the poor) nor a site (the slums), but a set of socio-spatial processes of which planning is a constitutive part. She considers how the informalized planning regime may be "one that is a state of deregulation, ambiguity, and exception" and outlines a paradoxical situation whereby strategic deregulation becomes a way in which powerful interests can influence the direction of urbanization. And yet, it is also because of such deliberate ambiguities that the "territorial impossibility of governance, justice and development" is created

---

2 "Transparency, scientificity, participatory".

(ibid, 76). Other scholars who adopt such a critical perspective similarly show how planning as institutionalized informality produces zones of elite illegalities and fluid systems of patronage that generate crises which are not solved through "better" forms of planning (Varley, 2013; McFarlane, 2012; Bunnell and Harris, 2012; Soliman, 2010).

The institutionalization of informality has many expressions in the historical development of Macau. Eadington and Siu (2007) focus on the "grey areas" as an intermediate space between law and custom, where casino capitalists could undertake illegal activities such as prostitution, coolie-trafficking, opium-trade and junkets as long as they contributed a share of the profits towards public projects and social welfare. The distribution of grey areas as privilege, particularly in the allotment of land and limited concessions, was often opaque and formed the basis of negotiation between the government, casino capitalists and other interest groups. Such practices should also be framed within the larger context of "luso-tropicalism" – a form of colonialism that was purportedly kinder, more tolerant and cosmopolitan than the Anglo-American version. The model of "sort-of sovereignty" that emerged in the context of Portuguese Macau, anthropologist Cathryn Clayton (2010: 51–58) argues, operates through "different assumptions about the value of ambivalence, and a greater reliance on the blurring of boundaries". Ao's downfall should be seen as a performance of a will to shift from one model of rule to another, where the value of ambivalence was increasingly discredited in public, though not necessarily expunged in practice.

Understanding informality as the result of specific planning practices also resists the tendency to associate casino development with neoliberal ideology, financial deregulation, weak states and urban fragmentation (Fu and Murray, 2014; Balsas, 2013; Mele 2011; Luke, 2010; Sheller 2008; Strange, 1986). Though there are many similarities across these "tourist utopias" (Simpson, 2017) and "casino cities" (Hannigan, 2007), the casino industry in Macau is distinct in that it performs the crucial role of social reproduction through the funding of schools, public infrastructure, tourist facilities and other welfare institutions.[3] Furthermore, China's geo-economic expansion in the new millennium has altered imaginaries and discourses of development in its Special Economic Zones and Administrative Regions. Casino development in the uplands of

---

3   This has historically been the case during the period of Portuguese rule when the casino monopoly was held by Stanley Ho. Today, casino developers have to contribute up to 3% of their revenue to charity and community causes as well as urban development, social security and the promotion of tourism. See http://www.dicj.gov.mo/web/en/contract/SJM/2002_BORAEM014S2Sup.html (accessed 2 Jan 2018).

Southeast Asia that accompanied the extension of Chinese capital into border regions and extraterritorial zones materialized and capitalized on the
promise of large-scale state-sponsored development (Lyttleton and Nyiri, 2011;
Nyiri, 2012; Tan 2012; Laungaramsri, 2015; Zhang 2017; Sims, 2017). The advent of
Singapore's model of "Integrated Resort" in 2007 further presents industry
players and governments with a sanitized version of casino development made
possible through strong state intervention (Lee, 2018). The Singapore state influenced the urban and architectural expression of the buildings, curtailed the
developers' typical practice of providing free shuttle buses to local residential
areas, and subjected junkets[4] to stringent surveillance. Developmentalism
seems to have forged a profitable partnership with an industry that thrives on
the deregulation of capital flow across borders and governments desperate for
tax revenue. The combination of the ideal of a developmental state, new transnational capitalists and entrenched local power structures may thus reinforce
or displace certain inherited institutions and practices.

The planning practices examined in this chapter range from master planning to development control and tender mechanisms. They represent different attempts by foreign and local agents to produce strategic ambivalence
in pursuit of political and economic objectives. In the first part, I discuss the
ramping up of modernizing visions towards the 1990s when the handover was
becoming more and more imminent. A sense of uncertainty and opportunity
had gripped the city even as Portuguese administrators strategized to leave a
positive legacy of its brand of luso-tropicalism through large-scale urban planning projects. These projects substantiate how planners responded and contributed to the regime of informality as they planned for a city where very little
could be controlled. In the second part, I analyze in detail the casino liberalization process after 1999, in particular the competitive tender mechanism which
determined who would be awarded the highly sought-after casino licenses.
Through selective disqualification and a restricted set of evaluation criteria,
the tender mechanism became an assemblage of technical rationality, neoliberal ethos and geopolitical calculations where the drive to maximize economic
gain come into a relationship with concerns over territorial sovereignty at the
urban and national scales. Straddling across the historic moment of 1999, such
practices should not be interpreted as evidence of the "failure" of planning – a
motif that the downfall of Ao dramatizes. Rather, they illustrate the specific
planning rationalities and techniques that allowed casino development to

---

4 Junkets are middle-men who bring in wealthy (usually foreign) gamblers to play in specific
   casinos. They typically provide credit (in the form of money or unexchangeable chips) for the
   gamblers and receive commissions from the hosting casino.

flourish in a context where broad frameworks of developmentalism *or* neoliberalism are limited in explanatory power.

1   The Impossibility and Possibility of Planning, 1990s

Though Ao was charged with tampering with the land sales mechanisms to favor specific parties, he was practicing no more than what had been standard procedure for some time. The Portuguese administration preferred closed-door negotiations to public auctions for the sale of land. This created over time an intimate relationship between the government and specific players who were able to cater to the agenda of the administration. Stanley Ho, who held the casino monopoly from 1960s to 2001, was one of the chief beneficiaries of the system as the government often sold land to him at lower-than-market value based on the argument that his company contributed most to the social and economic development of Macau. A documented case illustrates the extent to which ambivalence and porosity defined the politics of urban development in the 1990s.

In 1991, the Portuguese government decided to sell seven plots of outer harbor land at the Novos Aterros Porto Exterior (NAPE) through a public auction attached with a "favored party" rider. Under this mechanism, if the "favored party" is not the highest bidder, they have the opportunity to buy the land at the highest price. Stanley Ho, the operator of the casino monopoly in Macau since the 1960s, was listed as a "favored party" and was therefore able to buy six of the seven plots. This was heavily criticized by the pro-Chinese constituencies, which led to the auction being voided.[5] In the subsequent public auction, competitors were able to outbid Stanley Ho and buy several land parcels at prices far higher than was the norm. This led to a surge in property prices at the NAPE and subsequently several relaxations to urban planning controls as developers pressed for higher densities to make good their investments. However, when speculative Chinese capital was stemmed in 1993 by new government policies in the PRC to curb the outward flow of capital, many Chinese investors had to withdraw, resulting in 30,000 to 50,000 empty residential units at the NAPE (Clayton, 2010).

5   While it is not within the scope of this paper to delve into the specifics of the parties involved, some background information is useful. The political constituencies operating in Macau are extremely diverse and numerous. Scholars generally identify the Chinese General Chamber of Commerce, Federation of Labor Unions and Neighborhood Associations as amongst the most powerful groups. In the years leading up to the handover, Chinese businessmen with ties to the central government in Beijing were especially influential. See Chou, 2005.

During the auction of land at NAPE, Stanley Ho was careful enough to set up a conglomerate of pro-Portuguese and pro-Chinese parties so that he would not betray any political position. He repeated this strategy in the next big urban development project at the Nam Van Lake. It seems that the Portuguese government was sympathetic towards Ho, especially after voiding the auction of land at the NAPE, which caused him to "lose" what he had originally won. As such, there was an implicit agreement that the large development project would be awarded to him. Stanley Ho set up the Nam Van Company where he effectively owned about 40% of the shares and in 1991, the $43 Billion project encompassing 126 hectares of land was given to the company. Again, this came under much criticism from the pro-Chinese constituencies who saw this as an unfair arrangement that protected Portuguese interests. As a result, in 1992, the company underwent internal restructuring and the pro-Chinese constituencies were able to control 49% of the shares (Zu and Xin, 2005: 191–197).

Stanley Ho, referred to colloquially by the local Chinese as the "Crownless Governor of Macau" (无冕澳督), wielded considerable influence over which urban project moved ahead and which did not. The Portuguese government had hoped that Stanley Ho would develop the Nam Van Lake into a prestigious waterfront mixed use city by alienating land parcels to him. Yet, Stanley Ho was not keen to rush into developing these projects. In 1999, just before the handover, Stanley Ho and the government were only able to commit to building the "Macau Tourism Tower" which finally opened at the end of 2002. The uncertainty of the handover and rumors of the end of his monopoly made Ho cautious about overcommitting to Macau. In fact, Ho was strategically spreading his investments out into Taiwan, North Korea, Vietnam and the Philippines. Ho's control over land and this sense of uncertainty also affected the much-lauded Marine theme park at Taipa and the Airport Business City at Cotai. Both of these projects were heavily promoted before 1999 as projects destined to "change the face of Macau forever (Cairns, 1998). Land was reclaimed, but no construction ever began. A political analyst surmised that Ho held on to the land parcels without developing them so that he could use them to bargain with the new SAR government after handover (Leng, 2009: 194–203). It seems that his analysis is correct – during the bid for the casino license in 2001 when bidders had to compete based on how much they were willing to invest in Macau, Stanley Ho attempted to retrospectively include the half-completed Macau Tourism Tower as part of the total investment amount.[6]

These cases reveal the range of planning practices that allowed various parties to capitalize on the general state of ambivalence. This was especially

---

6 Interview (Anonymous) March 2011.

evident at NAPE, Nam Van Lake and Cotai because they were, ironically, the most visibly planned projects in the run-up to handover in 1999. Unlike all other proposals, master-plans with detailed development controls for these projects had been drawn up, publicly displayed and legally endorsed by the Portuguese administration (Daniell, 2015). A senior planner who had worked in Macau for many years interpreted the politics of visibility as a means to justify the direct alienation of land to Mr. Stanley Ho. His shrewd interpretation explains why planning can be most effective when it is opaque:

> If you ask what happened? What happened is that this was published because they needed this to be published. And this was published because that was published. And they needed to justify this portion [of land]. That was the only reason why. None of the other [plans] were ever published. And why? Because everywhere in the world, some places more than the others, they prefer not to have rules to have to comply with. Because if I have the flexibility to negotiate on a case by case basis, probably I will be in a better position to take advantages that I cannot take in another situation.[7]

Behind publicly visible and legally binding documents, opaque decision-making and political maneuvering *through* the planning process maintained the territorialized flexibility that defined a certain model of urban development. Due to the disjunction between the publicized plans and built reality, these projects had inadvertently become a concrete testament to the structural forces that make planning both possible and impossible in Macau – the overwhelming influence of a single industry in shaping political decisions and urban development, the geopolitical forces that undermine the capacity of any single party to claim absolute sovereignty over the territory and the monopolistic concessionaire-system that binds the interest of the government to the casino capitalist.

The disjunction between plan and reality should not be dismissed as a failure of planning. Rather, this disjunction was internal to the process of spatial production, and planners were cognizant of and worked with it. Planning changed its techniques and rationalities in order to capture value and secure political clout, even if at first glance, the master plans of NAPE, Nam Van Lake and Cotai bore typical geometries of modernist planning that assumes a developmentalist regime helmed by a powerful state. How did planners adapt

---

7   Interview with Mr. Campina Ferreira, Managing Director of Macau Professional Services, Nov 2010.

their craft to the context of Macau and contribute to a regime of ambivalence? Again, the two iconic projects of NAPE and Nam Van Lake provide some substantive material for analysis.

In the 1980s, Portuguese architects Alvaro Siza and Fernando Tàvora teamed up with Palmer and Turner Consultants from Hong Kong to prepare a plan for the NAPE, while a team led by architect Manuel Vicente prepared a plan for the Nam Van Lake Project.[8] They are drastically different visions. The former is a gridded platform that extends from the peninsula like a separate land mass. This separation is articulated both by its orthogonal geometry and a canal that cuts the reclaimed land from the peninsula. The plan for the NAPE bears some lineage to the modernist planning ideology of the Oporto school in Portugal, where Alvaro Siza and Fernando Tàvores taught.[9] The latter is a bold gestural curve that seamlessly extends the southern tip of the peninsula back to the NAPE, like a dyke that encloses the Praia Grande and transforms it into a lagoon (Figure 13.1). Unlike the plan for the NAPE, its geometries seem to be pulled out, rather than truncated, from the existing topography of the land. Yet, this juxtaposition of two radically different planning schemes did not happen by accident – the lead planner of the planning department had made the decision not to "impose an overall master plan on the incoherent city he had inherited", and instead "commissioned outside offices to produce designs for various districts, while his own team worked on solving the connections between them" (Daniell, 2015: 74). This separation of responsibilities between private and public planning was thus an acknowledgement of a context unamenable to comprehensive total planning. It also generated debates that foreshadowed the criticisms of casino development in 2010 – planners related to me how Manuel Vicente and Alvaro Siza did not cooperate with each other, and there were disputes over who was the rightful planner for the piece of land where the two plans overlapped.

The disjointedness of the Nam Van Lake and the NAPE attests not to the failure of planning but to the acknowledgement that a certain type of planning could not be accomplished in Macau. Though planners appeared to be passively responding to an "incoherent city" they had "inherited", they in fact

---

8 In contrast to Alvaro Siza, whose experience of Macau was limited to his plans for the NAPE and the Almeida Riberio, Manuel Vicente was prolific in Macau, being involved in over 60 buildings and urban plans between 1962 and 2004. See Lye (2006).

9 According to architectural scholar Hendrik Tieben (2009, 53), the NAPE plan was also influenced by "Marquis Pombal's reconstruction of Lisbon after the earthquake in 1955 or of contemporary plans for the International Building Exhibition in Berlin". Thomas Daniell (2015, 74) notes that Siza's initial proposal was influenced by 19th century Cerda plan for Barcelona, and the grid was typical of Spanish colonies.

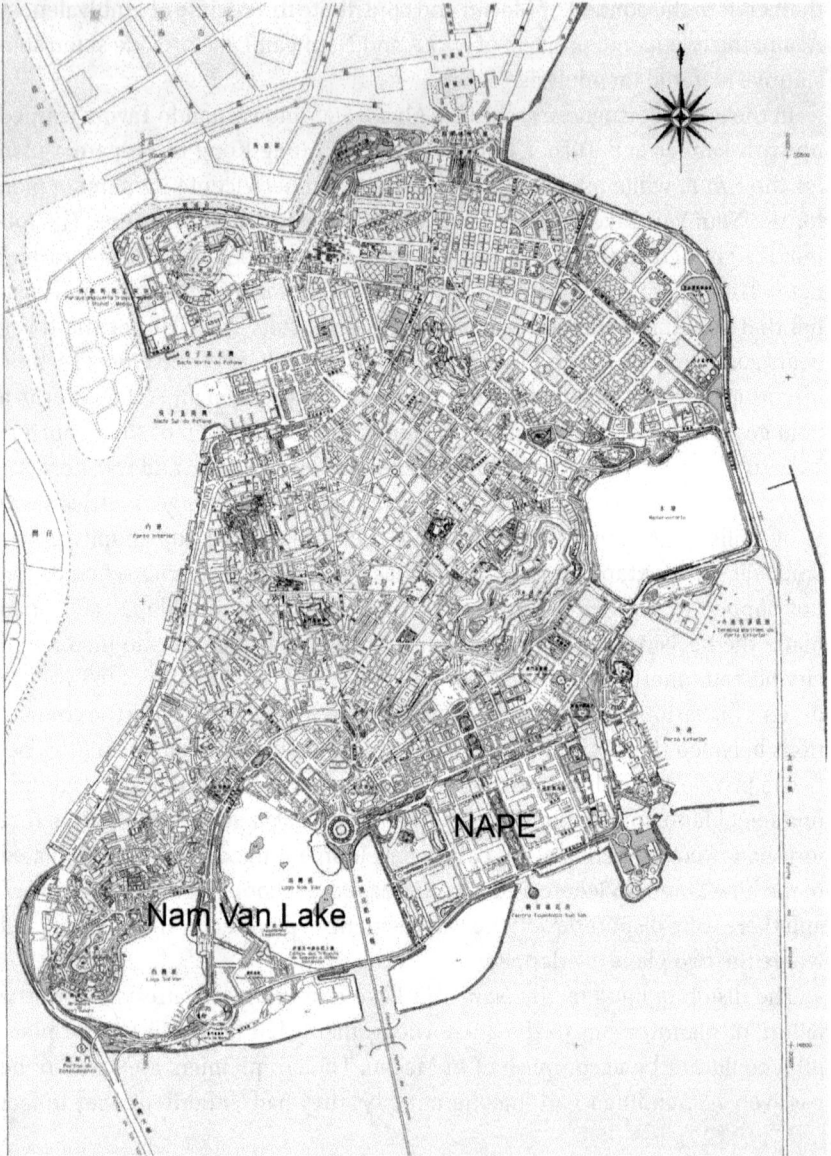

FIGURE 13.1   Nam Van Lake and Novos Aterros Porto Exterior, 2010
                SOURCE: MACAU SPECIAL ADMINISTRATIVE REGION GOVERNMENT—
                CARTOGRAPHY AND CADASTRE BUREAU

played an active role in sustaining it. The gridiron geometry of the NAPE bears only superficial similarity to the Modernist city of Brasilia or City Beautiful movements of Chicago because its intention was very different – planners in Macau saw their product as a disciplinary and flexible technology capable of mediating diverging interests without losing the overall spatial structure. This dual function is aptly captured in a short article about the plan for the NAPE in 1993 (Prescott, 1993: 52):

> As a basic disciplinary option, it was decided that the urban solutions to be proposed should be characterized by great clarity of principles and geometric rigor but sufficiently flexible to ensure the survival of those few disciplinary elements of the Plan even when confronted with eventual changes in programmes of occupation for the area.

Written shortly after this plan was gazetted as a legal document, the author felt optimistic enough to declare that the NAPE might finally be realized. For the lack of "flexibility", he was more pensive about Vicente's plan for the Nam Van Lake, wondering "how the developmental requirements of the individual enterprises, which will occupy these buildings, will be restricted by the strait jacket of prescribed, very detailed, layouts" (Prescott, 54–55). In his mind, urban speculation and weak political control appeared again and again as the preconditions of planning in Macau. Thus, flexibility and discipline were a planning tactic to maintain a basic spatial structure while accommodating the inevitable changes due to political maneuvering. This translated into a set of basic formal rules that governed road network, land parcellation, plot ratios, building heights and typologies (Prescott, 1993: 53):

> In this perspective, and in the case of the final version of NAPE, the following structuring elements were adopted: an urban grid of 144m x 72m measured along the axis of roads: a hierarchical arrangement of the road networks based on orientation and cross section; a disciplined occupation of the city blocks with definition of coverage and plot ratios tailored for the defined land uses; the control of maximum heights and the enforcement of perimetral development on a fixed podium in order to ensure consistency and visual unity between open areas and built volumes.

The relationship between formal rules and the informalization of planning is further elaborated by a group of Dutch planners from the Dutch Foundation for Architectural Research who collaborated on this project. Borrowing from system theory, their planning method was based on a hierarchy of controls that were both independent of and guided by one another, thus linking the idea of dynamic equilibrium in system theory to how a city functions. They broke down the urban fabric into "infill", "support" and "tissue" for analysis and proposed different rules for building height, green space ratio and land parcel sizes, as well as different urban prototypes for mixed-use developments in different parts of the city. All these could be generated through and within a "generic grid" (Bax and Knikkink, 1984):

> This type of grid contains information, qualities, in the most condensed form and from a point of view of architectural and urban planning and design also in the most essential way: dimension, position and function of spatial elements governed by rules. Plans on the urban level are notations in higher level grids. The grids are designed by structuring and generalization of lower level qualities. These qualities, in the form of objective standards and subjective historical and symbolic values, support the planning and design process, *even when only rude sketches are made for an overall plan on the level of the city* ... (italics mine)

Thus, the Dutch planners rationalized their work on the NAPE using very similar idioms of flexibility and discipline. In the Netherlands, this method was used for large housing projects, where the central question was how to accommodate diversity and choice introduced as a result of resident involvement in the design brief.[10] In Macau, it was an economical solution as well as a strategic tool to give a general order in an environment where little could be controlled. The generic grid and the hierarchy of rules reflected what the planners thought was a diminishing horizon of controllability. The strategy was thus to put in place a bare layer of structural controls which generated large amounts of grey zones where political bargaining, or in the language of planners, "diversity" could happen. The generic grid was a *response to*, rather than a *rejection of*, its context. Rather than an absolute geometry in the Modernist tradition of

---

10   "There is a structure in the existing diversity and there is a structure in the transformation. SAR has tried to make the structure of diversity and change explicit by introducing the concept of levels. Levels are units of control, of rules systems that are almost universally obeyed for the purpose of channeling diversity and change into desirable courses. Levels have as their basis the observation that some aspects of the environment are of a more general nature than others, have a longer lifespan than others, concern more people than others, etc." Carp J (1984, 15). For a thorough documentation of the planning philosophy of the group, see the work of its first director, John Habraken (1998) who later became the Head of the Department of Architecture at the MIT.

total planning, the grid, in the context of Macau, was a geometry of strategic ambivalence.

2   Geopolitics of Unmapping, Post-1999

Macau's handover to the PRC in 1999 and the subsequent liberalization of the casino industry unleashed an unprecedented scale of urban transformation and economic growth. The plans for Cotai and the NAPE created in the 1980s and 90s were scrapped in its wake, which contributed to the impression that urban planning was once again sacrificed in the development of Macau. This restricted conceptualization of planning ignores the fact that the scrapping of old plans, like the creation of flexible plans, was just as strategic a move to accommodate new sources and scales of foreign capital in the city. In place of old plans, the SAR government adapted planning practices to the task. Examining such practices and their rationalities shows how state-business networks continued to drive the production of urban space through channels of institutionalized informality, albeit in a different geopolitical environment.

In his response to the media in 2002 when the casino licenses were up for bidding, then-SAR chief executive Edmund Ho argued that putting strict upper or lower limits to the number of casinos and gaming tables would interfere with the business strategies of the concessionaires. Espousing a free market logic, he argued that role of the government was to encourage "benign competition" (良性競爭) among the concessionaires so as to serve the greater interest of Macau in terms of its urban development and tourism industry (Lin, 2002). In various Chinese media reports, liberalization was often conflated with modernization and competitiveness, and the way to do so was to import foreign capital and expertise and transform Macau into the gaming center of Asia.

Though Edmund Ho reiterated how the casino industry must contribute to the urban development of Macau, by the time the tenders were awarded and the conditions negotiated, the primary parameters of control were simplified to one of investment quantum – successful concessionaires were bound only by their commitment to invest a declared amount within a given period with some indication of the kinds of projects to be taken (see also Pinheiro and Wan, 2012). They were also required to build at least one flagship development, though the location and exact business model of such a development was not prescribed (Comissão, 2002a). This was a crucial moment in the dematerialization of land and the decanting of its socio-historical content. A lawyer who was involved in managing the tender process explains:

The problem, mind you, is that there was and there still is, a lack of land in Macau. So most of the proposals don't have [sites]. The subconcessions have executive summaries that state 'we intend to have a five-star hotel with 5000 rooms, three restaurants and so on' ... the interesting thing here is that one of the scoring weights of the tender was the investment [amount]. During the tender, we found out that most of the investments that were proposed by the bidders, candidates, were overpriced. A lot. So, the idea, instead of having them bound to a specific investment, they were bound to a specific amount of investment. This means that instead of having SJM build the Grand Lisboa, we don't care if it costs 100, 200 or 50 billion Patacas. You say that you are going to spend 10 billion, ok, so put it on the paper, and you are bound to spend at least 10 billion.[11]

Technical rationality in the form of legal reasoning and practical administration had the effect of deleting land and architecture from the calculations of government. In order that all 18 bidders who entered the field with unequal strengths be treated equally, in order that the government could extract the most benefit from the bidders based on what they could offer individually, and in order that all these be done with minimal effort in compressed time, an administrative procedure was set up that reduced the elements of consideration to monetary value.

The anti-politics of such administrative procedures produced political effects that were both contradictory and necessary to its smooth functioning. On the one hand, the bidders and the government negotiated and settled on a whole series of urban improvements and economic benefits that were specific to each bidder. Steve Wynn promised to invest $4 billion in a theme-park at Taipa and produce a total of 6,500 jobs in the casino industry while Sociedade de Jogos de Macau (SJM) promised to invest a total of $4.7 billion in 17 different projects around Macau and maintain the jobs of its current employees. On the other hand, these different promises were subsumed into a numerical score that determined who would win the bid, such that their very tangibility became irrelevant. Indeed, 54% of the total score was given to the company's track record in the casino and entertainment industry (Comissão, 2002b). This decontextualized the final product from the concrete materiality of the city of Macau. What the judges most valued was not so much a physical product as the intangible experience of building and running this product. This mode of

---

11   Interview with Mr. Antonio Lobo Vilela, March 2011. For the conditions imposed on concessionaires, see also Pinheiro and Wan, 2012.

valuation assumed the reproducibility of products and located corporate identity as a guarantee of reproducibility.

Similar to the contestations over land between the Portuguese government, pro-Chinese constituencies and the casino capitalist at NAPE in the 1990s, the tender mechanism was instrumental in creating an ambiguous space where power dynamics between old and new actors could be re-established in a new geopolitical environment. Though the criteria and scope of evaluation were public knowledge and designed as a performance of objectivity it functioned primarily as a gatekeeper that determined who could or could not participate in the casino industry based on considerations that had nothing to do with these openly declared criteria. Such considerations pursued objectives of capital accumulation, political autonomy and territorial consolidation, often in contradictory ways.

This ambiguous space opened up by the tender mechanism can be seen in how the incumbent monopolist, Stanley Ho, almost lost in his bid for a concession. For 40 years, the economy, social welfare and urban development of Macau was indivisible from the performance of Ho's casino monopoly. Based on the judging criteria, it would seem that his company SJM would have no problem winning one of the three concessions. As mentioned earlier, more than 50% of the score was given to track record in the casino and entertainment industry, thus favoring him heavily. Yet, in the context of postcolonial Macau, Stanley Ho's monopoly was suddenly seen as a legacy of weak Portuguese rule, triad violence and bureaucratic corruption (Lo, 2005). As the newspapers had picked up, SJM's position in the top three was a close shave (Macau Daily News, 2002). The original score given to the category of "experience in the industry" was a shockingly low figure of 63.09.[12] This score was only subsequently increased to 84.40, which barely won SJM a spot in the top three (Comissão, 2002b). As Lo (2005: 217) notes, the Macau SAR government had intended to reform the casino-government complex by maintaining "a degree of autonomy vis-à-vis all the casino capitalists". Even though Ho won a license, the tender mechanism delivered a symbolic slap indicative of the changing power dynamics in the post-colonial regime.

Through the tender mechanism, certain sources of capital and expertise that could reposition and rescale the economy of Macau in a global and regional context were privileged. Right from the beginning, the casino industry of Macau acquired an extra-national status: it was an industry to be run by foreigners, or Chinese capitalists from ex-colonies, for the greater good of one

---

12   In contrast, the top bidders Wynn Resorts, MGM Grand and Galaxy Entertainment scored
      75.33 , 70.62 and 60.46 respectively for this criterion.

of its own special administrative zones while casino gambling remained illegal in mainland China. The preferred sources were hinted at just before the tender was launched, when the SAR government approached casino developers in the United States, South Korea, Malaysia, Australia and Japan to gauge their interest in Macau (Lo, 2005: 215). Furthermore, the PRC was motivated to attract American and Australian operators as they were bound by the regulations from their home jurisdictions.

This strange set of geopolitics produced a series of contortions where bidders, governments and other investors sought to create and influence partnerships that would appeal to decision-makers at different levels of governance. Initially, Venetian, headed by chairman of Las Vegas Sands Sheldon Adelson, had partnered with Asian American Entertainment for the bid. The financial support for this joint bid was underwritten by the China Development Industrial Bank, a Taiwanese lender. However, in the midst of the bidding process, Adelson abruptly shifted his partnership to Galaxy Entertainment, a company run by a Hong Kong entrepreneur. This fueled speculations about the sensitivity of Taiwanese capital, particularly since the chairman of the underwriting bank was the chief finance officer of the Kuomingtang Party (Simpson, 2016).[13]

After winning one of the three concessions, the partnership between Galaxy Entertainment and Venetian eventually fell through. A sub-concession system was created so that Galaxy Entertainment could sell a sub-concession to its ex-partner, thus retaining Venetian as a market player in Macau. It was later revealed that Sheldon Adelson had allegedly gained access to high-ranking politicians in Beijing and worked his connections to help Beijing clinch the 2010 Olympics bid (Bruck, 2008). It was through this sleight of hand that three concessions doubled into six as the other two original winners insisted on this right to sell a sub-concession. Stanley Ho's daughter and son partnered with MGM Mirage and PBL/Melco respectively and managed to win both sub-concessions. In a bid to match the competition, local players also sought out foreign investors who had both the capital and expertise desired in the new geopolitical environment.

As scholars have shown, shifting geopolitical forces continue to shape the border-crossing development of China's Special Economic Zones and SARS (Yang, 2006; Ong, 2004). The geo-economic integration of Taiwan and China, for example, does not override geopolitical calculations concerning territorial

---

13   This abrupt change in partnership happened five days before the announcement of the
      results. Asian American Entertainment alleged that "this is proof the concessions was
      somehow rigged in Las Vegas Sands' favor, since Galaxy had already failed in its solo bid
      earlier in the process" (Ward, 2007).

consolidation and sovereignty (Lim 2012, Yang and Hsia 2007). The fact that Taiwanese companies had played an important role in the information technology and manufacturing industries of the Greater Suzhou Area since the 1990s and continue to do so into the 21st century suggests that a different set of geopolitics was at work in the context of Macau's casino industry. The tender mechanism became a way to reject Taiwanese capital while retaining an American product. It also became a way for local players to reemerge in a "modern" postcolonial guise through association with preferred foreign partners.

The erasure of existing plans was thus not a symptom of a lack of planning. Rather, a strategic move had been taken by the SAR administration to unmap the city of Macau so as to accommodate new sources and scales of foreign investment. Rolled out at the very start of the casino liberalization process, the tender mechanism took the place of flexible plans and reproduced the informalized regime of spatial production. In 2010, a government officer revealed during an interview that the three winners represented "a careful balance of local and foreign interests".[14] It is perhaps impossible to gauge if these decisions were indeed carefully orchestrated or contained a degree of short-sightedness and accident. Rather than neatly encapsulating a single developmental program, the doubling of casino concessionaires married the neoliberal ethos that "natural" market forces would create a dynamic equilibrium regardless of the number of competitors, with geopolitical calculations about the choice of competitors and a technical rationality that subsumed all variables under a quantitative metric.

3   Conclusion

Macau's urban transformation before and after its return to the PRC illustrates how states and experts constitute a regime of institutionalized informality in the production of space. Planning practices such as tender mechanisms, master planning and development control may seem to reign in chaos with a panoply of formalized rules and procedures, but they could also serve to rearrange

---

14   Interview (anonymous), Nov 2010. Explaining why the three winners were chosen, the interviewee said that Steve Wynn's concept of family entertainment was a "clear winner". Galaxy Entertainment represented a "local interest group." However, since it had no experience in the casino industry, it would not be able to win the concession by itself. "Someone from the top" spoke with Venetian and Galaxy Entertainment and encouraged them to submit a bid as partners. Finally, it was in the interest of "stability" to keep SJM. To dismiss Stanley Ho might create social chaos as his casinos employed many locals and were linked to many businesses and politicians.

existing power structures and generate ambiguous spaces for the recomposition of capital accumulation and real estate investment. Looking at such practices in detail reveals their specific intentions and effects and draws out the
relative positioning of different parties in critical moments of the urban development process. At this level of analysis, planning practices, inherited and
circulated, do not transmit ideologies or reflect political structures automati-
cally nor do they follow the same chronology as important historical events.
A standardized urban grid, as the case of the NAPE shows, need not always be
an expression of the Modernist ideal – it could also be a paradoxical effort at
accommodating disorder, a *response* to the unruly local context rather than
a *rejection* of it. If urban informality is to be conceptualized as a set of socio-
political processes rather than a status attached to an actor, site or ideology,
one needs to foreground the uses and values of ambivalence within the political calculations of states and experts.

The political value of ambivalence that Macau's case highlights is in mediating the production of space with a changing geopolitical environment. As
Ip (this volume) shows in the case of Hong Kong after 1997, the Beijing government plays a significant role in stimulating the urban economy of its SARs
through trans-border property speculation, business outsourcing and labor
flow. While Hong Kong serves primarily as a financial center in the Pearl River
Delta mega-region, Macau functions as an enclave of conspicuous consumption (Simpson, 2009). The liberalization of the casino monopoly and the re-
laxation of travel restrictions between mainland China and Macau radically
altered the spatial structure of the city of Macau and made it possible for unprecedented levels of foreign capital to enter the region and secure vast tracts
of land for casino development. This territorial flexibility continues to shape
Macau as its borders are contorted to absorb part of the neighboring province
of Zhuhai into its burgeoning economy, while casino developers continue to
buy existing properties and tracts of land in preparation for the renewal of the
concessions around 2020.

Yet, the casino industry is an industry unlike others. Its role in facilitating
capital inflow and outflow in the region is not as well understood as other
globally distributed institutions such as financial banking and manufacturing.
A distinct system of "concessions", "junkets" and gaming-specific taxes ce-
ments a special relationship between the operator and the host-city. In Manila,
Phnom Penh and Singapore, the other metropolitan centers of casino development in Asia-Pacific, state agents and local business elites have also been
indispensable in accommodating the needs of the industry by revising anti-
gaming laws and other urban planning or financial regulations (Lee, 2018; Saguin,

2017; Yamada, 2017). Yet, this partnership often ignites the flames of economic nationalism since its operation entails the transgression of an imaginary territorial boundary that demarcates one political community from its outside (Vlcek, 2015). Such transgressions can take the form of money laundering or the exporting of social harm or the dispossession of "local" wealth. Once a pariah industry controlled by state monopolies or sequestered in tourist enclaves, casino development in Asia has generated some of the most spectacular forms of urbanization over the last two decades. In the wake of its scandals and successes are writ large the territorial flexibility that enables vast amounts of surplus capital to flow in furtive ways across the region.

References

Balsas, C (2013) "Gaming anyone? A comparative study of recent urban development trends in Las Vegas and Macau" in *Cities* 31: 298–307.

Bax, MFT and H Knikkink (1984) "The Design of a Generic Grid: Urban Intervention Plans for Macau" in *Open House International* 9(4): 5–13.

Bruck, C (2008) "The Brass Ring: A multibillionaire's relentless quest for global influence" *The New Yorker*, 30 June, http://www.newyorker.com/reporting/2008/06/30/080630fa_fact_bruck

Bunnell, T and A Harris (2012) "Re-viewing Informality: perspectives from urban Asia" in *International Development Planning Review* 34(4): 339–348.

Carp, B (1984) "What-When A Practical Description of the Design Process" in :*Open House International* 9(4): 12–22.

Chou, B (2005) "Interest group politics in Macau after handover" *Journal of Contemporary China* 14(43): 191–206.

Chui, SP (2008) *21st Century Macau City Planning Guideline Study, 1999–2020*. Macau: Fundação para cooperação e desenvolvimento de Macau.

Clayton, C (2010) *Sovereignty at the Edge: Macau and the Question of Chineseness*. MA: Harvard University Press.

Comissão do primeiro concurso público para a atribuição de concessões para a exploração de jogos de fortuna ou azar em casino (娱乐场幸运博彩经营批给首次公开竞投委员会), (2002a) 娱乐场幸运博彩经营批给首次公开竞投方案. Macau: Macau SAR Government.

Comissão do primeiro concurso público para a atribuição de concessões para a exploração de jogos de fortuna ou azar em casino (娱乐场幸运博彩经营批给首次公开竞投委员会), (2002b) 应于考虑的标准及因素与相关加权系数综合表. Macau: Macau SAR Government.

Daniell, T (2015) "Artifice and Authenticity: Postcolonial Urbanism in Macau" in G Bracken (ed.) *Asian Cities: Colonial to Global.* (Amsterdam: Amsterdam University Press, pp. 69–93.

Eadington, W and R Siu (2007) "Between Law and Custom – Examining the Interaction between Legislative Chance and the Evolution of Macao's Casino Industry" in *International Gambling Studies* 4: 1–28.

Fu, AS and MJ Murray (2014) "Glorified Fantasies and Masterpieces of Deception on Importing Las Vegas into the 'New South Africa'" in *International Journal of Urban and Regional Research* 38(3): 843–863.

Habraken, J (1998) *The Structure of the Ordinary: Form and Control in the Built Environment.* J Teicher (ed.). Cambridge, MA: The MIT Press.

Hannigan, J (2007) "Casino Cities" in *Geography Compass* 1(4): 959–975.

Laungaramsri, P (2015) "Commodifying Sovereignty: Special Economic Zones and the Neoliberalization of the Lao Frontier". In Y Santasombat (ed.) *Impact of China's Rise on the Mekong Region.* US: Palgrave Macmillan, pp. 117–146.

Lee, K-W (2014) "Transforming Macau: planning as institutionalized informality and the spatial dynamics of hypercompetition" in *Environment and Planning A* 46(11): 2622–2637.

Lee, K-W (2018, forthcoming) *Las Vegas in Singapore: Violence, Progress and the Crisis of Nationalist Modernity.* Singapore: NUS Press.

Leng, X (2009) *Lengyan kan Aomen: Aomen huigui shi nian huigu ji fansi* [Lengyan looking at Macau: Reflections and Recollections 10 years after the Handover]. Hong Kong: Mingliu chubanshe.

Lin B H (12 January 2002) "赌场数目无硬性规定 [No fixed limit on number of casinos], Macau Daily News p. 1.

Lim, KF (2012) "What You See Is (Not) What You Get? The Taiwan Question, Geo-economic realities and the "China Threat" Imaginary" in *Antipode* 44(4): 1348–1373.

Lo, SH (2005) "Casino Politics, Organized Crime and the Post-Colonial State in Macau" in *Journal of Contemporary China* 14(43): 207–224.

Luke, T (2010) "Gaming Space: Casinopolitan Globalism from Las Vegas to Macau" in *Globalizations* 7(3): 395–405.

Lye, KC (2006) *Manuel Vicente: Caressing Trivia.* Hong Kong: MCCM Creations.

Lyttleton, C and P Nyíri (2011) "Dams, Casinos and Concessions: Chinese Megaprojects in Laos and Cambodia". In S D Brunn (ed.) *Engineering Earth: The Impacts of Mega-engineering Projects.* Dordrecht: Springer, pp. 1243–1265.

Macau Daily News (10 Feb 2002) "澳博WIN出险过剃头" [SJM wins by a shave], pp. B3.

McFarlane, C (2012) "Rethinking Informality: Politics, Crisis and the City" in *Planning Theory and Practice* 13(1): 89–108.

Mele, C (2011) "Casinos, Prisons, Incinerators, and Other Fragments of Neoliberal Urban Development" in *Social Science History* 35(3): 423–452.

Nyíri, P (2012) "Enclaves of Improvement: Sovereignty and Developmentalism in the Special Zones of the China-Lao Borderlands" in *Comparative Studies in Society and History* 54(3): 533–562.

Ong, AH (2004) "The Chinese Axis: Zoning Technologies and Variegated Sovereignty" in *Journal of East Asian Studies* 4:69–96.

Pinheiro, F and P Wan (2011) "The Development of the Gaming Industry and its Impact on Land Use" in Lam MKL and I Scott (eds). *Gaming, Governance and Public Policy in Macao.* Hong Kong: Hong Kong University Press), pp. 19–35.

Prescott, J A (ed.) (1993) *Macaensis Momentum: A Fragment of Architecture: A Moment in the History of Development of Macau.* Macau: Hewell Publications.

Robert Cairns (1998) "Macau: A Gateway to China" in Asian Architect and Contractor 27(1): 42–25.

Roy, A (2009) "Why India Cannot Plan Its Cities: Informality, Insurgence and the Idiom of Urbanization" in *Planning Theory* 8(1): 76–87.

Saguin, K (2017) "Actors in Global City Formation: The Case of the Entertainment City in Metro Manila" in *International Journal of Policy Studies* 8(1): 1–21.

Sheller, M (2008) "Always Turned On: Atlantic City as America's Accursed Share" in A M Cronin and K Hetherington (eds). *Consuming the Entrepreneurial City: Image, Memory, Spectacle.* New York and London: Routledge, pp. 107–126.

Simpson, T (2008) "Macao, Capital of the Twenty-First Century?" in *Environment and Planning D: Space and Society* 26: 1053–1079.

Simpson, T (2009) "Materialist Pedagogy: The Function of Themed Environments in Post-Socialist Consumption in Macau" in *Tourist Studies* 9(1): 60–80.

Simpson, T (2016) "Neoliberal Exception? The liberalization of Macau's casino gaming monopoly and the genealogy of the post-socialist Chinese subject" in *Planning Theory*, https://doi.org/10.1177/1473095216672499

Simpson, T (ed.) (2017) *Tourist Utopias: Offshore Islands, Enclaves Spaces, and Mobile Imaginaries.* Amsterdam: Amsterdam University Press.

Sims, K (2017) "Gambling on the Future: Casino Enclaves, Development, and Poverty Alleviation in Laos" in *Pacific Affairs* 90(4): 675–699.

Soliman, AM (2010) "Rethinking urban informality and the planning process in Egypt" in *International Development and Planning Review* 32(2): 119–143.

Strange, S [1986] (1997) *Casino Capitalism.* Manchester, UK: Manchester University Press.

Tan, D (2012) "'Small is Beautiful': Lessons from Laos for the Study of Chinese Overseas" in *Journal of Current Chinese Affairs* 41(2): 61–94.

Tieben, H (2009) "Urban Image Construction in Macau in the First Decade after the 'Handover'" in *Journal of Current Chinese Affairs* 38(1): 49–72.

Varley, A (2013) "Postcolonialising Informality?" in *Environment and Planning D* 31(1): 4–22.

Vlcek, W (2015) "Taking other people's money: development and the political economy of Asian casinos" in *The Pacific Review* 28(3): 323–345.

Ward, M (23 April 2007) "A gritty side of Las Vegas Sands" Las Vegas Business Press, p. 5.

Yamada, T (2017) "Phnom Penh's NagaWorld Resort and Casino" in *Pacific Affairs* 90(4): 743–765.

Yang, C (2006) "The geopolitics of cross-boundary goverance in the Greater Pearl River Delta, China: A case study of the proposed Hong Kong-Zhuhai-Macao Bridge" in *Political Geography* 25(7): 817–835.

Yang, Y and C Hsia (2007) "Spatial clustering and organizational dynamics of transborder production networks: A case study of Taiwanese information-technology companies in the Greater Suzhou Area" in *Environment and Planning A* 39: 1346–1363.

Zhang, J (2017) "Introduction: Integrated Mega-Casinos and Speculative Urbanism in Southeast Asia" in *Pacific Affairs* 90(4): 651–674.

Zu, CT and L Xin (2005) *Aomen Duwang: Hehongsheng quanzhuan* [Gambling King of Macau: The Complete Biography of Stanley Ho] (Wuhan: Hubei renming chubanshe).

CHAPTER 14

Translating a Fast Policy: Place Marketing and the Neoliberal Turn of Critical Urban Studies in South Korea

Laam Hae

How do policies travel across different locales in different countries?[1] Why have certain urban policies acquired a hegemonic position in the context of rapid globalization? This chapter examines these questions through the case of 'place marketing' (or 'city marketing'), a trend that generated a great buzz among geographers, urban planners and policy makers in the 1990s in South Korea (henceforth, Korea).[2] These actors prescribed place marketing as a promising local growth strategy in an era of expanding local autonomy in Korea. In Korean academic and policy circles, place marketing mainly re-ferred to culture-focused urban development policies and branding efforts used to enhance the image of a place – similar to the ways that it was used in the Western cities where it originated (Kearns and Philo 1993; Ward 1998). As members of various think-tanks and research institutes for local governments, groups of urban planners and geographers functioned as intermediaries who studied Western place marketing experiences, and consistently made a claim that place marketing could provide a 'new paradigm' (Lee MY 2006) for local growth in Korea that would rectify the urban problems generated by the devel-opmental statist urbanization that dominated in the previous decades.

How did the coterie of urban scholars and policy makers in Korea – which I call 'place marketers' in this chapter – come to learn place marketing policies implemented in Western countries? In particular, why did a significant seg-ment of *critical* urban scholars also participate in underlining the urgency of practicing place marketing in Korea? What political economic contexts have these actors been situated in and influenced by? How did they frame the ne-cessity of place marketing in the Korean urban context? This chapter explores these questions in relation to Korean cities' transition to a post-developmental

---

1 This work was supported by the National Research Foundation of Korea Grant funded by the Korean Government (NRF-2014S1A3A2044551).
2 In this paper, I use 'place marketing' instead of 'city marketing', as the former refers to mar-keting practices performed in varied geographical locations.

statist paradigm, and traces the contradictory outcomes of place marketing strategies implemented in different places in Korea. I show how traveling neo-liberal policies such as place marketing have, as a 'policy in motion' (Ward 2006), produced uneven and variegated outcomes between different land-scapes across different locales, rather than provoking their homogenization (Brenner, Peck, and Theodore 2010). Most importantly, I examine how place marketing – a good example of what Peck (2002) calls 'fast policy' – was trans-lated as an alternative paradigm of local development among a contingent of *critical* geographers and urban planners. I speculate upon several explanations as to why this contingent did so, especially ones that pertain to the particular way that this contingent problematized the urbanization pattern of the pre-vious developmental state period in Korea. That is, there were particular cir-cumstances that explain the enthusiastic endorsement of place marketing by this contingent, a trajectory that somewhat distinguishes the Korean origin of place marketing from that of the West. Nonetheless, the widespread and enthusiastic valorization of place marketing as the 'best practice' for local de-velopment in the 1990s should still be understood within the broader context of the gradual neoliberalization of the local development paradigm in Korea at that time. Unsurprisingly, the place marketing policies that have been im-plemented since then have produced struggles and contradictions similar to those that have unfolded in neoliberalizing cities in the West (and beyond), with the consequence of constraining the scope of an autonomous and demo-cratic politics of place in Korea.

This chapter, while built on the analysis of a body of literature on place marketing published both within and outside of Korea, is also founded on the author's previous experience in the mid-to-late 1990s as an urban planning practitioner and place marketer. Therefore, a crucial element of the writing and analysis here is also auto-ethnographical (Ellis and Bochner 2000), in the sense that it reflects my previous participation in place marketing policy circles and observation of their various practices. I wrote my master's degree thesis on place marketing, where I analyzed how place marketing strategies were gener-ating conflicts between different non-/local actors and prescribed normative solutions for what a better direction for place marketing might entail. After completing my master's degree, for a span of about eighteen months, I worked for an urban planning firm, and then the Seoul Research Institute (SRI), a re-search institute established to frame and assist policy-making processes by the Seoul municipal government. At the SRI, I was involved in a handful of place-marketing projects that aimed at the cultural revitalization of Seoul, and also co-authored an article that pleaded to the Seoul municipal government to adopt a marketing perspective to better promote Seoul's cultural assets (Hahn and Hae 2001). Therefore, this chapter contains an element of reflection and self-critique upon my previous role as a place marketer, and how I, like my colleagues, became an agent of the globalization of neoliberal urban policy in a non-Western context. That is, what this chapter attempts to do is part of what McCann (2011) calls 'a global ethnography of policy transfer', with self-critical retrospection as one of its main resources.

1   The Translocalization of Urban Cultural Policies

In post-industrial Western societies, culture has increasingly become seen as one of the essential elements that allegedly helped to resolve problems that cities confronted after deindustrialization in the 1960s and the fiscal crisis of the 1970s. The association of cities with playful cultures were said to help eliminate the image of dereliction of these cities (Holcomb 1993). The cultural vitality of cities was also deployed as a magnet to allure labor forces to high-end service businesses that enhance cities' economic competitiveness – the labor forces largely corresponding to Florida's (2004) 'creative class'. For groups like the creative class, it was argued, the prospect of experiencing urban 'authenticity' and the consumption of an urban lifestyle has become an important factor in their choice of habitats and workplaces (also see Ley 1996). Commerce and institutions associated with distinctive cultural styles are also often mobilized by realtors and developers to brand neighborhoods as chic, in the hopes of resuscitating derelict real estate markets (Harvey 2003; Tretter 2009).

For some urban scholars, these changes have been positive in the sense that urban diversity and vibrancy has finally been restored from the sort of modernist urban planning dominant in the post-war period that waged a relentless assault on the former. This celebration of urban cultural diversity and vibrancy, however, has been challenged. It was argued that positive appraisals of reclaimed urban vibrancy mask the reality that cultural vibrancy primarily functions to raise the competitiveness of cities (Peck 2005); that the urban management that these cultural strategies are part of is now heavily swayed by private interests (Hall and Hubbard 1998; Harvey 1989); and, that urban cultural landscapes strategically mask the deepening racialized and gendered impoverishment and erosion of democracy in public space under neoliberal urbanization (Lees, Slater and Wyly 2007; MacLeod 2002; Mitchell 2003; Taylor 2016). Others have also pointed out that certain expressive activities and vernacular cultures have been policed and priced out of redeveloped urban space – supposedly a space of 'cultural diversity' – and have been replaced with sanitized commerce for lifestyle consumption (Hae 2012; Mele 2000; Zukin 1982).

The importance of promotion and marketing urban cultures has been widely recognized in non-Western cities. For example, Yeoh (2005) shows how culture-led urban redevelopment and the facilitation of a culture industry sector have been major forces of change throughout Southeast Asian cities. These changes have been driven by 'place-wars' undertaken to attract mobile capital, international talent and tourists (Ibid., 946). Here, efforts of 'imagineering' cities have often involved the promotion of international modernity together with the post-colonial imperative of 'cultural self-determination', as illustrated by attempts to preserve local heritage values and a sense of 'Asian' identity. These changes, however, have also confronted challenges from local populations. For example, in Penang, Malaysia, residents contested the process of the city being transformed into a tourist or elite-oriented space, where they found themselves increasingly alienated from economic development (Teo 2003). Locals also contested the reified forms of their 'heritage' and 'history' that were marketed in these developments, raising questions about the local embeddedness of this heritage and history (see also Yeoh 2005, 952–953).

The universalization of the mandate to combine the cultural with the economic can be attributed to the reality that more and more cities in the world are now subject to intensifying global inter-urban competition (Harvey 1989), which pressures cities to adopt strategies 'that work' in this particular global milieu. This explains the increasing global mobilization of neoliberal policies between different cities as 'best practices'. While policy mobilization between cities is inter-referencing and not always unidirectional (Peck and Theodore 2010a, 170-1), in this context neoliberal policy paradigms from the West tend to maintain their hegemonic power in knowledge and policy production. Therefore, in addition to studies of coercive forms of policy impositions by international institutions such as the IMF and World Bank, recently there emerged a body of literature that interrogates how policies are made mobile through *competitive* forms of policy import – that is, the competitive learning of particular types of policies originating from elsewhere by policy intermediaries, such as technocrats, technocratic aides, policy experts and consultants, policy analysts, public intellectuals, and academics (Peck 2002; Peck and Theodore 2010a, 2010b; Peck and Theodore 2015). These policy intermediaries participate in various circuits and sites of knowledge distribution, such as conferences, and make fact-finding trips to model cities (McCann 2008; Peck and Theodore 2010a) to keep track of these programs and policies.

The imperatives of globalization often naturalize the urgency of implementing neoliberal policies among policy intermediaries, and these intermediaries, therefore, often form 'epistemic communities' (Peck and Theodore 2015, 21–2). Peck (2002, 344) further argues that the translocalization of neoliberal policies has been characterized by 'fast-policy' transfers *or* 'the importation of off-the-shelf program techniques'. That is, programs and policies are emulated even before in-depth, long-term studies of their effects in the original locale are conducted (Peck and Theodore 2010b, 199), as politicians that import these programs and policies seek to implement ones that produce quickly quantifiable results that can be used for the purposes of 'display politics'. Even if an impact study is conducted, evaluation institutions and specialists – which are often in direct or indirect institutional liaison with those who develop the policies – already have ideologically skewed standards of what constitute effective policies. They favor metrics that privilege short-term achievements and the reduction of costs in the public sector, and gloss over policies' unfavorable social repercussions (Peck 2002, 346, 352). While policy mobility has a long history, the recent translocalization of policies, it was argued, is characterized by the increasing intensity of mediation by intermediaries, crisis-driven policy transfer, the growing inter-referencing between different locales, and the accelerating velocity of policy learning (Clarke 2012; Peck and Theodore 2015, 3–4).

Closely related to the fast policy movement is 'selective learning'. That is, the learning tends to focus on policies and programs closely associated with fiscal pragmatism and other neoliberal precepts, and discourages scrutinizing the underlying ideological orientations of the policies (Peck 2001, 449). Learning also tends to be preoccupied with 'how-to pragmatism' (Peck 2002, 346), such as program design features, administrative routines, techniques, and even the slogans of specific programs (Peck 2002, 349). This type of selective learning takes on an ostensibly 'apolitical' or politically neutral form, although it actually furthers the normalization of neoliberal policy, and thus conforms to the general 'post-political' character of the neoliberal era (Peck 2001, 448; Swyngedouw 2011). In this process it is a daunting challenge for alternative, anti-neoliberal paradigms to be inserted into the major circuits of policy production, learning, and transfer.

There are certainly converging currents among policies implemented in different locales, but translocalization of neoliberal policies has also been uneven and variegated (Brenner, Peck, and Theodore 2010; Park, Hill and Saito 2012). This is because various neoliberal policies adopted by actors in specific locales only partially rework and mutate existing mechanisms (often exploiting them to their advantage), and do not alter the existing institutional landscapes in their entirety. However, Brenner, Peck, and Theodore (2010, 185) also note that successive sequences of neoliberalization in the last few decades have generated important cumulative impacts upon these uneven institutional landscapes, and that the 'uneven development of neoliberalization' in the 1980s across different locales was followed, in the 1990s, by a 'neoliberalization of uneven development'. The deepening of global neoliberalization, as such, has also been enabled by the 'growing inter-dependence, inter-referentiality and co-evolution' of neoliberal policies in the process of their circulation across different localities (Brenner, Peck, and Theodore 2010, 209). Therefore, while attending to how neoliberalization is variegated, path-dependently evolving, and multiple, locally contingent factors co-determine neoliberalization in particular places in the process of policy exchange, it is also important not to lose sight of how the unevenness of neoliberalization has been progressively re-patterned to form a broader neoliberal meta-regime across different locales.

On the other hand, some studies have examined the political, economic and social contexts out of which actors in non-Western locales opt to usher in culture-led developments. Kanai and Ortega-Alcázar (2009, 485), for instance, show how the popularity of culture-led urban regeneration in Latin America is the outcome of 'concurrent, contingent and often contradictory processes of democratization and neoliberalization'. Following political democratization and administrative decentralization, culture-led urban regeneration in Latin American cities emerged as one strategy of social development in disadvantaged areas that had been shorn of governmental subsidies for proper cultural resources. In cities like Mexico City, the culture-led urban regeneration was also expected to reinforce civic identities and the sense of belonging to the city through enhanced citizens' participation (Ibid., 487). Within these contexts, progressive social movements and grassroots activists in Latin American cities have taken up the initiatives of culture-led redevelopment, and have, on some occasions, been empowered by various public institutions to direct cultural policy towards socially inclusive goals (Ibid., 486). The cultural initiatives begun by these progressive groups, however, have been limited in their achievements. Their efforts were hindered as they were situated within the neoliberal context of limited public intervention, and these groups have, therefore, had to resort to the private sector, which transformed the process to make it congruent with the latter's interests. In addition, culture-oriented initiatives, even if developed by progressives with reformist objectives, have often been exploited to boost the competitiveness of cities at the expense of redistributive social goals and the empowerment of local cultural sectors (Ibid., 493).

The adoption of place marketing strategies among Korean scholars and policy makers has taken a similar trajectory. With democratization and administrative de-centralization in the mid-1990s and in scholarly objections to previous developmental statist urbanization, place marketing of locales was believed, especially among critical urbanists, to bring about an opportunity to develop the economic, social, and cultural capital of these locales. In the remainder of the chapter, I examine the mobilization of place marketing in Korea by this contingent of critical urbanists, local contexts that were facilitative of this mobilization, and the contradictory outcomes unfolding in Korean cities since their initiation.

2   The Emergence of Place Marketing in Korea

In 1995, in step with the increasing global popularity of neoliberal ideologies of decentralization and in response to democratization and associated regionalization of politics (Park BG 2008), the Korean central government introduced the local self-government system, whereby local politicians (e.g. mayors and local councilors) would be elected by local constituencies, contrary to the previous period in which they were appointed by the central government. The official initiation of the local self-government system triggered deliberations among economists, public policy academics, urban planners and geographers about what should be the priority policy of local governments in order to restore place identity among locals and most of all, to enhance the autonomy of local economies. Additionally, the slogan of globalization (*Segyehwa*) promoted by then president, Kim Young-Sam, added an urgency within local governments to build a city with global competitiveness. In accordance with the central government's championing of the culture industry as the new linchpin of national economic policy (Kang NH 2007), place marketing emerged as one of the prominent policy suggestions favored by these intellectuals. These intellectuals solicited local governments to pay renewed attention to each place's cultural assets, which, according to the former, had previously been neglected due to the central government's prioritization of industrialization (in a few privileged regions) during the developmental statist period. It was urged that places' cultural assets should be excavated, researched and marketed to improve their appeal to outsiders as well as to locals. As Kyoung Park (2002, 31) pointed out, place marketing surfaced among these intellectuals – among these 'place marketers' – as a panacea to the economic and social difficulties that local governments faced.

Quite a few local governments have implemented culture/tourism-oriented strategies since then.[3] The most popular strategies of place marketing were festivals in which cities' unique cultural artifacts, art forms, histories, traditions,

---

3   The ratio of budgets assigned to culture/arts among local governments reached 2.2% in 1996, whereas the ratio was 0.5% of the national budget (Cho 2000, 115).

vernacular cuisines or certain features of natural environments are featured (Cho 2000, 115; Paik 2006, 110). Creating symbolic landmarks, public spaces and cultural streets were also another popular strategy. In justifying the culture-oriented policies, place marketers argued that in the global milieu of inten-sifying inter-urban competition, creating culturally appealing environments and an associated 'quality of life' within places was important in enhancing the competitiveness of cities to global investors, private corporations and tour-ists (e.g. Lee HY 2005; Paik 2006; Park HS 2000). In the case of economically less developed cities, the primary goal of place marketing strategies has been to attract tourists (domestic or Chinese/Japanese/Taiwanese), as these local governments seriously lacked industrial/economic infrastructure, local capi-tal and professional expertise to allure global corporations or capital. Place marketers drew attention to the fact that locally based cultural strategies do not demand as prohibitive a sunk cost as other industrial investments would require, in the sense that it is primarily based on the cultural tradition, unique local ways of life and natural environment that already exist in a city (Park SH 1997). The Korean place marketing literature also repeatedly pointed out that with the post-Fordist and postmodern turn of global society, and as GDP had increased in major cities in Korea and in other East Asian countries, people in these countries were more interested in recreational and cultural enter-tainment and tourism, and therefore, cultural tourism, like many other post-industrial businesses, now promised a profitable future for cities. The same body of literature also contends that place marketing strategies would create a strong sense of belonging and local pride among locals, which would inculcate social capital among locals, and therefore amount to an ideal vehicle for per-fecting the local self-governance system.

As Bae-Gyoon Park (2010, 500) argues, place marketing in Korea was taken positively among many critical urbanists, as it was thought to help to restore a sense of community among locals and foster the cultural identities *embedded* in places, which had been neglected during the developmental statist urban-ization of the 1960s-80s – that is, economy-centric and central state led author-itarian urbanization. Developmental statist urbanization was now replaced with a culture-oriented paradigm, the latter of which was (perceived to be) more locally based, and therefore more humane and even democratic (e.g. Lee MY 2006, 34). The culture-oriented paradigm, 'place marketers' argued, would provide local actors with public spheres of reflexivity (if enacted properly), in which different local actors communicate with each other to establish the identity of a place (e.g. Lee HY 2005; Paik 2006, 109). Place marketing, it was argued, would provide locals with the power to shape the cultural, social and economic future of their city, and foster endogenous development. This was why place marketers saw place marketing as a potential instance of participatory democracy in the era of local autonomy (e.g. Chun and Shin 2004, 32–33; Jung 1999). This approach was in particular espoused by the younger generation of urbanists and geographers, who had studied among themselves critical and/or contemporary versions of Western urban theories (e.g. Marxist and postmodern urban theories), partly in protest to what they considered to be the apolitical curriculum offered at universities that focused on traditional Area Studies or quantitative spatial science type paradigms. The progressive minded student-run *Space and Environment Research Group* (SERG, *Kongkan-hwankyung-Yeonkuhoe*) that was based at Seoul National University (SNU), which the author was part of, led the trend. The graduate students primarily from Geography, Geographical Education and the Faculty of Environmental Studies at SNU that participated in SERG were deeply inspired by the Western place marketing literature in the early to mid 1990s.[4]

Like some urbanists in the West, who endorsed culture-led revitalization as a local development paradigm that would liberate urban vernacular cultures from suppressive modern planning, there was a general consensus among these would-be place marketers in the SERG over the progressive effects of place marketing, and conviction that place marketing would be one of the core urban paradigms in the post-developmental state period.[5] Certainly this younger generation – including the author – was aware, and actually studied, how place marketing as a neoliberal urban paradigm in the West had ushered in racialized and gendered disparity in various locales, and intensified the brutal mechanism of inter-urban competition at a global scale (e.g. Koo 2004; Lee HY 2005; Lee MY 2006, 8). However, while they (or we) would resist the form of neoliberalism that absolutely prioritized the market force over social considerations, place marketing strategies that prioritized the cultural embeddedness and the importance of 'place' (as supposed to abstract 'space') was taken as a benign form of market approach that would bring substantial benefits to the local majority. In other words, it can be said that these place marketers as 'social entrepreneurs' pursued the *progressive competitiveness* of places, and translated the otherwise neoliberal 'fast policy', such as place marketing, in a more progressive way. This was the reason why student members of SERG also

---

4   Many authors of the literature that I examine in this paper are also former members of the SERG.

5   Doucette (2016) defines the post-developmental state period in Korea as one when social formations that coalesced under the developmental state in the 1960s to 1980s were restructured and the central state's power decentered (although its power is still strong in some sectors), through the processes of democratization and neoliberalization that took place from the late 1980s to early 1990s.

vigorously looked into the theory of what was called 'social marketing', developed among Dutch scholars (e.g. Kotler 1971), in which social inclusiveness was set as a crucial principle of place marketing (see Koo 2004, 217; Lee HY 2005).

After completing their degrees these young critical urbanist students entered various government research institutes as researchers, including local government-subsidiary research institutes. From that time on, this became quite a normal career path for students in urban studies and geography, one the author also took.[6] At that time, their belief in the progressive and humane possibility of place marketing became the foundation of the policy direction that they proposed to local governments. As these institutes were more practice- and policy-oriented, there was not much room for critiques of place marketing, and researchers focused instead on studying pragmatic strategies for implementing place-marketing programs. Various research reports and academic articles authored by these researchers (many of who were former SERG students) voiced that if places cannot delink themselves from 'place wars' and 'place auctions' coming from the growing global competitive pressures, then it would make more sense that places try their best to respond to this pressure and succeed in it, but in a more locally based and humane way (Lee JH 2008, fn. 3; Lee SY 2009; Paik 2006, 109). Therefore, they opined that denouncing place marketing as merely a neoliberal policy would not help (Lee MY 2006). Jeong-Hoon Lee (2008, fn. 3) further contended that the criticism of place marketing was simply an academic distraction, and that when policy makers think through local policy fields they should develop a worldview based on practice rather than academic theory.

In this sense, it can be said that the emergence and popularization of place marketing in Korea was an embodied process, in which these particular actors' worldviews and aspirations for local autonomy and democracy were pursued through a neoliberal fast policy of place marketing, readily available as the standard best practice for these actors. In hindsight, this approach among critical urbanists to place marketing could also find a parallel with the broader liberal turn of the former progressive activists in the period of post-democratization in Korea. Those who had previously fought against the military authoritarian governments gradually embraced the 'softer' form of a free market system from the 1990s, in which principles of liberty, cultural consumption and creativity were celebrated (Kang NH 2007), or liberal economic paradigms prioritizing

---

6 Since the early to mid 1990s, research institutes for different municipal governments have been established to support local autonomy system and policy-making processes among local politicians.

the reform of the past politico-economic machine to usher in a freer form of market economy (Doucette 2015).

3   Policy Learning

The place marketers from SERG consistently advocated a more locally embedded and socially inclusive place marketing – which distinguished them from the place marketing strategies developed by experts in the fields of Public Administration, Economics and Business Administration, that had a more uncompromising, pro-market orientation (e.g. Park HS 2000; Yeom 2010). However, it is not difficult to spot commonalities between these two groups of place marketers, as this section later reveals.

The process of place marketing, which originated in Western cities, was adopted and implemented in Korea may best be described as 'voluntary' and 'competitive', as opposed to a coerced process. In the voluntary and competitive process, policy intermediaries actively benchmark the non-local policies and seek to apply them to their places, without explicit political pressure by non-local implementers, such as the IMF and World Bank. These intermediaries primarily respond to the external competitive pressure that places are situated within, and frame the solutions for urban problems according to the competition ideologies that this environment has naturalized. In other words, this external environment has disciplined Korean urbanists to 'voluntarily' defer to the policies that embody these ideologies.

Korean urbanists learned place marketing policies by studying academic/policy documents of model cities, participating in relevant conferences, consulting with model cities' technocrats and other experts, and often making business trips to these cities. While Korean place marketing may have been developed as a coalescence of 'multiple elsewhere' (Mbembé and Nuttall 2004 cited in Robinson 2015; 833), Western cities were certainly the most favored models among place marketers (Shin HR and Stevens 2013, fn.8).[7] This is especially true, on the one hand, of cities that have developed place marketing strategies as a response to the declining urban economy after deindustrialization, such as Glasgow, Edinburgh, Ipswich, Manchester and London (esp. Dockland) in the UK and Pittsburg and Oregon in the US, and, on the other hand, European 'cultural' cities such as Bilbao and Bologna (Lee HJ 2001; Lee

---

7   As McCann (2011, 121-2) explains, the reason why certain cities have risen as 'models' has much to do with the uneven access that different cities have to various resources that enable these cities to articulate their policies more widely.

HY 2005; Lee MY 2006; Paik 2006; Yeom 2010). Japanese cities with successful and popular cultural festivals and historic districts were also frequently emulated (Chun and Shin 2004; Lee HJ 2001; Paik 2006). Drawing upon the marketing theory developed in economics and MBA programs, policy learning tended to revolve around the following: what place marketing is constitutive of, e.g. visions, goals, consumer market surveys, competitors surveys, marketing mixes, organizations for execution, place brands, publicity channels, promotion, sales strategies and public private partnerships (Lee HJ 2001; Lee MY 2006; Lee SY 2009; Park HS 2000); typologies of different place marketing strategies (Lee MY 2006; Paik 2006); city slogans and brands, unique brand identities and linkages between branding, place making and development of human resources (Lee JH 2008); strategies to develop distinctive and unique place contents and niche markets (Chun and Shin 2004; Lee SY 2009; Paik 2006); place marketing evaluation criteria (Paik 2006); strategic market management and branding efforts (Yeom 2010); and development of backward and forward linkages of place marketing programs (Chun and Shin 2004).

It is quite striking to discover how these research reports and academic articles repeatedly make similar points and inter-reference each other to the point that they look like replicas of one another (whether it is one authored by former SERG members or scholars based in Public Administration, MBA or economics programs). The same was observed in these authors' suggestions of how to enact a successful place marketing strategy. Almost all these works concur that to be successful in place marketing each place should engage in the following acts: create unique cultural items and programs, and turn places into distinct assets (Lee HJ 2001; Paik 2006); these cultural items and programs should be strongly embedded in places and carry the authenticity of the place (especially, Lee MY 2006); place marketing should be planned and implemented through collaborative social networks and public and private partnerships (the private not only including businesses, but also local residents and especially cultural creatives in locales) (Cho 2000; Lee HJ 2001); local governments should be entrepreneurial and aggressively seek to create markets and demand (Park HS 2000); governments should be open-minded, their organizational structures and expertise should be professionalized, and they should support cultural initiatives by civil society (Cho 2000; Lee MY 2006); the developed items and programs should be implemented with institutional, spatial and economic sustainability (Paik 2006); and, economic and social effects should be maximized, and evaluation criteria should be established (Paik 2006).

The redistributive injustice and commodification of cultures associated with place marketing and related popular struggles that have occurred in 'model' cities are also mentioned in this body of literature, but these are mostly treated as a sidebar, and it is hard to find serious interrogations of these struggles. More interestingly, a number of authors cite Kearns and Philo (1993) (e.g. Chun and Shin 2004; Lee HY 2005; Paik 2006) or Hall and Hubbard (1998) (Lee JH 2008) – both of which are critical examinations of place marketing. But the majority of these authors only cite them to provide definitions of place marketing or simply to point out that place marketing emerged out of the deindustrialization experienced in the West during the 1980s. Ironically, Jeong-Hoon Lee (2008, 874) cites them, but only to conclude with the normative urgency of introducing an entrepreneurial turn in the Korean local governance system. These are perhaps the most apt examples of what Peck (2001) calls 'selective learning'.

The authors of these Korean place marketing works also make the ambiguous argument that cultural infrastructure provisioned through place marketing policies would eventually benefit everyone in the locale, including disenfranchised populations (Lee HJ 2001). They also often assert that well-established public-private-civil society networking would help to prevent marginalization of already marginalized groups in places (Lee MY 2006). More recently, culture-focused redevelopments have been articulated to, and packaged as a critical component of, the 'social economy', in which, advocates assert, culture can contribute to job creation especially for young local creatives and increase local social and cultural capital (Yuk forthcoming, 4). Worse still, illustrating place marketing strategies implemented in cities like Liverpool and San Francisco, Heung-Jae Lee (2001) argues that place marketing contributed to the demolition of eyesore ghettos, and that despite this demolition that must have displaced underclass populations, in the case of San Francisco the city achieved a unity among the different residents as the place marketing strategies successfully elicited the participation of local artists in the process. This shows how for certain place marketers, gentrification, even when leading to displacement, was taken as a benefit of place marketing.

4   The Unfolding Contradictions of Place Marketing in Korea

Since the mid-1990s when place marketing started to be widely implemented by local governments, locals have debated about the commodification of cultures involved in place marketing programs. Criticisms were raised over the promotion of manufactured cultures that, some locals perceived, were unrelated to the identity of specific places (Lee SY 2009, 90). Even when vernacular cultures and traditions were mobilized, they were limited to a few among a wide range of lived cultures in those places, a few that were deemed fit for commodification. Since a main goal of place marketing is to enhance the place's image, the selected cultures and traditions should not only resonate with a positive image, but also ideally an apolitical one, as political images of a place would narrow the possible types of tourists that a place can attract, and also shut out private capital's interests in the place. Such selectivity has become a prominent controversy in Kwangju, a city that has been known for its democratic movements and, more specifically, the 1980 Kwangju uprising against the military government, in which 165 people were killed by the government's army. From 1995, the Kwangju local government started to host Kwangju Biennale with a focus on fine art, but art related to the city's resistant history was excluded there. In response, *Minjung* artists[8] hosted an Anti-Biennale, where they attempted to rework the identity of the city by circulating images of what they perceived to be a *true* history of the city against those circulated by the Biennale organizing body (Shin HR 2004). Kwangju's case resonates with some of the place marketing practices in the Western cities that experienced deindustrialization, such as Glasgow in Scotland, where the local government promoted the 'city of culture' campaign and sought to erase the city's well-known identity associated with a history of a militant working class (Tretter 2009).

This type of place marketing strategy is problematic as it promotes cultures that are compatible with pro-market directives (like high-end fine arts that are politically less sensitive). It is also problematic because it reifies the notion of place and culture, and represents place as something fixed and closed for the purpose of commodification rather than positing it as a process (Park BG 2010). Additionally, place marketers' idealization of place marketing as a site of democracy, in which locals discuss the cultural identity of the place, has proved to be misleading. For example, in Ha-hoe Village in the city of An-dong, one of the officially designated Traditional Folk Villages, villagers problematized the process in which the identity of the place is reified into two tourism-oriented commodities, such as 'Ha-hoe Mask' and 'Ha-hoe Byul-shin Exorcism' (Noh 2007). Furthermore, the village has also painfully witnessed the rise of cutthroat competition among local residents who sought to profit by maximizing the commercialization of traditional festivals and patented commodities related to the village's traditions. Villagers voiced that such commercialization gradually defiled the sense of community among the villagers.

In my own master's thesis research on festivals in the city of Chun-cheon (Hae 1999), some festival organizers – who were mostly local artists – protested

---

8   *Minjung* refers to 'people', and *Minjung* artists produce political and resistant art that represents (the history of) people's struggles against governments and corporations in South Korea.

the local government's constant demand to increase the commercial viability of the festivals at the expense of artistic quality and community involvement. There were also persistent conflicts between local- and Seoul-based artists and cultural creatives, both of whom were involved in organizing local festivals in Chun-cheon. Seoul-based artists and cultural creatives were very often favored and empowered by the local government that was funding these festivals, as the former were deemed to possess a more professional cultural capital and a capacity for higher profit-making.[9] Place marketers' claim that local 'cultural renaissance' would be enabled by place marketing has been contradicted in these ways.

On the other hand, place marketers' call for a cultural renaissance does not clearly point out how this renaissance would also lead to enhancing the welfare of citizens at the local scale, especially when the Korean economy and society has been increasingly neoliberalized. Place marketers largely confine their discussions to the enhancement of 'cultural welfare', in the sense that place marketing would improve cultural infrastructure, public space and quality of life that local residents can now avail themselves of (Koo 2004, 222; Lee HJ 2001, 14). However, place marketers do not explain how enhanced cultural welfare would be translated into economic and social justice at the local scale (e.g. Lee JH 2008, 888). There is also no consideration of how the produced sense of place identity may elide forms of class consciousness that vary across different class fractions.

In Seoul, which increasingly saw a widening disparity between different classes of people, the local government's drive for place marketing and the beautification of urban space was coupled with expanding gentrification, the displacement of lower income households (Kwon 1994; Shin HB 2009) and the pricing-out of vernacular cultural institutions (Kim 2015). This was further paired with the local government's prohibition of political assembly in beautified public spaces, such as Seoul Square (Seoul Kwang-jang), showing how beautified landscapes can be used for the purpose of political control. Despite the increasing roll-back policies regarding the city's poor, the Seoul government engaged in branding efforts for the city, such as creating the logo of 'Hi Seoul', whose example is vigorously pursued by other local governments in Korea. The Seoul municipal government has also been funding artists to paint murals on dilapidated houses in rundown shantytowns, which have

---

9   According to Yuk (forthcoming, 3), Seoul, which in 2012 accounted for 19.2% of the whole population of Korea, had 50.1% of all cultural workers in the nation. Seoul is the capital of the cultural industry in Korea in terms of the size of the creative labor and the professional expertise of this labor.

invited an increasing number of curious 'tourists' visiting these neighbor-hoods to see the murals. This tourification of poverty increased the level of discontent among shantytown residents, and residents in some of these neigh-borhoods even mobilized themselves to erase all the murals painted in their neighborhoods.

In less affluent local governments that have been heavily dependent upon the central government's transfer fund and have suffered from a lack of interest from external private capital, the culture-oriented policies and place market-ing have been also used as a 'display politics' of newly elected local politicians (Chun and Shin 2004, 39), which further worsened fiscal balances (Park K 2002, 11). That is, politicians are using cultural revitalization in order to project an impression among residents that something positive has been done by these politicians for the benefit of local residents. For this ideological project, cul-tural festivals have been organized when it is politically convenient to do so, and often take on a crude commercial character without involving a wider participation among local residents. Local residents became a spectator of this spectacle, and were devoid of productive agency over these festivals (Cho 2000, 116; Lee SY 2009, 89). It is also frequently observed that, in order to pay back the local landed capital (*Toho*) that has been the most important politi-cal contributors to election campaigns of elected politicians, these politicians have created construction projects under the name of place marketing, such as the construction of new cultural amenities, or related culture/knowledge industry complex (Kang JY 2015; Park K 2002).

Some place marketers contended that the reason why some place marketing programs at the local scale failed is because of the locale's heavy dependence on the central government's local transfer (Park K 2002, 30), the absence of en-trepreneurial, long-term thinking among government officials and politicians (Chun and Shin 2004), and the replication of similar cultural items and pro-grams across different locales (Chun and Shin 2004, 41; Lee HY 2005, 36; Lee JH 2008, 876; Paik 2006), as well as crony capitalist liaisons between local politi-cians and the landed class. As a solution to these problems, these place market-ers have called for a more entrepreneurial, creative and free market approach and privatization (e.g. Chu 1998; Chun and Shin 2004, 43; for the critique of this approach, see Park K 2002, 11, 31), in which private capitals and corporations are actively sought after by effective and transparent local government machines. Place marketers have rarely pointed out how place marketing is often coupled with the governmental rollback of welfare services and the subsequent dispar-ity among different classes of locales (and act as an ideological mask for this disparity), as well as trigger gentrification (Yuk forthcoming, 9).

5 Conclusion

It is hard to conclude that place marketing presented a hopeful framework for local democracy, as place marketing has not necessarily assured the democratic process in which locals are empowered to meaningfully participate and deliberate over the future of their own places. Defining the image of a place has been influenced by considerations of market feasibility and political calculation, and alienated a good portion of local residents both in planning processes and from economic and social benefits of place marketing programs. In this chapter, based on both place marketing literature and my own past experience as a place marketer, I examined the political economic and institutional contexts (i.e. the post-developmental statist turn of Korean political economy) that were facilitative of the adoption of place marketing among scholars and policy makers in Korea. While the arrival of place marketing in Korea was a conjunctural outcome of particular changes in Korean political economy and institutions in the mid-1990s, place marketing as was implemented in different places in the past two decades has generated a maelstrom of contradictions similar (if not identical) to those faced by neoliberalizing Western cities that have implemented culture-oriented regeneration policies.

It is worth noting how in this process formerly critical urbanists, including myself, became unlikely participants on this place marketing bandwagon, and how they saw reformist potential from place marketing strategies and conceived it as a 'new' paradigm that would transcend the problems generated by the urbanization of previous decades. While this faction of urbanists as 'policy entrepreneur[s]' (Mintrom 1997, cited in McCann 2011, 114) have continued to study and pursue other versions of culture-oriented strategies since the 2000s – including the Creative City paradigm (e.g. Lee JH, 2008, 886; see also Yuk forthcoming) – a group of dissident, activist urbanists who have been opposed to neoliberal urbanization in Korea has also increasingly turned their attention to an alternative knowledge circuit. These latter urbanists have looked into approaches such as 'the right to the city', and started to debate how the activist inspiration associated with this paradigm could be rethought and reworked in the Korean context. While this recent move provides a hopeful glimpse into the fields of urban movement activisms in Korea, whether the alternative, resistant movements can succeed will depend upon the organizational capacity of these activist scholars, their solidarity with grassroots activists, and active participation in progressive international circuits of alternative knowledge production and formation of international solidarity with actors in other places.

Acknowledgements

I thank the participants of the panel session of the 2016 Inter-Asia Connection conference, where this chapter was originally presented. Without their stimulating questions and encouraging comments, it may not have survived. My tremendous thanks also go to the editors of this book, Jamie Doucette and Bae-Gyoon Park, who read my manuscript many times and helped me refine my arguments.

References

Brenner, NJ Peck and N Theodore 2010 "Variegated Neoliberalization: Geographies, Modalities Pathways", *Global Networks* 10 (2): 182–222.

Cho, MR 2000 "Cultural Economy and Cultural Urban Planning." [In Korean.] *Journal of Urban Studies* 6: 115–130.

Chu, MH 1998 "The Development of Event Tourism in the Case of Namdo Food Festival at Nakan." [In Korean.] *Journal of the Korean Geographical Society* 33(2): 339–351.

Chun, SW, and YC Shin 2004. "Changso Marketing-eul Tonghan Chibangdoshi-eui Pal-cheon-eh Kwanhan Yeonkoo (A Study of the Development of Cities through Place Marketing)." [In Korean.] *Korean Policy Sciences Review* 8(1): 26–45.

Clarke, N 2012 "Urban Policy Mobility, Anti-politics, and Histories of the Transnational Municipal Movement." *Progress in Human Geography* 36(1): 25–43.

Doucette, J 2015 "Debating Economic Democracy in South Korea: The Costs of Commensurability." *Critical Asian Studies* 47(3): 388–413.

Doucette, J 2016 "The Post-developmental State: Economic and Social Changes since 1997." In *Routledge Handbook of Modern Korean History*, edited by Michael J. Seth, 343–356. London: Routledge/Taylor & Francis Group.

Ellis, C S, and A Bochner 2000 "Autoethnography, Personal Narrative, Reflexivity: Researcher as Subject." In *Handbook of Qualitative Research*, 2nd Edition, edited by Norman K. Denzin, and Yvonna S Lincoln, 733–68. Thousand Oaks, CA: SAGE Publications.

Florida, RL 2004 *The Rise of the Creative Class: And How It's Transforming Work, Leisure, Community and Everyday life*. New York, NY: Basic Books.

Hae, L (as Heyman) 1999 "Festivals in Chun-chon and Place Marketing: Conflicts among Participating Agents." [In Korean.] Master's thesis, Seoul National University.

Hae, L 2012 *The Gentrification of Nightlife and the Right to the City: Regulating Spaces of Social Dancing in New York City*. New York, NY: Routledge.

Hahn, YJ and L Hae 2001 "The 2002 World Cup and City Marketing." *Journal of the Korean Regional Science Association* 17(1): 91–109.

Hall, Tand Hubbard P, (eds.) 1998 *The Entrepreneurial City: Geographies of Politics, Regime, and Representation*. Chichester: John Wiley and Sons.

Harvey, D 1989 "From Managerialism to Entrepreneurialism: The Transformation of Urban Governance in Late Capitalism." *Geografiska Annaler* 71(B): 3–17.

Harvey, D 2003 "The Art of Rent: Globalization, Monopoly and the Commodification of Culture." In *Socialist Register 2002: A World of Contradictions*, edited by Leo Panitch and Colin Leys, 93-110. Toronto: Fernwood Books Ltd.

Holcomb, B1993 "Revisioning Place: De-and Re-constructing the Image of the Industrial City." In *Selling Places: The City as Cultural Capital, Past and Present*, edited by Gerard Kearns and Chris Philo, 133–144. Oxford [England]: Pergamon Press.

Jung, KS, (ed.) 1999 *Chukje, Minjujueui, Chiyeok Hwalsunghwa (Festival, Democracy and Local Revitalisation)*. [In Korean.] Seoul: Saegil.

Kanai, M and I. Ortega-Alcázar 2009 "The Prospects for Progressive Culture led Urban Regeneration in Latin America: Cases from Mexico City and Buenos Aires." *International Journal of Urban and Regional Research* 33(2): 483–501.

Kang, JY 2015 "The Local Embeddedness of Stateness: The Rise of Construction-State and the Evolvement of Growth-Coalition in Korea." [In Korean.] *Society and History* 105: 319–355.

Kang, NH 2007 "The Cultural Movement in the Age of Neoliberalism: Its History and Tasks." [In Korean.] *Marxism21* 4(1): 278-303.

Kearns, G and C Philo, (eds.) 1993 *Selling Places: The City as Cultural Capital, Past and Present*. Oxford: Pergamon Press.

Kim, SA 2015 "Shingaebaljueui-wha Gentrification (Neodevelopmentalism and Gentrification)." [In Korean.] *Hwanghae Review* 86: 43–59.

Koo, DH 2004 "Place Marketing as an Urban Cultural Strategy and Quality of Life." [In Korean.] *The Geographical Journal of Korea* 38(3): 215–226.

Kotler, P and G Zaltman 1971 "Social Marketing: An Approach to Planned Social Change." *The Journal of Marketing* 35(3): 3–12.

Kwon, TJ 1994 "Localization of Politics vis-à-vis Globalization of Economy." [In Korean.] *Journal of Environmental Studies* 32: 1–13.

Lee, HJ 2001 "Doshi-wha Changsopanchok (Cities and Place Promotion)." [In Korean.] *Urban Affairs* 36(394): 11–20.

Lee, HY 2005 "The Meaning of Place Marketing and its Vitalization for Regional Studies in the Era of Globalization." [In Korean.] *Journal of the Korean Urban Geographical Society* 8(2): 35–53.

Lee, JH 2008 "A Theoretical Review on Place Branding as a Major Toolkit of Soft Regional Development." [In Korean.] *Journal of the Korean Geographical Society* 43(6): 873–893.

Lee, MY 2006 *Place Marketing Strategy, New Paradigm of Regional Development*. [In Korean.] Seoul: Non-Hyong.

Lee, SY 2009 "Implementing the Place Marketing Strategy in the Rural Development Projects." [In Korean.] *Journal of The Korean Regional Development Association* 21 (3): 71–101.

Lees, L, T Slater, and E Wyly 2007 "Gentrification: Positive or Negative?" In their *Gentrification*, 194–236. New York, NY; Routledge/Taylor and Francis Group.

Ley, D 1996 *The New Middle Class and the Remaking of the Central City*. Oxford: Oxford University Press.

MacLeod, G 2002 "From Urban Entrepreneurialism to a 'Revanchist City'? On the Spatial Injustices of Glasgow's Renaissance. *Antipode* 34(3): 602–24.

Mbembé, A, and S Nuttall 2004. "Writing the world from an African metropolis." *Public Culture* 16(3): 347–372.

McCann, EJ 2008 "Expertise, Truth, and Urban Policy Mobilities: Global Circuits of Knowledge in the Development of Vancouver, Canada's 'Four Pillar' Drug Strategy." *Environment and Planning A* 40(4): 885–904.

McCann, E 2011 "Urban Policy Mobilities and Global Circuits of Knowledge: Toward a Research Agenda." *Annals of the Association of American Geographers* 101(1): 107–130.

Mele, C 2000 *Selling the Lower East Side: Culture, Real Estate, and Resistance in New York City*. Minneapolis, MN: University of Minnesota Press.

Mintrom, M 1997 "Policy entrepreneurs and the diffusion of innovation." *American journal of political science* 41(3): 738–770.

Mitchell, D 2003 *The Right to the City: Social Justice and the Fight for Public Space*. New York: Guilford Press.

Noh, YS 2007 "A Study of Cultural Tourism of Traditional Folk Village: The Cases of Ha-hwe, Whe-am, and Nakan-eupseong Village." [In Korean.] PhD diss., Seoul National University.

Paik, SH 2006 "The Aims and Elements of Regional Festivals as an Urban Cultural Strategy: Based on the Comparative Analysis of Regional Festivals in the US, Japan and Korea." [In Korean.] *The Geographical Journal of Korea* 40(1): 107–125.

Park, BG 2008 "Uneven Development, Inter-scalar Tensions, and the Politics of Decentralization in South Korea." *International Journal of Urban and Regional Research* 32 (1): 40–59.

Park, BG 2010 "Place Marketing and Territorialization of Place: A Critique of the Essentialist Notion of Place". [In Korean.] *Journal of the Economic Geographical Society of Korea* 13(3): 498–513.

Park, BG, R Child Hill, and A Saiton 2012 *Locating Neoliberalism in East Asia: Neoliberalizing Spaces in Developmental States*. Hoboken: Wiley-Blackwell.

Park, HS 2000 "City Marketing as a New Managerial Tool." [In Korean.] *Chung-Ang Public Administration Review* 14(2): 239–258.

Park, K 2002 "Chibang-chachi Yi-hu Shin-chiyeok-jeong-chaek-eui Doyip-shiltae-wha Dae-an-jeok Cheollyak (The Problems of New Regional Policy after Local Autonomy

System and Alternative Strategies).” [In Korean.] *Economy and Society* 53 (Spring): 10–35.

Park, SH 1997 “Kyonggi-do Chukje-wha Event-eui Segyehwa Cheollyak (Kyonggi-do Festivals and the Globalisation Strategies of Events).” [In Korean.] *Kyonggi 21 Se-gi.* July-August: 9–25.

Peck, J 2001 “Neoliberalizing States: Thin Policies/Hard Outcomes.” *Progress in Human Geography* 25(3): 445–455.

Peck, J 2002 “Political Economies of Scale: Fast Policy, Interscalar Relations, and Neo-liberal Workfare.” *Economic Geography* 78(3): 331–360.

Peck, J 2005 “Struggling with the Creative Class.” *International Journal of Urban and Regional Research* 29(4): 740–770

Peck, J and N Theodore 2010a. “Mobilizing Policy: Models, Methods, and Mutations.” *Geoforum* 41(2): 169–174.

Peck, J and N Theodore 2010b “Recombinant Workfare, across the America: Transnationalizing ‘Fast’ Social Policy.” *Geoforum* 41(2): 195–208.

Peck, J and N Theodore 2015 *Fast Policy: Experimental Statecraft at the Thresholds of Neoliberalism.* Minneapolis, MN: University of Minnesota Press.

Robinson, J 2015 “‘Arriving at’ urban policies: The topological spaces of urban policy mobility.” *International Journal of Urban and Regional Research* 39(4): 831–834.

Shin, HB 2009 “Property-based Redevelopment and Gentrification: The Case of Seoul, South Korea.” *Geoforum* 40(5): 906–917.

Shin, HR 2004 “Cultural Festivals and Regional Identities in South Korea.” *Environment and Planning D: Society and Space* 22(4): 619–632.

Shin, HR and S Stevens 2013 “How Culture and Economy Meet in South Korea: The Politics of Cultural Economy in Culture-led Urban Regeneration.” *International Journal of Urban and Regional Research* 37 (5): 1707–1723

Swyngedouw, E 2011 “Interrogating Post-democratization: Reclaiming Egalitarian Political Spaces.” *Political Geography* 30(7): 370–380.

Taylor, KY 2016 *From #BlackLivesMatter to Black liberation.* Chicago, Illinois: Haymarket Books.

Teo, P 2003 “The Limits of Imagineering: A Case Study of Penang.” *International Journal of Urban and Regional Research* 27(3): 545–563.

Tretter, EM 2009 “The Cultures of Capitalism: Glasgow and the Monopoly of Culture.” *Antipode* 41(1): 111–132.

Ward, K 2006 “‘Policies in Motion’, Urban Management and State Restructuring: The Trans-local Expansion of Business Improvement Districts.” *International Journal of Urban and Regional Research* 30(1): 54–75.

Ward, S 1998 *Selling Places: The Marketing and Promotion of Towns and Cities, 1850–2000.* London: E & FN Spon.

Yeoh, B SA 2005 "The Global Cultural City? Spatial Imagineering and Politics in the (Multi) Cultural Marketplaces of South-east Asia." *Urban Studies* 42(5-6): 945–958.

Yeom, MB 2010 "Local Brand Value and Local Public Finance." [In Korean.] *The Korea Regional Economic Review* 16: 107–140.

Yuk, JW Forthcoming "Creating a Niche, Building a Community: A Case Study of Young Small-scale Creative Workers in Daegu, South Korea." *International Journal of Cultural Policy*, 1–13. https://doi.org/10.1080/10286632.2017.1343308

Zukin, S 1982 *Loft Living: Culture and Capital in Urban Change.* New Brunswick, NJ: Rutgers University Press.

CHAPTER 15

Fashioning the City: Trans-Pacific and Inter-Asian Connections in the Global Garment Industry

Christina Moon

1   Introduction

A couple of years ago, I was invited to speak at the Korean Apparel Manufacturing Association meetings in Seoul in my capacity as Director of the Fashion Studies program at Parsons, the design school I teach at in New York.[1] I was asked to speak of the rise of New York as a global fashion capital, and approached the talk naively, without realizing that there were government officials and policy makers in the room. The audience was interested in understanding how fashion was going to change the city of Seoul, bring in foreign investment and cultivate an image of Seoul as a global cultural center and symbol of modernity across Asia and beyond. The large audience asked questions on how the fashion industries in Seoul and New York were going to grow economically in the next ten, twenty years. Local business owners and associations from the local garment district were listening closely, anxious to learn what was at stake and how these changes to the city and manufacturing would affect the fragile ecosystem of design and labor in which they worked, in an area of the city that was fast disappearing.

I approached the talk through the lens of the history of the New York fashion industry. I narrated a key moment in New York in the 1970s that framed the historical, social and cultural changes that occurred within the last thirty years in the garment district – a period when multiple forces intensified the city's deindustrialization. At the same time the city's economic, political, and social powers transformed the city from a manufacturing hub to an iconic fashion city. Most people think of New York's transformation into a global fashion capital

---

1   I would like to thank those I have interviewed in the Los Angeles Jobber Market for my continuing research. I would also like to thank the editors of this volume Jamie Doucette and Bae-Gyoon Park for bringing together scholars in a SSRC funded workshop and for this special publication. Finally, I thank my fashion studies colleagues including the Fashion Praxis Working Group at Parsons; the India China Institute, Spatial Politics of Work at The New School; and the New School's Graduate Institute of Design, Ethnography, and Social Thought for continued support of this research.

as an overnight success. In truth the development of its fashion industry was part of the broader urban development ethos that changed the cultural identity of the metropolis in the following three decades. From the working class to the luxury high-class, from low culture to high culture, from manual labor to design, branding, and marketing, the meta-narrative of a transition "from garments to fashion" has indeed helped promote urban development in contemporary New York and help it to stylize itself as a global city, but it is also a narrative often at the disadvantage of working communities. Furthermore, this shift has also been the result of an inter-twined urban and industrial history linking the US fashion industry and garment and manufacturing centers in Asia from the 1970s onwards. Diasporic communities, in particular have placed an instrumental role in the shaping and development of fashion economies within and between the cities of New York, LA, Seoul, and Guangzhou.

In what ways has garment manufacturing in Asia shaped the transformation of the US garment industry into the creative fashion economy that it is known for today? It highlights the transformative role that fashion plays in urban development in cities and rural areas across the US and Asia, revealing how developmental forms of urbanization in Asia have been tightly connected to urban histories elsewhere, and in ways that invoke ongoing post-colonial and Cold War legacies. To do so, it highlights two important questions: 1) How has garment industrialization in Asia (in the development of earlier garment industrial districts, and zonal and industrial histories among East Asian tiger economies) informed, influenced, and cultivated the fashion economies in cities such as New York and Los Angeles, which are known as US fashion capitals today? 2) What effect does the continued development of fashion have on the transformations and geography of urban areas in Asia and beyond? In the contemporary moment, cities such as Hong Kong, Shenzhen, Shanghai, and Seoul are eager to both promote and upgrade their fashion culture industries and creative economies with the establishment of fashion weeks, fashion schools and programs, design centers, and "incubator" programs. In an era of hyper-mobile capital and heightened inter-urban competition, fashion is transforming the urban landscape and geography of the city. Understanding fashion's industrial histories – its role in the development of industrial districts and zones, the migration of fashion workers, and cultural intermediaries in the form of (Korean) diaspora – is thus important for grasping its continued legacy in shaping American and Asian cities.

The first section examines the role of fashion in New York's development as a global city. I then explore the role of garments in shaping urban development in Asia throughout the 1960s and 1970s. The following section then looks at the trans-Pacific and inter-Asian legacies of the fashion city, where diasporic communities became crucial to linking manufacturing in China with American and European investment capital, and consumers in the Global North. I specifically examine fast-fashion in Los Angeles and the familial logics of fashion. Finally, I discuss the refashioning of Asian cities through inter-urban competition in the fashion circuit, a process that has real material and economic consequences for the transformations of the urban landscape. Multi-sited and across cities and histories, I show how the inter-Asian and trans-Pacific migration of fashion workers have a continued legacy in shaping American and Asian cities in an intertwined and unexpected ways.

2   Fashioning the Global City

New York of the 1980s was the site of seemingly opposite economic forces to those fuelling rapid urbanization in East Asia. The city was undergoing deindustrialization, which nearly phased out all of its local manufacturing industries. To stem the flow, City governments across the U.S. began to look towards the development of its creative economies to replace manufacturing. This was also a key moment for New York's local business, political elites, and Wall Street financiers to capitalize on the reimagining and remaking a city they thought was inefficiently run by unionized middle-class workers (Moody, 2007). Embracing the tenets of free market individualism, privatization and deregulation of all industries (as espoused by Ronald Reagan and Margaret Thatcher of those times), new alliances flourished between real estate development, finance, tourism and fashion, which would put forth agendas that fostered the use of public funds towards private efforts and profit. Powerful local finance and real estate lobbies, including advocacy groups such as The Association for a Better New York (ABNY) emerged from this era, establishing enormous tax breaks for businesses which borrowed public funds originally set aside for housing, job training, and transportation. This money subsidized instead private offices and high-end residential real estate development in Manhattan (Greenberg, 2008).

Central to these lobbies was the idea that the city's cultural image abroad needed rebranding in order to stimulate business growth, protect financial markets, and increase real estate value in New York. Fashion would become a powerful tool throughout the 1980s and 1990s as a collaborative effort between elites, corporate media and advertising firms to "rebrand" the city for outside business travelers, convention goers, international tourists, and affluent elites. The most famous local New York fashion designers of the 1980s/1990s, including Bill Blass, Geoffrey Beene, Oscar de la Renta, Nicole Miller, Donna Karan,

Liz Claiborne, Anne Klein, and Eileen Fisher, joined the local industry leaders and government to transform the city's identity from a working class garment center to a global fashion capital that attracted international fashion designers and promoted shopping. They championed Rudolph Giuliani, the 1993 mayoral candidate who campaigned around "Made in New York" and "Designed in New York" campaigns to encourage new partnerships between manufacturing and design (Moon, 2009).

This coalitions would form the Fashion Center Business Improvement District, transform factory spaces into fashion showroom lofts, create high-end retail districts, and make Times Square the headquarters of Conde Nast, the largest publishing firm in global fashion. These activities went hand in hand with the liberalization of international trade laws and local pro-business policies with tax breaks that would permit small time companies to become globally recognizable American design corporations throughout the 1990s. American fashion companies of this era successfully acquired global licensing agreements and precipitated the offshoring of mass-production in clothing to overseas factories in Asia in rapid timing and in enormous scales. With the federal de-regularization of media and communications industries within the US (Telecommunications Act of 1996), new global media systems new platforms of communication emerged and aired television shows like *Sex and the City* and *Project Runway* to global audiences, largely advertising New York fashion and luxury retail to potentially new markets around the world. Fashion billboards soon vertically blanketed the walls of the pedestrian city, adding fashion and glamour to its everyday visual culture.

While New York adopted the producer services, luxury consumption, and festival atmosphere associated with its persona as a global city, low-wage manufacturing in its fashion district continued to exist through several economic crises of the city, including the 1970s oil crisis. Ironically, while the rest of the country experienced high unemployment, there existed a labor shortage within the New York garment industry. The changes to U.S. immigration law in 1965 saw the increase of Dominican and Chinese immigrants working in garment district and Chinatown garment factories (Waldinger 1986). In 1983, there were more than 500 sewing shops with more than twenty thousand Chinese workers in New York's Chinatown, and Koreans owned over 400 garment shops that employed nearly 14,000 Latinos working in the local New York garment district (Chin, 2005). Korean and Chinese factory owners bought their businesses from Jewish American factory owners looking to make their way out of the industry with the expiration of their 100 year old leases on factory space. In the next decade, Korean and Chinese-owned businesses would transform the local industry into a cottage industry of "sample-making," manufacturing high-end fashion labels in small batches of production, along with making the runway collections for a growing New York Fashion Week.

In tandem, local New York design schools also grew exponentially throughout this time period, providing a new workforce of design labor for growing multinationals on Seventh Avenue, who had offshored to Asia throughout the 1980s (Aspers and Godart, 2013). Student populations at The Fashion Institute of Technology, Parsons The New School for Design, and Pratt Institute were fast internationalizing throughout the late 1990s into the 2000s with newspaper reporters calling it the "Asian Invasion" of the New York fashion industry. Often, two different groups were conflated into one – Asian Americans who were the children of local New York Chinese and Korean factory owners, sewers, or even dry cleaners who had grown up in and around the garment districts in New York, Los Angeles, and San Francisco, and fashion design students from Asia, in particular Korea, whose migrations were influenced by 1997 IMF crisis (or Asian financial crisis) and the state's calls for globalization and the development of its "soft power" culture industries. This decade was marked by the movement of students, particularly young female students in fashion, driven by the desire to learn English in New York, obtain the prestige of a foreign American degree, gain work experience in famous American fashion companies, and take advantage of powerful alumni connections upon their return to Asia to start their own fashion labels. By 2000, 40% of Parsons comprised of students from Asia, the vast majority of them from Korea, on a campus that began to create global affiliations with design schools in Korea and eventually China (Wang, 2013). New York could not become the global fashion capital it is known for today, without the workforce of interns and technical design laborers, many of whom were Korean, who received their technical training in Korea. Further, Korean and Chinese-owned sample making factories had the technical, craft skills to create the runway collections for New York Fashion Week, while networked into garment production facilities in Korea and China and further in South and Southeast Asia. In fact, Korean contractors in manufacturing are major intermediaries for American and European fashion companies, and producing in South America, Southeast Asia, and South Asia.

3   Fashioning Labor, Fashioning Space

It is difficult to disentangle New York's rise as one of fashion's global cities without understanding the role of garments in shaping urban development in Asia throughout the 1960s and 1970s. Much of this production took place in newly made Export Processing Zones, a spatial form promoted by the World Bank and United Nations, among other actors. EPZs in Asia were thought to be a way for developing countries to enter into the global marketplace and attract foreign investment, culling foreign investment with highly attractive incentives, from tax holidays to cheap labor. Revolving around garment industries, EPZ construction occurred where industrial land was cheap – all that was required to build a garment factory was its four walls, the purchase of sewing machines, and a constant pool of cheap labor. Garment factories would be established in places where they could easily be relocated to attract new labor, relying heavily on a workforce of transient young women working for incredibly low wages in tedious and exhaustive work. These zoning technologies not only increased foreign investment and market activities, it created new political spaces and "conditions of variegated sovereignty aligned on an axis of trade, industrialization, and knowledge exchange" (Ong 2006:98). This very formula and path towards industrialization, a form of governance that attracts firms and foreign investors who have little interest in assisting host economies in the long term, relied on the labor of migrant female workforces, as the central form and site for experimental forms of labor exploitation throughout the 1970s (Yuan & Eden 1026–1045, 1992).

In 1965, post-war South Korea established six export-oriented industrial complexes in Seoul and neighboring Incheon, and in 1971, an EPZ was established at Masan. In Taiwan, Kaohsiung Export Processing Zone was established in 1965. The development of these EPZs in Korea and Taiwan was highly influenced by the success of free trade policies in Hong Kong and Singapore, and were primarily invested in by Japanese and American capital alongside Korean/Taiwanese partnerships (Warr, 1984). The sites and locations were chosen for their proximity to cities, harbors, and Japanese ports, and aimed to connect labor, goods, and highways to foreign buyers. Garments became a key export commodity in Korea beginning in the late 1960s, with large scale factories for mass production implemented by State policy, which saw a massive rural to urban migration, and the rapid industrialization and urbanization of Seoul. Mostly concentrated in Seoul and Pusan, the majority of firms were export companies producing for the U.S. and Japan. Workers worked within a system of "authoritarian patriachism," an elaborate system of subcontracting which included large firms with their own facilities that produced brand named products for US companies and small and medium sized firms and communities of informal producers (Lee and Hong 1994). These small firms could be found in the basement of four to five story buildings near industrial towns, employing small numbers of female workers using secondhand sewing machines. In 1985, eighty percent of Korea's firms relied on the assembly line system, the largest of factories employing hundreds of workers, supervisors, managers, and skilled male workers in cutting. Large numbers of nonunionized married women were the unskilled female workers on the assembly.

Under government funded export-promotion drives, Korean garment firms including the largest and leading knitwear exporters of the time (such as Hankuk Wool Textile Co., Masan Wool Textile Co., Samsung Moolsan, Miwon Industrial Co., and Samdo Trading company) aimed to dominate the U.S. market in the making of knits and sweaters (Kim, 1965). In fact, Macy's and May Department Stores headquartered in New York City and carrying American namesake design brands, considered the largest clothing retailers in the U.S. of that time, created new partnerships with Seoul knitting mills and plants throughout the 1970s. Using Korea's low-cost female labor and Japanese marketing networks, South Korean garment firms produced clothing for American companies such as Nike and Reebok, which saw their corporate dominance in American sportswear rise all throughout the 1980s. In sum, this era saw the development of all kinds of duty-free experimentations and arrangements involving American, Japanese, or foreign firms providing orders and raw materials for Koreans to process and send to American importers. By 1982, there existed eighty-three firms at Masan EPZ, where the average female worker between the ages of 17 and 25 was making 100,000 won a month (US $146) (Warr, 1984). The development of these EPZs (at both Masan and Kaosuhiang) catalyzed the industrialization, urbanization, and advancement of surrounding regions through the creation of garment industries. In Korea, nearly an entire generation of women cut their teeth, during the country's industrialization, working in garment factories.

Masan and Kaosuhiang would eventually become templates for SEZs throughout China in the 1980s under Deng Xiaoping's 1982 reforms of "one country, two systems" which would justify foreign investment and international trade as complementary to China's history of "self-reliance and socialism" (Lee, 1998). Using "a system of coexistence between capitalist and communist modes of production," the Open Door economic policies focused on developing areas of South China, which were given considerable degrees of autonomy and flexibility in soliciting foreign investment and trade, and included the first five Special Economic Zones (SEZs) of the 1980s in China – Shenzhen, Xiamen, Shangtou, Zhuhai, and the entire province of Hainan (Easterling, 2014). The success of these planned experiments with market economies would go on to create sixteen more zones all by 1984. And though industries were developed in electronics, hardware and furniture, foreign capital aimed to invest and develop labor-intensive export manufacturing industries that would include clothing and textiles.

As Ching Kwan Lee states, the economic reforms and the development of garment factories and industrial zones of South China was intentional and of no coincidence (Lee, 1998). The de-collectivization of communes and the breakdown of the socialist work unit had released a massive supply of surplus rural labor, and the migration of entire populations into urban areas occurred alongside the influx of foreign capital. Guangdong, in particular, had attained special national status within China, as it had historical ties with overseas Chinese communities and with Hong Kong, and its geographic distance from Beijing reduced the risk of political unrest and disruption to the central government. In these ways, the region had become an appealing site for foreign currency and national bids for foreign investment. As stated in her ethnography, "Guangdong was to be an airlock through which China dealt with the outside world. Shenzhen would be Guangdong's airlock to Hong Kong, and Hong Kong the direct window to the outside world. The example of Hong Kong's success was to attract Taiwan" (Lee, 1998, p. 41 citing Overholt 1993, p. 122).

There were further, particular circumstances that made China an attractive destination for foreign fashion companies and surplus capital investment throughout the 1980s and 1990s. The available workforce was educated, healthy because the state provided healthcare, and had a capacity for self-management. "Society had been shaped by the hierarchical and disciplined forms of social control, as well as the welfare advances established by the Communist Party of China (CPC) between 1949–1970s" (Brooks, 2015). Unlike Africa and South America, Chinese workers had come up through a system that guaranteed employment, food supplies, school enrollment, basic health care, and family planning, with outstanding life expectancy. Many of these migrant workers were structurally bounded by the state hukou system, a housing registry that tied one to the origin of birth. Named "mingong," once these peasant workers migrated from rural areas into the city, they were deprived of access to education, medical care, or other forms of social welfare available to urban hukou families (Ngai, 2005). Foreign and local ventures heavily capitalized on the non-citizen status of workers, building dormitories in industrial zones to maximize work time, without concern for the reproduction of labor power. It must be understood that these forms of labor exploitation were therefore institutionally legitimated by the Chinese state, using the hukou system to provide labor control for global and private capital.

Industrial areas and zones attracted migrant women in their mid to late twenties, who had come to urban areas to make wages for their families, with dreams of a cosmopolitan life in the city, and who were looking to delay the high cost of marriage. For most village girls, short-term wage work was expected during pre-marital life whereby women between the ages of eighteen and twenty-five were incorporated under the "expropriation of global capitalism and the state socialist system" which favored urban and industrial development (Ngai, 2005). In her ethnography *Made in China*, Pun Ngai shows how young women migrant workers were often faced with the choice between single life as a worker in the city, or married life within her husband's village. Central to this system of capitalist production and consumption was the use of sexual discourse and gender ideologies, which formed the basis for systematic hierarchies within the workplace (Ngai, 2005). Rural female migrants workers were recruited specifically because they were perceive to be cheaper and easier to regulate or control. As an example, Ngai cites foreign-owned electronic compounds in China, which were "metaphorically depicted as peach orchards, where female adolescents wait for men to pursue them" (Ngai 2005, p. 15). She concludes that the "bio-power" of the production machine has only interest in the "feminine body," which is imagined as "more obedient, tolerant and conforming to the factory machine" (Ngai 2005, p. 15). Though the state played a dominant role establishing the industry throughout the 1980s, it allowed private firms to gradually take over. With the exodus of Hong Kong manufacturers to Guangdong and Shenzhen, the Pearl River Delta grew in direct competition with Korea and Taiwan's EPZs, because of the low cost of South China's industrial lands and the continuous availability of a massive population of female workers.

4   The Trans-Pacific and Inter-Asian Legacies of the Fashion City

Diasporic communities became crucial to linking manufacturing in China with American and Europe investment capital, and consumers in the Global North. In cities like Hong Kong and Shenzhen, kin networks facilitated business for Hong Kong entrepreneurs who built garment factories in Shenzhen, where relatives were located. These "blood related" joint ventures were written as agreements based on mutual trust and without formal contracts, and called upon to deal with government regulations and labor disputes more "flexibly," alongside benefiting from special treatment and privileges (Brooks, 2015). Ethnic urban villages comprised of kinship networks influenced local power structures, and the former elites or cadres became managers from the same kin lines within local government and the factory system. The village corporations they ran benefited enormously from accommodating migrants – the rural peasants who had lived in these areas, suddenly found themselves to be rich landlords. Municipal governments planned infrastructure for industrial cities that would includes roads, communication, water, electricity, sewage system, and green space. But as township and village enterprises built on collectively owned rural land along major highways, mixing commercial with residential use, these particular factories often lacked infrastructure, discharging industrial waste directly into rivers.

Factories were continuously built along these kin networks and lines all throughout the Pearl River Delta and eastern seaboard of China in the 1980s and 1990s. Further, Taiwanese and Korean companies switched production to China in the late 1980s, attracted to the lower costs of labor, energy, and transport. This system would lead to the development of textile and clothing industries in the coastal regions of Fujian, Guangdong, Jiangsu, Shangdon and Shanghai provinces. Throughout the 1980s and at its height, Hong Kong, Singapore, South Korea, Taiwan, and South China collectively shared world clothing and textile production. Between 1980–1994, China's exports of clothing and textiles increased eightfold in less than two decades. EPZs continued to flourish in also Malaysia, Sri Lanka, Thailand, and Philippines by 1990 (Easterling, 2012). Today, Korean and Chinese contractors have spread their production networks and connected them to lead firms in global value chains across Southeast Asia and South Asia, but have also moved up the global value chain in the form of sending their kids to design schools in the US and Europe, moving between cities and making new connections while also shaping North American cities.

Fashion clusters thus sit within a constantly shifting network of industrial histories, production networks and diasporic connections that integrate cities across Asia but also across the Pacific. This networked, mobile geography of connections thus shapes not only the districts, zones, and enclaves of garment manufacturing but also the form and industries of America's fashion cities. As discussed above, Korean and Chinese diasporic cultural intermediaries played a significant role in transforming New York into a global fashion capital throughout the 1990s and 2000s. Recently, these industrialized legacies of garment industrialization in Asia are now powerfully shaping the city of Los Angeles, which has become a new center for fast-fashion in the U.S. and global fashion economy. Since 2013, my ethnographic fieldwork has traced the emergence of "fast-fashion" in L.A. and, in particular, the work of hundreds of Korean families who have, over the last decade, transformed the former L.A. garment district into the central hub for fast-fashion in the Americas (Moon, 2014). These Korean families – their migration, their knowledge, skills, and experience in garments, and their diasporic networks to manufacturing bases and wholesale clothing markets throughout Asia – are the culmination of these former industrializing histories in Asia and also a reflection of the continued ongoing industrializing histories being made today in Asia. They have subverted the buying structures of American retail, dramatically changed the material object of fashion, and established the growing fashion economy of Los Angeles. Their work in fashion has created new global routes in the making, marketing, distribution, communication, consumption, and pattern of disposal of this one commodity. Their work and livelihoods are the legacy of these earlier industrial garment and zonal histories that occurred in Korea of the 1970s as well as the creation of new zones of garment production throughout China and Southeast Asia today.

"Fast-fashion" has only emerged within the U.S. over the last decade but has transformed the global fashion industry in profound ways. Considered cheap and highly trendy clothing, its once stable three-month production cycle – the time it takes to design, manufacture, and distribute clothing to stores, in an extraordinary globe-spanning process – is now collapsed to just two weeks. As a material form, fast-fashion has transformed how clothing is made, what it is made of, how it is assembled, shipped, distributed, sold, and even the way consumers wear and buy it. Fast fashion is highly desirable because it puts trendy designs and details from high-fashion or the runway into production, making design and fashion accessible to the masses at incredibly affordable prices. As a material form, fast-fashion has powerfully transformed communities, technologies, economies, and the rural and urban landscape across the U.S. and Asia. It also only exists because of these Asian American immigrants within the US, their ties to both American retail and wholesale markets and manufacturing factories in Korea and China, and their histories and experiences in and around the EPZs and garment industrial districts of Asia.

In a neighborhood locally known as the "Jobber Market" in downtown Los Angeles, Korean families make their living by designing clothes, organizing the factory labor that will cut and sew them in countries like China and Vietnam, and selling them wholesale to many of the largest fast-fashion retailers in the U.S. – including Forever 21, Urban Outfitters, T.J. Maxx, Anthropologie, and Nordstrom. These families operate their showrooms in a sprawling, 30-square-block area where over 6,000 Korean-owned clothing labels are located. Some are multimillion-dollar enterprises, but the majority are mom-and-pop businesses. Korean husband-and-wife teams run these businesses alongside their designing children, while Mexican husband-and-wife teams serve as sales agents, inventory workers, and packers. Together, these small time producers design, manufacture, and wholesale their garments, supplying cheap and trendy designs for the most prominent clothing markets in across the Americas.

Older generations, having gained three decades of knowledge, experience, and skills in the making of garments (from patternmaking, fit, and quality control, etc.) across three continents from Asia, South America to the US, set up shop in the LA garment district throughout the 1980s and 1990s (see Buechler, 2004 for Koreans in Brazil). Their diasporic connections to other Koreans working abroad in the trade, whether in Korea, China, or Vietnam, connected them to fabric and trim sources, factories, managers, sample-makers, and sewers throughout Asia. Their children, having grown up in the family business, with degrees in design, business, marketing, and merchandising from American universities (including my employer Parsons School of Design in New York), with knowledge of design brands and trends along with American cultural identities, had come of age within the last decade, and were returning to Los Angeles to revamp their parents' failing garment businesses. Yet these families work within an environment that is increasingly precarious, as they represent new distributions of risk within the local L.A. industry, with much of it falling on the shoulders of the Korean and Mexican families in LA, and those near the bottom of the production chain in Asia. Working in a highly volatile market where consumer demands are unpredictable and finicky, these fast fashion manufacturers live at the mercy of powerful corporate retailers – families must invest cash and put thousands of styles (anywhere between 6–40 within a day) into production before knowing what will sell. In most cases, the family unit becomes both the site of intense trust (and perhaps exploitation) in order to survive such fast-fashion's ephemeral markets.

There's an uncanny resemblance in the L.A. Jobber Market to "Dongdaemun market," the famous wholesale clothing market-turned-retail market in Seoul, in which all the Korean vendors in L.A. cite or have some history or association with. Dongdaemun was born out of the export-centered economic development of Korea during the 1960s and 1970s and was at the front line of conflict between Korea's democratic labor movement and the authoritarian state. Since the 1997 Asian IMF crisis, it has become a revitalized retail cluster in Seoul, attracting tourists from China in search of cheap plastic surgery and trendy clothes. Yet its history is born out of a time when Korea was a still impoverished country with high unemployment and an oppressive military regime. Throughout the 1970s, many from this market community emigrated to the U.S. and South America – in particular to Brazil and Argentina – and without language skills or money, the majority ended up leveraging their ties back home to the textile trade. Today, there exists a diaspora of Korean-owned garment factories across Central and South America, East and Southeast Asia, and Korean immigrants have gone on to play large roles in the most important clothing markets across São Paulo, Buenos Aires, Guangzhou, L.A., and New York.[2]

---

2   The diaspora of Korean garment factory owners is found across Central and South America including Brazil, Argentina, Guatemala, Uruguay and across East and Southeast Asia, including

Though Koreans have worked in the L.A. garment district since the 1970s, buying up the garment sewing factories that were once owned by the Jewish and Persian communities, it wasn't until the 1990s that so many Korean-owned *fashion* manufacturers emerged and thus made up the Jobber Market that exists today. Some say that the 1992 Rodney King race riots were a turning point – with local Korean businesses burned down in Koreatown, with new racialized fears and a weakened local economy, Koreans living in downtown L.A. were looking for a way out of the industry. Occurring alongside a heightening peso crisis in South America, Koreans from Sao Paulo were looking to come to L.A. for better opportunities and better educations for their children. They wanted to escape the growing violence in their own cities and were in search of a more stable dollar.

5 Familial Logics of Fashion

The Kim family, whom I've been meeting regularly in my study of U.S. fast-fashion, is a typical "fast-fashion family" in that they first started their clothing business in Sao Paulo in the 1970s and 1980s, only to immigrate to L.A. in 1993. For a good while, they enjoyed a successful business selling garments, but by the 2000s, Magdalena the mother, noticed a lot of changes happening to the local industry, when sewing began being offshored to China. Clothing that was organized by style and function (pants, sweaters) on department store floors, was now organized by brand names. Gone were the days when a garment shop just took orders from companies like Gap to create basic designs that would continue to sell for several seasons. Big retailers were doing a lot less of their own designing, requiring more complicated details and features in trim and ornamentation from their suppliers. This is when her daughter Daniela and Daniela's husband Sung Joo decided to join the family business in 2005. Sung Joo, with his degree in Graphic Design from Parsons would give their little "mom and pop" operation a branded identity – re-designing the interior of their showroom, coming up with a company logo, and creating a sleek looking vendor's booth at the clothing trade shows. Back and forth to China from L.A. twice a month, he is being groomed to oversee production. Daniela, with her Fine Arts degree and love for fashion, would become heavily involved in the design process– keeping up-to-date on the latest trends, putting together

China, Vietnam, and Cambodia. See the following articles for reference: Buechler, 2014; Iberico-Lozada, 2013; Figueroa, 1996; Katz, 2013; Kim, Jaesok. 2013, 2016a; Kim, Junyoung Veronica, 2016b; Hsieh, 2014; Mosk et al., 2016; Sims, 1995. Sokhean, 2014; Son, 2016; Yoon, 2015.

lookbooks, producing photoshoots that visually narrate the clothes styled on Caucasian models, uploading images and publicizing her clothes on Instagram. Her multiple cultural identities – Korean, Brazilian and American – gives her the ability to speak Spanish with her Mexican employees, Korean to factory managers in China, Portuguese with her parents and other 1.5 generationers in the neighborhood, and perfect English with her American buyers and retailers (1.5 refers to those who had moved to the United States at a young age). Magdalena tells me that it's Daniela who has brought their fashions to the attention of the most prestigious American retail chains and department stores for the very first time and that their American Dream isn't just about getting into some Ivy League university, but rather, to have their clothes sold at the largest of American retailers like Nordstrom or Macy's.

For their part, Magdalena and her husband Fernando, a patternmaker and a fabric cutter, had gained decades of knowledge and experience in garment construction – they are responsible for smoothly translating Daniela's design ideas into actual material forms. Magdalena and Fernando have also created relationships to cut and sew in factories across China and now Vietnam, and among the Korean garment community within the U.S. who have shifted clothing production from South and Central America to Asia post 9/11 and recent changes in trade laws. Magdalena tells me of Korean Chinese agents and traders who run their businesses around fast-fashion – they provide a full package of services all ready for her when she shows up at Guangzhou Airport. She gets picked up by a Korean speaking driver, stays in a Korean-run hotel that serves her planned Korean meals, while being taken to different factory sources with young bilingual speaking intermediaries. Sung Joo's close friend from his military service days in Korea, fluent in Korean and Mandarin now serves as their quality control production manager at the factory in Guangzhou and permanently lives in China. And Sung-Joo himself makes the trip from L.A. to China, twice a month, to help oversee quality control and garment production.

The Kim family, among many other families in the L.A. Jobber Market, suggests that the fashion industry doesn't operate or occur on a single city or production site. Rather, its skill formations necessitate multi-sitedness – sites which are powerfully negotiated by families through backward and forward linkages. The Kim family's skills had been acquired in home countries but have also been invested in elsewhere, in terms of skill upgrading. How these fast fashion families negotiate geography is much different than how we might conventionally think about clusters as isolated or territorially confined. Rather, these fashion economic "clusters" involve a complex history that stretches across spaces and are negotiated by family and migrant networks. These intermediaries help link up these different geographies and also point to the need for multi-sited ethnography for the understanding of this global fashion system.

6   Refashioning Asian Cities

While just a few zones and industrial districts revolving around garment production existed in Asia in the 1960s, today these designated zones and industrial districts are increasing and offer, instead of factories, fantasies of luxury and fashion to attract foreign investment as destinations for shopping and entertainment. Garment factories are now built alongside green parks, dormitories, theme parks, resorts, corporate enclaves, and luxury shopping malls, reflecting the desire of garment cities to "upgrade" their labor-intensive garment industries, just as New York once had. Municipal governments of cities like Shenzhen have now identified high tech industries as new focuses for jumpstarting the economy, developing new sectors in textiles that produce high quality cloth and synthetic fibers (example, special functioning coated cloth and non-woven agricultural fabrics). In Shenzhen, as in many other Asian cities looking to "upgrade" from garment manufacturing, the municipal government has set up and established organizations such as the Shenzhen Garment Design Center, to offer training in software development to promote high-tech skills in fashion design. For instance, while more labor-intensive sections of the industry in Korea and China have now migrated inland to Guangdong Province, local workers in the Shenzhen EPZ have become skilled technicians in CAD/CAM techniques. This path of skilling and deskilling is now occurring across the industrializing and deindustrializing garment cities across Asia. Just as it did in New York and Seoul throughout the 1990s and 2000s, in China from 1978 to 2008, culture industries based on fashion, advertising and graphic design, film and television, art and design industries have proliferated and flourished (Chumley, 2016). In Korea but particularly in China, these culture industries have been cultivated by state interventions in the form of investment and the development of industrial districts.

Back in Seoul, speaking to this audience on the rise of New York as a fashion capital, I got the chance to revisit and walk the city after ten years from my first visit. In 2005, I spent much of my time in and around the Dongdaemun neighborhood, the old garment district of Seoul. So much of it had changed – the small time vendors that set up on the sidewalk or in the corridors of underground subway stations, selling supplies, notions, trims, muslin, and blankets, had nearly all disappeared. The hustle and bustle of motorbikes carrying fabric in and out of garment related buildings, were replaced with students and young fashion designers toting around their school design projects and portfolios. Department stores and retail spaces such as Doota and Migliore, which once attracted young Japanese female consumers and tourists in search of cheap fashions, were now replaced with hipper and catchier retail shops and department stores, attracting instead young Chinese female shoppers of a new middle class in search of trendy fashions and plastic surgery in clinics on the top floors of these same department stores.

Parts of the adjacent Changshindong neighborhood, which once housed a garment workers' rehabilitation center and featured a brass plaque commemorating the death of Chun Tae Il, a garment activist from the 1970s, was replaced with a large Design Center education facility. The Chongyecheon Stream, which snaked alongside the old Pyeongwha garment factories buried under a covered highway, was now restored as part of a completed urban redevelopment and city beautification project. Like New York's High Line, the neighborhood was "cleaned up" and made attractive for tourists. Perhaps the most noticeable change to the neighborhood was the construction of a giant, silver, saucer-like Design Plaza, built by the architect Zaha Hadid. The building looked like it had swooped in from outer space, demolishing the former Olympic soccer stadium it replaced and which was once filled with flea market hawkers, vendors, and antique dealers. In ways, the new building and plaza represents a more contemporary symbolic embodiment of Korea's modernity. It seems all across Korea and China, former manufacturing spaces, built during the former industrial district and zonal periods of the 1970s, were now repurposed for the biennales, theme parks, shopping malls, and luxury spaces of fashion consumption, that now mark these deindustrialized cities of Asia. Fashion and design proclaims the purchasing power of Asia.

It is no surprise, then, that "creativity" and "innovation" have become the hallmarks of government throughout Korea and China since the mid 2000s as a way to attract investment, develop infrastructure and real estate, as well as gain international prestige. In both Korea and China, "creativity" is the idea to attract talent that could develop "soft power" industries. Just as in New York's deindustrialization of the 1990s, governments in China and Korea are now focusing on tax revenues and real estate development as the means to stimulate urban growth despite state interventions in limiting political expression (Schwak 2016). First with town and village enterprises in the early 1980s, to then the building of economic and science technology parks throughout the 1990s, and the development of media conglomerates in the 2000s, Asian cities are rebranding themselves "from the world's factory" to "the world's tech lab or design studio." Throughout the 1990s, the focus in South China had always been on the development of industrial clusters and parks involving low cost manufacturing in the production of socks, clocks, toys, ties, shoes, belts, household appliances. These industries, as Mike Keane points out, were "locally born, locally rooted and locally embedded" and formed the global supply chains for incredibly complex markets (Keane, 2013).

Economic and technology zones (ETZs) with high-tech or innovation parks, first appeared southern coastal areas of China from 1988 onwards, also in an effort to attract foreign investment through diasporic networks (Keane, 2013). The emergence of creative industries throughout the 1990s reflect the ambitions of policymakers, reformers, local government officials, think tanks, and cultural scholars, and driven to reality by "land grabs" and real estate developers. The results are the proliferation of creative clusters and zones throughout China include Beijing's Songzhuang Capital Arts District and the 798 Art Zone, the Dafen Art Village in Shenzhen, and the "creative" province of Hangzhou – all commercial ventures supported by local governments as state administered contemporary art-communes and cultural districts meant to drive "creativity." Despite all the government rhetoric in cities such as Hong Kong, Shenzhen, and Seoul, to nationally promote its fashion culture industries and creative economies, the creation of new cultural zones and districts dedicated to incubating design talent with design centers and fashion weeks are not guaranteed to be successful. Nonetheless, these new development and their attendant dispossessions will alter the geography of InterAsia and the fashion city, but in ways yet to be fully grasped.

7   Conclusion

Fast fashion's inter-Asian and trans-Pacific networks of families, factories, and expertise form fragile ecologies of clothing that condition our twenty-first century globalized fashion industry – and act as a space for all kinds of intermediaries, risk takers, brokers – the buyers and sellers, nomads, and traders, the entrepreneurs whose ingenuity "grease" the linkages of the global supply chains and in actuality float the global fashion economy. This chapter attempts to use a multi-sited ethnographic lens to understanding inter-urban circuits in fashion, and, in particular, how diasporic networks mediate the connections between these locales and their positioning in global value chains, exploring the interplay of urban histories and urban forms. It allows us to grasp a different kind of creativity which emerges from the unmarked, invisible histories of garment workers, whose skills were nurtured in the export factories and whose wholesale markets in fashion that still thrive on the peripheries of Asia's cities. The fashion industry, in this way, doesn't just occur within one site: its skill formations are multi-sited and powerfully negotiated by families in its backward and forward linkages and therefore demand an ethnography of multi-sitedness. Skills may be acquired in home countries but also invested in for skill upgrading, mobile, transnational, and transfer to other places and geographic locales.

In conclusion, understanding how fast fashion families negotiate geography demands a different kind of lens to how we might approach the emergence of clusters, seeing them not as isolated or territorially confined, but rather as involving a complex history that stretches across spaces and constantly negotiated by multiple families and kin groups. We must therefore return to the importance of study of diasporic connections, which is integral for grasping the future of development and urbanization and its connections within Asia and across the Pacific. This chapter thus shows us how cities and urban forms are connected through migrant networks and knowledge flows, and by extension, points to the important contribution of ethnographic approaches for the study of "urban developmentalism" in East Asia by charting how families accumulate experience from and travel through the multiple spatial forms and geopolitical economic connections that have shaped urban development in the region.

References

Aspers, P and F Godart (2013) Sociology of Fashion: Order and Change. *Annual Review of Sociology* 39(1): 171–192.

Brooks, A (2015) *Clothing Poverty: The Hidden World of Fast Fashion and Second-hand Clothes*. London: Zed Books.

Buechler, S (2004) Sweating It in the Brazilian Garment Industry: Korean and Bolivian Immigrants and Global Economic Forces in Sao Paulo. *Latin American Perspectives* 31(3): 99–119.

Chin, M (2005) *Sewing Women: Immigrants and the New York City Garment Industry*. New York, NY: Columbia University Press.

Chumley, L (2016) *Creativity Class: Art School and Culture Work in Postsocialist China*. Princeton, NJ: Princeton University Press.

Easterling, K (2014) *Extrastatecraft: the power of infrastructure space*. New York, NY: Verso.

Easterling, K (2012) Zone: the Spatial Software of Extrastatecraft. *Places Journal*. June.

Figueroa, H (1996) *In the Name of Fashion: Exploitation in the Garment Industry*. NACLA Report on the Americas, January 1.

Greenberg, M (2008) *Branding New York: How a City in Crisis was Sold to the World*. New York, NY: Routledge.

Hsieh, S (2014) Guatemala Factory Supplying Walmart and Other US Retailers Stole $6 Million From Workers. *The Nation*. Available at https://www.thenation.com/article/ guatemala-factory-supplying-walmart-and-other-retailers-stole-6-million-workers/ (accessed 15 May 2017).

Iberico-Lozada, L (2013) In sweatshops, the 'Brazilian dream' goes awry. *Reuters*. Available at http://www.reuters.com/article/us-brazil-immigrants-idUSBRE98004 L20130901 (accessed 15 May 2017).

Katz, J (2013) A glittering industrial park in Haiti falls short. *Al Jazeera America*. Available at http://america.aljazeera.com/articles/2013/9/10/a-glittering-industrialparkfalls shortinhaiti.html (accessed 15 May 2017).

Keane, M (2013) *China's New Creative Clusters*. London: Routledge.

Kim, J (2016) Power, Space, and Subjectivity in a Transnational Garment Factory. In: M Liu and C Smith (eds.) *China at Work: A Labour Process Perspective on the Transformation of Work*. London: Palgrave.

Kim, JV (2016) Disrupting the White Myth: Korean immigration to Buenos Aires and National Imaginaries. In ZM Rivas and D Lee-DiStefano (eds.) *Imagining Asia in the Americas*. New Brunswick, NJ: Rutgers University Press, 36.

Kim, S (1965) The Sportswear and Leisure Living: Big Bulge in US Sweater Sales Stated by Korean Knitters. *WWD*. 29 December.

Lee, CK (1998) *Gender and the South China Miracle: Two Worlds of Factory Women*. Berkeley, CA: University of California.

Lee, SH and HK Hong (1994) The Korean Garment Industry: From Authoritarian Patriarchism to Industrial Paternalism in (eds.) E Bonacich, L Cheng, N Chinchilla, N Hamilton, P Ong's *Global Production: The Apparel Industry in the Pacific Rim*. Philadelphia, PA: Temple University Press.

Moody, K (2007) *From Welfare State to Real Estate Regime Change in New York City, 1974 to the Present*. New York, NY: The New Press.

Moon, C (2014) The Secret World of Fast Fashion. *Pacific Standard Magazine*. Available at https://psmag.com/the-secret-world-of-fast-fashion-9c899e0edb08 (accessed 15 May 2017).

Moon, C (2009) From Fashion to Factories: An Intern's Experience of New York as a Global Fashion Capital. In H Clark and E Paulicelli (eds.) *The Fabric of Cultures: Fashion, Identity, and Globalization*. London: Routledge.

Mosk, M, B Ross, B Epstein and C Park (2016) In Haiti, a Factory Where Big Money, State Department and the Clintons Meet. *ABC News*. Available at http://abcnews .go.com/Politics/haiti-factory-big-money-state-department-clintons-meet/ story?id=42729714 (accessed 15 May 2017).

Ngai, P (2005) *Made in China: Women Factory Workers in a Global Workplace*. Durham, NC: Duke University Press.

Ong, A., 2006. *Neoliberalism as exception: Mutations in citizenship and sovereignty*. Durham: Duke University Press.

Overholt, WH (1993) *China: The Next Economic Superpower*. London: Weildenfeld & Nicolson, pp. 122.

Schwak, J (2016) Branding South Korea in a Competitive World Order: Discourses and Dispositives in Neoliberal Governmentality. *Asian Studies Review* 40(3): 427–444.

Sims, C (1995) Buenos Aires Journal; Don't Cry, This Land Is Rich in Kims and Lees. *New York Times*. Available at: http://www.nytimes.com/1995/11/15/world/buenos-aires-journal-don-t-cry-this-land-is-rich-in-kims-and-lees.html (accessed 15 May 2017).

Sokhean, B (2014) Garment Workers Protest at South Korean Embassy. *Cambodia Daily*. Available at https://www.cambodiadaily.com/archives/garment-workers-protest-at-south-korean-embassy-75004/

Son, T (2016) Mass fainting halts production at South Korean garment factory in Vietnam. *VN Express*. Available at: http://e.vnexpress.net/news/news/mass-fainting-halts-production-at-south-korean-garment-factory-in-vietnam-3490995.html (accessed 15 May 2017).

Waldginer, R (1986) Through the Eye of the Needle: Immigrants and Enterprise in New York's Garment Trades. New York, NY: New York University Press.

Wang, J (2013) *Institutional Change and the Development of Industrial Clusters in China: Case Studies from the Textile and Clothing Industry*. Singapore: WSPC.

Warr, PG (1984) Korea's Masan Export Zone: benefits and costs. *The Developing Economies*. 22 (2): 169–172.

Yoon, WK (2015) *Global Pulls on the Korean Communities in Sao Paulo and Buenos Aires*. London: Lexington Books, 105.

Yuan, J and L Eden (1992) Export Processing Zones in Asia: A Comparative Study *Asian Survey*. 32 (11): 1026–1045.

Index